THE
CONFUCIAN CREATION
OF HEAVEN

SUNY Series in Chinese Philosophy and Culture
David L. Hall and Roger T. Ames, Editors

THE
CONFUCIAN CREATION
OF HEAVEN

PHILOSOPHY AND THE DEFENSE
OF RITUAL MASTERY

ROBERT ENO

State University of New York Press

Published by
State University of New York Press, Albany

© 1990   State University of New York

For information, address State University of New York
Press, State University Plaza, Albany, N.Y., 12246

Library of Congress Cataloging-in-Publication Data

Eno, Robert, 1949-
    The Confucian creation of heaven: philosophy and the defense of
ritual mastery/Robert Eno.
        p.   cm.–(SUNY series in Chinese philosophy and culture)
    Bibliography: p.
    Includes index.
    ISBN 0-7914-0190-1.   –ISBN 0-7914-0191-X (pbk.)
    1. Philosophy, Confucian–China–History.   2. Confucianism–China–
History.   3. Heaven–Confucianism–History of doctrines.
    4. Confucianism–China–Rituals–History of doctrines.   I. Title.
    II. Series.
B127.C65E56   1990
181'.112–dc20

                                                                              89-31194
                                                                                    CIP

10   9   8   7   6   5   4   3   2   1

to Dick,
my first teacher

Contents

Acknowledgments

Like the early Confucians whose ghosts inhabit these pages I feel very keenly the debt I owe to my teachers. For more than a decade, Donald Munro guided my studies with generosity and great liberality, and I am delighted whenever I am identified as his student. My specific focus on early Confucianism reflects the influence of Mr. Liu Yü-yun, with whom I studied for several years in Taiwan. Mr. Liu taught me to read the texts and to take them seriously as the artifacts of critical decisions that people have been forced to make, rather than as static models of theory or puzzles in philology.

Several people were instrumental in ensuring the success of research for this book in Taiwan and Japan. I would like to thank in particular Professors Wejen Chang and Ting Pang-hsin of the Institute of History and Philology at Academia Sinica in Taiwan, and Professor Kanaya Osamu and the members of the Chinese Philosophy Section at Tōhoku University in Sendai, Japan.

Portions of the research for this book were supported through grants from the Social Science Research Council and the Fulbright Fellowship Program, for which I am most grateful.

A number of scholars have read portions of this book at various stages; they have been generous in their comments and corrections. I would like to thank Irene Bloom, Kenneth DeWoskin, George Elison, Albert Feuerwerker, Luis Gomez, A. C. Graham, Chad Hansen, Charles Hucker, Virginia Kane, and Jack Meiland. I have benefited greatly from their suggestions; the errors that remain are my own. Yan Shoucheng has kindly provided the elegant Chinese characters for this book. A special debt of thanks is due to my former colleague Elsie Orb for her many editorial corrections.

Finally, I would like to thank Candice and Jared and Daniel for being a patient family and making this worthwhile.

Introduction

The figures whose words and actions stand at the center of this book are the first Confucians, men who lived between the sixth and third centuries B.C., famous for their austere humanist ethics and puristic political zealotry. Long after their deaths, their movement grew into the dominant philosophical school of traditional China—a philosophy by means of which an imperial bureaucracy, with increasingly infrequent interruptions, sustained itself and constrained the parameters of social action and dialogue throughout two millennia of cultural cohesion. This posterity has formed a thick lens through which we see these men as a particular archetypal company—the first Mandarins—the founders of social orthodoxy. Great men, great models—perhaps a little dull.

Nor is dullness the only failing to be seen in their traditional portrait. The shape of their philosophy, as interpreted by generations of later Confucians, appears to the critical Western eye to be little better than a collection of received dogma loosely linked by ad hoc rationalization—more an ideology than a philosophy. When John Passmore remarked that Chinese thought consisted of "pronouncements" rather than "philosophy," he surely had classical Confucians in mind (1967:217-218).

But these same men will appear differently here. In our portrait they are dressed in colorful robes, playing zithers or beating drums, chanting, dancing, and living their lives through an eccentric form of ritual playacting suggestive, perhaps, of nothing as much as Peking Opera. They performed this intricate choreography surrounded by the scorn of a society that viewed them as hopelessly out of step with the times—but for these first Confucians, their dance was part of an eternal pattern; it was the times that were out of step.

Austere their ethics may have been, but they were not dull. As for the political activism that so pervades the traditional image of these men, it will not be central to our portrait. To us it will appear that the extremity of Confucian purism performed the inverse function of isolating the ritual community of early Confucians from the political hazards of a chaotic era and endowed a style of social withdrawal with the ethical status of conscientious objection.

For us, then, the early Confucian will appear very different from his later descendants (so different that, before we have gone very far, we will feel the need to abandon the term"Confucian" itself, with all of its traditional

1

associations). A comprehensive ritual choreography stands at the focus of his portrait: his paradigmatic role is not the righteous politician, but the master of dance. Ritual and political facets of the first Confucians will be split in an asymmetrical disjunction, with righteous zealotry stifling political deeds and fostering increasingly complex ritual activity.

We will illustrate the structure of this disjunction in Confucianism by exploring the complex way in which Confucians employed a term derived from pre-Confucian religious practice, a word usually rendered in English as "Heaven." This term, which bore an unmatched ethical authority in the rhetoric of early Chinese traditions, had been cut free from its original moorings of meaning by abrupt social and intellectual changes predating the birth of Confucius, changes that had brought into question the adequacy of traditional ideas about Heaven. The problematic status of Heaven during this period of transition provided Confucians with an unusual degree of freedom to recreate Heaven in the image of their new philosophy.

As we pursue an initial inquiry into the sense in which Confucians conceived of Heaven, we will see that they created a Heaven essentially void of consistent features, and so free to reflect the growing image of their new philosophy and their unique lifestyle. Every attempt to anchor the meaning of the term in a static concept or set of images fails. This new Confucian Heaven was ultimately the moving reflection of a patterned choreography, elaborated by groups of masters and disciples increasingly alienated from a society in disruption.

Most surprising in this picture of early Confucianism is that despite the intellectually unlikely project of placing ritual practice at the center of philosophy, early Confucianism appears from this perspective fully philosophical, possessing coherence and intellectual discipline. However, the style of this philosophy is fundamentally different from that we have grown to expect from the analytic schools of Western tradition. It was not analytic, and it made no categorical distinction between the spheres of theory and practice.

To draw a portrait that reveals the coherence and interest of this philosophy, we will follow an interpretive approach that reflects the Confucian notion that a complete intellectual enterprise involves an essential integration of theory and practice. The ideas of the early Confucian school cannot be captured exclusively in terms of conceptual architecture. By exploring the role of Heaven in Confucian philosophy seen as a conjunction of articulate statements and historical practices, the unique structure of this species of philosophical enterprise will become visible.

❖   ❖   ❖   ❖

This prelude like a musical overture, has introduced with provoking brevity the most distinctive themes of the work to follow. Obviously any book that undertakes to characterize Confucius and his followers through their role as masters of dance has a lot of explaining to do. Those explanations will start with a discussion of the issues with which this study did, in fact, begin: the problematic functions of the word "*t'ien*" or "Heaven" in the primary texts of early Confucianism, the *Analects* of Confucius, the *Mencius*, and the *Hsun Tzu*.

Looking for the Ground of Heaven

The classical texts of early Confucianism are not distinguished by the systematic argumentation and sensitivity to logical justification that characterize Western philosophical texts from the era of Parmenides and Socrates on. Although both the *Mencius* and the *Hsun Tzu*, composed in response to intellectual challenges mounted by competing schools of thought, do employ techniques of argument to defend Confucian doctrine, the doctrine itself seems always a given, defended but unquestioned. Where post-Socratic philosophy in the West became a recurrent search for the ground of knowledge, Confucians, China's first philosophers, seem confident they have a map of that ground in hand, and the ground appears to bear the detailed contours of Chou Dynasty China (1045-221 B.C.).

We are, therefore, entitled to raise the question whether early Confucianism was truly a philosophy, or merely a well-rationalized cultural point of view. The initial basis of Confucian claims is unclear. Universal axioms of logical or ontological necessity are not formulated, and direct statements describing empirical bases for Confucian commitments are regularly permeated by vagueness at critical junctures where a modern reader will feel most in need of clarity.

Here is the point of departure for this study. Can careful probing of the vaguest sections of these texts elicit meanings clear enough to reveal some basis for the confidence of early Confucians that knowledge was attainable and lay in their possession? Among such passages, a single group emerges as at once philosophically provocative and deeply obscure: statements that include the traditional religious term "*t'ien*," or "Heaven."

An example from the *Mencius*, a text dating from the fourth century B.C., will illustrate the point. "He who exhausts his mind," Mencius tells us, "knows his nature; and knowing his nature, he knows Heaven" (*M*: 7A.1). This is a much-celebrated passage, and it suggests a philosophically provocative link between what we would identify as epistemological and metaphysical issues, but every phrase is problematic. The promise of the passage is a knowledge of Heaven, but the passage tells us nothing of what that knowledge might reveal Heaven to be.[1]

Such critical vagueness is a problem, but it presents a clear challenge: to seek the ground of Confucian certainty by pursuing the elusive Confucian Heaven.

The Term "T'ien"

Our first order of business is terminological. The English word "Heaven" translates the Chinese term "*t'ien*," and the translation is elegant because both words can denote a deity and also the sky. But just because the translation is so fortuitous, it may have obscured the fact that we know very little about what "*t'ien*" meant in early China, and we will not use it, choosing instead to leave the term untranslated to allow the variety of its meanings to appear.[2]

The pre-Confucian history of the term "*t'ien*" is marked by some of the same sorts of ambiguity we encounter in the Confucian texts. The origins of the term and its initial meanings are unclear. (These issues are discussed in detail in appendix A.) We do know that from the eleventh century B.C., T'ien was an object of great religious reverence and the focus of Chou Dynasty aristocratic religious practice. We know very little, however, about the intellectual image in which this T'ien was conceived.

In time, the word came to denote a complex of overlapping concepts. As far back as the twelfth century, the philosopher Chu Hsi tried to organize this complex by analyzing T'ien into three distinct aspects: T'ien as Ruler or God; T'ien as Ethical Law; T'ien as Nature (Ikeda 1968:31). More recently, Fung Yu-lan has expanded this analysis into five divisions: T'ien as the Physical Sky, as Ruler or God, as Fate, as Nature, as Ethical Principle (1931:55).[3]

These various facets of T'ien have suggested an evolutionary process through which an increasingly sophisticated intellectual tradition gradually moved from a highly anthropomorphic religious cosmology toward a more rational philosophical view. This model has governed the agenda of previous studies of the role of T'ien in Confucian texts. Historians of Chinese philosophy such as Fung Yu-lan, Hou Wai-lu, and T'ang Chün-yi, who have written extensively on the subject in the course of their longer works, and monographic writers in China and elsewhere (e.g., Dubs 1958; Ikeda 1965), generally have framed the issue of T'ien's role in early Confucianism by asking which of the various images of T'ien is appropriately assigned to each instance of the word in Confucian texts. They have tailored their interpretations to respond, either positively or negatively, to the hypothesis that the predominant image governing philosophical discussion of T'ien evolved from an anthropomorphic image in the mid-Chou period to an image of Nature by the end of the Chou.[4]

But what is striking in the Confucian texts is the apparent promiscuity with which the various images are employed. So terse a work as the *Analects*, which refers to T'ien only a handful of times, can be read as exemplifying the five dimensions in Fung's analysis. As the Sky: "The insurmountable height of Confucius' achievements is comparable to the sky, to which no staircase can ascend" (*A*:19.25); as Ruler: "At the age of fifty, I knew T'ien's command" (*A*:2.4); as Fate: "Wealth and status are up to T'ien" (*A*:12.5); as Nature: "T'ien does not speak, yet the four seasons turn, the myriad things are born" (*A*:17.17); as Ethical Principle: "Only T'ien is great, only the Emperor Yao emulated it" (*A*:8.19).[5] Even the *Hsun Tzu*, which devotes an entire chapter to a discussion of T'ien, proves upon analysis to employ the term in most of these senses (as we will discover in chapter VI), and as the passage from the *Mencius* cited earlier suggests, in some instances the texts employ the word with a vagueness so profound as to defy any conceptual limitation whatever.

Now, it would be unfair to demand that a philosophical text be consistent in its use of key terms; ambiguity may be central to a philosophical point.[6] For example, the *Analects* is notably inconsistent in its various discussions of the key term "*jen*" (sometimes translated as "humaneness"), and this obscurity represents precisely the problem that it seems Confucius wished to present to his disciples for reflection when he used the term (see chapter III). Those who can grasp a unity behind this diversity have presumably grasped the complex and partially ineffable meaning of "*jen*." The example of "*jen*" suggests that our best and perhaps only means of discovering the meaning of "*t'ien*" is to ponder the variety of statements about that term until we factor out, as a sort of algebraic constant common to all instances of the term, the esoteric concept the Confucians were trying to convey, independent of any specific images associated with T'ien.

But were Confucians using the art of ambiguity to make this sort of philosophical point in the case of "*t'ien*?" T'ien differs from "*jen*" because it is difficult to establish that it was a "key concept" for Confucians prior to the Han Dynasty. On the contrary, early Confucian philosophy seems directed away from metaphysics and religion, and historically, T'ien was first and foremost a metaphysical and religious idea.

If T'ien was not a defining interest of Confucianism, then a different sort of methodology is needed to elucidate the meaning of the term. The variety of expressions might not point to any single, ineffable unity, but might reflect the multifarious ways in which a complex traditional concept was functionally related to those things which *were* of central interest to Confucians. The long-established ambiguities associated with T'ien made the term extraordinarily malleable and ideally suited to serve as a rhetorical anchor to lay upon any philosophical ground whatever. In other words, if Confucianism was not "about" T'ien, the meaning of T'ien for Confucians ought to be expressed as a relation to what Confucianism *was* about.

This simple formula redirects our attention. Instead of searching directly for some unified concept of T'ien beneath a variety of expressions, we will search for a consistency in the relations between statements about T'ien and the core interests of early Confucianism. And because we will be exploring this relationship through texts written over several centuries (c. 500-200 B.C.), we will be looking, too, for its elaboration and development.

Early Confucianism and the Ru

Already, our project appears quite changed. We undertook to define the Heaven of early Confucianism; now it appears we must first define early Confucianism itself. Our guiding hypothesis will be this:

The extreme instability of the term *"t'ien"* in early Confucian texts, and the willingness to allow so rhetorically prominent a term to be employed without theoretical coherence, must reflect the force of a coherent set of core interests that governed formulations of doctrine and whose free expression could only be impeded by the friction of a fixed concept of T'ien.

A key element of this hypothesis is the introduction of the extra-theoretical notion of "interests." The reasoning here is that if the early Confucian enterprise were adequately definable as an attempt to build a theoretical construct, it is highly unlikely that Confucians would not have undertaken to devise a consistent theory to govern a term such as *"t'ien."* Our suggestion is that the volatility of Confucian theory in general, and of the term *"t'ien"* in particular, reflects the guiding influence of an extra-theoretical core of early Confucianism. This core we may suppose to represent the elusive ground of Confucian certainty and its contours should be reflected by the complex functions of T'ien in the texts.

To suggest that the core of early Confucianism may have lain outside Confucian theory is to imply that early Confucianism is not properly conceived as a philosophical enterprise in the Western sense. Surely the essential core of philosophies such as Platonism, Thomism, Rationalism, Idealism, and so forth, lies in the theoretical architectures articulated by the followers of each school.

Confucianism is different. The term "Confucianism" itself is highly confused, sometimes describing a set of doctrines or an ideology of state, sometimes a cultural point of view, sometimes a way of life.[7] In its earliest incarnation, the tangible constituents of Confucianism were the members of a small group of men known as "Ru," who viewed their distinguishing trait as a commitment to a particular set of ideas *and* well-defined practices, with no sharp division possible between the two. Any analysis that assumes that early Confucianism is adequately conceived as a set of ideas, on the model of Western philosophical enterprises, fails to approach the school on its own terms and cannot help but encounter a wealth of enigmatic problems.

It will be best for us to relinquish entirely the term "Confucian," burdened as it is with ambiguities and irrelevant traditional associations. As we turn toward a description of the school of Confucius, we will call its members by the name they originally bore, "Ru"; their philosophy we will call "Ruism."[8] The origins and nature of the Ruist school and its ritual focus will occupy us throughout the first portion of this book. Prior to embarking on a detailed exploration of the school, however, we should clarify precisely how our approach to Ruism will represent it as a nonanalytic philosophy and how this determines the strategies we will choose in examining the role of T'ien.

The Nonanalytic Agenda of Ruist Philosophy

The configurations of the revised portrait of Ruism that will emerge from this study have already been suggested. By drawing the outlines of the school in conformity with the notion that theory and practice were essentially integrated, we will be led to picture Ruism more as a community of men than as a body of doctrine. Programs of ritual activity will appear as the distinguishing core of that community. Consequently, the explicit doctrines that were articulated as a product of these activities will be most coherently expressed by their relation to the activities themselves: either as reports of perspectives generated through core practices, or as defensive rationalizations possessing the instrumental value of promoting and preserving the ritual core.

Clearly, if we describe Ruism in this fashion, we are effectively conceding that it was not philosophical in the Western analytic sense. In most branches of the Western tradition we find an implicit belief that the structure of the real world should, in principle, be subject to theoretical description. The philosophical enterprise is built on the notion that the natural world must make sense—that its structure is in some way parallel to the structures of human reason.[9] Ultimately, philosophical knowledge is knowledge of right theory. Philosophy might prescribe practices as a product of ethical theories of value, but practices, other than the practice of logical discipline in reason, are not a part of philosophy itself.

The centrality of practice in Ruism indicates that it was not a philosophy in this sense. Ruist texts, in fact, include statements that explicitly deny the ultimate value of logic and reason in the search for knowledge. The school rejects the analytic enterprise, and so, on the face of it, Ruism seems nonphilosophical.

However, Ruism had its own set of implicit assumptions about knowledge and the world, and when we examine these Ruism clearly was not nonphilosophical, but was rather a nonanalytic species of philosophy.

It has often been noted that early Confucian texts seem to use the word "knowledge" in the sense of "knowing how" more often than in the sense of "knowing that"; that is, in the sense of skill-knowledge rather than fact-knowledge or theory-knowledge (e.g., Lau 1979:43-44; Hansen 1983:64-65). This is not simply a matter of frequency; it a fundamental characteristic of Ruism as a nonanalytic philosophy. Ruists did not picture the world as an infinite collection of intrinsically atomic particular entities structured by a limited set of deterministic relational laws, such that every actual array of entities necessarily exemplified the universal structures of reality. Conceiving the things of the Ruist world as possessing intrinsic relational norms would be more accurate.[10] An actual array of things—an encountered situation—might fully exemplify these norms, but it might also exemplify a disorder in which things were displaced out of their natural relational positions. Chaos is possible. From such a viewpoint, the state of things in the world is not merely a matter of fact; it is intrinsically a matter of value. Knowledge in such a world must reflect this value dimension. The goal is not a search for descriptive theories that make sense of the world as an atemporal order, it is a search for the skills to configure the world according to its natural order, to perceive and fulfill a lifelong series of immediate imperatives.[11]

The project of the Ruist enterprise was to endow the individual with the skills needed to function in an ethical universe. What was necessary was not to analyze an underlying order to the world, but to synthesize the skills that could bring the world into natural order.

Skill Mastery and Ruism

The word "philosophy" was, of course, missing from the Ruist lexicon; the Ru described their program by a traditional word, "*tao*," and the meaning of the term reflects the nature of the program.

The word "*tao*" is probably best translated as "teaching," and in Chou Dynasty China, a *tao* was conceived as a coherent teaching that involved two elements: practices and statements.[12] The master of a *tao* viewed the practices as central because mastery of the practices generated a new perspective from which to view the world. To teach the practices, however, words were required, both to attract disciples and to instruct them, and eventually individual *tao*s became known through texts composed to persuade and to instruct.[13]

These texts included statements about the world subject to judgments of truth and falsity, but they differed from statements that characterize Western philosophy because the evidence of their validity could only be obtained through mastery of the practices that lay behind them. No test of theoretical cogency could be relevant because the practitioners of *tao*s assumed that the conceptual frameworks we use to determine truth are not generated analytically, but are the product of practical interaction with the world through experience. As a *tao* structures experience, it synthesizes a perspective, and the truth of a text's explicit claims cannot be evaluated outside that perspective.

The underlying hypothesis that an individual's repertoire of skills determines the interpretive options available to him for understanding the world is central to Ruism. Ruists had no faith in logical or ontological axioms that universally possessed powers of reason might confirm as self-evident (their philosophical adversaries, the Mohists, busied themselves in deriving these).[14] The masters of the Ruist *tao* saw truths in the world that reason did not reveal, and their concern as teachers was in transmitting to disciples their point of view. The core of the Ruist program was logically prior to an analytic agenda: their concern was not in analysis of the implications of self-evident axioms; it was in the synthesis of the axioms themselves.

In this sense, Ruism may be termed "synthetic philosophy." Its central methodology involved the careful design of a syllabus of practice rather than in rigor of rational argument. The heart of Ruism lay outside its texts in a detailed training course of ritual, music, and gymnastics. Masters and disciples spent considerable time discussing these practices and elaborating theories that rationalized their value. Such discussion was an ancillary activity. However, given the nature of texts, it is these discussions and theories that occupy the foreground of our view of Ruism.

The suggested link between one's repertoire of skills and one's natural perspective on the world that seems to underlie the Ruist enterprise was not a widely held tenet of traditional Western philosophies. The obvious relativistic implications would not have been congenial to most thinkers prior to this century, when the philosophical quest was generally cast as a search for objective absolutes. More recently, certain Western writers have examined the relationship between skill mastery and other forms of knowing and their work suggests the validity of Ruist assumptions.[15] Jean Piaget's studies of the way children learn illustrate links between the acquisition of basic motor skills and the construction of basic concepts of the world and time.[16] Michael Polanyi, a philosophical critic of science, developed detailed models describing the way individual growth involves a rhythm of attention to new skills as they are mastered followed by attention to the world through those mastered skills; in each instance, the newly acquired skills shape one's perception of structures, values, and imperatives.[17] One need only think of the identifiably idiosyncratic values and behaviors of people whose careers are shaped by commitments to well-defined "disengaged" arenas of skill, such as the arts or sports, to glimpse the manner in which skill configurations may govern both the perspectives and the "personali-

ties" of individuals.[18] So deeply may skill systems determine who we are
that we can analogize the mastery of a new skill to the extension of the
physical body.[19] The matrices of mastered skills create the pattern of possibilities through which we live, and in this sense, we can consider our skills
as the constituents of what we are as individual persons.

Ruist philosophical activity was predicated on this idea, and training
disciples in the Ruist syllabus was conceived very much as the creation of
new men. A passing comment in the *Hsun Tzu* conveys this notion well
enough: "Body is not so powerful as mind; mind is not so powerful as
art—once the proper arts are mastered, the mind will follow them" (*H*:5.3).
Thus, the ritual arts formed the core of the Ruist *tao*; once they were
mastered, the proper view of the world—the proper theory—would follow.

The Instrumental Role of Ruist Theory

If the core of Ruism was the body of ritual practice that dominated its
syllabus, then we are faced with a difficult interpretive problem when dealing with Ruist texts. Traditionally, these texts have been analyzed to elucidate the theoretical architecture their various statements imply. But if Ruist
philosophy was synthetic rather than analytic, then theory served only secondary functions for the school, and those functions did not necessarily
require or value the creation of a coherent theoretical archtecture. We may
have been reading the texts with irrelevant expectations.

The discursive component of the Ruist *tao* can be described as including
three different functional components: (1) an instructional function, (2) a
defensive rationalizing function, and (3) a reportative function.

The instructional function is reflected in the texts we possess by a
great wealth of admonitory statements and by innumerable statements of
and about ritual procedures (the text of the *Yi-li* is the best example of
the latter).

By far the greatest part of the Ruist texts, and the portion that has most
occupied interpreters, belongs to the second functional area, that of rationalization. From the start, Ruist texts must have performed a persuasive
function, attracting the ritually unwashed into the community of disciples,
and many statements in the texts are attempts to legitimize the Ruist enterprise to those who stand on the ground of common sense. Passages that
offer homely ad hoc explanations for Ruist practices would belong to this
group,[20] as might passages seeking to explain political failures of the school
(a group in which T'ien plays a major role, as we will discover). In addition,
as time elapsed, Ruist texts became to an increasing extent polemical
responses to the philosophical challenges of competing schools and of
sceptics, and in the process they began to incorporate sophisticated argumentation and theoretical constructs. This large body of Ruist theory, how-

ever, was not elaborated with any goal of systematic coherence. The goal was primarily instrumental: to defend the core of the school and its practices and lifestyle from attacks on its legitimacy that might lead to the dissolution of the Ruist community.

When we reformulate the program of this study by casting it as a search for the meaning of T'ien *as a function* of the core interests of Ruism, we anticipate that because of their lack of theoretical integration statements about T'ien most frequently performed a rationalizing role. Consequently, we abandon any effort to look for a consistent referential meaning of the term "*t'ien*" – any stable image or concept that could provide a dictionary-style gloss for the term in each text – and determine instead to look for coherence in the instrumental relation that Ruist statements about T'ien may have borne to the preservation and growth of the school's practical core.[21]

The primary nature of Ruist texts was instrumental; the noninstrumental practical core of the school lay elsewhere. But we should also be alert for the possibility that in some instances, the texts may not merely be engaged in legitimizing this core, but may be reporting directly what it was, and in such cases it may be that the term "*t'ien*" played a role in helping Ruists express their unique viewpoint. If Ruists were engaged in a prolonged and intensive process of skill acquisition, which was designed to generate a radically new perspective on the world, it would not be too surprising to find that they did in fact see things as others did not, and, recognizing this, simply reported what they saw. Nor, given the apparent willingness of individual Ru to devote entire lifetimes to the practice of ritual skills, should we be surprised to find that the Ruist perspective revealed a world of deep rewards, threaded together by a thematic logos paralleling the coherence of Ruist ritual practice. When we encounter passages in which Ruists claim knowledge of T'ien and in which T'ien appears so vague as to be linked to no particular traditional concept, we may ask whether the author simply sees something which we do not and cannot see, the Ruist ritual path being closed to us forever.

This leads us to the final theme of this introductory chapter: the notion of a coherent totalistic Ruist perspective, expressed by the concept of the Ruist Sage.

Philosophical Coherence: Ruist Sagehood

As noted above synthetic philosophy is inherently relativistic: it may well be so that self-evident truths are accessible only through the mastery of skills, but no criteria by which one could evaluate the relative merits of one set of skills and truths vis-à-vis another seem evident.

Ruists did not acknowledge the necessity of such relativism, and they claimed that their *tao* was the only valid one. Their claim rested on two elements, one theoretical and the other practical—history and Sagehood.

The historical claim rested on the sources of the specific content of the Ruist syllabus. The rituals that the Ru celebrated were not arbitrary: they were the intricate codes of the most successful political organization known to East Asian civilization to that date—the early Chou Dynasty. The enormous—in the Ruist view, perfect—success of the early Chou state was used to legitimize the absolute value of the codes (a process of transference that we will examine in chapter I). But more important, the early Chou was viewed by the Ruists as the culmination of an evolutionary process of universal history: the ordering of the natural world in conformity with the patterns of its inherent relational norms. Chou rituals were seen as the outcome of an inevitable learning process, a natural tendency of the human species to grasp and respond to the value imperatives that call through the disorder of the world as given.

An attractive theory, but merely a theory, after all. The practical element behind the Ruist claim to absolute knowledge was different in kind. From this angle, Ruists rested their claim of certainty on the evident comprehensiveness of the perspective that their *tao* generated. The Ruist texts report that the individual who mastered the multifaceted but thematically coherent ritual syllabus would discover powers of practical understanding of a degree far beyond those accessible to ordinary men. The trained Ru, it was maintained, could "read" the world much as someone possessed of proper language skills can read a book, easily interpreting each entirely new page according to the powers of understanding engendered by his mastery. Inherent structures of values and natural imperatives were clear to his eye, and response according to these norms had become as spontaneous as turning a page is for a reader.

Now, this too reads like a theory, but the difference here is that Ruists claimed to have empirical evidence of its truth from their own experience, and while none would claim to be himself a Sage, many clearly considered themselves to have glimpsed this perspective of totalistic coherence, and all agreed that certain great Ru, such as Confucius himself, embodied it fully.

The Ruist vision of Sagehood appears, in the final analysis, to be the bedrock of Ruist certainty, the center of gravity that kept the disparate doctrines and practices of the school from disintegrating into the ad hoc mass that they may appear to be from the outside. The pivotal role of the ideal of the Sage is reflected in the enormous importance that Ruists granted to the model of the master as an educational device. If the heart of Ruism lay in the transformation of men into ritual Sages, it followed that the teacher represented to a greater or lesser degree the embodiment of the philosophy, surpassing in importance not only texts, but even the rituals themselves. As the *Hsun Tzu* puts it: "In study, nothing is more helpful than to stay close to the man [i.e., one's model or teacher]. . . . The exaltation of ritual is next best. . . . If one merely memorizes exegeses of the *Poetry* and *Documents*, then forever unto death one can be no more than a base Ru" (*H*:1.35-37).[22]

Did Ruists actually become Sages—men whose perceptions of the world formed a perfect moral phenomenology? Well, we live in an age of scepticism, and can only suppose not. But whether Ruists possessed an experiential basis for their vision is another question. Certainly we encounter ostensibly reportative passages in the Ruist texts so vivid in their descriptions of what we might call "heightened states of consciousness" that it would require doltish insensitivity to ignore them. In chapter II, we will see that Ruist education aimed at transforming thought and behavior through a thoroughly prescribed choreography of daily living, extending from the most prosaic acts of personal conduct to an ultimate celebration in the splendor of ceremonial ritual and dance. In our conclusion, we will speculate on the way in which such skills may have generated experiences of certainty and control over delimited arenas of action that could well have formed the model for the idealized notion of totalistic Sagehood that disciples viewed as the self-evident legitimization of the Ruist *tao*.

Ultimately, we will describe this vision of Sage perfection of thought and motion in the everyday world through a metaphor meaningful to Ruist practice: the experience of dancing with complete command one's part in a grand ritual dance, able to evaluate every movement on the vast dance floor by its relation to one's own perfect motion. We will see the Ruist social ideal of ritual utopia as a vision of society transformed into an eternal and comprehensible field of dance, with each individual a Sage whose mastery of his or her determinate dance role allows the entire stage of society to appear as a predictable and understandable phenomenology.

Programmatic Summary

This introductory chapter has suggested the difficulties raised by the elusiveness of the Ruist notion of T'ien and outlined the model of Ruism that will be central to our approach to resolving them. In the body of this study we will separate rather sharply the projects of delineating the synthetic core of Ruism and of expressing the Ruist concept of T'ien as a function of that core structure.

Chapters I through III form a unified group devoted to outlining the origins, configuration, and philosophical implications of the Ruist ritual community. These three chapters respond to the baslc fact that the idea of a philosophy treating the accidental patterns of social and religious custom as its pivot of value is, in Western perspectives, somewhat implausible. Chapter I undertakes to establish the historical logic of Ruism's ritual commitment by examining the conditions under which Ruism and Chinese philosophy in general were born. We will see that critical thought in China grew out of an acute crisis in values that shaped the intellectual history of China from the eighth through the third centuries B.C. At the heart of this value crisis lay the issue of theodicy, and we will see that the rise of ritual as a category of philosophical significance was directly tied to the fall of T'ien as a stable ethical and religious foundation. In this context, the Ruist reconstruction of T'ien as the legitimizing ground for ritual makes sense.

Chapter II contains our historical portrait of the Ruist movement and its central interests. This portrait will be drawn largely from historical texts, the *Analects*, the *Mencius*, and various ritual books that circulated during the Han period. We will see that Ruism was not primarily a political movement, but was first and foremost groups of men meeting to practice and discuss ritual ceremonies and music, immediately motivated by the ideal expectation of attaining transcendent wisdom and the practical expectation of employment as a ritual Master. The expectation of political roles was secondary and to a great extent tactical, the professed expectation rather than the actual achievement serving to legitimize ritual interests.

Chapter III addresses in more detail the issue of how the individuals who joined the Ruist community could plausibly have believed that ritual practice could have been so ethically and practically efficacious. Our analysis will focus on the ideal of ritual Sagehood, which we will characterize as a comprehensive "totalistic" goal, which aimed to reshape every aspect of the individual. A discussion of Ruist notions of self revealed through the texts will illustrate the plausibility of such a totalistic goal, by illustrating that the "self" undergoing transformation in the Ruist model included malleable "public" dimensions excluded from traditional portraits of the self in Western thought.

Chapters IV through VI undertake close textual analysis of instances of the word "*t'ien*" in early Ruist texts. We begin in chapter IV by exploring the role of T'ien in the *Analects*. We will encounter there a structure of instrumental meaning that forms a theme throughout our three early texts. This structure rests on a dual role that T'ien played, acting both as a prescriptive authority legitimizing Ruist ritual interests, and as a descriptive historical force that provided a teleological explanation of the politically outcast status that Ruism was both forced to and preferred to play during the late Chou.

Chapter V will focus on the *Mencius*. The *Mencius* is the earliest Ruist text to discuss T'ien in theoretical terms, and we will explore the motivation for this interest in metaphysical speculation and the models that it generated. We will conclude that the metaphysical theory of the *Mencius* was an integral part of a strategy to mount a defensive structure of rhetoric that could protect Ruist ritual interests from powerful attacks launched by competing philosophical schools.

In chapter VI we will turn to the *Hsun Tzu*, a work whose views on T'ien have been much analyzed. Prior scholarship has yielded a consensus agreement that the *Hsun Tzu* conceived T'ien as Nature. We will suggest that this conclusion, while largely accurate, does not tell the whole story, and we will explore its limits. The *Hsun Tzu*'s equation of T'ien and Nature was largely a cooptation of ideas developed by a disparate variety of late Chou naturalistic philosophies. These schools presented the greatest challenges to Ruism during the third century B.C., and the *Hsun Tzu* employs notions of T'ien characteristic to them in order to defend Ruist ritual interests against their attack. Underlying the text's naturalistic portrait of T'ien, however, we discover a use of the prescriptive and descriptive roles of T'ien that has much continuity with the portraits of the *Analects* and *Mencius*. Once again, T'ien is described so as to legitimize Ruist ritual commitment. The form that description takes is in response to the philosophical environment of the day.

Finally, in the brief concluding chapter we will return to the theoretical issues of this introduction and discuss them in terms of what we have learned about the structure of early Ruism and the role of T'ien in Ruist doctrine. Our theme will be that the Ruist T'ien had always to be a function of a particular system of skills idealized by Ruists as Sagehood, and we will close with a speculative discussion of the structure of that Ruist ideal.

Part One

Setting the Ritual Stage

Pre-Confucian Heaven

Chapter I

The central theory of this study holds that it is not possible to understand the functional meaning of the term *"t'ien"* in early Ruist texts without grasping the depth of the intellectual and practical commitments of Ruists to Chou Dynasty ritual: *li*. That primary commitment is itself a puzzle. How is it possible that the foremost philosophy of China should be grounded on the ascription of cardinal value to what were, in the final analysis, accidental patterns of behavior particular to a single historical era? If we are to argue the cogency of a ritual-centered portrait of early Ruism, it is necessary to demonstrate not merely the evidence for such a claim, but its basic plausibility. In this chapter, we will sketch an outline account of the historical background that made Confucius' celebration of ritual a logical response to the intellectual demands of his time. Part of the analysis involves a discussion of the general pervasiveness of ritual behavior in pre-Confucian China and its social function. Concern with ritual was no Ruist innovation, although the notion of ritual as a focal category of value most likely was.

But the particular historical circumstances behind the emergence of ritual as a philosophical focus are also central to our inquiries concerning T'ien. Confucius' turn to ritual *li* was directly related to the discrediting of a belief that had served as the basic anchor of value during the early Chou: the belief in an omnipotent and omnibenevolent power guaranteeing social order—T'ien. The rise of *li* as a cardinal value can be seen as a function of the fall of T'ien.

1. The Ritual Antecedents of Ruism

The central role that ritual plays in the early stages of social organization is well known. One anthropologist has speculated that its symbolic systems of activity provide for human beings the sorts of coded information that are transmitted genetically as instinct in other animal species (Geertz 1973:92-3). Another point of view holds that ritual codes are one medium through which a human community is able to sustain an efficient interaction with the stable ecosystem in which it lives (Rappaport 1971:71).[1]

The nature of these theories alone suggests our growing awareness of the enormous importance that ritual can play in society. Paul Wheatley has discussed the role of ritual in the genesis of urban communities in these terms:

Whenever, in any of the seven regions of primary urban generation [including China] we trace back the characteristic urban form to its beginnings we arrive not at a settlement that is dominated by commercial relations, a primordial market, or at one that is focused on a citadel and archetypal fortress, but rather at a ceremonial complex (1971:225).

Evidence from the earliest period of Chinese civilization of which we have written record, the Shang Dynasty (c. 1766-1045 B.C.), suggests that Chinese culture was, from a very early time, highly ritualized. The Shang rulers, who presided for many centuries as hegemons over a confederacy of tribal units, left records in the form of divination inscriptions, known as oracle texts.[2] These inscriptions, unearthed by archeologists during this century, afford us a detailed view of certain aspects central to the concerns of the Shang ruling house, particularly matters of religious practice.[3]

The religious picture revealed through the oracle texts is extraordinarily complex, particularly in light of the fact that the baroque network of ritual we are shown pertains only to the royal house of the Shang: popular religion is not accessible to us. The Shang ruler was responsible for maintaining sacrifices to a bewildering number of nature deities, culture heroes, and royal ancestors, the last group ever growing.[4] By the eleventh century B.C. the king was obliged, on every day of the year, to stage a major ceremony marking the annual sacrifice to a prominent royal deity.[5]

The religious obligations of the Shang royal house reflected the ritual-centered nature of Shang society. Communities of priests and diviners bustled about the capital, and as Wheatley has noted, the demand for ritual artifacts of jade and bronze—which dazzle our eyes in museums today—made the ritual industries the focus of technological innovation for late Shang society (Wheatley 1971:73).[6]

During the eleventh century B.C. a tribe on the Western periphery of the Shang confederacy, the Chou, grew dissatisfied with its subordinate role. Under a leader known to history as King Wen, Chou political power seems to have begun a period of rapid growth.[7] Under King Wen's son, King Wu (The Martial King), the Chou revolted against their Shang overlords. In 1045 B.C., on the plain of Mu-yeh outside the walls of the Great City of Shang, King Wu, tradition tells us, led his troops in a great dance of war, and, on the following day, the Chou were the rulers of the Central Kingdom.[8]

With the coming of the Chou, Chinese civilization experienced fundamental changes in social and political structure. The early Chou rulers were not content to maintain the loose tribal hegemony that seems to have characterized the Shang. Immediately after the conquest, King Wu and his successors began policies of mass resettlement and political enfeoffment that soon resulted in direct control by members of the royal house or their stalwarts over most of the territory of the Chinese cultural sphere.[9]

This redrawing of the political landscape opened a remarkable period of stability in China. From the middle of the reign of King Ch'eng in the eleventh century B.C. to the reign of King Yi in the early ninth century, the historical record is remarkably blank. Although occasional crises of royal succession and military setbacks do occur, these seem to have been well-spaced in the overall context of political calm, and in the retrospective eye of historical tradition, they served only to accent the dominant theme of tranquility.[10] What stands out is the gradual consolidation and expansion of the Chou polity under a succession of comparatively capable kings and regents.[11] This century and a half, as featureless as utopia, is the true backdrop of the Ruist vision of the world.

1.1. The Three Pillars of the Western Chou

In the view of later Ruists, living amidst the decay of the Chou social order, the early centuries of the Chou Dynasty represented the acme of human potential.[12] This period of the Western Chou (1045-771 B.C.), as it is known, came to be regarded by later generations as a golden age of peace and virtue. This reverent view is not surprising. The Western Chou kings successfully administered a unified empire long before any entity of comparable size and duration had been created in the West. The early Chou Dynasty *was* remarkable.[13]

The architecture of the Chou polity was sustained by three pillars of social order: the institution of the kingship, the institution of hereditary succession to political office or social occupation, and the unifying force of a state religious system centered on the king and his god, T'ien. These constituted consensus foundations for value in Western Chou society.

The innovative political program of King Wu, along with salutary contributions of the Duke of Chou, who succeeded him as regent, served to strengthen the power and raise the prestige of the early kings far beyond their Shang predecessors.[14] In terms of the mechanics of social stability, the pseudofeudal structure of Chou political administration combined with normal forces of social inertia to produce a society firmly committed to the notion of hereditary social roles, a pattern that must have made Western Chou life comfortably predictable.

The kingship and hereditary "feudal" structure were the practical bases of Chou social order. But their legitimacy and intellectual power rested upon the third pillar of the early Chou: the explicit claim that Chou rule was no more than an agency for the benevolent will of T'ien, and that government was, in effect, an organ for the discharge of religious responsibilty. During the early centuries of social tranquility, the benign image of T'ien seemed plainly visible in a succession of adequate rulers. When the quality of Chou rule declined in the ninth century B.C. the nagging riddle that began to undermine beliefs and values was not how the House of Chou could decay, but how a benevolent T'ien could allow a decadent house to retain the throne. The debasement of the ruling king entailed the debasement of the ruling god, and this is the impetus that set philosophical thought in motion.

However, even during the brightest days of T'ien and the Chou kings, the ritual patterns to which philosophy would first turn as a new ground for value were being woven.

1.2. The Patterning of Chou Society

The three pillars of the Western Chou anchored that society for two centuries. And during that period, encircling each of these pillars grew a network of highly stylized political, religious, and social etiquette, mirroring throughout the Chou polity the affinity for ritual behavior that seems to have typified the Shang.

The intricacy of the ritual system of the Western Chou is probably difficult to overstate. Throughout the period we see a growing profusion of the paraphernalia of ritual, particularly bronze ritual vessels. Nearly all contemporary inscriptions of any length describe religious or political ceremonies, often in great detail and invariably in language itself highly stylized.[15] Even allowing for the exaggerated detail in later Ruist accounts of Chou ceremonies, the question can only be the degree to which ritual constituted the grammar of social intercourse among the elite, not the fact that it did.[16]

A single detail reveals much about this aspect of Chou culture. The ritual articulation of Chou society is reflected in a passage in the *Analects* in which Confucius comments: "The Chou was a mirror of the previous two eras; how rich were its patterns (*wen*)!" (*A*:3.14). The word "*wen*," which we will see later was a key term in Ruist ritual doctrines, was used in the Western Chou to denote a type of personal virtue.[17] The original meaning of the term is revealing. The early graph pictured an outstretched human body with an outsized chest, upon which appeared a pattern whose particular form might vary.[18] Inscriptional and later textual evidence indicates that the graph may have depicted a dancer costumed as a bird with a patterned feather breast.[19] On sacrificial vessels of the Western Chou period, the word commonly is used to honor a deceased ancestor, sometimes in parallel with the word "*huang*," a term also drawn from dance.[20]

"Pattern" denotes the original sense of the term "*wen*," and its positive connotations are conveyed by the choice of a ritual symbol for the graph.[21] The applications of the word in extended senses of "beautiful," "cultured" and "honored" reflect broadening of the term from an aesthetic notion to an ethical one. Its centrality to Western Chou civilization is reflected in the fact that "*wen*" was the word selected as the posthumous name of King Wen, the founder of the dynasty, father to King Wu.[22]

All this suggests the care with which the Chou ruling class relied upon aesthetic criteria of ritual conduct to shape social behavior. Yet the Western Chou people probably did not consciously view themselves as a "ritual society," or conceive of ritual as a distinct category. Our evidence suggests that not until later did the term used to mean "ritual," "*li*," come to have a generic sense.[23] During the period of the Western Chou itself, ritual codes were not likely stressed as sources legitimizing action and status. Positive bases of value were provided by the pillars of kingship, hereditary roles, and, ultimately, the sanction of T'ien. Ritual was not perceived as the distinguishing characteristic of the Western Chou until the pillars of the era had largely decayed. But once they had, it was logical that Chou ritual codes should inherit their role as value standards.

2. T'ien as the King's God

According to tradition, at the time of the Chou conquest, King Wu and his supporters legitimized their action in overthrowing the Shang by claiming that the Chou had simply acted as the agents of T'ien. This claim, known as the doctrine of the Mandate of Heaven, asserted that T'ien was an omnipotent guarantor of tranquility and justice in the Central Kingdom. T'ien fulfilled its guarantee by intervening occasionally in human affairs whenever the virtue of the ruling house of China declined beyond a critical level. On such occasions, the Chou founders explained, T'ien would effectively order the most virtuous house in the land to displace the offending royal line and succeed to the throne. The claim was simply proved: had omnipotent T'ien not wished the Chou to occupy the throne, it would not have enabled the conquest to occur.[24]

These arguments were effective in reconciling the peoples of the Shang polity to Chou rule. But they had yet another function. Whereas the Shang king had been merely chief priest to the high gods, the Mandate of Heaven theory made the Chou king T'ien's executor on earth.[25] T'ien and the king were now nearly indistinguishable.[26] During the period of vigorous Chou rule, T'ien was virtually the personal deity of the king. Only the king was permitted to have intercourse with T'ien through sacrifice. When T'ien was spoken of by others, it was always with reference to the king, or to affairs of state under the king's direction. People who were not members of the royal house neither sacrificed to nor prayed to T'ien. In terms of function, T'ien was practically reduced to the king.[27]

The identification of T'ien and king is marked by their significant coincidence of powers and interests, as is revealed in contemporary inscriptional texts. One of the kings, probably King K'ang (r. 1005-977 B.C.), exhorts an appointee in these terms: "Steady and diligent, remonstrate from dawn to dusk; exhaust yourself in service, fearing the awesomeness of T'ien."[28] T'ien will punish those who do not serve the king well, and the executor of that punishment will surely be the king himself.

The point is made even more clearly by the *Pan kuei* inscription. There the king sends his generals off to war with the order: "Within three years settle the eastern lands so that none is not peaceful, assured of the awesomeness of T'ien."[29] Yet it will not be T'ien they hold in awe, but the king's army. A general responds, "These people have foolishly courted disaster; they are all deaf to T'ien's orders, and so will perish."[30] Yet the orders they ignore are not T'ien's but the king's.[31]

The identification of T'ien and king naturally helped legitimize the Chou claim to the throne. What is often overlooked is that the stable rule provided by the early Chou kings legitimized T'ien's choice. The king and T'ien were linked in the action of good government, and under these conditions, it was possible for a sense of T'ien as an ethically prescriptive force to grow.[32] During the heyday of the Western Chou, political success gradually strengthened the dual belief in the legitimacy of the Chou order, and in the omnipotent goodness of the god who had mandated it.

2.1. T'ien as a Royal Adversary

The vigorous rule of the early Chou kings legitimized T'ien, the king's god. But from the mid-ninth century B.C. the fortunes of the royal house went into a steep decline. The border "barbarians" were no longer subjugated with ease, the Chou kings attracted increasing disrespect, one even being exiled, and internal dissension arose. In 771 B.C., the dynasty was forced to flee the capital and relocate in Lo-yang to the east. The Western Chou was at its end; it was followed by a prolonged period of war and suffering.

In some late Western Chou bronze inscriptions, the king continued to claim the protection of T'ien, as evidenced by a rather boastful inscription on a vessel apparently cast by King Li (r. 859-842) that refers both to T'ien and to "*ti*" the term used to denote a supreme deity in the Shang:

The king said: I am but a small child, yet unstintingly day and night, I act in harmony with the former kings to be worthy of august T'ien. . . . [I] make this sacrificial food vessel, this precious *kuei*-vessel, to succor those august paradigms, my brilliant ancestors. May it draw down [the spirits of] those exemplary men of old, who now render service at the court of Ti and carry forth the magnificent mandate of august Ti . . . .[33]

But other inscriptions tell a different story, a story of mounting military impotence and the abandonment of the king by T'ien. In the *Yü ting* inscription, the general Yü laments:

Alas! T'ien has sent great disasters down upon the lower countries. Yü-fang, Marquis of O, has led the southern tribes of the Huai and the Yi tribes of the east in a great attack on the southern and eastern lands, reaching to Li-han. Whereupon the king has ordered. . . . "Fiercely attack Yü-fang, Marquis of O, sparing neither young nor old."[34]

The general has seen here what the king may not yet have seen, that T'ien and the king were now fighting on opposite sides of the battle.

The new distance between T'ien and king is portrayed in the text of the *Mao Kung ting*, a vessel which may be dated to the reign of King Hsuan (r. 827-782 B.C.).[35] The king first recites how T'ien bestowed the mandate to rule upon Kings Wen and Wu, then he continues:

And so august T'ien unstintingly stood by us, watching over and protecting the Chou. There was no danger that the former kings would prove unworthy of the mandate. [But now] pitiless T'ien rises awesome, and if I, a small child succeeding [to the throne] am inadequate, how shall the state be blessed? The four quarters are in chaos, all following in unrest.[36]

Here again, the king stands in opposition to T'ien, and it is interesting to see that he faces an unjust fate. It is not because the king is weak that T'ien has wreaked havoc, but because T'ien is pitiless that the king fears his own inadequacy.[37] From the royal perspective, the issue is not kingly virtue, but the puzzling failure of T'ien's benevolence.

Another inscription of the same period tells the story even more plainly. The king speaks again of the past beneficence of T'ien, but then addresses his minister Shih P'ou with these words:

Alas, Shih P'ou! Now T'ien rises awesome and sends down disaster. Foremost virtue cannot overcome and control it, hence none can receive [the throne of absolute power] from the former kings.[38]

Within a few decades, T'ien had completed its subversion of the royal house. The king had fled the capital, and he and his successors would be no more than figureheads thereafter. Soon after we find evidence that the king's monopoly on T'ien has ended as well. Within a century of the Chou flight to the East, we find the Duke of Ch'in proclaiming:

Magnificent, my august ancestors received T'ien's mandate, receiving the reward of the Yü lands. The twelve [former] dukes now reside with Ti and look down; reverent in caring for T'ien's mandate, they protect their Ch'in and dispatch (?) the southern and central peoples.[39]

In another inscription, the ruler of the small state of Hsu, styling himself "king," dedicates a vessel for sacrifices to "august T'ien and my exemplary father; long may they guard my person."[40]

2.2. The Injustice of T'ien

When the Chou founders made their claim that the conquest of the Shang was by the grace of T'ien, the power of their assertion rested on the established authority of T'ien as a religious figure. We do not have clear evidence of the preconquest role of T'ien, or of the early meanings of the term "*t'ien.*"[41] There is evidence, however that during the Western Chou, the notion of T'ien as the benevolent god of state may have existed side by side with popular agricultural traditions, most likely very old, which cast T'ien as the unpredictable ruler of the sky, whose whims were as likely to be malevolent as otherwise (Eno 1984:91-94).

The firm rule of the Chou kings had demonstrated T'ien's political benevolence during the early years. Now that the kings had lost the power to restrain social chaos, T'ien's political behavior became as changeable as the weather. Instead of ruling with ethical perfection, T'ien now allowed injustice and suffering in human affairs, just as it had in natural affairs before. The king's god was coming more and more to resemble the popular sky god, blind to good and evil, a danger to man even as man depended upon it.

In the "Hsiao ya" section of the *Poetry*, there is a remarkable group of poems datable to soon after the fall of the western capital, which gives eloquent testimony to the change in T'ien:

> Bright T'ien so vast prolongs not its grace,
> Hurls misery and famine, beheading the states.
> Bright T'ien rises awesome, unthinking, unplanning,
> Lets the guilty go free; they have paid for their crimes—
> And the guiltless must join them, all drowning as one (194/1).

The poem continues, lamenting the fall of the capital, and it is clear that the sky god, who is causing famine here, is the same god who abandoned the king to his fate. The theme of these passages is the confusion of good and evil, and it is no accident that the poem's title is "Rain Without Justice."

Another poem with a similar theme begins by describing an ill-omened eclipse, a portent of the instability of nature. After describing the political situation, the poet says:

> The four quarters are sated, I alone am in anguish;
> All loose themselves from care, I alone dare not rest;
> T'ien's commands are all awry, I dare not obey (193/8).[42]

This poem is usually dated to the reign of King Yu, just prior to the fall of the capital (Wang 1968:407). Once again, the poet stands in opposition to T'ien, surrounded by evildoers whose conduct T'ien seems to condone, both by failing to punish them and by its own irregular course.

The fall of the Western Chou left T'ien morally bankrupt, and the language used to vilify the supreme deity is startling by Western standards:

> Now the people are in peril, they look to T'ien all darkened;
> Were there one who could bring peace, [T'ien] would overcome him.
> August god above, who is it you hate? (192/4).

In these poems, a clear distinction is drawn between human evil, which is caused by man, and the chaos that engulfs the innocent, caused by T'ien.[43] Guilt is assigned to man in the former case, but to T'ien in the latter.

As long as T'ien remained linked to a strong human king, it was a just and discerning deity. Once the world of man degenerated into injustice and blind suffering, the king's god disappeared into the tradition of the sky god, terrific, unjust, and blind. As social values collapsed, so did the value of T'ien.

2.3. Creating a New T'ien

The fall of T'ien raised an issue capable of stimulating a transformation of religious thought to philosophy. Simply put, it was the problem of theodicy: how can a deity prescriptively good allow a world descriptively evil?

T'ien had served as a mooring for value. During the early Chou, service to the king, the king's law and customs, and the might of the king's armies had all been tied to T'ien. But it was the success of these institutions that had, in fact, anchored T'ien. Now the moorings were cut, and T'ien itself was adrift; only by discovering other values to fasten to it could T'ien again be anchored. The task was to find the "real" values, ones that restored to T'ien its prescriptive perfection. Finding a new point of view from which even a chaotic world made moral sense was necessary. Whatever that logos was would become the new T'ien.

Nonphilosophical thought was not able to do this. It could, as the boastful Duke of Ch'in, simply claim that orderly rule, and T'ien, had been restored in the rule of a new leader, ignoring the contradictory facts of a chaotic world. Or, it could simply make do with T'ien as it appeared to be, descriptively amoral. Such a deity would be much like "fate": incomprehensible, commanding awe but not reverence. Nonphilosophical thought in the late Chou often chose such an option (Ikeda 1968:25-29).[44]

But early philosophical thought was tied to the attempt to restore T'ien's credibility by redefining values that could in some real way be upheld in the face of social disorder. We will see that for Ruists, this world of value was defined as ritual and the transformation of man into a perfect ritual being. It will not surprise us, then, to find Confucius reassure his companions of his safety by declaring, "If T'ien had wanted this pattern (*wen*) to die, [I] would not have been able to participate in it; what can [my enemies] do to me?" (*A*:9.5), where the "pattern" referred to is the network of Chou ritual norms. In Ruism, the first response of philosophy to the mid-Chou crisis in values, ritual *li* succeeded to the place vacated by the practical pillars of Chou value: the kingship and hereditary roles. And, in turn, T'ien was restored to its place as the ultimate ground of value, recast as the mandator of ritual.

Summary

In this chapter, we have prepared some of the groundwork necessary to demonstrate the claim that early Ruism revolved around a ritual focus, and that the role of T'ien can only be understood as a function of that ritual orientation. Our argument to this point has addressed the basic implausibilty, for the modern West, of conceiving a philosophy grounded on the ascription of cardinal value to a body of traditional ritual, by exploring the historical background that made the Ruist choice of philosophical focus logical. We have seen that, amidst the mid-Chou collapse of all stable value foundations, only the secondary elaboration of ritual codes survived as an existing basis on which to build philosophy. Moreover, having seen that the emergence of ritual as an intellectual category was tied to the decay of the existing notion of T'ien as a value standard, the reconstitution of T'ien as a legitimizing ground for ritual value seems more cogent.

But historical logic alone cannot rationalize a ritual basis for philosophy. We may still ask how a philosophy focused on ritual could be intellectually satisfying, and how a school built upon so problematical a base, could endure.

In the next chapter, our tasks will be to explore the intellectual dimensions of Ruist ritualism, and to describe the birth, structure, and social roles of the Ruist school.

Masters of the Dance

Chapter II

In our introduction we concluded that to elucidate the meaning of T'ien in Ruist texts we had to understand how T'ien "fit into" the central projects of early Ruism. Our immediate task was thus shifted from analyzing the varied uses of the word "*t'ien*" in the texts, with an eye to finding some unified concept or a set of concepts to which the word referred, to an exploration of the practical projects of Ruism. It is in light of these that the inconsistent uses of the word "*t'ien*" should make sense. Ruist discussions of T'ien were interested discussions; they were not reflections of "pure" inquiry, but part of an attempt to legitimize and elaborate in doctrine the activities and interests that were typical of early Ruists and that set them apart as a distinct element of society. Unity and diversity in the Ruist meanings of T'ien must derive from the evolving course of these activities and interests and not from a persistence or succession of inflexible "concepts."

Underlying all this is an implicit theory of what Ruism was, in a formal sense. Early Ruism was not so much an ideology as a way of life. It was a style of personal behavior cultivated through a long process of education. Ruists acquired a distinct repertoire of skills; their behavior and their thinking differed from that of their non-Ruist contemporaries as a consequence.

This chapter is our attempt to get at the core of early Ruism—to locate those interests and issues so central to the lives of early Ruists that virtually no part of their theories can be understood completely without reference to them. As we employ our instrumental method, we will be looking for the *non*instrumental core of Ruism: the things which were, for Ruists, of ultimate value, ends in themselves.

In this chapter, we will draw substantially upon historical sources to compose a portrait of Ruism in terms of what early Ruists actually did, as opposed to what they thought or said. This will not be a disinterested narrative. It has a point to prove and an interpretive framework that organizes the historical materials. The central issue involves the reformulation of a structural model basic to understanding early Ruism.

The doctrine of early Ruism is fundamentally bifurcated. Ruists spoke at great length about the need for self-cultivation and moral training, and they spoke at just as great a length about the need for political reform and governmental training (Schwartz 1964:5). These two aspects were theoretically linked, the linkage being most elegantly expressed in the *Ta-hsueh* (Great Learning), which teaches that the rectification of the mind through careful study is the first in a series of steps culminating in sagely government. Ruists held that self-cultivation and political activism were equally important, but that sequentially, self-cultivation was prior. Accounts of Ruism in the West have generally either accepted the Ruist claim that the two aspects were closely linked, or have leaned toward the view that despite its sequential position, political activism was ethically primary, and that early Ruism was fundamentally an activist political movement, whose ideology included an ethics of self-cultivation.

Our portrait of Ruism will differ. It interprets the instrumental functions of the two aspects of Ruist doctrine as having operated in different ways, and views the two doctrinal moieties not as linked but as radically disjoined. Our portrait will suggest that while rhetoric describing the perfection of the self served to commit Ruists to an ever deepening dedication to mastery of an educational syllabus, idealistic political rhetoric served to *discourage* Ruists from practical political ambitions, and legitimized a withdrawal from the world of political intrigue. In other words, although the two aspects of doctrine stressed distinct imperatives, one to study and one to change the world, they were reducible to a single message: study and keep on studying.

In our portrait, we will reject the notion that Ruists were political activists whose lives were devoted to seeking governmental responsibilities. We will, instead, picture the Ruist community as an archipelago of lifelong study groups, a brotherhood whose social insularity was tempered only by desires for social legitimacy and prestige, and by the need to maintain economic sustenance.

At the core of early Ruism we will find devotion to study and to the formation and perpetuation of study groups, which were the basic units of the early Ruist community. These groups were composed of disciples pledged to a prolonged course of personal improvement under the direction of a Ruist Master. The training that they received focused on mastering a broad set of traditional ritual formulas, known as *li*.[1] The varied syllabus of the Ruist school revolved around the theory and practice of *li*, and the end goal of self-cultivation was the complete ritualization of personal conduct.

This call for complete self-stylization was the aspect of early Ruist thought and practice that most clearly distinguished Ruism from other philosophical schools. Ruists advocated a totally choreographed lifestyle, where the formalities of ritual guided action from one's first step outdoors in the morning to the time one lay down at night.[2] The totality of the imperative cannot be underestimated. In the *Analects*, Confucius urges his disciple Yen Yuan not to see, hear, say, or do anything which is not *li* (*A*:12.1). For the *Mencius*:

"Every motion, every stance precise in *li* as one goes round: this is the acme of full virtue" (*M*:7B.33). And for the *Hsun Tzu*, even the flow of thought and the pulse of the blood must be governed by *li* (*H*:2.7-8). The goal of the Ruist was to strive toward this ideal and become a master of this enduring ritual dance.

In chapter I we explored the background that makes the Ruist ritual focus logical in the context of Chou intellectual history. Nevertheless, the dogmatic exaltation of *li* that is characteristic of Ruist texts of all periods tends to strike us in the West as arbitrary and unsophisticated. *Li* consisted of a set of particular codes that were culturally specific: the very antithesis of the universal propositions that we expect a philosophy to formulate and test. Some early Chinese texts themselves recognize that *li*, which were subject to change, were conventional, rather than universal norms.[3] Moreover, *li* must appear to non-Chinese as an arbitrary circumscription of human potential, stifling individualistic and innovative expression. The Ruist obsession with particularistic *li* appears to disqualify Ruism as a viable pan-human philosophy. Even if we interpret *li* in a broad sense as *any* set of culturally specific codes, the Ruist program is still alien to our modern stress on ethical individualism and the Kantian notion of the individual as the creator of universal law (see Lukes 1973:55, 99-105).

Our understanding of the philosophical significance of the Ruist commitment to *li* has been greatly enhanced by the innovative interpretations that Herbert Fingarette has presented in his *Confucius—the Secular as Sacred* (1972). Drawing on Fingarette's insights, we can begin to understand how *li* could have appeared so attractive and rewarding to Ruists and how commitment to a particular form of behavior may be compatible with philosophical ideas of broad value. Many of the ideas presented here were given focus by Fingarette's study. References to his work do not appear frequently on the pages that follow primarily because the overall outline of the argument here was developed independently and deals with some issues in a different way.

Our historical outline is divided into three sections: a brief discussion of the intellectual dimensions of ritual practice in early Chinese society and their role in the founding of Ruism, an analysis of the instrumentality of political idealism in preserving the ritual-centered and apolitical nature of Ruism, and a survey of the structure and social role of the Ruist community from the death of Confucius to the end of the Chou.

1. The Ritual Basis of Ruism

The Han historian Ssu-ma Ch'ien tells us that when Liu Pang, soon to become first emperor of the Han, was pursuing his war against his rival

Hsiang Yü, "He raised his troops, and encircled [the capital of the old state of] Lu. From within came the ceaseless sounds of strings and songs, for in that place the Ru still recited and chanted, practicing ceremony and music" (*SC*:121.3117).

Here is a glimpse of early Ruism that shows us features not often stressed in Western accounts. If there were such a thing as a pure behaviorist historian, he might describe pre-Ch'in Ruism not as a philosophy, but as a social phenomenon primarily involving the joining together of men in groups to chant ancient texts, sing ancient songs, and play ancient music. If he could take us in a time machine to view a single scene typifying what Ruism was, he might show us a group of eccentrically costumed disciples assembled at their Master's house, carefully stepping through an intricately scripted and choreographed ritual under the eye of their teacher: a band of men mastering an endless variety of ancient dances.

But there are other, more intellectual aspects of Ruism, aspects far more celebrated, some of which seem far removed from this scene of ritual dance. There is Confucius instructing the lords of Lu in the art of government. There is Mencius arguing the innate goodness of human nature, and trying to prove it by transforming corrupt warlords into universal Sages. There is Hsun Tzu devising intricate theories of social dynamics and the process of knowing.

In the account that follows, we will try to suggest how the variety of Ruist activity and doctrine grew from and remained rooted in the single paradigmatic image we have sketched here. Our thesis is that the central commitment of Ruists throughout the Warring States period was to the practice of *li* and to the notion that mastery of *li* was the path to Sagehood. The fervent political idealism and the wonderful variety of philosophical theories developed by the many Ruists of the Warring States should, in our view, generally be considered as the intellectual manifestations of the central Ruist concern: to legitimize and perpetuate their chosen lifestyle as students and Masters of *li*.

Our first task is to explain how ritual could provide intellectual rewards on a scale adequate to place them at the heart of philosophy. I would like to begin by sketching a highly schematic picture of some general features of ritual, and then use this schema to suggest some basic changes that may have occurred in the ideological rationale for ritual behavior during the Chou, as a result of the collapse of the kingship and the discrediting of T'ien that we discussed in chapter I. These changes, if the model is valid, help to explain the way in which Ruists of the late Chou regarded ritual, and make somewhat clearer how their interpretation of *li* represents a significant transformation of the traditional approach to ritual, a transformation that made the category of *li* a rich one for intellectual exploration.

1.1. Rationales for Ritual

Our simple model begins by dividing ritual into three main categories: its religious, social and aesthetic dimensions.[4] The religious aspect of ritual is most apparent in activities such as sacrificial worship. It is based on the premise that there can be an entailment between symbolic action and supernatural or natural consequences. Thus, ritual can be used to manipulate the gods or Nature.[5]

The use of religious ritual generally has deep ethical significance, whether we speak of holy rite or black magic. This sort of ritual is sacred, except perhaps at the simplest levels of superstition (e.g., knocking on wood). During the Western Chou, religious rituals were ethically legitimate if they were practiced within the sanctioned structures of state or clan religion. These areas of ritual practice contributed to the body of lore called *li*. Religious *li* was thus ethically legitimized by belief in its natural efficacy and by the sanctioned morality of state and clan religions.

The social aspect of ritual refers to the power of ritual to delineate meanings in hierarchical society. For example, what it means to be politically subordinate is directly expressed in the ritual injunction: "When one's lord orders one to receive guests, one's countenance suddenly changes, one's legs seem to give way" (A:10.2). This sort of playacting is not trivial. It is a powerful aspect of ritual, and, when it is understood by all the actors involved, it can make ritual a field of remarkably subtle communication.[6]

Although ritual severely constrains one's responses in some situations, ritual communication may allow complex discretionary action. In early China, it was customary at banquets for guests to express their sentiments by selecting stanzas from a corpus of classical poetry to sing to one another. This ritual could become quite intimate and stirring, as the sanctity of the texts give great weight to the chanting of even ordinary people. The interplay of aesthetic skill, shared erudition, and sincere expression could produce a moving encounter.[7]

But the subtlety of ritual communication goes further. The intricacy with which ritual action can be scripted and choreographed is limitless. Anyone who has read the *Yi-li* (*Ceremonies of Ritual*) will recognize that formal ritual encounters have a tendency to elaborate ritualized movements to the point where all non-ritual action is necessarily banished—there is simply no room.[8] Like a choreographed ballet which does not have gaps where the dancers revert to the ordinary movements of everyday action, a ritual encounter lifts the actors into a distinct medium of interaction, a medium of entailed symbolism.[9]

Within such an intricately determined network, small actions that initi-

ate complex patterns of response may accomplish far-reaching consequences. A story in the *Analects* illustrates this (*A*:17.1). We are told that the
usurper Yang Huo wished to employ Confucius, but Confucius refused to
meet with him to discuss it. To meet thus without compulsion would have
implicitly acknowledged Yang Huo's right to request service of Confucius,
that is, his legitimacy as a sovereign. Yang Huo solved the problem of induc-
ing Confucius to visit him by sending Confucius a pig. According to *li*, when
a man of Yang Huo's *legitimate* rank sent such a gift to a man of Confucius'
rank, the latter was obliged to pay a courtesy call on the former. Confucius
had no choice but to visit Yang Huo, and though he carefully timed his visit
in order that Yang Huo was away from home, to Confucius' dismay he
encountered him on the road. Thus Yang Huo was able to solve a problem
of political pragmatism by a brief adventure into the world of *li*.[10]

This simple power of ritual action would theoretically be magnified
according to the breadth and intricacy of the field of ritual action and the
skill of the actor. The *Analects* recounts the ultimate ideal: "The Master
said, ' "He did nothing and all was ruled": would this not charaterize the
Emperor Shun? What did he do? He merely set himself with reverence and
faced due South; that was all' " (*A*:15.5).[11]

This aspect of ritual behavior is also generally linked to ethical values.
Social ritual is not inherently ethical – games are examples of social ritual –
but because social ritual is so central to articulating and confirming roles
in a hierarchical society, it becomes entailed with the ethical nature of that
society. If it is a society sanctioned by tradition and myth, its social rituals
are equally sanctioned.

In Western Chou society, powerful central rule created a consensus valuation of Chou social institutions, which were founded on the premise of
hereditary assumption of social roles and the pyramidal structure of Chou
feudal authority. Perhaps the single largest category of *li* was comprised of
the social rituals that articulated and confirmed the ordered hierarchical
society of the Chou.

The third aspect of ritual behavior is its aesthetic dimension, which is
not so much distinct from the religious and social dimensions as characteristic of both. Ritual activity is scripted and choreographed; it is prescribed
by formulas. These are generally rationalized on religious or ethical grounds,
but in practice they tend to respond to aesthetic criteria as well. While
ritual is not necessarily aesthetic, as it was elaborated in Chinese society it
tended to be so.

The clearest indications of this are the frequent links we find between
ritual and manifestly artistic activities, such as music, song, and dance.
Prayers for rain took the form of rain dances in both the Shang and Chou,[12]
and Shima Kunio has identified numerous oracle graphs that may denote a

range of other types of ritual dance (1958:206-7, 289-93).[13]

Major state rituals were marked by complex artistic displays. The *Li-chi*, a late text, describes a royal sacrifice as a grand ballet: "As the altar is mounted, 'The Bright Temple' is sung. Descending, the pipes play and the Hsiang Dance is performed. Then the cinnebar shields and jade spears are brought out for the Great War Dance. Next, eight ranks of dancers perform the Great Hsia Dance" (*Chi-t'ung*:14.23b). The *Yi-li* documents the elaborate costume, heightened speech, and frequent use of music and song that pervaded all forms of ritual activity.

There is, in ritual, a significant overlap between the ethical and aesthetic. In ritual activity, what is "right" to do is often what is in "good form." A spontaneous intrusion into a ritual procedure, for instance a complacent belch at a society dinner, can offend equally for its display of disrespect for social rule and for its ugliness.[14] This overlap is reflected in Chinese in the cognate relationship between the words "*yi*": "right," and "*yi*ª": "form; manner; standard.'"[15]

Aesthetics acts to reinforce the ethical meanings of religious and social ritual. It permeates the aura of sanctity of religious activity, and, as the example of ritual poetry chanting indicates, it adds to the affective power of social ritual. The very nature of group ritual activity as a smooth interaction of cognate roles expresses an aesthetic ideal.

However, the aesthetic aspect of ritual does not, in itself, ethically legitimize ritual, although it may be ritual's most attractive aspect. Without the ethical sanctions that legitimize religious and social rituals, the beauty of ritual action would possess no moral meanings beyond any accorded to spontaneous artistic expression. Keeping this point in mind may help us better understand the role of *li* in early Ruism. Ruist texts abound in ethical rationalizations of *li*—we will explore some of them further on. But to accept that Ruists *loved* ritual as they seem to have, one must believe that their sensitivity to it was largely aesthetic. The intellectual labors that Ruists performed to legitimize *li* may have been efforts to sustain an intuition of the goodness of *li* that was fundamentally aesthetic.

1.2. The Decline of Ritual

In chapter I we saw how the decline of royal power at the end of the Western Chou led to major dislocations in social order and ideology. The Chou king had stood not only at the apex of a political system, but of a religious system as well. His decline led to the appearance of religious scepticism and political chaos. Our simple model of the functions of ritual might lead us to expect that the decline of royal power and social order would undermine the ethical legitimacy of religious and social ritual; there is ample evidence that it did.

At once a symptom and a cause of this was the usurpation of ritual forms by those not entitled to them. We have already noted in chapter I instances where feudal lords presumed to pray to and claim the support of T'ien, the king's god. The third book of the *Analects* is peppered with other examples (*A*:3.1, 3.2, 3.6, 3.22). Further symptoms of the decline of ritual during the Eastern Chou include the discarding of the finer points of ritual performance[16] and the appearance of critical and even hostile attitudes toward *li*.[17]

Our simple hypothesis, then, is that dislocations in the religious and socio-political systems undermined the ethical legitimacy of ritual. While faith in the natural efficacy of symbolic action certainly persisted in forms of shamanism and superstition, that aspect of religious ritual which had possessed the greatest stability and social sanction, state religious practice, had been discredited.

As for the legitimacy of social ritual, during the prolonged social chaos of the Eastern Chou, the traditional determinant of social hierarchy—hereditary privilege—was deeply undermined (Hsu 1965:26-31). In its place, less formalized criteria, such as military prowess, wealth, talent, and ruthlessness came to shape the social network. Warlord rulers and swashbuckling knights found an ethics that stressed bravery and personal loyalty more congenial than the morality of ritual norms.[18] As the moorings of religious and social value slipped away, ad hoc values proliferated without any systematic ethical base.

Confucius and Ruism were born in this milieu, and Confucius himself embraced the plurality of simple values that had become so prized in the period of chaos. The *Analects* celebrates a variety of homely virtues: righteousness (*yi*), courage (*yung*), trustworthiness (*hsin*), devotion (*chung*), and many more. But Confucius celebrated these in the context of his attempt to describe a unified vision of enduring value, and that value was anchored in complete dedication to the obsolescent rituals of a bygone era: *li*.

1.3. Confucius' Career[19]

Confucius was born in the small state of Lu about 550 B.C.[20] His background and early career are variously but not reliably reported in our historical sources.[21] What seems clear, however, is that Confucius was not a member of the hereditary nobility of Lu,[22] that he possessed a basic training in traditional ritual behavior,[23] and that he aspired to political office in Lu. Although the *Analects* does not mention Confucius holding any specific official post,[24] other sources claim for him exalted political titles.[25]

About the year 498 B.C., Confucius left Lu, possibly forced to leave on account of actions he took as a political official.[26] He subsequently traveled among the feudal states of eastern China, perhaps seeking employment in government, possibly looking for a nonadministrative position as an honored senior advisor at a feudal court.[27]

Late in life, Confucius returned to Lu at the invitation, it is said, of the leading warlord of Lu, one of whose retainers was a disciple of Confucius who had recently contributed to a great military victory.[28] Confucius spent his last years in Lu, quietly teaching his sizable entourage of disciples. He died about 479 B.C.[29]

At some time during his life, Confucius began to attract around him a group of men who regarded him as their teacher.[30] Among these men were several who achieved considerable political prominence, most notably Chi Yu, styled Tzu-lu, and Jan Ch'iu, both of whom became stewards for the Chi clan, the single greatest power group in Lu.[31]

The many accounts of Confucius' political activities and the political prominence of some of his disciples makes it clear that the movement that grew out of Confucius' teachings had its roots in political activism. There seems no doubt that, at one time, Confucius thought that he just might be able to change the world if only he could attain enough political leverage.

That did not come to pass, however, and although Confucius' political activism influenced all later Ruists, an even greater influence was exerted by his ultimate failure. For what distinguished Confucius from other men with praiseworthy political impulses was the fact that his political goals were linked to a systematic value standpoint rooted in his special reverence for ritual action. In his own career, he demonstrated repeatedly that his ethical idealism could in no way be compromised in the name of political expediency, and his political failure may have largely been due to this rigid stance. Generations of later Ru would follow his example and content themselves with political obscurity in order to carry on Confucius' absolute commitment to the ethics of ritual action.

1.4. Legitimizing *Li*

Philosophy was born in China amidst a pervasive atmosphere of social and intellectual crisis, and these conditions determined its agenda.[32] Philosophers shared a common goal of articulating a stable structure of value that would prescribe and legitimize social action as Western Chou religious and political ideologies once had. The Mohists built such a structure upon a strict utilitarian ethic, which upheld a moral imperative to engage in any type of political activity that might relieve suffering to any degree. Taoists like Chuang Tzu embraced a systematic ethical relativism, objectifying their ideas as a transcendent principle of existence that challenged the value of any political action whatever.

Confucius came before these thinkers, and his approach was to embrace the ritual system of *li* as a stable value foundation. In doing so, Confucius followed a different path from most subsequent thinkers because he adopted as fundamental a particular and relative form of behavior, rather than a universal ethical principle. *Li* was not a body of principles: it was a collection of specific codes associated with the institutions of a specific dynasty.[33]

What led Confucius to feel that *li* was a viable basis for an ethical teaching preached seriously in times of trouble? The answer lies, in part, in the aesthetic values of ritual that we discussed earlier. The Confucius of the *Analects* is a man predisposed to value *li* for its beauty. The *Analects* tells us that he was so moved by a performance of ritual music that for three months he was not conscious of the taste of food (*A:7.14*), and other passages confirm his deep feeling for ritual dance and song (*A:3.23, 3.25, 7.32, 8.15, 11.24*). Commitment to *li* was inextricably linked to immersion in its aesthetic forms: "The Master said, 'Rise up with the songs, stand with *li*, and be fulfilled in music'" (*A:8.8*).[34]

Aesthetics was not ethically trivial for Confucius. The early Chou term *"wen"* had linked patterns drawn from ritual artistry to personal virtues and social norms (see chapter 1). In Ruism, this commitment to patterned action deepened and the aesthetic qualities of *"wen,"* a term which in Ruist texts is generally best rendered as "style," were a central quality of Ruism's potraits of the ideal person. *"Wen,"* or "style," denoted among other things the aesthetic skills that equipped an individual to apply the narrow codes of ritual, skills that were cultivated by studying written texts, music, dance, and the martial arts. In the *Analects*, this aesthetic aspect of ritual is sometimes contrasted with explicit prescriptive rules—*"li"* in the narrow sense—as in the thrice repeated formula that a person should be "broadened with style, constrained by *li*" (*A:6.27, 9.11, 12.15*).[35]

This formula reminds us that the aesthetics of ritual, although deeply attractive, cannot legitimize ritual as an ethical category. In the Ruist case, because the religious and social legitimations of *li* had eroded with the decline of the Chou rule and social order, it was not enough for Confucius and his followers to celebrate the beauty of ritual forms. It was necessary for them to reformulate the ethical bases of ritual to justify their claim that *li* could serve as a cardinal principle of value. Although we obviously cannot trace their thinking, we can give a brief schematic summary of how early Ruists solved this problem in terms of our simple model of the dimensions of ritual.

In attacking this problem, Confucius and his followers developed a series of innovative ideas. The first of these was so basic that it sometimes escapes the attention of interpreters. This is the fundamental Ruist tenet that *li* is, in itself, a category of intellectual and ethical significance. As we noted earlier, prior to Ruist thought, we have little evidence to indicate that *li* was understood as a general category, a common property shared by the many individual rites and rules. Confucius was, if not the first, then among the first to pay attention to *li* as a universal category to which particular *li* belonged.

This understanding of *li* in an abstract sense allowed the Ruists to value the formal aspects of *li*. Whereas the basis of much of the Western Chou interest in *li* had been tied to confidence in the supernatural efficacy of individual religious rites, Ruism did not require that any rite prove its value through magical utility; it could possess value as an instance representing a larger ethical category.[36] The proper practice of *li* was inherently good.

The second innovation that Confucius and his followers used to legitimize *li* was to invert the ethical basis of social *li*. Originally, the stable social order of the Western Chou provided a consensus value base legitimizing social ritual. This base had disintegrated leaving the significance of *li* in question. Confucius' solution was to treat *li* not as a property of social order, but as the genesis of social order. The value of Chou *li* was not diminished by the decline of the Chou social order, just the opposite: Chou *li* was if anything more valuable now, for the perished social order existed latent in the *li*. In a sense, Confucius reinterpreted the basis of Chou institutions: their essence no longer lay in hereditary privilege, it lay in the behavioral norms that characterized them.[37] These were the seeds of revived social order, and Confucius' mastery of them was the basis of his political mission: "King Wen is dead, but his style lives on here [in me], does it not? If T'ien wished this style to perish, [I] would not have been able to partake of it" (*A*:9.5).

The claim that social order existed latently in ritual was defended with reference to the extraordinary ethical leverage that social ritual could provide. Although Chou ritual was lying dormant, it remained an interconnected network whose outlines were well known. The initiation of a single properly performed act of *li* might be sufficient to engage others in a steadily broadening circle of ritual action—just as Yang Huo engaged Confucius in the instance discussed earlier. One person, one continuing source of *li*, could ritualize the world: "Conquer yourself and return to *li* for one day, and the world will respond to you with *jen* [humanity]" (*A*:12.1).[38] If that person were in a position of political power, the process would be swift and simple indeed:

Can *li* and deference be used to rule a state? Why, there is nothing to it! (*A*:4.13).

When a ruler loves *li*, the people are easy to rule (*A*:14.41).

If the lord directs his ministers with *li*, the ministers will serve their lord with devotion (*A*:3.19).

By arguments such as these, Confucius and his followers promised to replace, through ritual, the stable social order that had been supported by the institutional pillars of kingship and heredity.

The religious pillar, to the degree that it rested on the notion that religious ritual possessed magical efficacy, Confucius did not attempt to restore, although, as we will see, Ruists employed T'ien to sanction their ritual claims. Instead, the third innovative idea of early Ruism was to erect an entirely new basis for *li*, a fourth dimension of ritual apart from its religious, social, and aesthetic aspects. This was an educational dimension, which legitimized ritual forms on the basis of their spiritual effect upon the ritual actor himself. Confucius and later Ruists claimed that the practice of *li* and its related aesthetic forms was inherently edifying, and could transform individuals into ethical and wise beings. This was an evolving claim in early Ruism, which grew from an implicit theme in the *Analects*, where devotion to *li* and personal virtue are loosely but consistently linked, to an explicit and central doctrine in the *Hsun Tzu*. In its most positive form, this idea was expressed as the claim that mastery of ritual and ritual style transformed a person into a perfect being: a Sage. And even where the claim is expressed in softer terms, the practical obsession with ritual, which we will see was characteristic of all early Ruism, suggests that the notion of *li* as the path to Sagehood was a powerful motivating force behind the dedication that Masters and disciples showed to their ritual vocation.

Thus, in establishing *li* as a cardinal value, early Ruism reformulated the bases upon which *li* was legitimized. No longer was ritual sanctioned by its magical efficacy or its place in an established social order. Now, aesthetically celebrated and understood as a universal category of action, *li* was legitimized by its power to generate order in society and Sagehood in individuals.

This new dual legitimation of *li* was fundamental to the structure of Ruism throughout the Warring States period and for thousands of years after. The social rationale yielded a political imperative: to transform society into a field of ritual action.[39] The educational rationale compelled the student to devote his days to transforming himself into a perfect ritual actor. Theoretically, these two imperatives were not in conflict, and Ruist doctrine embraced both. But practically speaking, the political imperative was beyond the powers of the Ru; doomed to failure, it was not a rewarding path to follow. The path of self-cultivation in ritual study, on the other hand, offered many sorts of rewards, both spiritual and, as we will see, material as well.

Even during Confucius' lifetime, the political claim seems to have increasingly become a rhetorical device, whose primary function was to legitimize the Ruists' pursuit of their personal educational goals. While it was always a centerpiece of Ruist doctrine, the political claim did not become a guiding imperative of Ruist practice until after the Warring States period had come to a close and political realities had changed. In the following sections, I hope to demonstrate that this was so, as we evaluate the frequently held hypothesis that early Ruism was fundamentally a political movement.

2. The Political Role of Ruism

As we saw in the last section, Ruist doctrine was born in a context of
political action. Confucius himself may have held important political posts,
and several of his disciples were politically prominent. Furthermore, Confucius' advocacy of *li*, central to all aspects of his teachings, was supported
by a claim that government by *li* was the key to social order. For disciples,
this entailed an imperative to engineer the implementation of *li* in the
world, an imperative that was clearly political.

Interpreters of Ruism have drawn two conclusions from all this. The first
is that Ruism was fundamentally a political ideology. H. G. Creel has identified the two enduring principles of Ruism as "the insistence that those who
govern should be chosen not for their birth but for their virtue and ability,
and that the true end of government is the welfare and happiness of the
people (1949:4).[40] These were certainly important and impressive political
doctrines, frequently–although not always–proclaimed by Ruists. But we
will argue here that the central core of early Ruism lay in an entirely different direction. The second conclusion is that Ruists were political activists
who sought and frequently occupied positions in government from which
they could implement their various social policies. Frederick Mote has
adopted this interpretation:

It became known that [Confucius'] students were a cut above the ordinary job seek-
ers, and that made them eminently employable. . . . [M]any of his students advanced
rapidly in government. Within a few generations the students of his widely proliferated school commanded the market–they had the talent, they got the positions
(1971:41).

In the last section we noted that Confucius' dual legitimation of *li* resulted
in a certain bifurcation in his philosophy, which stressed imperatives both
to perfect oneself and to transform society. In the course of this section, we
will suggest how this bifurcation acted to render Ruism essentially *apolitical*
despite its political rhetoric. This hypothesis will be supported first by a
survey of historical records, which indicate that during the Warring States
period Ruists did not, in fact, actually hold positions of political responsibility, and second by a reexamination of the attitudes expressed by the
Ruist texts themselves. We will see that these consistently maintain a negative attitude toward practical political involvement, even as they espouse
doctrines of political idealism.

Our conclusion will be that political idealism acted to shield Ruists from
the unpredictable results of practical political activism, and to legitimize
the withdrawal of the Ruist community into a cult focused on group education and the quest for personal Sagehood.

2.1. The Bifurcated Doctrine of Ruism

The portrait of early Ruism as a political ideology derives, I think, from a series of uncritical assumptions that have guided the interpretation of Ruist texts. The most fundamental of these is the assumption that Ruism was first and foremost an ideology, or set of ideas.

To contemporaries, the Ru were most likely not so much distinguished by their ideas as by their obsession with *li*: their archaic dress and scrupulous bearing, their precise speech, their tendency to gather and bring out their zithers, chant poetry, and practice ceremonial dance. (We will explore these activities in detail later.) Although it may seem to be a fine distinction, our picture of early Ruism will vary enormously depending on whether we concentrate only on what early Ruists said or also on what they did.

The conception of Ruism as a body of doctrine arises from our historical perspective. When the Ru proselytized, recruited new disciples, or defended their activities against attack, they elaborated an ever-growing body of philosophical material, which formed topics for discussion within each group and between Ru and outsiders. This material is virtually all that is left to us; we can view early Ruism through no medium other than its words. Furthermore, few of those words directly describe what the Ru were actually doing; the texts are overwhelmingly concerned with articulating ideal doctrine. Thus, the nature of our source material has predisposed us to regard early Ruism as a set of ideas.[41]

Because our sources give us access to ideas but not to activities, there is a temptation to fill in the gap by implicitly translating the stated aims of the texts into social action. Ruist texts repeatedly describe Ruist education as preparation for political activity; should we not conclude that Ruists were politically ambitious? Ruist doctrine advocates a utopian social program; does it not follow that the Ru sought political posts in order to achieve their goals?

These inferences reflect a simplistic equation between rhetoric and action. It is sometimes the case that energetic verbal inquiry or posturing relieves pressures for practical action about which the speaker may actually feel ambivalent. If we reexamine the role of political doctrine in early Ruism, we can see the plausibility of applying such a principle in this case.

Early Ruism, as we have already seen, is fundamentally bifurcated. Its central ideology links two sets of doctrines which are not necessarily entailed. The first is a body of self-cultivation theory. These statements prescribe methods—primarily involving self-ritualization—for becoming a superior person and ultimately a Sage, with a Sage being defined as a man whose perfect moral intelligence is displayed in action.[42] The second set of doctrines consists of statements concerning a wide variety of political

ideas. These include criticisms of contemporary society along with prescriptive political programs, governance by *li* being one of these.

Ruist texts link these two sets of doctrines in three primary ways. The
first link is sequential: self-cultivation precedes political action. Good government was not just a matter of running a feudal court according to ritual
rules. Without the correct spirit, ritual action would not engage others in
the broadening matrix of symbolic activity. For ritual to fulfill its political
potential, ritual actors had to understand the values that governed the application of *li*. They had to become ethical themselves: "The Master said,
'How can a man who is not *jen* [humane] manage *li*? How can a man who is
not *jen* manage music?' " (*A*:3.3).[43] For the master of ritual, government is
simple. But a man unskilled in the art of ritual will only blunder if he attempts
to exploit the political power of *li*: "Can *li* and deference be used to rule a
state? Why, there is nothing to it. He who cannot use *li* and deference to
rule a state, how can he manage *li* at all?" (*A*:4.13).[44] For the Ruist, then, the
study of ritual and a grasp of the values that govern the application of *li*
must precede ritual government. The Ruist disciple must begin by cultivating his virtue within the Ruist group: political action must be deferred.

The second link is predictive. The man whose virtue has been cultivated
through ritual education is supremely competent to oversee the restora-
tion of political order, either as a ruler, or as the administrator of enlightened
policy.[45] Thus in the *Analects*, Confucius claims that given a genuine
opportunitity, he could reform a state in three years or create a new Chou
in the east (*A*:13.10, 17.4). Mencius claims that, given the chance, he could
bring peace and order to the entire empire (*M*:2B.13). The success of true
Ruist government would be limitless and ensured.

The third link is proscriptive. Being moral, the Ruist Sage or *chün-tzu* will
not participate in corrupt government, lest he set a bad example, needlessly
expose himself to danger, become himself corrupted, or legitimize corruption by his presence. Instead, he will bide his time, perfecting himself, until
the proper opportunity for political action presents itself. This is the doctrine of "timeliness" (*shih*): "When the Way prevails in the world, appear;
when it does not, hide" (*A*:8.13).[46]

Our immediate concern here is with the first and third links between the
two doctrinal moieties: that self-cultivation must precede political action,
and that one must not accept political responsibilities in a state not morally governed. Within the context of Warring States China, these two doctrines provided a practical implication somewhat different from their explicit
content. Because true opportunities for joining moral government were
virtually nonexistent at the time, the functional message which these doctrines conveyed to disciples was to enter and persist in Ruist training for
ideal political opportunities, while avoiding involvement in actual govern-

ment. Coincidentally, as long as this course of action was followed, the second assertion— predicting the limitless political success of Ruist Sages and Ruist policies—could never be tested and disproven.

According to this analysis, rather than being a political movement whose essential message lay in political doctrine and whose followers were groomed to enter the governments of the times, Ruism was in its early days a cult directed toward self-improvement in which political doctrines played a legitimizing role. The instrumental function of these political doctrines was to rationalize and encourage abstinence from non-Ruist government in favor of participation in the activities of the Ruist community. Political idealism both explained a Ruist withdrawal into cult studies, and justified it in the eyes of society. Rather than appearing eccentric and selfish, Ruists could portray themselves in terms of the Warring States values of righteousness, courage, and honesty.

In the next section, we will test this analysis against the alternative interpretation of Ruism as a political movement by examining the historical record to determine, first, whether explicit records are found documenting substantial numbers of Ru participating in government and, second, whether the use of Ruist rhetoric by political actors of the Warring States period implicitly indicates the presence of Ru in government.

2.2. The Missing History of the Ru

The school of Confucius was founded in a political context, but after the death of Confucius, there is little evidence of Ruist participation in government. A change seems to have come over the school of Ruism, and this change may have begun during Confucius' lifetime.

After leaving his home state of Lu, Confucius spent almost fifteen years traveling through the various feudal states of eastern China looking for a ruler who would employ him in government. This is generally taken to demonstrate that Confucius' commitment to political activism remained undiminished. But we can look at it another way. If we rely on the evidence of the *Analects*, at least part of the reason for Confucius' failure to find a political position was his unwillingness to be flexible about the conditions under which he would seek office. It might not be that valuable political opportunities were not available to him, but that he kept his ethical standards too high to seize them.

For example, the *Analects* suggests that Confucius had numerous opportunities to establish a political base in the state of Wei. He was called into audience with an influential consort of the ruler, but he regarded her as immoral, and shunned any political relationship (*A*:6.28). The leading military figure in Wei proposed a political alliance; Confucius snubbed him (*A*:3.13). The ruler himself granted him an audience, but Confucius formed a low opinion of him and left the state (A:15.1). Yet Confucius himself remarked later that although the ruler was without virtue, his government included men of talent and honor—they, at least, could see their way clear to serving under him (A:14.19). Following the death of the ruler there ensued a bitter succession dispute, and some of Confucius' disciples wondered whether this might not provide a political opportunity for their Master. Confucius, however, declined to become involved (A:7.15).

The case of Wei is the clearest example, but there are other instances where Confucius seems to have been more concerned with maintaining his political purity than in attempting to turn political opportunity to ethical advantage (e.g., A:14.36). In the *Analects*, we see him walk out on no less than three rulers (A:15.1, 18.3, 18.4). One cannot help but wonder whether his travels were as much a quest for ethical opportunity as a way of proving that it could not be found.

As far as the disciples are concerned, several of them did hold political office, and it is reasonable to follow traditional interpretations that suggest that Confucius taught these men because he wished to train a new breed of political actors. But the disciples who achieved political prominence were all among the most senior of Confucius' students. The younger disciples, who knew Confucius only after his political career in Lu came to a close, appear to have moved in a different direction.[47] Although some of them, such as Tzu-hsia and Tzu-yu, are said to have taken positions as town magistrates in Lu during Confucius' lifetime, we find no evidence that they rose in government— or even persisted in it.[48] Other prominent members of the younger generation of disciples, such as Tzu-chang and Tseng Shen, apparently never held political office. They, along with Tzu-hsia and Tzu-yu, made their reputations as teachers in the style of Confucius, taking on students of their own after their Master's death.[49]

Thus, even in Confucius' lifetime, the character of formative Ruism may have been changing from political activism to a withdrawn cult of self-improvement. After Confucius' death, we find little evidence of any of his disciples finding employment in politics.[50] And, as we look down the course of Ruist history during the Warring States period, there is even less evidence to indicate that this tendency toward political withdrawal was reversed prior to the Ch'in conquest. On the contrary, a survey of our best historical sources for the period, the *Chan-kuo ts'e* and the *Shih-chi*, along with the testimony of early Ruist texts such as the *Mencius* and *Hsun Tzu*, indicates a near total absence of Ruists from the ranks of government.[51] In fact, were it not for the two great Ru, Mencius and Hsun Tzu, whose biographies have been preserved to some degree, the history of the Ruist community after Confucius would be nearly blank. Ruists simply left no mark on the political annals of the period. Over the course of two and one half centuries, the record lists no more than a handful of Ru in positions of administrative responsibility, and the circumstances in even these few cases are often unclear.[52] The evidence to support the positive claim of Ruist political activism simply does not exist.[53]

How, then, did the impression arise that Ruists were a major, albeit ultimately unsuccessful political faction prior to the Ch'in? Partially, no doubt, because of the uncritical assumptions that linked Ruist rhetoric to supposed actions. But another reason might exist. That is that interpreters have not adequately stressed the distinction between serving feudal governments in an administrative capacity and accepting other types of court positions. For while we do not see Ruists occupying administrative posts, we not infrequently see them serving as court tutors, as special emissaries, as ritual masters, or as occasional advisors, invited to impart their teachings to rulers anxious to enhance their own reputations for wisdom. Duties such as these did not interfere with a Ruist's primary occupation as a Master of disciples. Their administrative burdens were nil and, most important, this sort of activity did not implicate Ruists in the general immorality of contemporary government because they were never in positions of political responsibility.

Still, one might wonder why, if Ruists were serious about following Confucius' injunction to "hide" in times of immoral rule, they were willing to be associated with feudal courts at all. The answer is probably that feudal courts were centers of economic surplus, and for Ruist groups—as for Mohist and other groups—patronage by members of a court was the surest path to economic sustenance. In addition to gaining a position as a teacher or ritualist, a well-known Ru might receive court patronage simply for being a "wise man" and residing nearby.[54]

During the Warring States period, rulers commonly displayed their virtue by patronizing "worthies" of all descriptions. Wise men arriving at the capitals of such rulers could be assured of being granted audiences and stipends as well.[55] Ruists gravitated to such states, and the portrait of early Ruists as politically ambitious men has certainly been enhanced by the fact that many Ru did maintain close ties with a court. Confucius' disciple Tzu-hsia, for example, responded to the first recorded instance of such patronage. When Marquis Wen of Wei[a] put out a call for worthies, Tzu-hsia joined a number of his contemporaries in traveling to Wei[a], where he was appointed court tutor (SC:67.2203).[56] Some years later, the Marquis' descendant King Hui, battered by bad fortunes in war, revived the policy in order to attract fresh political talent (SC:44.1847). Among those responding was Mencius, who, needless to say, was not the sort of man the King was casting for when he dangled the bait of large stipends.

Mencius may have been among those most disposed to respond to opportunities of this sort. Aside from his tenure in Wei[a] (Liang), his travels to

Ch'i, T'eng, and perhaps Sung all may have initially been in response to or in expectation of such general patronage policies.[57]

In the state of Ch'i, the policy became institutionalized in the form of a government sponsored academy, where wise men of every stripe received salaries and gathered disciples without any political responsibilities whatever (Ch'ien 1956:321-34). Hsun Tzu taught at this academy, where he was revered as senior teacher (*SC*:74.2348).

During this period, Ruists did not serve as officers of government, but as the personal retainers of whatever lord was willing to support them. The *Han Fei Tzu* gives a credible portrait when it lumps Ruists together with knights-errant: both groups lived off the patronage of politically prominent leaders, but just as wandering knights of martial skill were not appointed to lead regular armies, so Ruists skilled in ritual arts were not appointed to lead governments (*Hsien-hsueh*:19.9b-10a).[58]

The advantages of this arrangement for political leaders were manifold. The ruler of a feudal state could justify the actions of his government by pointing to the panoply of worthies who were attracted to his court. From these men, a ruler or his spokesmen could learn facile rhetorical formulas to rationalize their pragmatic acts.[59]

The proximity of Ru to Warring States courts resulted in a general diffusion of Ruist political ideas and rhetoric. Ruist rhetoric was particularly well-suited to political manipulation. The Ru were, after all, revivalists. Many of their ideas could be seen as little more than a restatement of traditional values. Few non-Ru would challenge the Ruist stress on righteousness, courage, and reverence. Even the most particular of Ruist values, *li*, was not controversial if taken in a weak sense as proper and seemly action. Ruists were distinct only in taking these values seriously; most everybody paid them lip service.

Because Ruist rhetoric was so well-suited for political manipulation, it is not unusual to encounter in our historical sources Ruist-style speeches uttered by non-Ru political actors.[60] We should not conclude that the incidence of such Ruist rhetoric in the political language of the times indicates significant Ruist participation in policy-making or administration.

A particularly apt historical example illustrates perfectly this need to distinguish between rhetorical and political influence. It involves the civil war in the state of Yen (316-314 B.C.). Every aspect of this affair involves the manipulation of Ruist rhetoric by pragmatic politicians.

The crisis in Yen began when unscrupulous ministers, interested in elevating one of their number to supreme power, employed Ruist arguments to persuade the ruler of Yen to cede his throne to his Prime Minister (*CKT*:9.11b-12a).[61] The legitimate heir raised a rebellion, whereupon the border state of Chung-shan seized on the chaotic situation to invade and capture land from Yen. This invasion was justified in Ruist language, as a proper punishment for the "wayward" rulers of Yen. They had "violated *li* and righteousness" and confused "the *li* which distinguish superior from inferior."[62]

Meanwhile, the giant state of Ch'i decided that this was an opportune time to launch its own invasion of Yen. Just at that time, the Ruist Master Mencius was in Ch'i, where he had been granted the exalted rank of high minister, a rare instance of a Ru holding a political title—although the accounts of the *Mencius* indicate that Mencius took no part in the actual administration of government, and his high rank was probably honorary (see below). According to the account of the *Chan-kuo ts'e*, Mencius urged the King of Ch'i to invade Yen on ethical grounds (*CKT*:9.13a). But the *Mencius* painstakingly explains that the government of Ch'i actually tricked Mencius and distorted the meaning of his words (*M*:2B.8-9).[63] Apparently, Ch'i manipulated the words of its token Ruist minister in order to launch its invasion with a claim of Ruist sanction. Mencius properly awaited the end of hostilities and then resigned his post (*M*:2B.14).

Ch'i succeeded in conquering Yen and proceded to install the legitimate heir as its puppet. But the new prince turned on Ch'i, and, seeking to revive the strength of Yen, he issued a Ruist-style call for wise men to come to his aid. Many responded, but the ones chosen for political posts were not Ruists, but militarists, who rebuilt the armies of Yen.[64]

So much Ruist rhetoric! But all to serve the practical interests of non-Ruist government. No incident in pre-Ch'in history better demonstrates the mistake of assuming that the use of Ruist political rhetoric indicates that an individual was a Ru or that a government was Ruist.[65]

In sum, we find virtually no record of Ruists occupying political positions during the Warring States period. But they did gravitate toward feudal courts, where their ideas became well known. Their presence on the fringes of political power led to the absorption of some of the less controversial aspects of Ruist rhetoric into the political mainstream. This does not indicate that Ruists exerted significant influence in government, or that they generally aspired to do so. It reflects an increasing skill on the part of political actors in coopting the issues of Ruist idealism, and in binding Ruists to their courts in nonpolitical roles by paying lip service to their doctrines.

Our historical survey does not confirm the interpretation of early Ruism as a political movement. This does not prove that Ruists did withdraw from the political arena; our negative evidence can yield only an argument from silence, and such an argument cannot be conclusive. It can, however, surprise our traditional assumptions about Ruist activism and shift the burden of proof to claims for substantive Ruist political involvement. Moreover, negative evidence concerning Ruist political efforts is by no means the sole basis for the claim of Ruist withdrawal. A reexamination of the Ruist texts themselves shows that the principles that guided Ruists away from political involvement are clearly and prominently articulated in the texts. No disciple who employed the lessons of these texts as a guide could mistake their message.

2.3. The Textual Imperative of Withdrawal

Many passages in Ruist texts tell us that government service is an imperative, but that imperative is always modified by the proviso that it only applies when a practical chance exists that such service will have its intended moral effect. The formula: "When the Way prevails, appear; when it does not, hide," is repeated at least six times in the *Analects*, in a variety of forms (*A*:5.21, 7.11, 8.13, 14.1, 14.3, 15.7). The message is conveyed in other ways as well.

Many Ruist recruits may have begun their studies with the aim of obtaining political posts.[66] Confucius is said to have lamented that, "A student willing to study three years without accepting a post is hard to find!" (*A*:8.12). It makes sense to believe that Ruist political rhetoric attracted ambitious men as well as idealists to the Ruist fold. One of the Ruist Master's tasks was to bring such ambition under control and reorient the student's primary goals toward study, the quest for Sagehood, and the rewards of sharing in the life of the Ruist community.

Many passages in the *Analects* appear designed to redirect goals in this way. For example: "The Master said, 'To eat coarse greens and drink water, to crook one's elbow for a pillow: joy also lies therein. If they are not got by righteous means, wealth and rank are to me like the floating clouds' "(*A*:7.16).

This sort of idea was never raised to an ascetic code that might alienate potential disciples. The lesson was framed in terms of a choice between shoddy immorality and the rewards of a life of righteousness: "The Master said, 'If the path to wealth is honest, then I follow it, even if it means being the lowly bearer of the whip. If it is not, I follow my own pleasures' " (*A*:7.12.)[67]

In the *Analects*, the message of political withdrawal is conveyed most effectively through the judgments made on positive and negative models. The leading positive model in the *Analects* is the disciple Yen Yuan. He is the only disciple portrayed as having approached Sagehood (*A*:6.7). He is nowhere criticized and everywhere idealized—Confucius even implies that Yen Yuan was ethically superior to himself (*A*:5.9). Yet Yen Yuan is never connected with political office, nor even shown considering one. He apparently chose voluntarily to live in poverty and obscurity (*A*:6.11). Confucius said to him, "When [the Way] prevails, act; when it is discarded, hide: only you and I can follow this" (*A*:7.11). Yen Yuan achieved nothing in the eyes of the world. All his achievements were within the confines of Confucius' small coterie.

Other disciples followed Yen Yuan's example of refraining from political employment. The *Analects* tells us that when the warlord Chi family wished to employ one disciple as magistrate of their fortress city, he replied to their emissary: "Make it clear I must decline. If they pursue me, I shall surely be found on the far side of the river Wen [i.e., out of reach]" (*A*:6.9).[68]

On the other hand, disciples who did, in fact, hold positions of political authority almost invariably serve as negative models whenever their conduct in government is touched on, usually because they have shown themselves impotent to effect changes in bad policies. The disciples Tzu-lu and Jan Ch'iu, the most politically successful of the disciples, come in for particularly harsh criticism (*A*:3.6, 6.4, 11.23, 16.1). At one point Confucius even suggests that the other disciples "sound the drums" and drive Jan Ch'iu from their midst (*A*:11.17). Another disciple, whom the *Shih-chi* records as having lost his life in a political intrigue, is the most denigrated disciple in the *Analects*.[69]

Confucius' own actions, as portrayed in the *Analects*, reinforce the message of political withdrawal. The *Analects* never portrays Confucius accepting a post in government (although *A*:17.1 does come close to it). But it cites three instances of his turning his back on rulers who do not meet his high ethical standards (*A*:15.1, 18.3-4).

The situation is similar in the *Mencius*. Mencius formulates three alternative principles of entering government: a puritanism that allows participation in nothing less than utopian rule, a missionary attitude that accepts employment under any circumstances, and Confucius' principle of accepting employment only when the time is ripe. History records good men who have followed each principle, but Mencius endorses only the last: "Confucius was the Sage of timeliness. He represents the great cadence . . . where the gongs resound and the jade bells chime" (*M*:5B.1).

The example of Mencius himself seems to be somewhat contrary to the principle of avoiding entanglements with corrupt governments. After all, Mencius, like Confucius, traveled from state to state in search of a ruler who would use him, and unlike Confucius, he did accept a post, becoming a high minister in Ch'i. But this picture is not quite complete.

Mencius was an eccentric among Ru because he supplemented the doctrine of "timeliness"—accept employment only when the times are ripe— with a millennial belief in the immanence of the appearance of a New King (a point we will discuss further in chapter V). This did lead him to seek a ruler-patron with exceptional zeal, but not with as much zeal as is often believed.

First of all, we find no indication that Mencius had ever seen fit to acquire experience in government. We do not hear of an ambitious young Mencius seeking out a magistrate level post as a way of gaining political leverage. The old man we see in the *Mencius* is not a frustrated politician, but an aging philosopher hoping to use the leverage of his reputation as a wise man to break into politics at the highest levels.

Mencius pursued this quest in a most unadventuresome way, generally traveling only to courts that had promulgated policies of patronizing wise men or appeared to be on the verge of doing so. He was not willing to seek out audiences elsewhere (*M*:3B.1, 3B.3).[70]

Nor was Mencius seeking political responsibility. His post in Ch'i, apparently the only one he ever accepted, as mentioned earlier, was almost certainly an advisory position without administrative duties.[71] He held it only briefly, and, what is more, he declined to accept his salary because from early on he was set on leaving as soon as possible (*M*:2B.14).[72] Mencius differed from other Ru only in that his style of political withdrawal depended on proving rather than assuming the futility of political activism.

Returning to the *Analects*, we noted earlier that one task of the Master was to redirect the personal ambitions of disciples from goals of wealth and status to goals oriented toward self-perfection and success within the Ruist group. One of the most prominent themes in the *Analects* addresses this issue directly: "Without anxiety about having no position, be anxious for the wherewithal with which to take your stand. Without anxiety that no one knows you, seek that by which you may be known" (*A*:4.14).

This message is repeated with variations in at least four other *Analects* passages (*A*:1.1, 1.16, 14.30, 15.19). The opening book of the text, which may have been composed somewhat later than most other chapters and been designed as an overall summary of Ruist doctrine, both begins and ends with passages on this theme.[73] No statement better affirms the inner-directedness of the Ruist community than the opening words of the *Analects*:

To study and ever practice: is this not contentment! To have comrades come from afar: is this not joy! Unknown and unsoured: is this not a *chün-tzu*! (*A*:1.1).

3. The Community of Ru

We have spoken several times of the "Ruist community" without explaining just what the expression means. In this section, we will describe in more detail what the early Ru were like and the role they played in Warring States society.

Perhaps the best starting point would be to recall Ssu-ma Ch'ien's description of the sounds of music and song that were ever heard in the Ruist homeland of Lu. The types of practice which that picture reflects marked

Ruists as social eccentrics. These ritual practices became the focus of attacks by hostile schools such as Mohism, and devotion to them came to be, for the disciple, perhaps the most prominent mark of his personal identity.

The eccentricity of the Ru was manifest in their appearance. Ruists dressed in an archaic style that came to be known as "Ru-clothing."[74] They were fluent in the ancient Chou court dialect, and their speech was filled with archaic phrases (*A*:7.18; *MT, Fei Ju*:9.17b; *Kung Meng*:12.9b).[75]

And then there was their obsession with the ceremonies of *li* and their associated aesthetic forms. The *Mo Tzu* expresses its disgust with the Ru in this way:

[They] bedeck themselves with elaborate dress to poison the world. They strum and sing and beat out dance rhythms to gather disciples. They proliferate *li* of ascending and descending to display their manners. They labor over the niceties of ceremonial gaits and wing-like gestures to impress the multitudes (*Fei Ju*:9.40-41).

An odd group of people indeed.

Perhaps because few Ruists became politically prominent prior to the Han, information about the lives of Warring States Ru is scarce. But in this section we will try to piece together whatever information we can and discuss the Ruist community in terms of its internal structure as a socially distinct cult, in terms of the syllabus that Ruists studied and taught, and in terms of the social roles that Ruists played in order to sustain a place for themselves in the general community.

3.1. The Ruist Study Group

As best we can determine, Ruism as a social entity began with the group of disciples who first gathered around Confucius sometime near 500 B.C. Of course, Confucius' thought did not arise in a vacuum; he had been steeped in the complex traditions of Chou society. Nor was Confucius the only man of his day deeply versed in ritual arts. Ritual specialists such as shamans, liturgists, and court scribes all carried on elements of early Chou ritual tradition. Confucius absorbed much from ritual specialists and from other traditional sources; he himself viewed his teachings as wholly derivative (*A*:7.1). Nevertheless, they mark the start of a new tradition, and the *Analects* makes this clear when it tells us that Confucius himself was the disciple of no teacher (*A*:19.22).[76]

Confucius and his disciples created a new type of social unit, an enduring group organized not on hereditary, political, or economic bases, but on the basis of a common commitment to a course of study. The general structure of Ruism continued to be modeled on the pattern of Confucius' study group. The only way to become a Ru was to do what the original disciples did: study for many years with a Master.

The *Analects* shows us what a tightly knit brotherhood the study group could be. The text is more than a collection of sayings, it is a version of primary Ruist mythology, and its appeal goes beyond its philosophical interest. It stands as a remarkable piece of literature, and its literary value lies largely in the interplay between its ideas and its characters. Disciples who read the text were instructed as much in the sentiment of belonging to a Ruist family as they were in doctrine. The authors of the *Analects* seem to have embraced this aspect of their book. The text is peppered with entries having little function other than to portray the touching personal relationships of the Ruist group.[77]

Creel has speculated that Confucius' disciples lived with him (1949:78). While there is no certain evidence that this was so, it is clear that during his exile they traveled with him, and shared his frequently ill-fortuned lot (*A*:15.2). The relationship between Master and disciple was close to that between father and son. The *Analects* tells us that when Confucius was ill, Tzu-lu asked permission to offer up prayers for him, and staged ceremonies intended to make the spirits grant Confucius greater respect after his death (*A*:7.35, 9.12).[78] In the *Mencius* we hear that after Confucius' death the disciple Tzu-kung performed the three-year mourning rites of a son, living in a hut by the side of his Master's grave (*M*:3A.4).[79]

After Confucius' death, the disciples perpetuated the life of the study group. At first, it is said, they chose one of the senior disciples to honor as they had Confucius, but subsequently they parted company, many of the major disciples becoming Masters of their own study groups (*M*:3A.4).[80] In this way, the Ruist community began to disperse into independent units, each modeled on the example of the first study group.

The commitment of disciple to Master was lifelong. Although disciples might reject their Master and leave, or decline to join him in travel, judging from the *Analects* and the *Mencius*, many did not. In the *Mencius*, we encounter two disciples of a recently deceased Ruist Master who have abandoned their Master's teaching to follow a heterodox school. In berating them for their treachery, Mencius mentions that they had served their former teacher for "decades" until his death (*M*:3A.4). Even poor students never left the group!

Mencius traveled with an entourage of disciples, and although they are not extensively portrayed in the *Mencius*, the core members of his group appear to have stayed by him for many years.[81] In the state of Ch'i, Mencius seems to have encountered another prominent Ru named Kao Tzu.[82] The *Mencius* shows us the clash between the study groups of these two Ruist Masters, with Mencius coaching one of his disciples in the art of besting Kao Tzu's disciples in debate (*M*:6A.5).[83]

Although the early Ruist community can be conceived as a network of study groups, it was by no means a united network, as the conflicts between Mencius and Kao Tzu show. Factionalism among Ruists appeared early; the seeds are evident even in the *Analects*, which records disputes among disciples after Confucius' death (*A*:19.3, 19.12, 19.15-16). By the late Warring States period, factional disputes had become bitter indeed. In the *Hsun Tzu*, rival Ruist factions are attacked with a venom as virulent as that directed against heterodox schools.[84] The *Han Fei Tzu* records that as many as eight major Ruist factions existed by the end of the Chou (*Hsien-hsueh*:19.7b).[85]

3.2. The Ruist Syllabus

The Ruist stress on study was absolute. "Study" (*hsueh*) is the first word of the *Analects*, and when Confucius recounts his thumbnail autobiography, the first event is, "At fifteen I set my heart on study" (*A*:2.4).[86] Confucius regarded his love of study as what set him apart from other people (*A*:5.28). For him, study was as basic as thought, if not prior to it: "I have spent whole days without eating and whole nights without sleeping in order to think. It was useless—not like study!" (*A*:15.31). In this section we will try to describe just what study entailed for a Ru.

The Ruists did not invent formal education in China, but they may have been among the first to grasp intellectually the tremendous importance of education in shaping every aspect of a person's character. Some question exists as to whether formal education was either intensive or widespread prior to Confucius' time. Late sources, such as the various Ruist ritual manuals, recount in exquisite and contradictory detail the structure and syllabi of early Chou education.[87] The detail of these books clearly labels them as idealizations, and, if they are indicative of any actual education practices, they are more likely to have been those of early Ruist study groups than those of the early Chou aristocracy.[88]

Whether the need for broad formal education was recognized prior to the Ruists or not, it seems likely that no other group had such faith in the transforming power of education: "If I wished to change from base to noble, stupid to wise, poor to rich, could I? I say: Study … Just now I was a muddled man in the street; a moment later and I am the equal of Yao and Yü!" (*H*:8.39-41). Just what did this study entail?

Basically, the Ruist syllabus consisted of four elements: the study of the gymnastic arts of war, the study and interpretation of texts, the study of *li*, and the study of associated aesthetic forms, such as music and dance. Formal and informal ethical discussion—the aspect of study that is recorded in our texts—accompanied all four elements. As we explore the syllabus here, we will find that all four elements—not only the last two—were directed toward cultivating in the Ruist student an all-encompassing mastery of stylized, ritual action.

Of the four areas, the one least discussed in the texts is the first: the martial arts, including archery and charioteering.[89] These skills were probably acquired by every member of the aristocracy, and it is likely that most or all Ruist students would have been proficient in these arts prior to joining the Ruist group.

Nevertheless, archery practice, at least, seems to have been included in the Ruist syllabus; we can draw this conclusion from the fact that Ruist texts speak of archery as a means of self-improvement. The *Analects*, for example, discusses archery as a field for manifesting the proper spirit of ritual conduct among equals. Archery contests are where men "compete at being gentlemen" (*A*:3.7).

The *Mencius* expands on this somewhat, and makes it clear that archery was seen as an ethical type of motor training: the quality of the physical shot was a reflection of the quality of one's moral attitudes (*M*:2A.7). The late Ruist text *Li-chi* contains a detailed interpretation of archery as an ethical medium of conduct. The central idea is that archery should be a perfect display of virtue because the arrows are shot from the midst of a completely ritualized setting (*She yi*:20.8a).[90]

The second category, the study of texts, is usually overemphasized in the West. Again, this is probably due to the bias of our sources, which are themselves texts, and are better suited to recording discussions of *Poetry* passages than to describing archery or other ritual practices that occurred on an uninteresting daily basis.

Nevertheless, although it has been overemphasized, the study of texts did become central to Ruism. The *Hsun Tzu* includes citations from the *Poetry, Documents, Spring and Autumn Annals,* and *Yi ching,* as well as from ritual books and other texts. At the start, in the *Analects,* the list is much briefer. The *Poetry* was certainly studied; it is frequently cited and discussed. We also find several references to "Documents," but whether this refers to the text we now know by that name or not is uncertain (Matsumoto 1966:17-20).[91]

The most discussed text in all Ruist works is the *Poetry,* and this alerts us to a seldom-stressed facet of Ruist textual study. We know from a variety of sources that the *Poetry* was not simply a group of songs collected for readers' pleasure and edification. The poems were employed as "scripts" on formal occasions. Skill in citing the *Poetry* was a form of ritual mastery. The speaker had to understand rules of citation and had to be creative within them.[92] This is why the *Analects* can say, "If you do not study the *Poetry,* you have no means whereby to speak" (*A*:16.13).[93]

Mastery of the *Poetry* was not an abstract scholarly interest; it was one aspect of self-ritualization. It provided the disciple with weighty scripts upon which to rely in general social intercourse. Of course, the subtlety of citing the *Poetry* lay in the speaker's ability to reveal a deep understanding of the meaning of the text, hence memorization was only the beginning; exegesis was a central concern. This is evident even in the *Analects* (*A*:1.15, 3.8); in the *Mencius* we find general rules of exegesis discussed (*M*:5A.4). By the time of the *Hsun Tzu*, the exegetical traditions that characterize Han Ruism are already in evidence, with elaborate moral interpretations attached to even the simplest poems (e.g., *H*:21.47-49). But this tradition should be viewed as an extension of the earlier one. The interest was not academic, it remained tied to ritual social action.

From Mencius' time on, at least, Ruists also studied the *Documents*. Such study was important because it informed disciples of "historical" precedents for Ruist doctrines, which could be used to legitimize Ruist ideas and actions. But as with *Poetry* study, the primary use of the *Documents* was probably as a vehicle for scripting speech. We can see this when we contrast the way in which the *Documents* is generally employed in Ruist texts and in the *Mo Tzu* (Mohists also studied the *Documents*, although the two schools seem to have read different versions of the text). While Ruist texts tend to employ the *Documents* much as they do the *Poetry*, citing brief passages (often out of context) to convey a moral point elegantly, the *Mo Tzu* frequently cites the *Documents* at length, treating the text as a narrative with a moral (e.g., *Shang-hsien* II:2.11b; *Chien-ai* III:4.14b [but cf. *A*:20.1]; *Ming kuei*:8.9a; *Fei ming*:9.13). The Ruist style of usage reflects the role of textual citation as an ornament of speech.

Thus, Ruist textual study grew out of an aim to incorporate those texts in conduct. Certainly more abstract intellectual rewards were found, and, by the Han period, Ruist study was undoubtedly bookish.[94] Even during the early period, we find the *Hsun Tzu* attacking Ruists who placed too great an emphasis on textual study at the expense of the study of *li* (*H*:8.91-92). But basically, textual study was part of the Ruist process of moral self-stylization, which Mencius described thus: "If you wear Yao's clothes, chant Yao's words, and act as Yao acted, then you are simply Yao" (*M*:6B.2).

The third topic of the Ruist syllabus was *li*, and although we list it here as one of four topics, it should be understood that *li* was, in fact, what the entire educational program was about. The point of studying archery was to learn physical and emotional control in a ritualized context; the point of studying texts was to ritualize one's speech. All aspects of Ruist study were directed toward ritualizing the student; study of the explicit codes of *li* was only one aspect.

Once again, the texts we possess tend to report things said rather than things done. Works such as the *Analects* do not list the types of *li* studied or discuss the frequency of practice. But the evidence of the Ruist obsession with *li* is quite visible: it is embodied in the tomes of ritual codes the Ruists compiled during the late Chou and early Han. Some of these, such as the *Yi-li*, were probably used as workbooks. The more theoretical texts are most likely to have grown from group discussions in which Masters recounted or improvised increasingly elaborate ethical meanings of the rituals they performed.

But Ruists did not merely memorize and theorize about ritual codes, they learned to do ritual, and they aimed at a complete stylization of their persons according to *li*. In the *Analects*, Confucius tells Yen Yuan never to look at, listen to, say, or do anything that is not *li* (*A*:12.1). For Hsun Tzu, the role of *li* was to mold people into ideal types. Ritual food molds the sense of taste, ritual fragrances mold the sense of smell, ritual ornamentation molds the eye, ritual music the ear, and ritual halls and furniture mold the body (*H*:19.3-5).[95] The role of *li* goes beyond codes, because *li* molds every aspect of a man.

According to the *Hsun Tzu*, "The course of study begins with the chanting of texts and culminates in the study of *li*" (*H*:1.26).[96] The ideal man is portrayed as a completely stylized being: "His cap is high, his robes billow about him, his expression is benevolent. Dignified and stately, free from care and want, boundless, vast, bright, serene—thus does he present the role of father and elder"(*H*:6.42-43).

As we discussed, ritual is generally formulated according to aesthetic criteria, and the Ruist process of self-ritualization was also a training in aesthetic skills. Some of these skills were simple, such as learning to execute *li* with precision and grace.[97] But Ruists also delighted in and practiced the more artistic skills associated with *li*.

We find considerable evidence of this in the *Analects*. We learn there that Confucius was accomplished on the zither (*A*:17.18), and that zithers and drums were played during group meetings (*A*:11.17, 11.24). There is even a metonymic reference to a disciple by his zither, indicating the importance of the instrument to the group (*A*:11.15). And we hear of Confucius' scrupulous delicacy in joining in song with others (*A*:7.32).

Confucius did not just like music; he was expert in it. When we see him in discussion with the Grand Music Master of Lu, it is Confucius who lectures the Music Master, not the other way around (*A*:3.23).[98] Elsewhere, Confucius claims to have "properly ordered" the music of the *Poetry*, though just what this means is uncertain (*A*:9.15).[99]

In early China, no clear distinction was made between poetry, song, and music, such as we make today. "Poetry" (*shih*[c]) was not spoken, it was chanted and sung; "music" (*yueh*) was often accompanied by lyrics. When we picture the Ruist citing a poem in the midst of an argument, we must realize that not only was he gracing his speech with ancient words, but he was ornamenting it with music as well. And in addition to this, a number of sources testify that the verses of the *Poetry* were meant to be danced as well as sung.[100]

Although our portrait of Ruist practice pictures it as an all-encompassing ritual dance, the role of formal dance in the Ruist syllabus is somewhat elusive. Perhaps because dance was subsumed under the categories of *li* and music, it is not much discussed as a discrete activity in our three early Ruist texts. But the probability that it occupied a significant place in the syllabus is indicated by the role that dance plays in the idealized education syllabi described in Ruist ritual texts. Although most of these texts are generally believed to have attained their current form during the Han, they include a great deal of late Chou material. They frequently purport to describe early Chou practice. The idealistic portraits they present most likely reflect forms and values that characterized not the early Chou royal house, but the late Chou Ruist community.

The *Chou-li* reports that in ancient practice, the Grand Supervisor of Music was the chief officer of education. It was his task, we are told, to assemble all promising noble youths at the Ch'eng-chün Academy, where they were instructed in music and dance (*Ch'un-kuan*, Ta ssu-yueh:6.1). Under him was the Music Master, who was in charge of all elementary education, which consisted primarily of the teaching of "minor" dances (Yueh-shih:6.7b).

Another Ruist text, the *Wen Wang shih-tzu* chapter of the *Li-chi*, begins its syllabus by proclaiming "One must teach noble heirs and cadets according to the proper season. In spring and summer they learn dances of the shield and spear; in autumn and winter, dances of feather and flute" (*LC*:6.13a). Their teachers, as in the *Chou-li*, are music masters.

The *Nei tse* chapter of the *Li-chi* does not place music and dance at the head of the curriculum as do these other texts, but in its graded syllabus it notes precisely which dances are studied at each age, beginning at age thirteen (*LC*:8.25b-26a). In the *Wang-chih* chapter, dance is not specifically mentioned; the curriculum for higher education consists of poetry, texts, *li*, and music. But here again, the teaching is under the aegis of an Officer of Music, and the evaluation of the students for purposes of advancement in government is in the hands of the Grand Officer of Music (*LC*:4.10b).

These texts reflect a belief in the primary importance of music and dance to education, and, in light of their idealizations of Chou education practice, it seems very likely indeed that Ruist disciples were instructed in dance as well as in poetry and music. The *Hsun Tzu* seems to refer to such instruction when it explains that the only way to understand the meaning of a dance is to practice the dance repeatedly (*H*:20.39-40).

I have dwelt at some length on the aesthetic aspects of Ruist education because I feel that these elements make plausible the Ruist dedication to *li*.

It is my experience that Westerners find the Ruist interest in *li* puzzling and assume that the real heart of their teaching must lie elsewhere. I think that the center of Ruism is unmistakably *li*, and that the problem is not the incongruity of educated men constricting their lives into a ritual mold, but is our frequent misunderstanding of what ritual entails.

Every rite that a disciple memorized, every poem, every zither tune, every intricately choreographed ceremony constituted a new skill in artistry, one that he could apply in social life. The Ruists were specialists in the human arts. Their study encompassed nearly every major aesthetic form of their day: poetry, music, costume, dance, and the infinite crafted objects of ritual. Can we doubt the rewards of mastering these arts?

The Master Ru was essentially an artist, and his love for his ritual art was not a pose. It was in ritual living that he found his greatest satisfaction.

A passage in the *Analects* expresses this feeling perfectly. In it, Confucius asks four disciples to confide to him their dreams: "You are always complaining that nobody knows you. If someone were to recognize your abilities, what would you want to do?"

The first three disciples describe various feats they would like to perform: to regenerate a state through revitalizing its armies (a caricature of Tzu-lu), or to do it through good policies, or to be a high court ritualist. But when it comes to the fourth disciple, Tseng Tien, the answer is different:

"Tien, what about you?" The rhythm of his zither slowed; it rang as he laid it down and rose. "My thoughts differ from the others'," he said. "There is no harm in that," said the Master. "After all, each of us is simply speaking his heart." "In late spring," said Tseng Tien, "after the spring garments have been sewn, I would go out with five-times six capped young men, and six-times seven boys. We would bathe in the River Yi, and stand in the wind on the stage of the great rain dance. Then chanting, we would return." The Master sighed deeply. "I am with Tien," he said (*A*:11.24).[101]

3.3. Philosophers and Funeral Directors

Before closing our description of the early Ruist community, we should briefly note another sphere of noninstrumental Ruist interests: the necessities of economic sustenance. In some respects, these factors can be seen as the ultimate heart of Ruism: modern history tends to regard economic motives as fundamental. We accord them only a secondary position here because Ruism, being a nonhereditary sect, did not encounter its economic needs as givens, but created them as a consequence of its primary commitment to ritualism and group study. While an awareness of economic factors can enhance our understanding of Ruist practice and doctrines, ultimately these economic needs grew out of the decisions of individual disciples to adopt the Ruist lifestyle. Because we find no evidence that the economic rewards of early Ruism were great, we may suppose that, at least initially, idealistic interests were prior to economic ones for most Ru.

Although Ruism was in many ways a socially insular community, its political doctrines and the desire to maintain legitimacy prevented most Ru from adopting an eremetic lifestyle. Economic necessity also required Ruists to play roles in society, ones that would earn them their keep without destroying the fabric of their cult organization.

There is only the barest information in our sources concerning how they managed this. Four major methods are discernable: they could find regular employment as teachers, they could seek out gratuitous patronage, they could find posts as family or court ritualists, or they could hire out as masters of ceremony for important ritual occasions. We will discuss each of these alternatives and their implications for Ruist doctrine very briefly here.

Several dimensions of teaching were open to the talented Ru. He could form his own study group by attracting disciples, who may have contributed to their teacher's well-being by bringing him tuition or gifts.[102] A large enough entourage might raise a teacher's reputation and lead to other opportunities.

Because Ruists were accomplished in many of the traditional arts of China, they were logical choices for wealthy non-Ruist families or courts to hire as private tutors for their sons (as Tzu-hsia became court tutor in Wei[a]). The pervasive Ruist advocacy of universal education might have been related to their talents as teachers. If Ruist Masters were at all successful in lobbying for broadened education programs, they might have been able to provide their students with salaried positions as local teachers.[103]

The quickest way for a Ru to secure a steady income for himself and for his disciples was to be patronized as a "wise man" at a feudal court or by a great warlord.[104] But naturally, few Ruists were able to attract such patronage, and the quest for gratuitous support may have frequently taken less seemly forms. The *Mo Tzu* states flatly that Ruists supported themselves by begging (*Fei Ju*:9.17b).

If a Ruist lived near a feudal court where ritual forms were carefully observed, he might find employment there as a court ritualist.[105] But Ruists who were feudal retainers might not have had much say about the nature of their duties. The *Han Fei Tzu* tells the tale of one old Ru who was directed to go pick medicinal herbs on a mountain side (*Nei ch'u-shuo II*:10.5b).

Perhaps the most common form of employment for Ru was as occasional masters of ceremony, or presiding priests, particularly for funeral ceremonies. Ruists advocated funeral rites of remarkable length and complexity.[106] They justified their position on ethical and historical grounds, but they were deeply interested in the issue on economic grounds. They were probably the only people qualified to perform these rites in full detail—their specialization in funerals was truly esoteric; discussions of these rites comprise perhaps the largest single category in the Ruist corpus (Shirakawa 1972:67). By promoting the practice of elaborate funerals, Ruists were, in effect, creating employment for their talents.[107]

Even in this brief section we have touched on economic motivations for several aspects of Ruist doctrine. Their political doctrines endowed Ruists with social credibility, giving them the necessary status to seek respectable employment. Their advocacy of intense and widespread education was abetted by an interest in employment of teachers. Their obsession with *li* was coordinated with their availability as official or occasional ritualists.

It was precisely this linkage of cult doctrine and practice with economic interest which did, in the end, create a place for Ruists in Warring States society.[108] Ruists perfected a particular set of skills within the confines of their insular community, and they created a demand for those skills with a well-designed set of doctrines that appealed to people by invoking the authority of semi-mythical culture heroes, traditionalism, homely contemporary ethics, and lofty idealism. Simply put, Ruist doctrine reflected Ruist interests, and this should not surprise us because it is a truism that such linkages can be demonstrated of any philosophical school. It neither affects the value of the doctrine itself, nor shows unethical intent on the part of the philosophers—although it might make them seem less heroic.

Summary

In order to be able to see how T'ien "fit in" to Ruist interests and practice we have been trying to discover just what early Ruism was all about. We have argued that Ruism was not so much an ideology as a way of life, which centered around a devotion to traditional forms of ritual conduct called *li*. In a brief analysis of *li*, we argued that they were traditionally legitimized on the basis of religious beliefs in their magical powers, and also on the basis of their confirming an established social order. And we noted that in addition to these ethical dimensions, they were also associated with aesthetic values.

When Confucius and his followers addressed the crisis in values that had been created by the decline of Chou rule, their solution was to focus on *li* as a cardinal value. To do this, they rebuilt the foundations of *li*, legitimizing it on the basis of its ability to generate social order and to transform people into Sages. This dual legitimization created a bifurcation in Ruist philosophy, yielding conflicting political and personal imperatives.

In Ruist theory, the dimensions of self-cultivation and political activism were closely linked. They were sequential: response to the personal imperactive of self-perfection preceded response to the political imperative to change he world. In effect, however, the two dimensions were radically disjoined. The idealistic conditions imposed on political activism effectively ruled out political action. Political doctrine was actually employed to legitimaze a withdrawal from politics in favor of prepetual self-cultivation, in accord with the example of the ideal disciple Yen Yuan.

As a result, the network of Ruist study groups that flourished during the Warring States period tended to become socially insular, students concentrating on the tasks of self-ritualization, and delighting in the rewards of participation in a brotherhood preoccupied with perfecting highminded and aesthetic skills. The syllabus they studied was varied, and included martial arts and textual study, along with formulaic and aesthetic ritual study. But, in fact, all elements of the syllabus were directed toward the end of ritualizing every aspect of speech and conduct.

The social insularity of the Ruist community was tempered by needs for social credibility and economic sustenance. Much of Ruist doctrine was shaped by these needs. The result was a balance, where Ruists pursued an eccentric social course, but created and maintained for themselves a viable role in society.

The Sage and the Self

Chapter III

In the portrait of Ruism we have developed to this point, we have sketched the historical background that made ritual *li* an eligible choice as a philosophical focus. We have also delineated the parameters of Ruism as a school that provided structures of ritual initiation and as a social institution that provided professional roles, enhancing in both aspects the appeal of ritual as a source of personal and social rewards.

In this chapter, we will complete our portrait of Ruism by concentrating on an aspect of explicit doctrine: the ideal of the Sage. Our discussion will clarify the manner in which the ethical dimensions of Ruist ritual were broadened through linkage with a personal ideal of Sagehood, a linkage forged through the innovation of a comprehensive ethical virtue: *jen.* Through ritual self-cultivation, disciples were to subdue their attachment to the perspectives of self-interest, and strengthen their devotion to the interests of the human community. This new perspective, identifying self and other, was the basis of the personal ideal of the Sage.

This process was viewed as a fundamental transformation of the self, and we will see how the plausibility of the claim that such a transformation could be achieved was greatly enhanced by the portrait of the empirical self which emerges from Ruist texts. In contrast to traditional Western ideas of the self, the implicit picture of the self in Ruist texts is intrinsically social, and this accounts for the cogency of the notion of molding personal identity through commitment to the social institution of *li.*

1. Practical Totalism: The Ruist Doctrine of Sagehood

Early Ruism shares with a number of other systems of thought the belief that an extraordinary level of understanding exists, attainable by man, which can comprehend the phenomenal world as a whole. When this level of understanding is attained, any significant phenomenon will be perceived as possessing a clear meaning because it will be understood in its relation to the whole. In other words, the multiplicity of the world makes sense, and it is possible to understand the holistic sense of it, and so to understand any part in relation to the whole.

We will refer to this type of doctrine as "totalistic," a term that signals both the impulse toward holism in the portrait of a universal level of meaning in the world and the force of the associated imperative to grasp the universe in its entirety.[1]

Most Western philosophies do not posit any such ideal human type, but the case was quite different in early China. During the pre-Ch'in period, we see doctrines of this sort expressed in texts representing several schools of thought. These texts reflect what we might call "the cult of the Sage." We see it in the *Tao te ching*, which praises the Sage as one who "knows the world without going out his door, and sees the Way of T'ien without looking out his window" (chap. 47), words echoed by the *Hsun Tzu*, which tells us that "without leaving his halls, the *chün-tzu* has assembled therein all the truths of the world" (*H*:3.38-39).[2] Perhaps the simplest statement of such a totalistic vision appears in what Fung Yu-lan calls the "materialist" chapters of the *Kuan Tzu*, which tell us that the Sage knows the outcome of events without divining.[3] The ideal of Sagehood as a totalism cuts across the philosophies of disparate pre-Ch'in schools.

Thomas Metzger has used the term "totalism" to describe the neo-Confucian "ideal of total, rationalistic knowledge of ultimate reality" (1977:61). Metzger's description points explicitly toward a model of totalistic understanding conceived in terms of its cognitive properties. In the case of early Ruism, and of some other varieties of the cult of the Sage, such an emphasis on mentalistic processes would be misleading.[4] The true Sage was not merely a repository of facts and theories; he was a perfect actor, a person who always chose the appropriate response to concrete situations, and so could protect himself from danger, seize every opportunity to exert an ethical influence on the world, and set an example for others. We will see this active aspect of Sagehood stressed repeatedly as we explore our Ruist texts, where every Sage is a perfect master of ritual action. Because of the overlap between the dimensions of thinking and acting in the Ruist portrait of the Sage, we may call Ruism a "practical totalism," signifying the Ruist belief in a personal ideal who not only understands the meaning of every phenomenon in the universe, but also can respond to phenomena with perfect appropriateness.

One significant aspect of such a notion of totalism is that it implies a closed notion of human perfection. In the modern West, most people would probably agree that no individual, no matter how knowledgeable or mature, can exhaust all potential avenues of human growth. Neither the Nobel scientist nor his counterpart poet can represent *the* single model of human fulfillment. But a doctrine of practical totalism tends to envision human perfection in a single mold: those who have attained totalistic understanding are Sages, those who are looking for values in another direction are

misguided. The proper goals of self-development are reduced to a single
option. Doctrines of Sagehood do not generally allow for a pluralism of
values.[5] As the *Analects* quotes Confucius, "Who can go out except by the
door? Why, then, does no one follow this Way?" (*A*:6.17).

1.1. *Jen* as a Totalism

Nowhere in the *Analects* is there a systematic description of a totalistic
consciousness, and the text can be read without introducing the idea. However, to read the text in this way is to encounter a bewildering concatena-
tion of independent moral virtues and imperatives, which leaves the
impression that Confucius' philosophical achievement was the laborious
piling on of ad hoc rules. It has traditionally been recognized, however, that
an important unity is created by the textual dominance of the word *"jen"* in
the *Analects*, and this is, in fact, the key to discerning the notion of the
Sagely totalism in that text.[6]

The essential role of *jen* in the *Analects* is to be a mystery.[7] Only Confucius—
and perhaps Yen Yuan—seems to know what *jen* is. Its elusiveness makes it
the focus of the text. Disciples repeatedly try to pin down the meaning of
the word. They offer descriptions of virtue and ask Confucius whether these
constitute *jen*; Confucius almost never says yes (*A*:5.5, 5.8, 5.19, 14.1).[8] But
when disciples suggest that some person is certainly not *jen*, Confucius
suddenly finds grounds for calling that person *jen* (*A*:14.17-18).[9] *Jen* is a
paradox, and the disciple's task is to resolve it.

The word *"jen"* is not used with complete consistency in the text. At
times, it appears to be only one of several cardinal virtues: "The *jen* man is
free from anxiety; the wise man is free from confusion; the courageous man
is free from fear" (*A*:14.28; cf. 9.29). But as we explore the entire body of the
text, we find that *jen* is given a clear priority over other virtues, such as
wisdom and courage: "To dwell in *jen* is the fairest course; if one chooses
not to reside in *jen*, whence will come wisdom?" (*A*:4.1).[10] "The man of *jen*
will certainly be courageous; the man of courage will not necessarily be
jen" (*A*:14.4). The panoply of individual virtues we find in the *Analects* all
seem, in one passage or another, to be defined as manifestations of *jen*.[11]

1.2. The Single Thread

In Ruist texts, a persistent tension exists between the notions of having
broad knowledge and being a Sage. While all Ruist texts agree that narrow-
mindedness is a bad trait, they are just as clear in holding that human
perfection lies not in a comprehensive knowledge of facts, but in a comprehensive ability to understand ethical meanings and to act accordingly. This
tension reflects the antithetical opposition of the closed boundaries of
Sagehood conceived as a totalism to the openmindedness of fact accumu-

lation. The *Hsun Tzu* is most articulate on this matter; it offers a variety of arguments to the effect that "study is precisely the study of limits" (*H*:21.81). Although the *Analects* is not this articulate, it makes a similar point. Wisdom is not "knowing-that"; it is "knowing-how."

> The Master said, "Do I possess knowledge? No, I have none at all. If some simple fellow came to me with a problem, I would—all empty—just strike at it pro and con, and solve it so" (*A*:9.8).[12]

The linkage of this skill of wisdom to the totalism is apparent in the following passage, wherein Confucius confides a lesson to the disciple Tzu-kung:

> The Master said, "Ssu, do you take me for one who studies much and remembers it all?" "Yes," was the reply. "Is it not so?" "No. I link all upon a single thread" (*A*:15.3).

A common response of readers to this passage is frustration because Confucius does not say what the "single thread" is. But in light of *A*:9.8 this may be unfair. If Confucius is referring to a cultivated skill of understanding rather than to a fact or explicit principle, then we cannot expect to be told what it is—a skill cannot be told, only taught. We must not think that Confucius withheld information from Tzu-kung by speaking cryptically of the single thread. Perhaps there was nothing to tell but that the thread was there, and to alert Tzu-kung to the value of finding it himself.[13] In his simple statement, Confucius describes the difference between studying facts and studying Sagehood.

The *Analects* conveniently supplies us with an alternate version of the same passage, involving a different disciple, Tseng Shen, and considerably expands our understanding of the single thread.

> The Master said, "Shen, my Way links all upon a single thread." "Yes," replied Tseng Tzu. When the Master had gone, the other disciples asked, "What did he mean?" Tseng Tzu said, "The Master's teaching is no more than this: devotion and reciprocity" (*A*:4.15).

Here, at least, we learn one disciple's confident interpretation of the single thread.[14] What does it mean?

Some traditional interpretations have taken a clue from the unifying role *jen* plays in the text and have viewed "devotion and reciprocity" as a gloss for *jen*.[15] I think this is essentially correct, and it gives us insight into the meaning of *jen*.

"Devotion" translates "*chung*." Cognate graphs are "*chung*[a]": "center," and "*chung*[b]": "inner recesses,"[16] and these suggest a root meaning of "one's inner self." The common sense of the word "*chung*" is often translated "loyalty" but in the *Analects*, a more precise gloss would be "singleminded devotion to fullfilling one's responsibilities."[17]

"Reciprocity" translates *"shu,"* a word defined in the *Analects* by a negative formulation of the Golden Rule: "Do not do to others what you would not wish done to you" (*A*:15.24).[18] The graph is built on the phonetic/semantic element *"ju*ᵃ*,"* variant *"ju*ᵇ*,"* which share a gloss as the second person pronoun "you."[19]

"Chung-shu," then, denotes a reciprocal externalizing of one's inner self in devoted action while internalizing the needs and interests of others as one's own.[20] This exchange of self-interest for a socially objective viewpoint is central to the meaning of *jen* and to the skill of perfect wisdom and action. It is the "single thread" that denotes, in the *Analects*, the Ruist ideal of Sagehood. But as we have been speaking of it, it remains abstract and impractical. Without a concrete program of action, "externalizing the self" and "internalizing the needs of others" are little more than jargon.

1.3. The Ritual Path

The crucial difference between the Ruist doctrine of practical totalism and those of other schools lies in the prescribed means of cultivating Sagehood. For Ruists, the path to Sagehood was the study of *li*. By refining the style of his life through *li*, the Ruist hoped to train both body and mind to achieve a perfection of social action described in the *Hsun Tzu* in dance-like terms: "He moves along with time; he bows or arches as the times change. [Fast or slow, curled or stretched,] a thousand moves, ten thousand changes: his Way is one" (*H*:8.86-87).[21]

The relationship between *li* and the totalism is not always clearly drawn in the *Analects*. Some passages are straightforward:

Yen Yuan asked about *jen*. The Master said, "Conquer yourself and return to *li*: that is *jen* . . . If it is not *li*, don't look at it; if it is not *li*, don't listen to it; if it is not *li*, don't say it; if it is not *li*, don't do it . . ." (*A*:12.1).[22]

Chung-kung asked about *jen*. The Master said, "Whenever you go out your front gate, [continue to treat all] as if you were receiving them as great guests. Whenever you direct the actions of others, do so as though officiating at a great sacrifice . . ." (*A*:12.2).

The primary element of *jen* here is clearly mastery of *li*, hence *li* seems necessarily prior to *jen*.

But some passages in the *Analects* suggest that, in fact, *jen* is prior to *li*: "How can the man who is not *jen* manage *li*?" (*A*:3.3); "*Li* comes after" (*A*:3.8). Passages such as these have led some interpreters to speak of *jen* as if it were a principle of interior self-realization independent of external influences, with *li* as an active manifestation of this mental maturation.[23] In effect, such a model suggests that Sagehood is prior to *li* and leaves blank the prescription for attaining Sagehood.

This sort of thinking confuses theory and practice, and is a product of the approach that views Ruist texts as reflections of structured doctrine rather than as guides for disciples undertaking a practical syllabus. It is quite true that in the *Analects jen* is ethically prior to *li*: the value of *li* derives from its power to generate *jen*, which is intrinsically good. Once the totalism of Sagehood is grasped, the disciple can throw away his *li*-books; he will be a perfect ritual actor naturally. But *li* is sequentially prior, as *A*:12.1-2 makes clear.[24] Disciples did not cultivate their inner virtue by means other than *li* and then choose to adopt *li* as their own. Joining a Ruist group, they stepped into an environment of enforced ritual regimen, and it was through ritual practice that they pursued the Ruist vision of the totalism, the Sagehood of *jen*.[25] The intense Ruist dedication to *li* suggests that it was through the habitual stylization of outer actions that disciples trained themselves in "devotion and reciprocity," the elements of *jen* that constituted the Sage's impartial and all-knowing social perspective. Through this intricate discipline of body and style, the disciple largely exchanged the narrow self of the "small man" for the all-encompassing self of the Sage.

2. Sagehood and the Self

In introducing the notion that striving toward Sagehood involved a transformation of the self through ritual practice, we must ask in what sense we mean to use the term "self." Not all definitions of the term will allow that the self is subject to alteration through practice, and we have not asked how we can apply the term in Ruism such that the totalistic goals of Sagehood would seem plausible.

Herbert Fingarette has investigated how the *Analects* seems to picture the self in relation to the ideal of Sagehood. He describes a model of the self as a composite of the will (*chih*[e]) and a self-regarding disposition. Fingarette suggests that the attainment of Sagehood involved complete identification of the will with the prescripts of ritual, or the Ruist Tao, along with the annihilation of self-regarding tendencies (1979:134-36). This simple picture of the ideal self of the Sage resonates with theories Fingarette has developed concerning the empirical experience of self reflected by the statements of the *Analects*. Focusing on discussions of moral responsibility and decision-making, Fingarette concludes that the tone of untroubled certainty that pervades the text, and its view of choice as no more than a perennial option to follow or not follow the Ruist Tao, reflects a psychological fact: that Confucius and his followers simply had not experienced the type of anguished psychic struggles that are so central to the Western experience of selfhood (1972:18-36, 44-45).[26] Fingarette's model effectively argues the plausibility of the totalistic ideal of Sagehood by removing from it its most implausible elements and reassigning these to the psychology of Chou China.

Fingarette's reasoning is easy to attack. As he does so often, Fingarette uses the argument from silence, and compounds it with the questionable tactic of reasoning from statements to their psychological background. It is unlikely that he is correct. The failure of the *Analects* to portray the inner psychic life probably reflects norms of what one articulates in literary form rather than the existence of an internal vacuum. Chinese histories and fiction are notorious for laconic narration of events of great drama without reference to the tortured thoughts of the actors; the agony is supplied empathetically by the reader, with, at most, a deep sigh from the narrator.

Nevertheless, Fingarette has focused on an important issue. Ruist texts and the totalistic ideal of Sagehood may indeed reflect a portrait of the self significantly different from those we customarily fashion in the West. Different definitions of the person lead to different judgments of what is valuable in the self and what is important to discuss. This will, in turn, influence the types of personal ideals that will be appealing and plausible.

In this section, we will analyze the configuration of the self as it seems to appear in the *Analects* and other Ruist texts and consider how this picture makes the totalistic goal of ritual Sagehood reasonable. We will find that the Ruist picture of the self—which may reflect no more than consensus Chou views—incorporates social dimensions incompatible with some Western ideas of the self, but highly compatible with the intrinsically social nature of *li*.

2.1. The Public Self

When Descartes stripped away from experience all that could be doubted, he found, in the *cogito*, bedrock certainty of existence proved by the fact of thought. But, as often noted, Descartes went further and made the unguarded assumption that the thought at the center of experience was personal thought, the thinking self. The assumption escaped his notice because for Descartes the search for the core of the subjective world was precisely a search for the self.

Plato was one of the first to exemplify the Western habit of conceiving of the self as an unchanging inner entity. For Plato—and many after him—the self was an immortal soul.[27] Later thinkers reconstituted it as a spiritual substance (e.g., Descartes, Locke), as configurations of psychic functions (e.g., Freud), as the stream of consciousness (e.g., James), and in any number of other forms, until very recently entirely mentalistic. Although suspicion of mind-body dualism has made it unfashionable to think of the self as a substance, our tendency is still to conceive of the self as an inalienable interior core: a private cell impervious to the eyes of the public world.

Ruist texts seem to draw the self differently, and this becomes evident in passages where aspects of the person, which we tend to envision as necessarily private, emerge into public view. In one such passage, Confucius describes the mind of his best disciple, Yen Yuan: "The Master said, 'Hui will go for three months without his mind (*hsin*[a]) ever deviating from *jen*. As for the others', they reach *jen* only occasionally' " (*A*:6.7).

It is puzzling that Confucius describes the minds of his disciples in this way. It cannot be that he has access into their thought; surely he is judging their conduct, and the word "*hsin*[a]" ("mind," or "heart") is a rhetorical flourish.

But other passages are found in which the anomolous visibility of the self is harder to dismiss. The most illustrative of these again involves Confucius' description of Yen Yuan. In it, the process of introspection appears to become interpersonal.

Inner reflection is denoted in the *Analects* by the term "*hsing*[a]": "survey," as in surveying land. The interiority of the process is indicated in phrases such as "surveying oneself inside" (*nei tzu hsing*).[28] The passage in question connects reflection to the word "*ssu*": "self," "selfish," "private." The etymology of "*ssu*," links it, like "*hsing*[a]," with geography: it originally denoted the crop of a privately assigned field.[29] These two words work together in the passage, along with another word (*fa*[a]) which can mean "to bloom" or "to issue forth," to create a central metaphor. The text reads literally:

> The Master said, "When I talk with Hui, he may go all day without contradicting me, as though he were stupid. But retiring and surveying the grain of his private field, after all it is ready to bloom. Hui is not stupid!" (*A*:2.9).[30]

The central phrase can be read: "But retiring and looking into his self, after all [my teachings] are ready to issue forth." The language seems outlandish— how can Confucius see into Yen Yuan's inmost self? But there is no great mystery. The self one examines simply includes public dimensions excluded from the Western self. The aspect of self under observation here includes public conduct. It is not that the only dimensions of the self are external, but that the text is calling up a unified notion of self that bridges dimensions we would discriminate categorically.[31]

This close linkage between inner and outer dimensions of a unified self is reflected in statements that claim that people's inmost selves are, in fact, open to scrutiny. The passage that follows the one just discussed instructs us: "See what he does, look at his reasons, observe what pleases him—where shall he hide? Where shall he hide?" (*A*:2.10). The *Mencius* makes a similar point: "Listen to his words, look at his eyes—where shall he hide?" (*M*:4A.16).[32]

The Ruist texts do seem to reflect a notion of the person very different from our own, one in which the external attributes of people are as important to the constitution of their selves as mental phenomena. We do not need to infer that this reveals a lacuna in the psychology of Chou individuals, but it does alert us to the possibility that they defined their identities differently from the way we do ours. Rather than suggesting that there was less complexity within the scope of their selves, we will do better to picture them drawing the borders of their "private fields" at some distance outside their bodies, so that a portion of their selves was in public view. This does not imply that people were unable to distinguish between the spheres we call private and public—the passages cited make clear that they did. But the distinction was not regarded as categorical, and the person was entified in a holistic manner.

That this broad self may have ranged well beyond the confines of the body is suggested by the use of the term "person" (*jen*ᵃ). Francis Hsu has argued cogently that even in modern Chinese, the term "person" incorporates relational aspects such as family membership, place of origin, and social role, alien to Western portraits of the self (1971). This social constitution of the person may easily have made normal processes of internal dialogue appear less significant than they appear in the West, where they so dominate the experience of selfhood. This would be particularly true if social dimensions of the self were viewed as more valuable and, in the final analysis, more real than the transient stream of consciousness.

In the next section, which examines the Ruist portrait of human nature as innately social, we will find that this was, indeed, the case. And we will see that weighting the substance of the self toward the public sphere in this way also made both plausible and appealing the idea of transforming the self through *li*.

2.2. The Social Self

Traditional Western theories of the self are rooted in beliefs about the ontological status of human beings. We tend to picture people as fundamentally atomic entities, separated in space. Social relations are not intrinsic to the self.[33] This implies a description of social structures on the model of social contract theory—a confederacy of ontologically independent beings; and from Hobbes to Sartre, this is a dominant view. Even if we grant social organization the status of the inevitable, we still tend to regard social relations as accidental contexts for a self intrinsically unentailed in their net. Our picture is firmly rooted in common ontology: as Aristotle put it, "Relatedness is, as it were, an offshoot or logical accident of substance" (*NE*:I.1096a).

Chinese views, traditional and modern, conventional and philosophical, have tended to stress the fact that much of what comprises individual identity is constituted in a social context. The portrait of human nature as intrisically social is a consensus position (see Munro 1977:15-19).[34] This common view was rejected by Taoists, and perhaps by Mohists as well,[35] but for Ruists, these ideas were congenial to their interest in social *li*, and they became defenders of what was probably contemporary common sense (see Munro 1969:74-81).[36] The most famous defense of the social portrait of man was offered by Mencius, who claimed that the social patterns of ethical conduct were innate dispositions of the human mind (*M*:2A.6; 6A.6). However, Mencius' notion of the innately ethical self was not a mainstream view, even among early Ruists.

The picture that probably best represented contemporary views of man is that presented in the *Hsun Tzu*. Hsun Tzu grants man at birth no more than certain biological needs: "His mind is nothing but a mouth and a belly" (*H*:4.52). This is an animal being, not yet a "human" one. The human element is formed through socialization, and this is made possible by the characteristic that distinguishes the species from other animals: the ability to form social groups on the basis of appropriate allotment of roles (*H*:5.23; 9.70-71).[37] These roles, the conventional patterns of society, constitute the social web in which the selves of individuals are nurtured.

Human qualitites do not emerge until the animal is socialized, first in the family context and later through the discipline of social roles. Thus, the human self is intrinsically relational, and this is reflected in the normative use of the term "person" to denote one whose social accomplishments are great (e.g., *A*:14.9). These ideas also lie at the basis of the frequent claim that the words "person" (*jen*[a]) and "*jen*" form a mutual gloss.[38] From this model the Ruists derive the centrality of filial action: the family is given to each individual as the context for personal humanization. Failure to master the role of child means failure to master the capacity for fulfilling social roles. The unfilial person is not a person at all. The *Chung-yung* tells us: " '*Jen*' means to be a person; cleaving to parents is the key" (20).[39]

Thus, whereas the Western tradition has sought the distinguishing characteristic of man through an inventory of his subjective consciousness, Chinese tradition has tended to describe it through patterns of social action, both for individuals, and for the species as a whole.[40] An analogy from nature may make the Chinese position clearer. Were we to ask about the essential nature of a "social insect" such as the honey bee, we would be unsatisfied with an answer that did not go beyond a biological inventory of the individual bee. The most distinctive and important aspects of an individual bee cannot be described without reference to the hive, and in an analogous way, for Ruists the most important aspects of mankind and of individuals do not emerge until humanity is viewed at the level of the group.[41]

All this is of a piece with our evidence concerning the public dimension of the self. But once again, although the social portrait of man is likely to affect attitudes toward the self, influencing both personal norms and what is considered worthy of recognition, it does not imply any impoverishment of mental life.

The moral status of the mental complex of inner mind was uncertain for Ruists, and here we may return to Fingarette's model of a self bifurcated into realms of will and a self-regarding disposition. The latter, Ruists tended to identify with the prehuman qualities of man: the mind of mouth and belly. In the will lay the potential to realize truly human qualities, and Fingarette is correct in pointing to the Ruist focus on the choice between following the path to humanity or remaining mired in animal urges. Mencius specifically recognized both the dimensions and the alternatives, and he spoke of the two selves (*t'i*) of the person: the great self and the small self (*M*:6A.15). Of these selves, only the former was considered a human self, and its boundaries were drawn well into the social sphere.[42]

One aspect of the self, crucial to Western views, seems to be ignored in the Ruist account: the uniqueness of qualities and capacities inherent in individuals.[43] As we noted near the outset of this chapter, Ruism, as a totalistic philosophy, tends to cast the images of human perfection in a single mold, and rules out acceptance of plualistic values. In view of the close linkage we in the West tend to make between personal identity and idiosyncratic qualities, it would be disturbing indeed to find that the holistic self of the Ruist Sage may leave no room for variety. And we might wonder whether such an ideal could have provided for disciples the sort of affective attraction that could sustain them in their long studies, whatever their notions of the empirical self may have been. Fingarette, a defender of the Ruist faith, attempts to address such issues by suggesting that the ritual actor expresses creativity in the manner of the performing artist (1979:137; 1983:345). I believe the analogy to be useful, and in the conclusion of this book we will discuss it further in terms of the rewards of skill mastery. However, one must allow that the field demarcated for uniqueness and creativity is rather narrow.

What seems to be lacking in the totalistic portrait of the ritual Sage is that aspect of the person that we usually denote by the word "personality." Although Mencius makes some motions toward acknowledging the possibility of variety among Sages,[44] and Hsun Tzu describes a utopian vision where each member of society is able to "give free rein to his abilities" (*H*:12.51-2), they fail to convince us that, in everyday language, Sages could have interesting personalities. This would have been a difficult point to establish in a doctrine that exalts the power of social ritual to shape the self, and Ruist theory does not, in fact, leave much room for the personality of the Sage.

But here, again, distinguishing between doctrine and practice is useful. If Ruists could not articulate the individuality of the Sage in theory, they nevertheless conveyed it vividly in the portrait of their patron Sage, Confucius, presented in their primary "textbook": the *Analects*. The doctrinal purist must always find it a little puzzling to see Confucius ridiculing students, racing after Taoist hermits, rapping the heels of old men, and losing control at the funeral of his best disciple. And, in the *Analects*, variety and uniqueness among selves is both acknowledged as a fact and celebtated as a value through the characters of the disciples, whose integral role in the text is, I believe, unique in philosophical literature.

If one considers Ruism as a tradition rather than merely as a body of doctrine, one finds the notion of the actual person recognizable, and the picture of the ideal person attractive and plausible. Endowing the Sage with a unique personality may have been beyond the parameters of consistent Ruist theory, but Ruist philosophy was more than theory, and the message was conveyed through other strategies.[45]

Summary

In the last three chapters, we have articulated a description of the ritual focus of early Ruism. In chapter I, we discussed how historical context made ritual plausible as a philosophical value. In chapter II, we described how Ruism functioned as a ritual sect. In this chapter, we have dealt with issues concerning the ethical legitimacy of ritual and the psychological plausibility of the personal ideal of the ritual Sage.

We are now ready to turn to the topic that will occupy us for most of the remainder of this book: the interpretation of the function of T'ien in the context of this ritual doctrine. As we predicted in chapter I, we will find that the Ruist choice of ritual as a new value pillar served to reconstitute the nature of T'ien, which continued to serve as a value ground, as it had during the early Chou. But our examination of the *Analects, Mencius*, and *Hsun Tzu* will also show that T'ien's legitimizing function was complex. T'ien was required to authenticate both of the disjoined moieties of Ruist doctrine and practice: ritual self-cultivation and political withdrawal. The bifurcated structure of Ruist doctrine yields a bifurcated portrait of T'ien.

Part Two

The Confucian Creation of Heaven

Two Levels of Meaning
The Role of T'ien in the *Analects*

Chapter IV

The conclusions of the last three chapters sharpen our understanding of what early Ruism was. We will refer to them frequently as we explore the role which T'ien plays in early Ruist texts. The aim of our analysis will be to examine the ways in which statements about T'ien reflect the concrete interests and goals of the early Ruist community.

Because our primary concern lies in the instrumental function of these statements rather than in the choice of conventional beliefs or preexisting theories that they may reflect, our approach will be somewhat different from that taken by most interpreters. Most previous analyses of the role of T'ien in Ruist texts have focused upon determining which of several conventional images or "concepts" of T'ien (god, fate, nature, and so forth) is reflected in each use of the word. These questions are of great importance in tracing the evolution of religious and protoscientific theories in early China, but answering them does not necessarily give us insight into the type of meaning we are seeking. Certainly, when a statement about T'ien relies upon a conventional image, it is best to be clear about which one it is. But we must not think that in detecting the operative image we have articulated the meaning of T'ien in the statement, much less the meaning of the statement. And we must also beware classifying statements according to a limited variety of imagistic options. To do so may be to overlook the very ambiguities and nuances that make a statement or a theory interesting.

As we proceed in our analysis, we will find that each of our three texts employs a variety of conventional images when speaking about T'ien. They are all inconsistent, and this should alert us to the fact that their primary concern is not to fashion a theory of T'ien that can stand as an intellectual artifact. They borrow or invent in each instance any theory which serves their immediate purposes—purposes which do not relate to T'ien at all, but rather to the concrete aims of each philosopher as spokesman for the Ruist point of view. What all uses of the word "*t'ien*" share is the rhetorical force which that word possessed as a primary term of Chou religious and political practice. It is of greater importance for us to understand how and why philosophers manipulated this rhetorical force than to reconstruct the image that appeared in their minds' eyes when they did so.

Having said this by way of a general introduction to analyses of our three early Ruist texts, we will now turn to the first of these, the *Analects* of Confucius, and explore the role of T'ien in it. We will begin with a brief discussion of the nature of the text, and some general problems of interpretation that it presents.

1. The Nature of the Text

The content of the *Analects*,[1] for the most part, purports to be a record of statements made by Confucius and his immediate disciples. But the nature and history of the text itself has been a matter of persistent doubt and speculation,[2] particularly since the mid-Ch'ing scholar Ts'ui Shu demonstrated the significance of stylistic inconsistencies in the text.[3] Modern scholarly opinion tends to agree that the various component parts of the *Analects* probably vary widely in date of authorship and also in the dates at which they were incorporated into the text as we have it today. A number of systematic attempts to trace the provenance of individual books and entries have been made, but none can yet be judged completely successful.[4]

The complex problem of the origins of the *Analects* has raised questions as to whether the statements recorded in the text truly reflect the words of Confucius and his disciples. Once we admit that a significant portion of the text is not what it purports to be, proving that any particular part of the text must be accepted as an authentic record of Confucius' own words becomes difficult.[5]

Thus, we are offered two radically different ways of looking at the text. We can view it as the first text of Ruism, which records, more or less, the ideas of Confucius and other Ruists of the early fifth century B.C. Or, we can see it as a collection of enduring thematic material, the product of many strata of composition and editing, representing a rough consensus text, whose contents were more or less endorsed by all factions of the Ruist community over a period of time.[6] This latter view—which sees the *Analects* as containing many stages of an evolving Warring States portrait of "original" Ruism—suggests that the priority of the *Analects* is not so much temporal as doctrinal. The text is rather like a Ruist bible. While Ruists always have been able to take issue with other early works, the *Analects* has traditionally been treated as Ruism's essential teaching, the property of no particular faction.

These two levels present both a problem and an opportunity for the interpreter. The meaning of a passage can vary according to whether it is interpreted in its narrative context, as the word of Confucius, or in the context of its inclusion in an edited text of canonical teachings. Traditionally, only the former context has been viewed as "authentic," but in light of the problematic relation of the text to Confucius, in many cases an original meaning might be provided by the latter context alone. Previous analyses of the role of T'ien in the *Analects* have suffered, in my view, because they have not distinguished these two levels. As we will see in this chapter, significantly different portraits of the role of T'ien emerge depending upon which of these two levels we choose.

In general, our approach to the contextual interpretation of the *Analects* will be this: because the text probably underwent an extensive and disparate developmental history, it is valid to interpret the text as an expression of the enduring interests of early Ruism, rather than as an essentially random gathering of independent micro-texts, each properly understood only in terms of its instrumental value to an original author and/or editor. We will view the *Analects* as the cumulative attempt of Warring States Ruists to portray their philosophical origins, pursued in part by preserving the words of the original Ru, as they knew them, and in part by ascribing to or inventing for these men statements which—from the Warring States perspective—they surely *would* have said in one way or another.

From this point of view, we will discuss the *Analects* as a philosophically self-conscious text, and we will interpret its instrumental meaning in terms of the largely synchronic model of Ruism presented in chapter II. We will employ this perspective to elucidate an implicit theory of T'ien which must be attributed not to Confucius, but to the collective editors of the text.

Having done this, we will alter our perspective and speculate as to how the *Analects* may provide us access to Confucius' own views concerning T'ien, and the role T'ien may have played in "original" Ruism. The conclusions we reach will indicate that Confucius' view of T'ien and the views of the editors of the text were probably not the same.

We turn first to analyze the implicit theory of T'ien in the *Analects* (the editors' theory). Our discussion will reveal that, predictably, the *Analects'* portrait of T'ien has two discrete aspects: a function of the bifurcated doctrine of early Ruism. On the one hand, T'ien forms a ground for the possibility of totalistic virtue and for the ritual forms which provide a path to it. On the other, T'ien prescribes the puristic idealism of Ruist political policies, determines the failure of those policies, and ensures that this failure must be understood as of ultimate ethical value.

2. The Implicit Theory of T'ien in the Analects

Considering the fact that the entries in the *Analects* which refer to T'ien are scattered throughout the text in books that might have originated among disparate factions and at different times, the portrait of T'ien that emerges is remarkably consistent.[7] The fact that this is so suggests that this view of

T'ien was deeply ingrained in early Ruism. Despite important differences in emphasis and in the imagery associated with T'ien, we will find that the major elements of the portrait remain visible in the more detailed and philosophically self-conscious discussions of T'ien in the *Mencius* and the *Hsun Tzu.*

One more preliminary: some remarks about the analytic approach we will take here. In organizing our discussion, we will lay great stress on the distinction between prescriptive and descriptive aspects of T'ien. This distinction is a function of the double duty that T'ien performs as an explanatory fiction. Prescriptively, T'ien provides reasons to act in certain ways in the future: we should do *X* because T'ien wants us to and/or will reward us. T'ien serves here as a normative value standard. Descriptively, T'ien provides a reason why events in the past occurred as they did: T'ien wished it so.

Often these two roles cannot be rationally reconciled. We saw earlier how this contradiction lay at the heart of the mid-Chou crisis of value. When good is not rewarded or evil goes unpunished, a gap occurs between T'ien as a value standard and T'ien as an efficient cause of amoral events. In the case of Ruism, a prescriptive/descriptive gap existed from the start, as a result of the political failure of Confucius' moral mission.

Where such a gap develops, the three basic alternatives for bridging it are: (1) it can be ignored,[8] (2) the ethical or the causal primacy of T'ien can be compromised (which may lead to ethical relativism or determinism),[9] or (3) a new explanatory fiction can be introduced: for example, a teleological plan.

Explicitly, the *Analects* may appear to select the first option: it does not address the issue directly. But we will find that implicitly it chooses the third option. It introduces the notion of a teleological course of events, and this restores to the descriptive events of the empirical world their "proper" value, which in turn preserves the ethical value of the T'ien-supported prescripts of Ruist practice.

2.1. The Prescriptive Role of T'ien

As a prescriptive force, T'ien plays two major roles in the *Analects*.[10] First, it provides a ground for the Ruist notion of transcendent wisdom, and legitimizes the Ruist claim that traditional ritual forms provide the path to attaining it. Second, it legitimizes Ruist political idealism and the rejection of practical politics. We can organize relevant passages into sets corresponding to these two functions, and we begin with those that employ T'ien to promote the Ruist commitment to seek Sagehood through self-stylization.

The first of these is a cryptic fragment. It reads in full:

The Master said, 'T'ien has engendered virtue (*te*) in me. What harm can Huan T'ui do me?" (*A*:7.23).

The passage makes little sense unless one accepts contextual material found in the *Shih-chi*, where we learn that Huan T'ui was Minister of War in the state of Sung and Confucius' enemy, at one time threatening his life (*SC*:47.1921).

The T'ien pictured here is ethically prescriptive. It is the genetic basis of virtue, protects the virtuous, and punishes, or at least renders nugatory, actions directed against them.[11] Perhaps we may also conclude that Confucius himself is implicitly pictured as the agent of T'ien, suggesting that the action of T'ien goes beyond responsive reward and punishment and reflects ongoing purpose. But the passage is altogether vague. Any practical lesson that it may have been meant to convey is vitiated by the notorious vagueness of the word "virtue" (*te*).[12] Nor are any interpretive clues provided by adjacent entries in the text, which seem to have nothing to do with our passage (a fact that has led at least one writer to regard this cryptic fragment as a late insertion in the text [Takeuchi 1939:135]).

Perhaps the *Shih-chi* account provides a clue to the concrete meaning of "virtue" here. The text reads:

Confucius departed Ts'ao and went to Sung, where, with his disciples, he practiced *li* beneath a great tree. The Sung Minister of War, Huan T'ui, wanted to kill Confucius, and cut down the tree. Confucius departed. The disciples said to him, "Let us go quickly." Confucius replied, "T'ien has engendered virtue in me. What harm can Huan T'ui do me?"

This stylized account, with the great ritual tree standing as a sort of icon, seems to suggest that Confucius' virtue was tied to his ritual action, the object of Huan T'ui's attack. Could this notion lie behind the *Analects* passage?

There is not much basis for this conjecture as it stands; *Shih-chi* material cannot generally be relied upon in this way.[13] But we are fortunate that the same tale appears to have survived in a different form, which appears in another book of the *Analects*. In this second version, the function that "virtue" performed in *A*:7.23 is performed by mastery of aesthetic ritual forms.

When the Master was in danger in the state of K'uang, he said, "King Wen is dead, but his style (*wen*) lives on here [in me], does it not? If T'ien wished this style to perish, [I] would not have been able to partake of it. Since T'ien has not destroyed this style, what harm can the people of K'uang do to me?" (*A*:9.5).[14]

Together, *A*:7.23 and *A*:9.5 convey two important points about T'ien. T'ien generates a virtue embodied in individuals, and it legitimizes the ancient behavioral patterns that were so central to Ruist interests.[15] The fact that the two passages seem to be versions of a single legend suggests that these two points are alternate formulations of the same message: that the way T'ien "engendered virtue" in Confucius was by allowing him to "partake of the style" of the ancient Sages.

A:9.5 is followed in the text by another passage that refers to T'ien.

The Grand Steward asked Tzu-kung, "Your Master is surely a Sage, is he not? He is skilled in so many things!" Tzu-kung replied, "It is actually T'ien which allows him to be a great Sage; he is skilled in many things besides." The Master heard of it. "What does the Grand Steward know of me?" he said. "When I was young I was of humble station, and so I became skilled in many rude things. Is the *chün-tzu* skilled in many things? No, not many" (*A*:9.6).[16]

The Grand Steward of this passage mistakes—perhaps maliciously—the meaning of "Sage" (*sheng*). He takes the disciples' claim that Confucius is a Sage to refer to his many skills, and from Confucius' remark, we can understand that the skills of which this passage speaks were "rude" things, talents of no ethical significance. We can envision a contemporary usage of the word "sage" to denote the sort of person handy enough to solve almost any practical problem—a jack-of-all-trades.[17] Tzu-kung replies that the Sagehood he means is of a different sort. It is a Sagehood guided by T'ien and quite apart from rude talents.[18]

We can learn more about this Sagehood from Confucius' remark. In the text, *A*:9.6 is followed by a brief entry that gives every indication of being a late insertion.[19] If we pass over it and turn to *A*:9.8 we find that it begins with phrasing almost precisely parallel to that which concludes *A*:9.6: "Do I possess knowledge? No, I have none at all." We have already seen how the import of this statement is not to deny that Confucius was wise, but to tell us that wisdom lies in totalistic understanding, a skill, rather than in accumulated knowledge of facts. The message of *A*:9.6 is essentially the same: virtue lies in attaining the totalistic perspective of the Sage, a master skill, not in the proliferation of individual skills. It is the quality, not the quantity of his skills that defines the *chün-tzu*.[20]

Reviewing the passages we have considered thus far, we can say this much about T'ien: we are to understand that the "virtue" of Confucius was "engendered" by T'ien (*A*:7.23), and that his Sagehood was "allowed" (*tsung*) by T'ien (*A*:9.6).[21] The nature of his virtue we interpret to be his mastery of the "style" (*wen*) of traditional ritual forms (*A*:9.5). The basis of his Sagehood is his mastery of the "single thread," the totalism that links and governs skills and knowledge (*A*:9.6 in light of 9.8). These three passages already show us the role of T'ien as a basis for the Ruist totalism and its ritual path.

The linkage between T'ien and *wen* that we found in *A*:9.5 appears in other passages as well. In Book 5, for example, we hear the disciple Tzu-kung make this apparently retrospective remark:

We are able to learn of the Master's paradigm of style (*wen-chang*), but his words concerning man's nature and the Way of T'ien we are not able to hear (*A*:5.13).

What is of immediate interest to us here is the juxtaposition of the "paradigm of style" against the more abstract notions of human nature and T'ien.[22] On the surface, the passage appears to tell us that Confucius' teachings about T'ien and about the nature that T'ien has engendered in man are either secret or lost, and many interpreters have read the passage in this way.[23] But this interpretation renders the first phrase superficial. If we look for the meaning of the passage in the balanced contrast between the two phrases, it appears to say something such as: "Don't ask about theories of T'ien or man's nature; you will find all there is to know about these matters in the Master's program of self-stylization." In other words, T'ien's existence "out there" does not matter; it gives us no clues as to what we are meant to be. For us, T'ien is manifest in and prescribes those behavioral forms that Confucius laid down as the basis for Ruist practice.

If this interpretation is correct, then *A*:5.13 reassigns the considerable rhetorical force of the word *"t'ien"* from images of the heavens or of spirits to the everyday practice of ritual forms. This certainly brings T'ien into the Ruist classroom.

A similar reformulation of T'ien appears to guide another *Analects* passage, which can be seen as forging a link between T'ien as the astronomical sky and T'ien as manifest in traditional ritual forms.

The Master said, "How grand was the rule of the Emperor Yao! Towering is the grandeur of T'ien; only Yao could emulate it. . . . Towering were his achievements; shining, they formed a paradigm of style" (*A*:8.19).

Yao—in Ruist lore the first Sage King—is said in other sources, such as the *Yao tien* section of the *Documents*, to have established a calendar and social order on the basis of astronomical observations.[24] This passage should probably be understood in light of such myths. And we should also note the opening passage of the final book of the *Analects*, which appears to quote the text of some lost book of the *Documents* or a similar scriptural work. The rhymed phrases supposedly record Yao's instructions to his successor, the Emperor Shun.

Oh Shun! The calendar of T'ien rests upon your person. Hold to its central [course]. Should the four quarters fall destitute, the wages of T'ien will forever end (*A*:20.1).[25]

As in *A*:8.19 this passage suggests that the institution of the kingship was founded upon the ability to translate regularities of the astronomical sky into prescripts of social order, leading to enduring peace and prosperity.

A:5.13 and 8.19 both speak of the "paradigm of style," and they are the only passages in the text which do. The "paradigm of style" means, more literally, "pattern-insignia." It is generally used in early texts to denote colorful patterns on ritual costumes.[26] In these two passages, the achievements of Confucius and the Emperor Yao are pictured as extensions of a ritual aesthetic, and this aesthetic is, in turn, linked to T'ien. In *A*:5.13, according to our interpretation, it is pictured as a manifestation of T'ien. In *A*:8.19, it is modeled upon the more concrete manifestations of T'ien as Nature or as the astronomical sky. In both instances, the notion of T'ien becomes intimately tied to the phenomenon of conventionally styled ritual patterns that are keys to Sage learning and to Sage rule.[27]

There remains only one passage in which T'ien plays a prescriptive role linking it to the Ruist totalism. It reads:

The Master said, "I wish never to speak." "If you never spoke," replied Tzu-kung, "then what would we disciples have to pass on?" The Master said, "Does T'ien speak? Yet the seasons turn and the creatures of the world are born. Does T'ien speak?" (*A*:17.17).[28]

It is enlightening to view this passage in the context of the entries that surround it. *A*:17.15 and 17.16 both deplore those who use glib speech to attain their ends. In contrast, *A*:17.18 describes how Confucius conveys a message to an unwelcome visitor without speaking to him. Throughout Ruist texts, there is a tendency to view words with suspicion because they are subject to sophistic distortion.[29] The ideal of the Sage often includes a notion that the perfect actor does not need words to transform the minds of the people.[30] In *A*:17.17, T'ien is pictured as the model for the idealized action of the Sage (approximated by Confucius in the subsequent passage). There is a parallel between the action of the Sage, which is a function of his totalistic understanding, and the action of T'ien. T'ien itself—whether pictured as Nature or god—seems almost to be a cosmic version of the Ruist Sage.

To sum up: passages such as *A*:7.23 and 9.6 portray T'ien as the source of the Sagely totalism. *A*:5.13, 8.19, and 9.5 portray it as the source of or as manifest in the ritual style that forms the path to the totalism. And *A*:17.17 seems to make T'ien the direct model for the totalism itself. T'ien prescribes in various ways, but regardless of how it does so, it is clear that what it prescribes is the ideal of Sagehood and the Ruist path to it. The linkage of T'ien to the everyday practice of Ruism is unmistakable: the *Analects* makes T'ien both the headmaster and the syllabus of the Ruist school.

❖ ❖ ❖ ❖

The prescriptive role of T'ien in legitimizing Ruist political idealism can be detailed more briefly, as it is explicit in only two passages. Both of these portray Confucius declining to take advantage of concrete political opportunities in the state of Wei, because such action would involve unsavory political alliances that would compromise Confucius' puristic idealism.

The first of these refers to an audience which, according to the *Shih-chi* (47.1920), Confucius was obliged to have with a notorious consort of the Wei ruler.[31]

The Master was presented to Nan Tzu. Tzu-lu was displeased. The Master swore an oath: "That which I deny, may T'ien detest it! May T'ien detest it.!" (*A*:6.28).

We may rephrase Confucius' oath for the sake of clarity: "May T'ien punish me if, contrary to my denial, I acted to compromise our ideals." The passage aligns the prescriptive action of T'ien with the ethics of Tzu-lu and Confucius, both of whom disapprove of any notion that political means can be any less exalted than political ends.[32]

The same theme is repeated in another passage, in which Confucius diplomatically declines a pragmatic political alliance offered by a powerful minister in Wei.[33] The offer is made through a thinly veiled metaphor in which the minister likens his ruler to the guardian spirit whose altar sits in the southwest corner of households, and himself to the god of the kitchen.

Wang-sun Chia asked,"What is the sense of that saying, 'Better to pay court to the kitchen than to the dark corner?' " "Not so!" replied the Master. "If one offends against T'ien, there will be no place at which to pray" (*A*:3.13).

Wang-sun Chia claims to be the power behind the throne. Why be a stickler for political legitimacy, he suggests; throw in your lot with me and you will achieve your political goals. Confucius skillfully employs Wang-sun Chia's own metaphor in picturing T'ien as an ethical arbiter, overseeing the course of political action. T'ien prescribes a moral course and punishes immoral action. What success could grow out of T'ien's punishment? Ethical purism is the only possible road to success. Hence, *A*:3.13, like *A*:6.28, employs

T'ien in order to legitimize the Ruist policy of devotion to political purism and the absolute rejection of the methods of political intrigue.[34]

This completes our discussion of the function of T'ien as a prescriptive force in the *Analects*. Our analysis has indicated that T'ien's prescriptive role is to legitimize the distinct moieties of Ruist practical doctrine: the commitment to pursue the Sagely totalism through ritual self-cultivation and the withdrawal from practical politics in favor of idealistic rhetoric.

We turn now to passages that deal more directly with T'ien as a descriptive force—as the entity or force that is accountable for the moral unintelligibility of the empirical social world.

2.2. The Descriptive Role of T'ien

The last section shows us that the editors of the *Analects* did little more than ascribe their own values to T'ien in dealing with its prescriptive aspect. The descriptive aspect presented more difficulties. From a descriptive angle, it was inadequate merely to assert that T'ien conformed to Ruist values. It was necessary to show that empirical events confirmed that this was so.

Given the amoral nature of empirical experience, and the particularly evident injustices of the late Chou period, the notion that events were shaped by T'ien in accord with Ruist values was clearly a difficult one to support. The *Analects*' solution to the problem—a solution which, like the statement of the problem, is only implicit in the text—was to rely on a further explanatory fiction, the notion of a teleological plan that T'ien follows. This notion shifts the evaluative standard against which events are judged from the present into the distant future, and, in essence, subordinates the descriptive values of experience to prescriptive dogma.[35] Regardless of the evidence, all must be for the good.

The creators of the *Analects* use the teleological notion to explain why T'ien did not bring it about that Confucius—T'ien's own ethical agent (*A*:7.23, 9.5)—should triumph over chaos and bring peace and order to the world, rather than being reduced to powerlessness and occasional destitution.

For the *Analects*, Confucius' failure was T'ien's means of arranging that his teachings be spread. It contributed more to T'ien's teleological plan for a just future than his political success would have. This position is presented in the text through the words of a border officer in the state of Wei, whom Confucius is said to have encountered either upon entering Wei after losing office in Lu, or upon leaving Wei without having achieved his political goals.

The border officer at Yi requested an interview, saying, "I have never been denied an interview by any gentleman coming to this place." The followers presented him. When he emerged, he said, "What need have you disciples to be anxious over your Master's loss? The world has long been without the Way. T'ien means to employ your Master as a wooden bell" (*A*:3.24).

The "wooden bell" refers to an instrument used by heralds and criers to alert the populace to an important message.[36] So obscure has the Way become that T'ien has judged it more appropriate to employ Confucius as a teacher than as a political leader. It is precisely through political failure that Confucius is able to serve as T'ien's agent.[37]

This type of reasoning does explain events in a way consistent with Ruist values, but in another way it creates a huge gap between prescriptive and descriptive value. If the value of an individual's actions derives from the contribution that those actions make to a teleological plan, of what relevance is it whether they accord with ethical prescripts? A:3.24 contains the seeds of a metaphysical utilitarianism.[38]

It is important to the *Analects*, and to Ruism in general, that the teleological determinism that it uses to explain Ruist political failures not devalue action according to the ethical prescripts that are legitimized by T'ien in its prescriptive role. Several passages in the *Analects* assert the value of following prescript without regard for empirical consequences.[39] Two of these relate the issue directly to T'ien, and we will consider them in some detail here. They are of particular interest to us because in different ways, both suggest that Sagehood–the end of the prescriptive path–is itself the bridge over the prescriptive/descriptive gap. This adds a new dimension to the value of ethical action: it creates an understanding of itself. And by suggesting that the answer to the prescriptive/descriptive problem lies in Sagehood, the *Analects*–however embryonically–adopts a position true to the enduring nature of Ruism: the intellectual solution is arrived at not analytically through logical reasoning, but synthetically, precisely by following the prescripts of Ruism (and of T'ien) to reach an understanding of truth.

The more famous of these two passages recounts Confucius' thumbnail autobiography.

At fifteen, I set my heart on study. At thirty, I was able to stand. At forty, I was free from confusion. At fifty, I learned the decree of T'ien. At sixty, I heard it with an obedient ear. At seventy, I follow the desires of my heart and do not overstep the proper bounds (A:2.4).[40]

Many things about this passage suggest that it is not a record of Confucius' own speech, but a late, retrospective look at the career of Confucius from the vantage point of a developed Ruist ideology.[41] Whether or not this is so, the passage eloquently articulates the relationship between the two doctrinal moieties of Ruism: self-cultivation and political idealism, and, in doing so, it illustrates the *Analects*' approach to reconciling the prescriptive and descriptive aspects of T'ien. I hope to make this clear in the analysis that follows.

Passing over the first phrase for the moment, let us begin by trying to make sense of the vague statement, "I was able to stand," or more literally, "I stood." The verb "to stand" (*li^c*) can carry a sense of assuming an occupational post, and it is used in that sense in the *Analects* (4.14, 6.30). However, the text also repeatedly links the word to the practice of *li*: ritual; for example, "Stand with *li*" (*A*:8.8); "If you do not study *li*, you will have no means whereby to stand" (*A*:16.13; cf. 20.3).[42]

These ritual overtones in the second phrase create a resonance with the first, which speaks of "study." As we saw in chapter II, the Ruist meaning of "study" was deeply entailed with ritual practice. The two phrases are linked. The first describes the initial commitment to ritual study, the second pictures a sort of graduation to an initial application of ritual skills in assuming occupational and other social responsibilities.

Giving concrete meaning to the third phrase is difficult; let us pass it by for the moment.

The fourth phrase, Confucius at fifty, refers to the "decree of T'ien" (*t'ien-ming*), a term whose wealth of textual associations may do more to obscure than clarify its meaning here (it is the term used to denote the Chou Dynasty's "Mandate of Heaven"). Commentators have been divided on the significance of this reference to the decree,[43] but the text itself provides two clues, and I think they are sufficient to solve the mystery. The first clue appears in the subsequent phrase, "At sixty, I heard [the decree] with an obedient ear." If I have translated this correctly, it indicates that the decree was something that Confucius initially found unpleasant to hear.[44] The second clue involves the age at which Confucius heard the decree. According to our historical sources, Confucius was slightly older than fifty at the time of the great crisis in his life, his loss of position in Lu and his subsequent self-exile (Dubs 1946). We may reasonably assume that this piece of chronology was known to the author of the passage, and that the phrase refers to that event. If so, then it is clear that T'ien is used here in its descriptive sense, its decree being the failure of Confucius' political mission.

With this in mind, let us return to the third phrase, which speaks of being free from confusion at forty. We can see now that the preceding two phrases chart Confucius' progress in ritual self-cultivation, while the subsequent phrases record the failure of his political mission. The claim of freedom from confusion stands as a pivot between the phases of preparatory education and political effort. It resembles an understated claim of Sage wisdom; elsewhere the text tells us that it is the wise man who is free from confusion (*A*:9.29, 14.28). I think that what the phrase must represent is Confucius' attainment of the totalistic perspective, and his embarkation, as a Sage, upon his political mission.[45]

Looking at the passage as a whole, we can begin to see that it is really composed of two halves. The first half in itself takes us the full length of the prescriptive path of Ruist Sagehood, from the first stages of study to the resolution of all uncertainty. In contrast, the second half opens by introducing the descriptive obstacles that confront the Sage as he steps into the world of political action. We can anticipate that the logic of the passage is to set the descriptive action of T'ien against the prescriptive path of Ruism in order to instruct us how to reconcile the two.

Confucius heard the decree at fifty, but we learn that it took him ten years to accept it. By acknowledging this, the text seems to emphasize how deeply unintelligible Confucius' failure appears from the Ruist standpoint. We must understand the force of the concluding phrase in this light.

This last phrase is generally taken to mean that Confucius had completely internalized prescriptive principle by age seventy.[46] I think that this interpretation falls short of the mark by half. We have seen that at fifty and sixty, the desires of Confucius' heart were not in tension with prescriptive rules but with the descriptive limits to which he was able to extend those rules. Now at seventy, his heart's desire has changed; he no longer wishes to overstep the limits drawn by the descriptive action of T'ien. The culmination of his Sagehood does not lie in internalizing the rules—we might expect that of Confucius at forty. It lies in his reconciliation of ethical imperatives with descriptive limitations, in adopting the limits that T'ien and the world impose as ethical principles of his life. This is Confucius in retirement, tirelessly and joyously playing the part of the wooden bell.

The passage depicts political failure as a stage in the full maturation of the Sage. T'ien's descriptive role does not undermine the value of ethical prescript; it educates the heart to embrace the empirical consequences of adopting those prescripts.

This theme, with its message that the Sage understands the necessity of embracing T'ien's teleological plan rather than one's own ethical ambitions, is repeated in a very different way in Book 14.

The Master said, "No one knows me." "How is it that this is so?" asked Tzu-kung. "I do not complain against T'ien," replied the Master, "nor do I blame men. I study what is lowly and so get through to what is exalted. Is it not T'ien who knows me?" (*A*:14.35).

Like the last passage, this one is carefully crafted, and rewards detailed interpretation.

The phrase "No one knows me" has a particular meaning in the *Analects*. It is the complaint of the thwarted office seeker, and the phrase Confucius is most eager to banish from his disciples' speech (e.g., *A*:14.30). The word "know" (*chih*) carries a double meaning, both as "to recognize" and as "to employ." Hence, the complaint can be paraphrased, "No one employs my talents."

The term "get through" (*ta*) carries a similar ambiguity. It is most frequently used in the senses of "understand" or "make oneself understood," but it can also mean to gain access to a ruler or to have one's talents generally recognized (*A*:6.30, 12.20).[47]

The logic of the passage runs like this. Confucius, the noble political failure, voices the complaint we associate with immature disciples. This is a paradox, and Tzu-kung helpfully asks for an explanation. Confucius responds with the true meaning of political failure: "I have no complaint against T'ien, nor do I feel men are to blame. I have applied myself to the study of basic things rather than high-flown speculation, and in doing so, I have come to understand and to be recognized by what is exalted. Is it not T'ien who employs my talents?" No ruler employs Confucius because he is already employed by T'ien. The failure to achieve political success is reinterpreted as an appointment to T'ien's court, a reward for following the proper path of study: perfecting the basic paradigm of style rather than chasing after "higher" things, such as theories of T'ien and man's nature.

As in *A*:7.23 and 9.5, Confucius is pictured as T'ien's agent. But *A*:14.35 goes further in reconciling Confucius' failure with his role as agent.[48] In light of this, it is probably not coincidental that *A*:14.35 is followed by a passage that closely parallels *A*:7.23 and 9.5, but which takes as its main object of attention not T'ien but *ming*, "fate," or the "decree" that expresses descriptive reality.

Kung-po Liao denounced Tzu-lu to Chi-sun. Tzu-fu Ching-po reported it. "My master has long harbored doubts about Kung-po Liao," he said. "It is still within my power to have his carcass exposed in market and court." The Master replied, "Should the Way prevail, it will be due to *ming*; should it be cast aside, it will be due to *ming*. What can Kung-po Liao do about *ming*?" (*A*:14.36).[49]

Here Confucius is pictured using *ming* in much the way he used T'ien in *A*:3.13, as a defensive political fatalism that protects him from compromising his ideals and engaging in political intrigue.[50] Its particular interest for us here lies in its proximity to *A*:14.35. If the two are taken together, the first can be seen as an embrace of T'ien's teleological plan in which the values of political success are rejected, while the second can be seen as an illustration of this attitude, as it harmonizes a "fatalistic" acceptance of Confucius' action with the prescriptive idealism of Ruist politics.

There is a sense here that the decree that determines the failure of the Ruist political mission almost frees the Ruist, extricating him from the toils of political responsibilities and allowing him to retire, at least partially, into the pure ritual practice of the Ruist community. The three passages that follow *A*:14.36 all deal with the balance one must strike between fulfilling the prescripts of political idealism through futile political preaching, and through complete political withdrawal.[51]

In sum, T'ien's descriptive role, once accepted and understood by the Ru, ceases to be an obstacle and becomes a new ethical opportunity. The community of politically impotent ritual actors forms an elite society of T'ien's agents: men who bow to the descriptive action of T'ien while pursuing the prescriptive ritual path. The *Analects* quotes Tzu-hsia's words to a fellow disciple whose political fortunes have been destroyed by the actions of his brother, Confucius' enemy Huan T'ui:

I have heard it said: Life and death are determined by decree; wealth and rank are up to T'ien. The *chün-tzu* is unstintingly diligent: he treats people reverently and with *li*, and all within the four quarters are his brothers (*A*:12.5).[52]

Man cannot control the descriptive action of T'ien; he cannot determine his fate in the world. But he can fulfill the ethical prescripts of ritual action, and so enter into the alternative community of ritual actors. The descriptive role of T'ien in no way alters the ethical value of this prescriptive course.

The model presented here sets forth, I think, the important themes of the *Analects*' treatment of T'ien. Of the seventeen entries that refer to T'ien, we have discussed thirteen in the text and one other in the notes. Of the remaining three, one employs T'ien in a nonphilosophical sense as "sky" (*A*:19.25), and we need not consider it here. Another is rather cryptic, and I feel that a precise interpretation of it is not possible. It reads:

Confucius said, "The *chün-tzu* holds three things in awe. He holds the decree of T'ien in awe, he holds great men in awe, and he holds the words of the Sage in awe. The small man does not know the decree of T'ien and so does not hold it in awe, he is disrespectful towards great men, and he disgraces the words of the Sage" (*A*:16.8).

Some commentators have read great significance into this reference to the decree of T'ien,[53] but my feeling is that the passage is so formulaic as to allow almost any interpretation, and I prefer not to treat it here.[54]

The last remaining passage describes Confucius' cry of despair upon the death of Yen Yuan: "Ah! T'ien destroys me! T'ien destroys me!" (*A*:11.9). If it were the intention of the editors of the *Analects* that we should believe the truth of Confucius' charge, then this passage would clash with our overall model. In this one case, however, I feel we must suspend our principles of interpretation and conclude that the passage does not contribute to the text's implicit theory of T'ien. The sole purpose of the passage, I believe, is to celebrate the virtue of Yen Yuan by illustrating the depth of Confucius' grief, which is also the theme of the subsequent entry.[55]

❖ ❖ ❖ ❖

The analysis we have presented here is intended to show that the editors of the *Analects*–in concrete terms, the generations of Ruists who recorded, composed, selected, and arranged the text as we have it today–can be shown to have portrayed T'ien in a consistent way, which expressed the enduring interests and goals of early Ruism.

In its prescriptive role, T'ien was essentially identical with the "Way" or "*tao*" of Ruism.[56] It was the ground that supported the totalistic notion of Sagehood. It was the model for and manifest in the ritual path to Sagehood. And it legitimized the political idealism that for Ruists characterized the wisdom of the Sage. The prescriptive role of T'ien brought T'ien into the Ruist classroom. The devoted disciple could feel that as he watched the perfect ritual action of his fellow Ru, he looked upon T'ien. When he himself participated in that ritual style, he could feel that T'ien was acting through his agency. In this sense, the word "*t'ien*" merely hypostatized Ruist prescript in the terminology of early Chou religion.

In its descriptive role, T'ien accounted for the political failure of Confucius and of all early Ru, and it gave that failure meaning. Because T'ien was spoken of in teleological terms, it could guarantee the rightness of Ruist idealism in the face of its empirical political wrongness. With T'ien on his side, the disciple could be assured that the rejection of Ruist doctrine by an amoral society actually confirmed the rightness of the Ruist stance. In this sense, the word "*t'ien*" denoted the political repulsion that actually freed the Ruists to follow their ritual path in ethical and partial social isolation.

T'ien was revealed to the disciple every day, when he looked upon the beauty of ritual practice among the Ru and when he considered his ethical distance from the self-destructive immorality of society at large. T'ien was the growing ritual mastery within him; it was the perfect world of the future whose foundations he was helping to lay.

3. Confucius' Doctrinal Silence

We have been exploring the function of T'ien in the *Analects* by treating each relevant passage of the text as a carefully chosen expression of the views of its many creators. The view of T'ien that we have pictured in this way can be said to represent a mainstream Ruist theory of T'ien, a theory that would have possessed consistent instrumental value throughout the development of early Ruism.

This is the *Analects*' view of T'ien, but that does not mean that it was Confucius'. To explore the *Analects* for Confucius' own view requires a different interpretive method. Even were we to grant that Confucius uttered every statement ascribed to him in the *Analects*—and we are very far from doing that—the meaning of his statements could only be brought out by elucidating the situational contexts in which they were uttered, and this level of meaning is quite different from the meaning the same statements may bear as elements of an edited text.

Many attempts have been made to analyze Confucius' view of T'ien. Fung Yu-lan has made two, and has arrived at different conclusions. In his earlier work, he concludes that Confucius maintained a conservative position on T'ien, and the T'ien he spoke of was an anthropomorphic ruling god of Chou tradition (1931:82-83). Later, in the communist period, Fung came to view Confucius as a man whose class standpoint was in transition, and who had consequently moved from a completely spiritualistic concept of T'ien to one which was predominantly fatalistic (1962:93-97, 102). Another writer who sees Confucius' view of T'ien as a transition between early and late Chou concepts is Li Tu, a noncommunist writer who stresses that although Confucius' T'ien seems modeled on Chou religious notions, it had evolved from an aristocratic to a democratic god, whose decrees any man, not just kings, could know (1961:39-41).

Relatively doctrinaire communist writers tend to see a reactionary quality in Confucius' view of T'ien. They see Confucius as using the Chou establishment portrait of T'ien to legitimize archaic social divisions (Hou 1957: chapter 6; Yang 1973:115-17). T'ien represents an ideal notion of history diametrically opposed to the true revolutionary direction that history takes (Hou 1957:152).

Those who are less committed to preconceived models of Chinese history differ widely on what Confucius' view was. Ikeda Suetoshi, for instance, argues that Confucius' view of T'ien not only borrowed Chou religious concepts, but was deeply religious and spiritualistic (1965:4-5). H.G. Creel, on the other hand, interprets the same material as indicating that Confucius thought of T'ien as "an impersonal ethical force, a cosmic counterpart of the ethical sense in man" (1949:117).

I feel that such interpretations suffer because they do not make a distinction between Confucius' view of T'ien and the *Analects*'. As a result, all fail to consider whether the statements attributed to Confucius in the *Analects* carry philosophical significance when viewed as Confucius' own words. It does not follow that because Confucius may have uttered a statement about T'ien and a disciple recalled it, resulting in its eventual inclusion in a canonical text, that Confucius uttered the statement with canonical intent.

In fact, when we explore the text for Confucius' original teachings about T'ien, we find considerable evidence that it might have been very different from that of the *Analects*. It is entirely possible that Confucius avoided including any significant statement about T'ien in his teaching, perhaps regarding metaphysical speculation to be inimical to the spirit of his philosophy.

The most striking piece of evidence in this regard is the simple fact that the text of the *Analects* contains so few references to T'ien. Only seventeen of the 500-odd entries mention T'ien at all.[57] The reticence of the text concerning T'ien may reflect an enduring tradition about Confucius' teaching. As we noted earlier, the text tells us that "[Confucius'] words concerning man's nature and the Way of T'ien we are not able to hear" (*A*:5.13).[58] A strong tradition that Confucius avoided metaphysical speculation may have constrained the editors of the *Analects*, and militated against including in the text late teachings about T'ien that may have been popularly attributed to Confucius. We will see that the *Analects* does suggest the plausibility of such an idea.

The *Analects* includes eleven passages that purport to record remarks Confucius himself made concerning T'ien. Some of these, if taken as accurate records of his speech, would seem to show that Confucius did express philosophical views about T'ien (e.g., *A*:2.4, 8.19). But in the majority of cases, when taken in the context of their narrative content, the passages appear to reflect no more than Confucius' skillful ability to employ traditional religious rhetoric in order to say something about matters other than T'ien. We would not be warranted in drawing conclusions about Confucius' view of T'ien from such statements. What makes them subjects for deep analysis is not their content, but their inclusion in a canonical text.

Several passages in the *Analects* support the notion that whatever his inmost thoughts may have been, Confucius conscientiously avoided entangling his teachings in religious and metaphysical speculations. The antispiritualist message of these passages is well known. They tell us that Confucius did not generally speak of spirits (*A*:7.21, 11.12),[59] and when they recount what he did say, his statements sound meticulously agnostic, as when he tells his disciples to "show respect for ghosts and spirits, but keep them at a distance" (*A*:6.22). Despite the great value that he placed on the rite of sacrifice (e.g., *A*:2.5, 3.12),[60] Confucius appears sceptical about the ability of prayer to influence events (*A*:7.35).

All this is in tune with the early Ruist approach to ritual, which stressed the social and psychological utility of *li* while adopting a stance of silence or scepticism concerning the magical efficacy of religious action. Generally, the central philosophy of Ruism, as outlined in the last two chapters, forms a complete system without any need to introduce spiritualist or metaphysical speculation, apart from unexamined teleological assumptions. It cannot be surprising, then, to find evidence that the earliest Ruist teachings avoided entanglements with issues of that nature.

If we turn to the remarks concerning T'ien that the *Analects* ascribes to Confucius, we find that the tenor of a majority of these does not conflict with such an attitude. For example, we are told that once when Confucius was seriously ill, Tzu-lu ordered the disciples to perform tasks appropriate to retainers of a high official. Confucius, upon learning of this, asked Tzu-lu, "Whom do I deceive by pretending to have retainers when I have none? Do I deceive T'ien?" (*A*:9.12). Such a remark merely addresses the foolishness of Tzu-lu's charade. It employs a conventional notion of T'ien as all-knowing in order to make a point—but that point is not that T'ien is all-knowing. It says nothing about T'ien.[61]

A number of the passages we examined earlier are of a similar character. In his response to Wang-sun Chia's proposal (*A*:3.13), Confucius manipulates the notion of T'ien as a supreme deity to turn the politician's metaphor back on him.[62] When invoking T'ien to swear an oath (*A*:6.28), Confucius does no more than clothe his words in appropriate religious garb.[63] In bewailing the loss of Yen Yuan (*A*:11.9), his complaint against T'ien should be considered no more than an expression of deep grief through mannered sacrilege. Finally, in interpreting the two versions of Confucius' defiant claim of T'ien's protection (*A*:7.23, 9.5), if they do echo an actual statement made by Confucius, it was one uttered as a cry of bravado to lift the spirits in the face of great personal danger. It would be as inappropriate to infer philosophical attitudes from this as to suppose that they indicate that Confucius anticipated the intervention of a *deus ex machina* or believed himself invulnerable to physical injury.

This leaves us with five passages that purport to record Confucius' own words about T'ien. At least three seem to carry indubitable philosophical intent (*A*:2.4, 8.19, 16.8). The other two (*A*:14.35, 17.17) can be interpreted as philosophical or as playful uses of conventional imagery with about equal cogency.[64] I do not wish to carry this argument too far and impose trivial meanings on philosophically interesting passages. My point is simply this: modern scholars tend to agree that the relation of the statements attributed to Confucius in the *Analects* to what Confucius may really have said is problematical. If we hypothesize that some *Analects* passages are reasonably accurate records of Confucius' speech while others are late distortions, inventions, or wrong attributions, then it may be significant that slightly more than one-half of Confucius' statements about T'ien are consistent with the testimony of *A*:5.13, supported elsewhere in the text, to the effect that Confucius excluded metaphysical speculation from his teaching. I feel this view is essentially a correct one, and that the contradictory passages *A*:2.4, 8.19, and 16.8 are all, almost certainly, late inventions, while of the remaining relevant entries, some might not be.[65]

Therefore, I think that without doing unjust violence to the spirit of the *Analects*, we can propose that T'ien probably performed no significant function in the philosophy of Confucius. This theory can be supported, although not conclusively, on the basis of the *Analects*' own evidence. It does not, however, affect the significance of our earlier model of the *Analects*' implicit theory of T'ien, which uses the same body of evidence and represents not the thinking of Confucius himself, but of the collective authors and editors of the text.

Tactics of Metaphysics
The Role of T'ien in the *Mencius*

Chapter V

We come now to the *Mencius*, and as we do so, our analysis becomes at once more abstract and more concrete. Abstract because with the *Mencius* we begin to encounter developed theories about T'ien, and we have to grapple with the logic of these notions of metaphysics; concrete because unlike the *Analects* (and the *Hsun Tzu*), the text of the *Mencius* seems firmly tied to the incidents of history, and we are presented the challenge of illustrating the pragmatic instrumentality of philosophical theory in Mencius' life. Our goal will be to elucidate the doctrinal function of T'ien within the text and to show how these doctrines might have been practical expressions of Mencius' personal goals and interests as a Ru.

1. The Nature of the Text

The *Mencius*[1] might be the only pre-Ch'in text that is essentially what it claims to be: the teachings of a single philosopher.[2] There are few evident corruptions or insertions in the text (Lau 1970:222).[3] The doctrines expressed in it are relatively consistent throughout, although they may reflect views that Mencius held at different times in his life.[4]

About Mencius himself, not a great deal is known apart from what we learn in the text of the *Mencius* itself. His dates are not known, but the major incidents of his life occurred late in the fourth century B. C., and Mencius was apparently considered old at that time.[5] Ch'ien Mu has argued that the best evidence points toward a birth date between 389 and 382 B. C. (1956:187-88).

Mencius is said to have been a native of the small state of Tsou, which bordered on the Ruist homeland of Lu (*SC*:74.2343). He seems to have trained as a Ru under an unidentified disciple of Tzu-ssu, Confucius' grandson, who had in turn studied under the great original disciple Tseng Shen.[6]

We know nothing of Mencius' early career.[7] Judging by the honors accorded him during the travels of his late years, he must have gained a considerable reputation as a Ruist Master in Shantung before setting out on his journeys.

Some time prior to 320 B.C., at the age of perhaps sixty, Mencius reached the conclusion that the times were ripe for the appearance of a new Sage King, who would unify China under ethical rule as had the Ruist heroes Yao, Shun, and the founders of the Shang and Chou Dynasties. Mencius–and presumably other Ru of his time–claimed that the idealistic political doctrines of Ruism were no more than the ethical policies of these great rulers of the past.

Confident of his own mastery of these policies, Mencius set out to find an existing feudal ruler whom he could convert into a Sage King by instructing him in their implementation. For a period of fifteen years or so, Mencius traveled from court to court in pursuit of his new King.[8] The high point of his career came during a stay in Ch'i c.317-312 B. C., where he was honored as a high minister (*ch'ing*[b]). This official post–as far as we know the only one he ever held–he soon resigned on principle. After leaving Ch'i, Mencius probably retired from his wandering career.[9]

The *Shih-chi* tells us that Mencius himself, aided by disciples, composed the text of the *Mencius* (*SC*:74.2343). While many traditional scholars have accepted this view (*MTCY*:7), modern scholarship tends to view the text as the work of disciples after Mencius' death, based on their experiences traveling with their Master and on his teachings in retirement (Lau 1970:220-22).[10] The work is in seven books, and stylistic differences among the books may suggest independent authorship. For example, in Book 2, which may have been written by the disciple Kung-sun Ch'ou, the King (or Kings) of Ch'i are referred to only as "the King," whereas in other books, kings and other rulers are generally referred to by their posthumous titles.[11] This may indicate that the book was completed earlier than the other books. The *Shih-chi* account of Mencius' life says that after the collapse of his political mission, Mencius retired with a group of disciples. Perhaps Kung-sun Ch'ou did not join Mencius in retirement, but wrote Book 2 independently of the other disciples, completing it before the other books were edited into their present form (we will return to this point later in this chapter). We should note also that the *Mencius* divides rather well into two halves. Through Book 3, the text seems to place most statements in the context of Mencius' travels. The later books are written in a style closer to that of the *Analects*, and generally present statements outside of their historical context.[12] The division will help guide the organization of this chapter. As we discuss the role of T'ien in the *Mencius*, we will make a clear distinction between the instrumental functions that statements concerning T'ien may have had with regard to Mencius' political mission, and the functions that they may have had with regard to the doctrines and practice that typified the Mencian study group as a branch of the Ruist community.

❖   ❖   ❖   ❖

Our analytic procedure for this chapter will be somewhat different from that of the last, and, as indicated above, it will take its cue from the divided interests of the text itself. In order to trace the instrumental function that statements concerning T'ien may have performed, we will discuss separately the role of T'ien in Mencius' political statements—a role we will conclude to have been minor—and the important role T'ien plays in Mencius' more theoretical statements, concerning the nature of man and man's place in the universe. In the case of Mencius' political statements, their instrumental functions will be related to his political goals, and they are rather straightforward. The instrumental functions of relevant theoretical statements are not, however, so simply traced. Devising a model to illuminate them will occupy most of this chapter.

The complexity of this latter analysis is what has prompted the division of political and theoretical interests we will employ here. The main purpose of the division is to winnow out references to T'ien in a political context that might otherwise unnecessarily complicate or confuse our more difficult problem. For the sake of clarity, then, we will outline the major analytic themes of this chapter after first discussing rather summarily the role of T'ien in Mencius' political doctrines.

2. The Role of T'ien in Mencius' Political Doctrines and Career

The key to understanding the role of T'ien in Mencius' political doctrines is to bear in mind that its role was marginal and of little intrinsic importance to the doctrines themselves or to Mencius' concrete political goals. Because Mencius' attention was not focused on articulating a consistent theory of T'ien in this regard, the meaning of T'ien in relevant statements varies with particular fluidity according to the instrumental context in which T'ien was discussed.

The heart of Mencius' political theory, in my view, lay in his idealistic populism, and the belief that the proper function of political leaders and institutions was to serve the needs and interests of the people (e.g., *M*:1A.7, 1B.1, 3A.3, 7B.14). Mencius elaborated this praiseworthy ethical bias with an important predictive corollary: the ruler who demonstrates in action his commitment to these principles will quickly receive the support of all the peoples of the empire (e.g., 1A.3, 2A.3, 2A.5). He will rule as the successor to the Kings of Chou. Hence, Mencius' brand of humane government was "right" both ethically and politically.

It may be that many Ruists held political views similar to Mencius'.[13] What made Mencius famous was not so much his views as his energetic search for a ruler who would adopt them. In this, he was somewhat unusual, given the tendency of early Ruism to opt for political withdrawal.

What seems to have motivated Mencius to pursue concrete political goals as he did was a belief in a type of millennial prophecy and a conviction that the millennium was imminent.

Apparently, in Mencius' time there was a widespread belief that dynastic rule was a cyclical process that obeyed set rules of timing. The *Tso-chuan* recounts how the second ruler of the Chou divined about the length of his dynasty's mandate to rule, and learned that it had been allotted a term of 700 years (Hsuan 3:10.20). Mencius, who lived at the expiration of this term, thought that the normal cycle called for five centuries between the rise of Sage Kings.[14] In his view, "According to calculations the term is past, and if we judge by the times, they are ripe for it" (*M*:2B.13).

The pivot of Mencius' decision to pursue political action probably lies in the phrase "the times are ripe." "Time" (*shih*) is an important word in the *Mencius*; it refers to the Ruist doctrine of "timeliness," which meant accepting political responsibilities only when they presented true moral opportunities (*M*:5B.1). Because Warring States governments were universally corrupt, they were not viewed as presenting moral opportunities for political action. As we saw earlier, the *Analects* makes clear that for early Ruism, the doctrine of timeliness meant withdrawal from politics; the times doomed ethical activism to failure.[15]

When Mencius says that "the times are ripe," he is saying that the rules have changed. Even though governments remain immoral, the desperate state that society has reached, viewed through the expectations of the millennial rise of the new King, creates a unique type of moral opportunity: "With half the effort of the men of old, their achievements can be doubled" (*M*:2A.1). This was Ruism's great chance: a time so desperate that an old man such as Mencius, without, so far as we know, a shred of political experience, might expect to transform the world. It was with this belief that Mencius breached the political passivity of Ruism and set out to find among the rulers of his day the one who would adopt Mencian policies and fulfill prophecy.

❖ ❖ ❖ ❖

To understand the small role that T'ien played in Mencius' political "persuasions" to rulers and in the political theory that underlay them, we must again distinguish between the prescriptive and descriptive roles that were ascribed to T'ien.[16] It is in the shifts between the two dimensions that the pragmatic basis of statements about T'ien becomes clear.*

---

* The terms "prescriptive" and "descriptive" occur frequently in the discussion below, and it may be helpful to restate the sense in which they are used. "Prescriptive" uses of T'ien include passages where T'ien is invoked to urge imperatives for future action. "Descriptive" uses are those in which T'ien is invoked to explain past events. The two dimensions diverge because the former suggests a T'ien that is freely ethical, while in the latter case, T'ien's ethical image is fettered by the moral ambiguities of events as they have actually occurred.

The prescriptive aspect of T'ien in this regard is quite simple. T'ien is manifest in humane government in accord with Mencius' policies. The ruler who adopts these policies will find the people of surrounding states flocking to his domain. "He will have no enemy in the world. He who has no enemy in the world is the agent of T'ien. Never has there been such a one who has not ruled as true King" (*M*:2A.5).[17] Note that in this formula, T'ien plays no active role. The humane ruler is T'ien's agent, but his political success is adequately explained by the virtue of his policies and the consequence that he ceases to have enemies. No barriers would then remain between him and the Imperial throne that would require the intervention of a transcendent power. T'ien's role is passive; it adds nothing to the power of virtue.

T'ien is prescriptive in that it approves of or is manifest in ethical government. But T'ien also has a descriptive aspect. The two contrasting dimensions of T'ien are evident in another passage, which purports to record Mencius' words to the ruler of the great state of Ch'i.

Only a ruler who is *jen* is able to render service to states smaller than his own . . . . Only a ruler who is wise is able to render service to states greater than his own . . . . To serve a state smaller than one's own is to take joy in T'ien; to serve a state larger than one's own is to hold T'ien in awe. He who takes joy in T'ien will protect the world [i.e., rule as King]; he who holds T'ien in awe will protect his state (*M*:1B.3).

The phrases omitted here cite historical examples, and these make it clear that the two uses of "render service" (*shih*[b]) are not at all equivalent. The powerful ruler merely honors states weaker than his; the weak ruler propitiates states stronger than his.[18]

Consequently, the two uses of "*t'ien*" are not equivalent. In the case of the strong ruler, who acts ethically even though not forced to do so, "*t'ien*" represents the prescripts of *jen*, one of which is honoring the weak. But for the ruler of a small state, "*t'ien*" represents the descriptive position of being under the sword of the mighty. For the ruler of the strong state, T'ien is the ethical opportunity to earn the throne. For the ruler of a weak state, T'ien is the threat of annihilation without regard to ethical effort.

This distinction between two entirely different T'iens, one T'ien seen from the perspective of political strength, the other seen from the perspective of weakness, reveals the pragmatic nature of the role of T'ien in Mencius' political thought. Mencius' political metaphysics recognizes political reality and does not challenge it. Mencius felt that political realities were such that if a strong state such as Ch'i were to adopt his program, it would rapidly be able to unify China under moral government.[19] He was anxious to put his programs to a crucial test in Ch'i, and so in lecturing the ruler of Ch'i he could picture T'ien as prescriptive. He urges the ruler to take as his model King Wu, who founded the Chou Dynasty by conquest, and, quoting the *Documents*, he pictures King Wu as T'ien's appointed agent on earth.[20]

But when speaking to the young ruler of the tiny state of T'eng—perhaps the only ruler who ever seriously considered adopting Mencius' programs—Mencius suggests a different model and describes a different T'ien:

Duke Wen of T'eng asked, "Ch'i is about to fortify Hsueh, and I am deeply alarmed. How should I deal with this?" Mencius replied, "At one time, King T'ai ruled in Pin. When it was invaded by the Ti tribes, he quit Pin and moved to live beneath Mt. Ch'i. This was not by choice but from necessity. If one does what is good, surely there will be some among one's descendants who will rule as true Kings. The *chün-tzu* initiates the task and lays down guidelines that it may be carried on. As for its success, that is with T'ien. What should you do about Ch'i? Strive to do good, that is all (*M*:1B.14).

King T'ai was the great-grandfather of King Wu, founder of the Chou. By prescribing him as a model for the Duke, Mencius has effectively removed from immediate view the consequences which, in theory, he predicts his programs will have if adopted by a feudal ruler. The T'ien of this passage is entirely descriptive. Mencius makes no claim that T'ien will aid the Duke if he practices virtue, and so steers clear of any hint that his social programs will work wonders that he knows to be politically impossible. Mencius interpreted prophecy within the bounds of reason, and he does not expect any more of T'ien than he expects of human political effort.[21]

M:1B.3 and 1B.14 are the only instances where Mencius discusses T'ien with rulers or other political actors, and this illustrates the minor role that T'ien played in Mencius' practical political rhetoric. Judging from them, T'ien represents political realities as Mencius saw them: prescriptive opportunities for the strong, descriptive perils for the weak. In this sense, T'ien is reduced to Mencius' view of practical reality—we could say that it disappears in the interplay between Mencius' prescriptive program and the descriptive social conditions under which he sought to put it to a test.

Two important passages remain which, although they record Mencius' political ideas in the context of his theoretical teachings rather than in the context of his political quest, we may profit by considering here. The passages show us Mencius' ideas about the general relation of T'ien to the office of Kingship, and they are of interest because they illustrate that even in theory Mencius was attached to no firm view of T'ien that would distinguish it from political realities.

The two passages are contiguous and both contain Mencius' comments about legends concerning the Sage Kings Yao, Shun, and Yü.[22] The first two of these Kings were said to have passed on their throne to an extralineal successor, rather than to their sons, and in *M*:5A.5, the disciple Wan Chang questions Mencius about this. Mencius replies that the transmission of the throne depends not on the ruler's whim, but on T'ien.

Wan Chang responds to this by asking what it means in practical terms. "Does T'ien [transfer the throne] through explicit decree?" "No," replies Mencius, "T'ien does not speak; it manifests its decree through action and event." Mencius proceeds to describe what this involves, and as he does so, T'ien once again seems to disappear into descriptive political realities.

Mencius begins by telling Wan Chang that before a ruler can pass the throne to a chosen successor, that successor must be approved first by T'ien—which means that the spirits accept his sacrifices—and second by the people, who may submit to his rule.[23] This appears to give T'ien a very minor role indeed: not T'ien but the people seem to be the crucial factor. But as the discussion proceeds, Mencius seems to ascribe both the spirits' approval and the people's to T'ien.[24] In the end, it seems to be T'ien alone that bestows the throne, but it is also true that "T'ien sees through the sight of my people; T'ien hears through the hearing of my people."[25]

In the course of this single passage, Mencius employs three different notions of T'ien: T'ien is a single purposive deity; it is functionally the sum of all the spirits; it is the collective will of the people. Clearly what he is trying to do is to identify the notion of a purposive deity with descriptive political realities, and he is willing to recast the image of T'ien in any way that will help him to do so. His fixed philosophical point seems to be to legitimize the will of the people through historical precedent. His "concept" of T'ien must be flexible enough to allow this.

In M:5A.6 this highly descriptive view of T'ien is broadened to legitimize the Chou tradition of hereditary political office, a position that seems in some ways contradictory to the populism of M:5A.5. Wan Chang opens the passage by citing those who say that the golden age of the Kingship ended with Yü, who passed his throne to his son rather than to a worthy. Mencius proceeds to argue why this view is incorrect. *All* royal successions, he claims, are guided by T'ien, and he explains apparent ethical anomalies in T'ien's descriptive action by matching them to a series of nonintuitive rules. Why did Confucius not become King? It is a rule that the reigning King must recommend his successor to T'ien; Confucius lacked this recommendation.[26] Who did the great ministers of the various dynastic founders fail to become Kings? It is a rule that unless an heir apparent is as wicked as were Chieh and Chou—historical heirs who were, in fact, deposed—T'ien will not depose him.

By these arguments, Mencius manages to bring the prescriptive notion of the "Mandate of Heaven" in line with descriptive history. Both T'ien and the Mandate are portrayed in completely descriptive terms: "What is done without anyone doing it is T'ien; what comes without anyone bestowing it is the Mandate (*ming*)."[27] Once again, T'ien is reduced to descriptive political realities.

M:5A.5 and 5A.6 show Mencius elaborating theories of history that rationalize his populist political theories and an acceptance of the existing insti-

tutions of hereditary privilege. Mencius' motives for doing this are not
explicit in the passages, but they are not, perhaps, unimaginable.[28] But what
is significant for us is that in these passages, as in those discussed earlier,
T'ien is not a stable concept but a chameleon-like notion that resembles
nothing more than a convenient rhetorical device. To construct from these
passages a theory of T'ien would be to misunderstand their import; the
resulting theory would be a shapeless grouping of conflicting ideas. What is
intriguing about the passages is precisely that they are governed by no
theory of T'ien at all. T'ien had little to contribute to Mencius' political
ideas other than to be available as a piece of rhetoric to help Mencius
express those ideas however he could.

3. The Mencian Theory of T'ien: Human Nature and the Personal Decree

The remainder of this chapter will be devoted to a discussion of the role
of T'ien in that portion of Mencius' teachings primarily directed toward
issues of personal values and conduct, rather than toward Mencius' political activities. All but a few of the passages we will discuss here are found in
the second, more theoretical half of the text, and deal with issues of greater
philosophical generality than the discussions of kingship analyzed in the
last section.

Our project will be to locate the role of T'ien in the web of theories that
comprise Mencius' general ethical philosophy and to explore how those
doctrines and T'ien related to Ruism as Mencius and his disciples practiced it. To do this, however, we must be able to describe in some detail
what we take the Mencian practice of Ruism to have been, and here we
encounter a problem that will be the starting point of our discussion: the
Mencius itself provides very few clues as to what that practice was. Although
we know that Mencius traveled with an impressive retinue of disciples
(*M*:3B.4), we know almost nothing about who they were or what they did.[29]

In chapter II we presented a portrait of the early Ruist community as a
group of men primarily occupied with the study and practice of *li*. But the
Mencius is remarkably reticent about *li*. It is not discussed nearly as often
as we might expect, and more important, the claim that the study of *li* is the
path to Sagehood is simply not made in the text. It is not that the Mencius
does not claim the existence of a totalistic level of understanding. It makes
this claim far more explicitly than does the *Analects*, in statements such as:
"The world of things is complete in me" (*M*:7A.4); "There is nothing that
the wise do not know" (*M*:7A.46); "Whatever the *chün-tzu* passes is transformed; what he nourishes is spirit-power *(shen)*; above and below he flows
in a single current with T'ien and earth" (*M*:7A.13), as well as in a number

of other formulas (see, e.g., *M*:2A.2, 4B.13, 7B.25).[30] But the genetic linkage of *li* to this perfection of mind is unclear at best.

In our discussion here, we will begin by trying to learn more about Mencian practice by exploring this changed role of *li*. We will conclude that this change was primarily a change in rhetoric rather than a change in practice, and that the Mencian practice of Ruism is unlikely to have differed greatly from the model of mainstream Ruist practice outlined in chapter II. We will argue that the major problems facing Ruism as a sect during Mencius' time were attacks mounted against it by the competing schools of Mohism and Taoism, which ridiculed the Ruist obsession with *li* and the claim that the practice of an ethically relative code of behavior—ritual—could generate an absolute category of mind: Sagehood. Sensitivity to issues such as these, particularly as they were raised by the analytically oriented Mohist school, dictated that Mencius supplement the synthetic structure of Ruist teachings with rationalizing arguments that could relieve *li* of its analytically unsupported role at the center of the quest for Sagehood. In the context of fourth century B.C. polemics, Ruism needed to develop analytically defensible doctrines that could remove from *li* the theoretical burden of engendering the Sagely totalism, but which would not interfere with its practical role at the center of Ruist education.

The new structure that Mencius created is the pivot of his ethical philosophy: his portrait of the universal ethical potential of the human mind. The first outlines of this portrait were probably sketched early in Mencius' career. They are visible in his persuasions of rulers, and help explain the particular nature of his millennial expectations. When these ideas evolved into their ultimate formulation as Mencius' doctrine of the innate goodness of the *hsing*, or human nature, this portrait became a new framework into which *li* could be integrated as a universal category of mind, rather than as the ritual code of a particular dynasty.

We will discuss this reformulation of *li* as a category of mind in terms of the twin doctrines of the "internality of righteousness" (*yi tsai nei*) and the innateness of the "four sprouts" (*ssu tuan*).

Having linked the practical Ruist interest in ritual to the theory of the goodness of human nature, we will discuss the notion of the good *hsing* as a prescriptive concept, representing essentially the same totalistic ideal as that denoted in the *Analects* by "*jen*." Because the *hsing* is directly tied to T'ien in the *Mencius*, T'ien becomes—as in the *Analects*—the prescriptive basis of both the totalistic ideal and the path of *li*.

Also as in the *Analects*, the conflicts between normative ethics and empirical experience create tensions in the meaning of T'ien. These are expressed in the Mencius through the twin doctrines of the good *hsing* and the personal decree (*ming*), both of which are tied to T'ien. We will see that these two related doctrines are complementary facets of the bifurcated doctrine of Ruism: the T'ien-engendered *hsing* prescribing the action of ritual self-cultivation, and the T'ien-ordained *ming* explaining the failure of political action and rationalizing persistence in ritual ethical conduct.

3.1. Mencius and *Li*

If the *Analects* and *Hsun Tzu* did not exist as standards of comparison, we might feel that the *Mencius* does, indeed, give an important role to *li*. The word itself appears often enough. It is included among the four cardinal virtues formulated by Mencius (*M*:2A.6, 6A.6).[31] It is an aspect of Mencius' idealized portrait of Confucius (*M*:5A.8). Mencius himself shows a preoccupation with rationalizing his sometimes peculiar behavior by reconciling it with *li* (e.g., *M*:2B.2). But when we compare the *Mencius* with the *Analects* and the *Hsun Tzu*, we cannot help but be struck by the absence of any claim that the practice of *li* is the path to Sagehood.

Because of this distinction between the *Mencius* and other important early Ruist texts, there has been a conception of pre-Ch'in Ruism as fundamentally divided into two traditions. The tradition to which Mencius belonged is seen as rejecting the pedantry that overconcentration on ritual detail generated, becoming increasingly oriented towards subjective contemplation. This tradition is sometimes viewed as culminating in the two *Li-chi* texts *Ta-hsueh* and *Chung-yung*, both of which are generally associated with the Mencian school of thought.[32] Contrary to this Mencian school stood a tradition sometimes epitomized by Hsun Tzu, with his great stress on the importance of scrupulous study of ritual and ceremony.[33]

This model has several problems. For example, it cannot account for important passages in the *Hsun Tzu* that are similar to those in the "Mencian" works that seem to point to an abandonment of *li* in favor of more "mystical" contemplation.[34] Nor can it explain the fact that extant textual traditions concerning the great Masters of Mencius' school feature a general preoccupation with ritual, particularly with funeral rites.[35]

But the most important problem with this model of two schools divided on the importance of *li* practice is that it offers us no insight into the concrete practice of Mencian Ruism. Mencius, as with Confucius and Hsun Tzu, was a teacher with disciples who studied and traveled with him for many years. We can infer from the *Analects* and the *Hsun Tzu* that the syllabus *they* reflect consisted largely of the daily practice of various ritual skills: speech, song, instruments, dance, and so forth. But if the Mencian school did not stress this sort of practice, what did Mencius and his disciples do with their time? What did Mencius teach? If we rely on the "two-schools" model, we are left only with the old answers of textual exegesis and moral discussion, plus a sense of some vague meditational component never directly described.

The two-schools model seems inadequate.[36] But if we reject it and maintain that *li* practice was for Mencius, as for other Ruist Masters, the core of his education syllabus, we are still faced with the task of accounting for the peculiarly small role accorded to *li* in the text of the *Mencius*. I think that we have to approach this problem by examining the position in which Ruism found itself at the time that the text was compiled. If we do, we will find that the tendency of the *Mencius* to stress theory and metaphysics rather than practical issues of education may simply reflect the fact that the text was written primarily to provide tools for sectarian disputation, rather than to instruct disciples in self-cultivation.

In Mencius' day, the new competing schools of Taoism and Mohism were reaching the zenith of their early development and were launching vigorous attacks upon the early established Ruist school.[37] A primary target of their attacks was the role of *li* in Ruism.[38] The philosophically embattled state of Ruism in Mencius' time is not only specifically noted in the *Mencius* (*M*:3B.9, 7B.26), but is evident in the composition of the text itself.

The *Mencius* is distinguished among Ruist texts by its stridently polemical style.[39] While the *Analects* seems designed to serve as a primer in Ruist self-cultivation, the *Mencius* contains little concrete instruction for disciples, relative to its bulk. The greater part of the text is devoted to arguments used to debate and persuade "outsiders"–kings nobles, and philosophical disputants–rather than to instruct "insiders." It does *not* reflect the practice of Mencius and his disciples. Although Mencius' featureless disciples do occasionally appear and question Mencius, their questions seem designed to present Mencius with rhetorical opportunities to rationalize apparent contradictions in his doctrines or actions. The theme of the *Mencius* text is argument rather than instruction and the spirit of the text is defensive. Its most evident raison d'être is to provide disciples with arguments and debating techniques to use against those who would attack Ruism, and with the doctrines that Mencius developed to defend it.

In accord with its defensive nature, the *Mencius* seems to have been compiled in such a way as to downplay the single most vulnerable aspect of Ruism as a philosophy: its claim that the relative cultural forms of *li* could generate a universal category of mind: *jen*, or the totalistic wisdom of the Sage. In the *Mencius*, we miss the linkage between *li* and the totalism. At the same time, we do not find any new practical linkage, but only abstract theories that make T'ien, as god or Nature, the basis for the totalism.

The failure of the two-schools model, the disputatious spirit of the *Mencius* as a text, and the absence of any alternate path to the Sagely totalism that the *Mencius* clearly envisions, all suggest that the diminished role of *li* in the text does not reflect any fundamental divergence of Mencian practice from the model of mainstream Ruist practice presented in chapter II, but reflects instead a change in rhetoric dictated by the sectarian interests of the text.

Mencius' Opponents

A brief note is called for here to explain how I intend to discuss the effects of outside attacks on Mencian Ruism. The *Mencius* itself indicates in three places that the enemies of Ruism, as perceived by Mencius, were the schools of Mo Tzu and Yang Chu (*M*:3B.9 7A.26, 7B.26). A. C. Graham has written a superbly argued analysis of Mencius' doctrine of human nature seen in response to an individualist doctrine of *hsing*, which Graham attributes to Yang Chu (1967).[40] In his article, Graham reconstructs the philosophy of Yang Chu, whose original writings have long since perished. Now, if Graham's view were granted, little would be left to be said on the issue, but I feel that it contains so many unresolved problems and depends upon so many contingent issues that it cannot now be accepted in its entirety.[41] My view is that the essential nature of Mencius' position on the *hsing* lies in that position's responsiveness to Taoist, and more particularly Mohist ideas, which did not involve a theory of *hsing* at all.

In the following pages, I will portray Mencius' theory of human nature solely in terms of the Mohist challenge. I do believe that Taoist ideas may have contributed to its creation, but I feel that to explore their possible role would add little to the elucidation of the import of Mencius' doctrines, and would only make this essay somewhat redundant.

The Mohist Challenge

There is a tradition preserved in the *Huai-nan Tzu* that Mo Tzu was a Ruist disciple who became disgruntled with the pedantry and wastefulness of Ruist *li* practice. We are told that he rejected the ethical authority of Chou Dynasty institutions, and traced his doctrine to the Emperor Yü, founder of the first dynasty, the Hsia (*HNT*:21.7a).

Whether or not this tale has any factual basis, it captures an important truth about Mohism. The threat that Mohism posed to Ruism stemmed largely from the fact that Mohism coopted substantial portions of Ruist doctrine, assimilating many of Ruism's most appealing ideas in order to attack its weaker aspects. Most significant was the Mohist adaptation of the Ruist terms "*jen*" and "*yi*."[42] By using these terms, Mohism borrowed their rhetorical authority, but significantly altered their meanings. "*Jen*," for example, does not denote a holistic virtue of mind in the *Mo Tzu*; it denotes "compassion," a restricted meaning that excludes any necessary entailment with *li*. "*Yi*" is used much as it is in the *Analects*,[43] but with one important difference, which applies to *jen* as well. In the *Mo Tzu*, *jen* and *yi* are considered ethically universal, as they are in the *Analects*. They are ethically universal because they are always good. But they are not ethical absolutes as they are in the *Analects*. Their goodness is not intrinsic, but is derived from their function in promoting an absolute standard—li^b: "welfare" or "profit."[44] For the *Mo Tzu*, it is human welfare that is intrinsically good; *jen* and *yi* are of value in that they help society maximize li^b. This utilitarian criterion is Mohism's most distinctive feature. It is significant that li^b, as an absolute standard, can never be necessarily entailed with a relative cultural form such as ritual *li*. For Ruism, the functional import of its ideology was to make *jen* and *yi* dependent on the practical action standard of ritual *li*. Mohism set against this an entailment of *jen* and *yi* with the absolute and abstract standard of maximized welfare. It makes sense that the *Huainan Tzu* portrays Mo Tzu as consciously removing his historical authority from the particular and limited Chou Dynasty to the ultimately prior and abstract Hsia.[45]

Armed with the borrowed sanctity of these key terms, using the Ruist method of relying on agreeable texts of questionable antiquity to legitimize their ideas, the Mohists organized into cohesive cults rivaling the Ruists. They were distinguished by their devotion to training in the martial arts and in crafts applicable to defensive warfare, and also by their ascetic practices.[46] Although they challenged Ruism in many ways, the favored method was to ridicule the role that *li* played in Ruist doctrine and practice, as is most evident in the *Fei Ju*, *Chieh tsang*, and *Kung Meng* chapters of the *Mo Tzu*.

Now, I do not mean to picture early philosophers debating the cultural relativity of *li*. The issue was not generally articulated in this way. For non-Ru, like the Mohists, the notion of ritual *li* was simply not in the same category of philosophical importance as universals like *jen* and *yi*. Its cultural—or rather dynastic—relativity was known to all (see, e.g., *A*:2.23, 3.9). Only Ruism elected to raise ritual to philosophical significance, and its position was theoretically tenuous intrinsically. (One can imagine how untenable a philosophy of propriety would have been in the Western tradition.)

The philosophical difference between the Ruist valuation of ritual *li* and value standards adopted by Mohism is well illustrated in the following passage, where a Ruist who is probably a caricature of Mencius is satirized for his ethical commitment to the relative value of Chou ritual:

Kung Meng Tzu said: "Only if the *chün-tzu* speaks the ancient words and dresses in ancient costume can he be *jen*." Master Mo Tzu replied: "In the past, the Shang King Chou and his minister Pi Chung were the worst tyrants in the world; Chi Tzu and Wei Tzu were the greatest Sages. They all spoke the same tongue, but some were *jen* and others not. Tan, Duke of Chou was a Sage and Kuan Shu a tyrant. They wore the same dress, but one was *jen*, the other not. Hence *jen* does not lie in wearing ancient costume or uttering ancient words. Moreover, you do not even emulate the Hsia, but rather the Chou—your "ancient" is not really ancient at all!" (*MT Kung Meng*:12.10b).[47]

The issue of universality of standards was a crucial one for the Mohists, whose case for their own utilitarianism rests heavily upon asserting its universal applicability. Their position is clearly demonstrated by the parable of the creation of government in the *Shang-t'ung* chapters of the *Mo Tzu*. In this parable, man's original "state of nature" is portrayed as one of complete value relativity. The creation of society is described as the elimination of value relativity under a government ordered according to principles of T'ien-ordained utilitarianism.[48]

Thus, the Mohists rested their case on the intuitive universality of the abstract utilitarian value of maximizing human welfare, or profit. This philosophical presupposition was a powerful challenge to Ruist practice and ideology. Ruist theory was saddled with the demand to justify the value of particular, culturally relative forms of ritual behavior—forms that were largely outdated and unpopular. This philosophical challenge was formidable indeed.

From its opening passage, which attacks the standard of "profit," the *Mencius* is preoccupied with undermining the Mohist position. But frontal attack is by no means its most important response to the Mohist challenge. Instead, an intricate reformulation of Ruist ideas, which deemphasized the importance of concrete *li* practice in favor of a new emphasis on the term "*yi*," borrowed back from the Mohists, provided the main line of defense.

The Meaning of "*Yi*" in the *Mencius*

The word "*yi*," "right" or "righteousness," plays a limited role in the *Analects*. It denotes an ambiguous ethical value, assigned to character, actions, or situations. It is not consistently linked with any other ethical term, such as "*jen*" or "*li*." The situation is very different in the *Mencius*. There "*yi*" has become the single most important ethical term, outstripping in frequency of use both "*jen*" and "*li*." We find "*yi*" regularly linked in compound ethical phrases such as "*jen-yi*" and "*li-yi*." In addition, the term carries new and important meanings.

The expanded role of "*yi*" complements the reduced role of "*li*," and this is a key to understanding one of its new meanings. In many instances, we find that "*yi*" is functionally equivalent to "*li*." Its primary role in the *Mencius* is as a universal abstraction of *li*.[49] "*Yi*" shares with "*li*" the meaning of "what is right to do," but it is not limited by reference to Chou codes of conduct, and so appears to have a universal sense, as opposed to the restricted sense of "*li*." In its actual function, however, the term "*yi*" often comes to be subjected to much the same limits as "*li*." The way in which the text accomplishes this is to select as a prototypical example of *yi* a basic form of ceremonial behavior stressed in Chou *li*: deference to elders.

The *Mencius* develops the following formulas as its most consistent definition of *"yi"*: "Love of parents is *jen*; respect for elders is *yi*" (*M*:7A.15);
"Service to parents is the realization of *jen*; deference to elders is the realization of *yi*" (*M*:4A.27, cf. 1A.4, 1A.7). When engaged in close analysis of
behavior according to *yi*, the examples raised are not issues of universal
moral import, but are all issues of ceremonial proprieties (*M*:6A.5). In this
way, the text repeatedly reveals a practical equivalence between *"yi"* and
"li," and we will see in the next section how this role of *yi* is crucial to the
famous debate between Mencius and the philosopher Kao Tzu over the
nature of man.

The *Mencius*, then, presents a frontline defense against Mohism by means
of a simple rhetorical device. It has, as with the *Mo Tzu*, greatly increased
the importance of the term *"yi,"* which in the *Mo Tzu* is a universal standard often inimical to ritual *li*. But the *Mencius* has also implicitly submerged
the concept of *li* within the term *"yi,"* in a way similar to that with which
the term "proper" can be integrated into the term "right."[50] Specific instances
of *li* behavior are thus analytically legitimate.

Before we turn to see the application of this to the Mencian doctrine of
human nature, it is interesting to note one instance in which it relates to
the way in which the Ruist totalism is discussed in the *Mencius*.

Perhaps the most poetic expression of the holistic consciousness that
Ruism idealized is Mencius' discussion of the "flood-like energy" (*hao-jan
chih ch'i*) (*M*:2A.2). Interpretations of this passage have frequently portrayed
the "flood-like energy" as a semimystical force of mind, cultivated in some
unstated, esoteric way (Chan 1963:63). Actually, Mencius tells us very clearly
how it is cultivated: "It arises from the interweaving of many acts of *yi*; it
cannot be grasped by putting *yi* on like a suit of clothes."[51] Bearing in mind
the close linkage of *yi* and *li* in the text, the path to the flood-like energy
does not appear far removed from the mainstream Ruist path to Sagehood:
mastery of the ritual syllabus and identification of self and ritual norms.
The flood-like energy seems to be very close to the totalistic ideal. Like
the comprehension of Sagehood, "it fills all between heaven and earth,"
and similar to the portrait of *jen* emerging from the *Analects*, it is cultivated
through ritual practice.[52] In concrete terms, *li*, rather than the more abstract *yi*, would be the basis of the energy. But consider the advantages
of the Mencian formula! Compare, for example, the following two English
sentences, and the force of the Mencian reformulation will become clear:
"By ceremony, I build my inner power"; "By righteousness, I build my
inner power."

In sum, the defensive nature of the *Mencius*, its responsiveness to the
Mohist challenge, and the frequent functional equivalence of *yi* and *li* adequately explain the diminished role of *li* in the text. Because the *Mencius*

does not point to any pursuits that could have replaced the dominant role
of *li*, we have no reason to doubt that the cultic activities of Mencian Ruism
conformed to the general model presented in chapter II.

3.2. The Mencian Theory of Human Nature

Mencius' description of the flood-like energy leads him, in the original
text, to pause for a brief attack on the philosopher Kao Tzu, whose concept
of *yi* differed from Mencius'. The debates between Mencius and Kao Tzu, as
they appear in the *Mencius*, will form the starting point of the next phase of
our discussion here, an examination of Mencius' doctrine that human nature
(*hsing*) is good. That doctrine can actually be analyzed into three separate
elements, and we will discuss each in turn. The three elements are these:
First, the assertion that "*yi* is internal," which makes *li* a universal category
of mind, thus refuting the Mohist attack on *li* as a relative phenomenon.
Second, the theory of the "four sprouts" (*ssu tuan*), which served to legitimize the messianic convictions that motivated Mencius' personal political
ambitions. This doctrine required a diminution in the scope of the concept
of *jen*, leaving the Ruist totalism without any designating term. Finally, the
prescriptive notion of *hsing*, which we will find to be a reconstruction of
the Ruist totalism as a universal category of human ethical potential.

The Debate With Kao Tzu

Although Mencius is probably best known for his doctrine that human
nature is good, that doctrine is asserted formally in only one section of one
chapter of the *Mencius*: the first eight entries of the Kao Tzu chapter
(*M*:6A.1-8).[53] These entries describe a debate between Mencius and Kao
Tzu, a philosopher about whom we know practically nothing. Kao Tzu was
almost certainly a Ru,[54] and he was probably senior to Mencius.[55] He held a
doctrine that *jen* was a virtue of mind, while *yi* was a characteristic of
external circumstances. His position on *jen* was clearly directed against
Mohism. As noted earlier, Mohism made *jen* reducible to welfare (*li*[b]) thus
placing the locus of *jen* outside the individual. Mohism needed this theory
in order to accommodate its doctrine of "universal love," which required
that feelings of *jen* be extendable without limit. Kao Tzu argued that *jen*
could not be extended in that way because it was a spontaneous response
of mind; it could never be consciously redirected to accord with an external criterion (*M*:6A.4). Having developed the theory that *jen* was "internal,"
Kao Tzu rounded it out by concluding that *yi* was "external," that is to say,
the locus of "right" lies in public standards or situations and not in a moral
faculty of mind. Kao Tzu's position on *yi* was probably intended primarily
to underscore his position on *jen* by contrast.[56]

Kao Tzu's ideas, while suitable for attacking certain Mohist claims, leave Ruism as vulnerable as ever on the issue of *li*, and this appears to be the reason that Mencius felt obliged to refute him.

The first reference to Kao Tzu in the *Mencius* occurs during the discussion of the flood-like energy. After making his remarks about the way in which this energy is cultivated through the accumulation of *yi*, Mencius adds, "That is why I say that Kao Tzu does not understand *yi*: because he externalizes it" (*M*:2A.2). What Mencius is trying to do is to take *yi*—now incorporating *li*—and make it a universal category of mind, a faculty possessed by all men. In this way, he will be able to refute the Mohist attack on *li*.

The debate with Kao Tzu, which appears later in the book, is on precisely this issue.[57] Despite the fame of this debate over *hsing*, the four passages where Mencius and Kao Tzu argue face-to-face are not very informative about what their conceptions of *hsing* actually were. These passages seem primarily intended to demonstrate the use of logic and rhetoric, and they were probably studied by disciples learning how to refute attacks on Mencius' doctrine.[58] Of these four passages, the first three need not concern us here. They are actually arguments over the logical consistency of analogies and syllogisms that Kao Tzu chooses to express his view that *hsing* is morally neutral. The substance of his view is never touched upon.[59]

The fourth passage is somewhat different. Its topic is the following statement by Kao Tzu: "Appetites and lusts are *hsing*. *Jen* is internal, not external; *yi* is external, not internal." The debate then proceeds upon the issue of the internality of *yi*. No further mention is made of *hsing* (*M*:6A.4).

The passage following this one shows Mencius coaching a pupil on the way to refute the doctrine that *yi* is external. The illustrative examples of what *yi* is are these: the proper treatment of elders; order of precedence in serving wine to elders; the priority of respect according to ceremonial role at sacrifices over respect according to age (*M*:6A.5). All these are issues of *li*. Mencius' point is that behavior according to *li* is actually dictated by a moral faculty of mind, expressed spontaneously in feelings of respect and deference.

These five entries form the first part of the *Mencius*' discussion of the doctrine that human nature is good. The only issue that is dealt with in any substantial way is the question of the interiority of *yi*. What the debate section represents is Mencius' attempt to rectify a major strategic error in Kao Tzu's battle against the Mohists—the admission that *yi* is determinate, relative, and therefore incompetent to provide a safe haven for Ruists interested in demonstrating the absolute value of *li* practice. Here, when Mencius argues that human nature is good, his ultimate meaning is that *li* is a natural expression of the human mind.

The sixth and most complex entry in the *Kao Tzu* chapter involves an exposition of non-Mencian doctrines about *hsing*, followed by a two-part statement by Mencius summarizing his position. The first part of this statement recapitulates Mencius' theory of the "four sprouts," a theory that appears elsewhere in the *Mencius*, completely independent of any entailment with a theory of *hsing*. The second part concerns the relationship between the *hsing* and T'ien. In the following two sections, we will concentrate on the first part of Mencius' stated doctrine of *hsing*. Subsequently, we will explore its links to T'ien.

Mencius' Millenarian Beliefs and the "Four Sprouts"

Mencius set out upon his travels with a conviction: given that by prophecy and the signs of the times the appearance of the new King was imminent, and given that Mencius himself possessed the understanding of the way such a King would rule, then what was imminent was not necessarily the birth of a particular individual who was destined to conquer because he was a Sage, but might merely involve a decision by an ordinary ruler to adopt the teachings of Mencius as his guide and Mencius as his minister. This new King would not necessarily be a man of superhuman virtue; he could be any man, given the right conditions of timing and political opportunity. This expectation provided a rationale for Mencius' career as a wandering Sage, as the requirement of the advent of a perfect ruler could not have.[60]

Mencius' personal ambitions rested upon the premise that any actual ruler might become an ideal ruler.[61] It is important to imagine the implausibility of this idea to men of Mencius' time. Mythical emperors such as Yao and Shun, warriors such as T'ang and Wu had been transformed by hagiographers into perfect saints, men like gods. It was too much to expect the debauched feudal lords of Warring States China to step into the shoes of heroes such as these. As one native of Ch'i remarked, watching Mencius depart from that state in failure: "If he did not realize that our king could not be made into a T'ang or a Wu, then he was rather unperceptive" (*M*:2B.12).[62]

To make his expectations convincing, both to himself and to the rulers whose teacher he sought to become, Mencius required carefully devised doctrines that he could argue with force. The doctrine of the "four sprouts" was the ultimate answer to this need. It was intended to persuade any ruler that he possessed in his mind the single most important attribute characteristic of the Sage King: the virtue *jen*.

All men possess a mind that cannot be indifferent to the sufferings of others. The former kings possessed such a mind, and their governments were ones which cared for the people. When a ruler governs according to his natural care for others, he can rule the world as though it lay in the palm of his hand. Why do I say all men possess such a mind? Suppose a man were suddenly to see a child about to fall into a well; any man would feel distress and compassion.... The sense of compassion is the sprout of *jen*; the sense of shame is the sprout of *yi*; the sense of deference is the sprout of *li*; the sense of right and wrong is the sprout of *chih*[a]. Men possess these four sprouts as they possess their four limbs.... If a man brings these sprouts to fruit, he can protect the four quarters of the world. If he does not, he cannot even serve his parents (*M*:2A.6).

This is one of several arguments in which Mencius appeals for recognition of the spontaneity of sudden, "moral" anxiety, to persuade listeners of the innateness of moral dispositions (see also *M*:3A.5).

The message spoken here reverberates through the accounts of Mencius' conversations with rulers. He tells King Hsuan of Ch'i that his tenderness toward an ox being led to slaughter is a manifestation of the virtue of *jen* that can make him a true King (*M*:1A.7). The King's love of debased music is identified as the seed of a love for his people (*M*:1B.1). His greed for wealth and lust for sex are transformed into the true King's delight in the prosperity of his state and the beauty of his queen (*M*:1B.5).

Although the theory of the four sprouts asserts the universal possession of four different qualities of mind, the demonstration of its truth involves only a single virtue: *jen*. Apparently, at the time the discussion of *M*:2A.6 was first recorded Mencius was unable to arrive at proofs for the other three virtues, or at least we can speculate that his proofs were too weak to convince, or to merit inclusion in the text. In fact, the only piece of convincing material that Mencius was able to offer to prove the theory of the four sprouts was the occasional arousal of unselfish feelings of compassion in people. From this single thread, Mencius spun his doctrine of the identity of actual and ideal man.

It was natural, then, that Mencius identify this compassionate response with *jen*. *Jen* was certainly the most important of the Ruist virtues, and demonstrating its innate existence in the mind greatly helped Mencius' theory bear the weight of the other three sprouts, whose innate existence hung upon the single proof of *jen*. But by making this absolute identification between *jen* and the compassionate response, Mencius acquiesced to a considerable change in the Ruist meaning of *"jen."* No longer did it have the broad range of the *Analects'* totalistic virtue. Instead, *"jen"* in the *Mencius* is generally restricted to the meaning of "compassion," identical with Mohist usage. It is no longer a comprehensive virtue, but only the first among many cardinal virtues.

Thus, in the course of arguing the existence of Sage qualities in actual rulers, Mencius implicitly lowered his expectations of what a Sage should be. The totalism—the true goal of Ruists who aspired to Sagehood—was lost in the accommodating identification of *jen* with compassionate feelings. This could have had a serious effect on Ruism if it had remained the last word on the goal of Sagehood. But in fact, it was not that the ideal of the totalism had been lost, but only that it had been displaced into new terminology, which may not yet have been formulated at the time *M*:2A.6 was first recorded.

As we noted in section 1 above, Book 2 of the *Mencius* might have been authored independently of and earlier than some of the other books of the text, and might not record the doctrines that Mencius formulated after his retirement. One piece of supporting evidence is that Book 2 includes no mention of the *hsing* or of Mencius' position concerning the *hsing*.[63]

When we reencounter the four sprouts in the *Kao Tzu* chapter, which may have been compiled with a more detailed knowledge of Mencius' last teachings, the context of the doctrine has altered considerably. For one thing, in the passages of the text that immediately precede its restatement we see Mencius arrive at a proof that demonstrates simultaneously the existence of the sprouts of *yi* and *li*: the proof that *yi* is internal and is manifested as the sense of respect, or *li*.[64] Mencius has filled out his theory, and, what is more, he is now citing it as a general proof of the existence of a comprehensive category of mind: the good *hsing*. In the *hsing*, which incorporates all four cardinal virtues, we find reconstituted the totalism that in the *Analects* had been signified by the term "*jen*." As with *jen*, the *hsing* was something that had to be cultivated, and we will see that when the *hsing* was fully realized, holistic understanding was achieved ("To know one's nature is to know T'ien").

The term "*hsing*," then, has a somewhat unexpected function in the *Mencius*. Although the portrait of what is innate to a species is generally considered to be descriptive, here we find the idea standing in the place of the prescriptive Ruist virtue of *jen*, as found in the *Analects*. What actually was the meaning of the term around which Mencius built his most famous doctrine?

The Meaning of "*Hsing*" in the *Mencius*

As noted many times, a fundamental reason why Mencius was able to maintain the doctrine that people are good by nature—a thesis in conflict with the observations of normal experience—was because he used the word "*hsing*," "innate nature," in an unusual way. As Graham states, "Mencius . . . seems never to be looking back towards birth, always forward to the maturation of a continuing growth" (1967:216).[65] The *hsing* is innate in that all people share the moral senses that provide the opportunity to achieve personal perfection. But it often appears that Mencius does not envision a person as "possessing" the *hsing* until after that path to perfection has been traveled.

"*Hsing*" does not seem to denote either the capacities of the mind at birth, or a composite of all capacities that a person could conceivably develop in a lifetime, both of which are descriptive notions. *Hsing* points toward a particular type of being to which man can aspire. It is a prescriptive term, denoting the Ruist totalism, the holistic comprehension of all phenomena and all action imperatives, attainable through ritual self-cultivation.

Mencius was perfectly aware that his use of the word "*hsing*" was not conventional. We find several such acknowledgements in the *Mencius*. The most important is also, unfortunately, the most obscurely phrased. In order to make its meaning clear, I will first translate it here, and then offer a periphrastic restatement.[66]

When people speak of "*hsing*," they refer only to our primitive being, and that is moved only by profit. What they dislike about intelligence is that it forces its way. If intelligence acted as Yü did in guiding the rivers, then they would not dislike it. When Yü guided the rivers, he followed their spontaneous courses. If intelligence also followed its spontaneous course, it would be great wisdom indeed. Heaven is high and the stars are distant, but if we seek after their primitive being, we can predict the solstices for a thousand years (*M*:4B.26).[67]

When people talk about "human nature," they restrict the meaning of the term to our most primitive thoughts, and these are moved only by profit. They refuse to allow that intelligence is a part of the nature because they see it as a distorting, rather than a spontaneous force. But if intelligence were to act as Yü did when he dredged the rivers of China, then they could have no objection to including intelligence in their concept of the nature. When Yü dredged the rivers, he followed their spontaneous courses. If intelligence also followed its spontaneous course, it would be great wisdom indeed. Heaven is high and the stars are distant. But if we apply our intelligence in the study of their spontaneous courses, our intelligence can run ahead of their spontaneity without distortion, and the solstices of the next thousand years will merely verify our intelligence.

Thus, Mencius does not wish to exclude a priori any aspect of human self-cultivation from the notion of what is innate to man, provided that the activity accords with what he feels to be man's spontaneous course.

Examples of men who have displayed this type of natural self-cultivation include the Ruist models the Emperors Yao and Shun, and the dynastic founders T'ang and Wu. Their type of self-cultivation is linked to the Ruist ideal in the following passage:

Yao and Shun did it by nature; T'ang and Wu returned to it. Every motion, every stance precise in *li* as one goes round: this is the acme of full virtue (*M*:7B.33).

The emergence of man's nature is in fact a transformation from actual to ideal man by an act of decision:

Vast territories densely peopled: the *chün-tzu* wants them, but his joy does not lie therein. To stand at the center of the world and settle the people of the four quarters: the *chün-tzu* rejoices in it, but his nature does not lie therein. What the *chün-tzu* *takes as his nature* is not increased by great achievements, nor decreased by retirement in failure; its place is set. What he *takes as his nature* are *jen, yi, li,* and *chih,* rooted in his mind, blooming brightly over his face, coursing through his spine, flowing through his limbs. Silent, he is understood (*M*:7A.21).

The *chün-tzu* does not possess his nature passively, as an inevitable property granted at birth. He determines it actively, seizing it as an opportunity that has been afforded him through his constitution at birth.

Mencius conceived of man's nature as identical with the nature of Sagehood, right down to the ritual precision of the Sage's style of action. The four sprouts are possessed by all actual people, but man's nature is realized—exists—only in the person of the Sage who achieves the Ruist ideal of totalistic comprehension.

The concept of *hsing* reconstitutes the Ruist totalism that Mencius seemed to put aside when he set his goals on idealizing actual rulers and limited the scope of *jen*. It would make perfect sense, then, for Mencius to claim that man's nature was good. Its goodness had become imbedded analytically in the term for "nature" itself. And this goodness was nothing abstract. It consisted specifically of the Ruist categories of mind: *jen, yi,* and most important, *li,* which had been incorporated into this universal ideal, the mind of the Sage. Mencius had managed to implant the homunculus of the chanting, dancing Ru in the universal mind possessed by all men.

3.3. *Hsing* and *Ming*:
The Interface of the Prescriptive and Descriptive Dimensions of T'ien

We have been describing the prescriptive doctrine of the goodness of human nature, and its functionality in reconstituting the particular ritual values of Ruism as human universals. For Mencius, the disposition to act according to ritual and right (*li-yi*) is a universal property of men's minds.

The linkage of the good nature to T'ien is not frequently discussed in the text of the *Mencius*, but it is clear and logical. In the last part of *M*:6A.6, the passage in which the four sprouts are incorporated into the theory of the good *hsing*, Mencius concludes his discussion with a citation from the *Poetry* that ties the universal dispositions of the *hsing* to the absolute authority of T'ien:

The *Poetry* says:

> T'ien gave birth to the teeming masses;
> Every thing has its law.
> The norm which people possess
> Is love of splendid virtue. . . .

Therefore, for every thing there must be a law, and "the norm which people possess" is innately, "the love of splendid virtue."[68]

The context in which the poem is cited makes it clear that for Mencius, this is an authority proving that T'ien created the *hsing* as a moral property. T'ien engenders in people their moral predispositions; it is the source of ethical value.

Other passages point more explicitly to T'ien as the source of the particular moral dispositions. For example, in contrasting the Mohist imperative to love all equally with the spontaneous impulse to love those closest to one, Mencius remarks: "When T'ien gives birth to a thing, it roots it in a single source [its parents]; [the Mohists] would give it a split source" (*M*:3A.5).

Furthermore, by linking man's moral dispositions to T'ien, Mencius is able to guarantee the absolute value of those dispositions, because in these discussions, T'ien stands as an ethical absolute, fulfilling the original ethical role it played in Chou religion. It is a teleological force—as it was in the poliltical discussions of *M*:5A.5-6—and its engendering of the good *hsing* in man indicates what man's purpose, or "final cause," is to be.

There are offices which T'ien bestows and offices which men bestow. *Jen, yi*, devotion and trust, and the untiring love of good are the offices of T'ien. High ministries and councilorships are the offices of men (*M*:6A.16, cf. 2A.7).

If one cultivates the offices that T'ien bestows, one can take one's proper place as T'ien's agent (*M*:2A.5).

Moreover, T'ien has engendered in man the abilities that he needs to cultivate his moral dispositions and achieve Sagely understanding.

The organs of the ear and eye cannot think, but are enveloped by objects. When they, as objects, encounter objects, there is merely a force of attraction. But the organ of the mind can think. If it thinks, it can understand (*te chih*); if it does not think, it will not understand—this is what T'ien has given us (*M*:6A.15).

The ethical potential of man precisely parallels the ethical nature of T'ien.

There is a path to becoming ethically complete (*ch'eng*[a]): if one does not comprehend goodness, one cannot be ethically complete. Thus, ethical completion is the Way of T'ien; to concentrate on ethical completion is the Way of man (*M*:4A.13).

This symmetry of human potential and the nature of T'ien creates the possibility of a direct experience of T'ien as comprehensive ethical perfection.

He who exhausts his mind knows his nature (*hsing*). To know one's nature is to know T'ien (*M*:7A.1).

Thus, T'ien is both the prior source of man's potential to become a Sage and immanent in the exercise of the totalistic understanding of the Sage. This is the metaphysical model that Mencius employs as a framework for his universalization of Ruist value.

Our discussion has taken us from the role of *li* in the *Mencius* to the role of T'ien, and we have tried to explore how the web of metaphysical doctrine, of which T'ien was a part, was tied to the practical interest of defending the value of *li* and the ritual lifestyle of Ruism. Because the text of the *Mencius* is so reticent about the actual activities of Mencius' extensive study group, our discussion has necessarily been speculative. But in it we have reconciled Mencian Ruism with the mainstream practice of Ruism portrayed in chapter II, and it has yielded a portrait of the prescriptive role of T'ien in the *Mencius* closely resembling that found in the *Analects*. In both the *Analects* and the *Mencius* T'ien is the source and the supporting ground for the Ruist path to Sagehood (ethical self-cultivation through ritual study) and for the Ruist ideal of the Sagely totalism. This is the central meaning of T'ien in its prescriptive sense.

But Mencius discovered, as had Confucius, that the assurance that T'ien had prescriptively ordained his ethical values did nothing to explain the failure of his political actions. We have still to consider how Mencius used T'ien to explain the descriptive amorality of the empirical world, manifest in the failure of Ruist principles to influence society and bring an end to the chaos of the Warring States.

Mencius' Failure and the Descriptive Role of T'ien

We saw earlier, in section 2, that Mencius was prepared to subscribe to an extreme descriptivist view of T'ien in order to rationalize views of history that supported his political doctrines. In doing this, however, Mencius did not relinquish the implicit claim that T'ien, in directing history, pursued a teleological plan. On the contrary, the contorted arguments of *M*:5A.5-6 are designed to show, against all odds, that history reveals the ethical premises of T'ien's action.

Mencius had himself become, through his own ambitions, a significant actor in the history of his day. Convinced of the opportunities prophesied by numerology and manifest in the desperation of the times, Mencius risked putting Ruist political doctrines to their great test and had been willing to become a part—in name at least—of the amoral political system of the Warring States. Mencius was convinced that his personal virtue was so complete as to allow him to link, in practice, the moieties of Ruist doctrine: self-cultivation and political action. Mencius put to the test the assertion that generations of Ru had avoided testing: that a truly virtuous Ru, given the opportunities of the times, could transform the world.[69]

He failed completely. And he did not hesitate to attribute his failure to the workings of T'ien's ultimate teleological plan:

As Mencius was traveling after his departure from Ch'i, Ch'ung Yü questioned him. "Sir, you seem to be unhappy. Yet formerly I have heard you say, 'The *chün-tzu* does not complain against T'ien or blame men.' " "That was one time," Mencius replied, "this is another.[70] Every five hundred years a true King should arise, and in the interval there will be those who bring fame to their generations. Since the Chou it has now been over seven hundred years. According to calculation, the term is past, and if we judge by the times, they are ripe. It is that T'ien does not yet wish to bring peace and order to the world. If it did, in this age, who besides myself [could do so]? Why, then, should I be unhappy?" (*M*:2B.13).

The attribution of his own political failure to T'ien parallels the way the *Analects* handles the similar problem of Confucius' failure, but it seems clear that for Mencius this was a bitter pill to swallow. After all, Mencius had Confucius' example to work from, and he was not simply acting on a voluntaristic imperative: he had judged that the times were ripe, and he was wrong. He had mishandled the doctrine of timeliness, and there were those who regarded him as having acted either foolishly or inconsistently (e.g., *M*:2B.12, 6B.6). And, perhaps most important, his test of the Ruist assumption that a great Ru, given the opportunity, could transform the world had not only misfired, but had resulted in Ruism becoming entangled in the immoral rape of Yen by the armies of Ch'i (see chapter II, section 2.2). His personal failure was potentially a severe blow to the Ruist community.

But Mencius' political failure was most likely the spur that led him to develop one of the most intriguing aspects of his philosophy, the complex doctrine of the "personal decree," or *ming*.[71] This doctrine is spelled out in a number of passages in the *Mencius*, all appearing in the final *Chin-hsin* chapter. Kanaya Osamu has speculated that this chapter is probably the latest in date of all the books of the *Mencius*, and represents primarily the last teachings of Mencius in retirement (1950-51:24). If Kanaya is correct, then we are justified in taking the confinement of the doctrine of the personal decree to that chapter as indicating its late development as a response to the practical problem of rationalizing Mencius' political failure, so as to minimize that failure's detrimental effect upon both Mencius' personal stature and the stature of Ruism as a sect.

The doctrine of the personal decree represents Mencius' most sophisticated position on the ethical ambiguity of empirical society and the stance that the morally committed individual must take in light of it. By exploring this doctrine in detail, we will be able to understand more fully not only the descriptive role of T'ien in the *Mencius*, but also the occasionally dynamic interplay between that role and the prescriptive role exemplified by the *hsing* that Mencian theory entails.

The doctrines of *hsing* and *ming* represent complementary models explaining in metaphysical theory the prescriptive and descriptive action of T'ien. As we have seen, elements of the theory of the good *hsing* were initially prompted by Mencius' need to show that the existing feudal rulers of his day possessed the potential to become Sage Kings and so fulfill millennial prophecy. The theory itself became fully developed as a part of Mencius' tactical use of metaphysics and ethical epistemology to defend the ritual basis of Ruism against philosophical attacks launched by competing schools. The theory of *ming*, probably developed by Mencius after the collapse of his political mission, was designed to rationalize that defeat and to protect Ruist doctrine from the implications of his own action in putting those doctrines to a test they essentially failed.

The Personal Decree

In our discussion of Mencius' political ideas, we saw that in *M*:5A.6 he explained the notion of the Mandate of Heaven in completely descriptive terms: "What is done without anyone doing it is T'ien; what comes without anyone bestowing it is the Mandate (*ming*)." A little further on in the same chapter, we find a hint that this "*ming*" can be relevant to people who are not destined to be rulers as well as to Kings. Responding to rumors that Confucius had twice compromised his political integrity by accepting the patronage of unsavory characters in the states of Wei and Ch'i, Mencius replies:

Confucius advanced according to *li* and retired according to *yi*. As to whether or not he received employment, "That is *ming*," he said. Now to take as patrons Yung

Chü or the eunuch Chi Huan would have been to act without either *yi* or *ming* . . . . If Confucius had done so, wherein would he have been Confucius? (*M*:5A.8).

In this passage, we can discern three principles guiding action: *li, yi,* and *ming.* The first two we have already discussed; they are completely intelligible in the context of Mencian doctrine. But the use of *ming* here is unusual. When we encountered *ming* in the *Analects* it was a purely descriptive term, denoting the limits of individual ethical endeavor. The most conspicuous use of the term appears in *A*:14.36, where it is used in the same way as it is used in the first instance in the passage above. However, when Mencius goes on to say that to have acted immorally would have been to be "without *ming*," he is giving *ming* a *prescriptive* sense that is not easy to understand. In this prescriptive dimension, *ming* seems to encroach upon the province of *hsing,* confusing the neat complementary relation between the two. This prescriptive/descriptive ambiguity is crucial to the Mencian doctrine of the personal decree developed in the *Chin-hsin* chapter.

The ambiguity can be traced to the root meanings of the word "*ming.*" The most common meaning of the word is "command" or "decree" and it is used in this sense throughout early bronze inscriptions.[72] Commands have descriptive dimensions to the degree that they "must" be obeyed, but they are basically prescripts, and can be contravened. "Must" means "must—or else!" The *purely* descriptive sense of "*ming*" derives from an early and important second meaning: "lifespan." The word is occasionally used in this sense in bronze inscriptions, as well as in later texts, such as the *Analects* (e.g., *A*:6.2, 6.10).[73] It is only this latter meaning that carries the exclusively descriptive sense that allows "*ming*" to be properly translated at times as "fate."

Now, the *Mo Tzu* attacks Ruism as a "fatalistic" doctrine, and there is some basis to the charge.[74] It is difficult to ignore the deterministic implications of passages such as *A*:14.36 or *M*:5A.8 that seem to attribute the outcome of events to *ming* rather than to human effort, and also passages such as *M*:2B.13 and *M*:1B.16 that cite the descriptive action of T'ien in the same spirit. However, although Ruist texts occasionally choose the option of fatalistic rhetoric to explain Ruist political failures, systematic Ruist doctrine was not fatalistic, and the prescriptive dimension of Mencius' use of *ming* illustrates this.

Mencius' use of *ming* derives strictly from the root meaning of "command" and is governed by a political metaphor. T'ien issues decrees, as does a ruler, and man is obliged to obey them, as is a subject. That obligation is ethical and occasionally coercive; it is not, however, related to predetermined or inevitable circumstance. T'ien rules as does a human ruler. Its will shall be done, but it is a responsive will, not a predetermined one, and the effectiveness of T'ien's commands in no way removes from its subjects the responsibility to obey, nor does it follow that they will be obeying commands even if they exert no effort to do so. It is descriptively true that T'ien's commands shall be fulfilled, as is true of great earthly rulers, but obeying them is prescriptive.

The metaphor of the ruler and the subject pervades the *Mencius'* discussions of the relation between T'ien and man.

He who exhausts his mind knows his nature; to know one's nature is to know T'ien. The way to serve T'ien is to preserve the mind and nourish the nature. The way to stand [waiting] for T'ien's commands (*ming*) is this: never waver for fear of death, just cultivate your self and await them (*M:*7A.1).[75]

Everything is decreed (*ming*): obey by receiving [those commands] proper [to you]. Thus, those who know their commands do not stand beneath high walls. A man's proper command is to follow the Way to the end and die. To die in shackles [cannot be] a man's proper command (*M:* 7A.2).[76]

These passages, which open the *Chin hsin* chapter, illustrate the balance of prescriptive and descriptive implications that follow from the picture of T'ien as ruler. *M:*7A.1 begins with the purely prescriptive imperative to cultivate the good *hsing*, following the Ruist path to Sagehood. The hallmark of the Sage is the complete selfconscious development of the moral nature, which is identical to a knowledge of T'ien or the ethical order of the world.This prescriptive path leads to an understanding of how to read personal imperatives out of the course of events. T'ien, acting through people and events, is constantly issuing commands, but not all commands are directed towards any one individual. The passages picture the individual as one of many subjects of T'ien, standing in the rain of descriptive events that are T'ien's decrees, watching them for the moral opportunities that constitute his own prescriptive orders.[77]

The ruler/subject metaphor that governs the discussion of the *ming* is effective in theoretically reconciling Ruist political failure with the value of Ruist practice. By assigning to man the role of subject, this portrait reinforces his ethical obligations (study and await ethical opportunity) without demanding that those be in any way entailed with the actual outcome of events. T'ien guarantees to no one person that obedience to its orders will result in a preconceived outcome. The ethically absolute nature of T'ien merely guarantees that obeying its decrees is a moral obligation and that the course of the T'ien-guided world is, in sum, ethical. Thus, the Ruist persistence in ethical conduct in the face of political futility is fully rationalized by this model.

The interplay between prescriptive dimensions of *hsing* and *ming* forms a complex doctrinal web. The passages of the *Chin hsin* chapter that are concerned with the doctrine of the personal decree tend to contrast, explicitly or implicitly, the prescriptive notion of *hsing* (which, as man's "innate nature," would seem to be an intuitively descriptive notion) with *ming*, which Mencius endows with a substantial prescriptive component. The third passage of the chapter stresses the distinct dimensions of *hsing* and *ming*. It comments on two platitudes, the first describing the cultivation of the *hsing*, or the totalism, the second describing the quest for political influence.

"Strive for it and get it; let it go and lose it": here striving helps to get it, because what I strive for lies within me. "There is a way to strive for it; getting it lies with *ming*": here striving does not help to get it, because what I strive for lies outside of me (*M*:7A.3).[78]

Hsing is the utmost to which a man can strive, and by developing his *hsing* a man becomes fit to take on his role in the teleological course of history. But his is only the role of a single person. *Ming* represents the circumscribing limit to the practical powers of individual effort, a boundary beyond which one cannot reach.[79] Regardless of one's determination, the infinite contingencies of actual social existence restrict what any one person can achieve. *Ming* possesses a descriptive meaning here, representing the plenitude of society and history faced from the perspective of the individual. Because it appears in this way as a limit, it could be translated as "fate" or "inevitability," in that it acknowledges the inability of an individual to exercise complete control over the world he faces. But the same notion also supplies an imperative because, by being the outward bound of *hsing*, it presents the goal to be reached. It is the duty of the individual to reach it, to exhaust himself and encounter the inevitable limit that is entailed with existence as a determinate entity.

Later in the *Chin hsin* chapter we find a passage that straightforwardly addresses the ambiguities that exist in the doctrines of both *hsing* and *ming*. In it, Mencius uses the descriptive dimension of *ming* as a foil to make clear his special use of "*hsing*" (as we discussed it earlier in connection with *M*:4B.26).

The response of the mouth to flavor, of the eye to beauty, of the ear to music, of the nose to fragrance, of the body to ease: these belong to the nature. But they are inescapable (*ming*), and the *chün-tzu* does not speak of them as the nature. The response of the sense of *jen* to one's father or son, of the sense of *yi* to one's lord or minister, of the sense of *li* to one's host or guest, of the sense of *chih*ᵃ to able men, of the Sage person to the Way of T'ien: these are inescapable. But they belong to our nature, and the *chün-tzu* does not speak of them as inescapable (*M*:7B.24).

To understand this passage properly, it is useful to recall that Mencius pictures the four sprouts as responsive organs of the body, just as an eye or ear would be (*M*:2A.6). In this passage, the "moral tropism" of each of the four sprouts is described by a parallel with the spontaneous action of a sense organ.[80] The ethical comprehension of the Sage is then likened to the sensory role of the body, which integrates the various senses. Thus, the totalism, which spontaneously embraces the holistic Way of T'ien, is precisely the coordinated development of the cardinal moral dispositions of the "greater body" of each individual, as opposed to his "lesser" biological dimensions (see *M*:6A:14-15).

The overall point of *M*:7B.24 is to acknowledge that *hsing* can refer descriptively to the nature of our physical endowment, but that because we cannot ever develop this endowment beyond its primitive state, it is better classified as *ming*, in its descriptive sense.

Now, the four sprouts are as responsive and universal as the other sense organs; they, too, operate without our conscious direction, as is illustrated in *M*:2A.6 by the example of the child falling into the well. Their affective operation is innate and spontaneous, and they are in this sense a "decree" beyond our power to evade. However, rather than limiting us, these represent our opportunity to participate in life as T'ien's agents, and their development depends upon our volitionally seizing that opportunity. Thus, they are presented to us prescriptively as ethical imperatives, and Mencius labels them with the prescriptive term: "*hsing*."

The contrasting import of these prescriptive and descriptive aspects of human nature are summed up elsewhere in the epigram: "A man's looks and figure are T'ien-endowed *hsing*, but only after becoming a Sage does a man know how to move his figure" (*M*:7A.38).

We can summarize Mencius' doctrine of the personal decree in diagrammatic form:

Dimensions of *Hsing, Ming*, and T'ien in the *Mencius*

	Prescriptive Dimension	Descriptive Dimension
Hsing	Moral nature (four sprouts)	Biological nature (body, appetites)
Ming	Course of events within one's power to determine (self-cultivation; ethical opportunity)	Course of events outside one's power to determine (acts of others in T'ien's teleological plan)
T'ien	Endows moral nature in man	Ordains events according to teleological plan, not to reward the virtue of any one person

The effect of the complementary relation between *hsing* and *ming* is to maintain the ethical imperatives of self-cultivation and timely political effort for the individual, guarantee the success of personal endeavors to reach Sagehood, and account for political failures that may result in spite of that success. Although the style in which the *Mencius* achieves this result differs considerably from that of the *Analects*, which avoids involvement in metaphysical doctrines such as *hsing* and *ming* (explicitly noted in *A*:4.15 and 9.1), the structures of the doctrines involved are similar in the two texts. And the portrait of T'ien that emerges in the *Mencius* is not much different from that of the *Analects*.

In both texts, T'ien represents the source and enduring foundation of the Ruist ritual path and the Ruist Sagely totalism. In both texts, T'ien plays a descriptive role in explaining through a teleological model the ultimately ethical nature of Ruist political failures. Where the *Mencius* differs most markedly from the *Analects* is in its elaboration of largely metaphysical doctrines to represent the prescriptive and descriptive roles of T'ien, and in its attempt, in its final chapter, to describe a dynamic interaction between the two, which helps to reconcile the seeming contradictions in T'ien's relation to man.

Summary

The *Mencius* presents a portrait of T'ien very close to the "mainstream" portrait found in the *Analects* interpreted as an edited text.

T'ien's prescriptive role in the *Mencius* is to serve as a central element in a web of doctrine revolving around the notion of the good *hsing*, which represents the totalistic ideal of Sagehood in much the same way that *jen* does in the *Analects*.

Although the *Mencius* is reticent about the role of *li* in the concrete practice of Mencian Ruism, this probably reflects the polemical objectives of the text rather than a significant deviation from the general model of Ruist practice presented in chapter II. Mencius' theory of *hsing* incorporated Ruist predispositions towards ritual action as a universal category of mind. By treating *li* as an innate tendency rather than as a positive code, Mencius defended Ruist ritual practice against the criticism that it absurdly sought an absolute perfection of mind, Sagehood, through an arbitrary dynastic code. While avoiding the claim that Chou *li* constituted the path to Sagehood, Mencius' theory of *hsing* preserved an essential theoretical linkage between *li* and the ideal of Sagehood. The ritual totalism was reformulated in it as the simple realization of innate predispositions.

The voluntaristic spirit of Mencius' doctrine of the good *hsing* was modified by Mencius' personal experiences of political failure. This failure probably spurred him to elaborate a theory of T'ien's descriptive action, the theory of *ming*, or the "personal decree." The effect of this doctrine was, as in the *Analects*, to align Ruist political failure with the teleological plan of T'ien. Its impact on the Ruist community was to help protect it against the negative philosophical implications of Mencius' political failure. It identified the political impotence of the community with its future, T'ien-guided ascendance:

When T'ien intends to place great responsibility upon a person, inevitably it first steeps his will in bitterness and subjects to toil his muscle and bone, withers his skin with hunger and exhausts his person with poverty. In every action it frustrates his design, and in this way it motivates his mind, toughens his nature to endure, and so nurtures in him the abilities he lacked (*M*:6B.15).

The bitter failure of Mencius' mission was just one more test administered by T'ien to prepare the Ruist community for its destined role.

Ritual as a Natural Art
The Role of T'ien in the *Hsun Tzu*

Chapter VI

U nlike the *Analects* and the *Mencius*, the *Hsun Tzu* includes a direct, detailed, and analytical discussion of T'ien, known as the *T'ien-lun*, or "Treatise on T'ien." this essay addresses a broad range of issues, such as whether T'ien determines events in the human sphere, responds to human action, or reveals its will in symbolic form through portents.

Modern scholars have focused on the "Treatise" to find Hsun Tzu's implicit answer to a question central to their interpretive frameworks: was T'ien, for Hsun Tzu, a god or a natural force? A consensus has emerged which characterizes Hsun Tzu's postition on T'ien by stressing that he saw T'ien not as an anthropomorphic god, but as an impersonal force of Nature (Fung 1931:355, Hou 1957:531-32; Fung 1962:498-99; Hsia 1979:45; Fu 1984:167-70), or as natural or universal law (Dubs 1927:62).

There is a great deal of truth in this consensus view, but this might have obscured the fact that it is not the whole story, nor, perhaps, even the central theme of the role of T'ien in the *Hsun Tzu*. Some recent Japanese writers have pointed out that certain spiritualist elements in the text's view of T'ien contradict the consensus view (Ikeda 1965:19-21; Itano 1968).[1] Matsuda Hiroshi, in particular, has stressed that the normative way in which T'ien is frequently spoken of in the "Treatise" and elsewhere in the *Hsun Tzu* should warn us against making an oversimplified equation between T'ien and Nature, scientifically conceived (1975).

One of the problems with the consensus view is that it implicitly assumes that the *Hsun Tzu*'s theories about T'ien reflect an abstract philosophical interest in T'ien. Scholars holding to the consensus view have tended to identify the *Hsun Tzu*'s philosophical agenda with their own. We have seen in our other two early Ruist texts that the authors of those texts did not discuss T'ien out of abstract theoretical interest, but because they were anxious to use traditional notions about T'ien to rationalize their commitment to ritual and self-ritualization. We will see that the same can be said of the authors of the *Hsun Tzu*. And, as in the other texts, an important indication that this is so is the fact that major inconsistencies are found in the way in which the text discusses T'ien, inconsistencies which appear even within the confines of the "Treatise on T'ien."

We will find in our analysis that the theory of T'ien that is the focus of the "consensus" view is only one of several implicit and explicit theories that appear in the text. These theories are in many respects mutually contradictory. They are linked, however, by a common instrumental function: all serve to legitimize ritual and ritual self-cultivation.

Broadly described, we will encounter three theories of T'ien in this chapter. The first is the theory of T'ien as nonpurposive, non-normative Nature— the theory recognized by the consensus view. This theory, which is central to the *Hsun Tzu*'s doctrine of human nature as evil, effectively maintains that that which is of ethical value to man cannot be found in the natural world, which is non-ethical, but must be sought in the world of human effort, a non-natural world, where ethical value is created. *Li* is the epitome of such value.

This first theory, which in its denial of purpose and value to T'ien as Nature seems to carry protoscientific overtones, has traditionally commanded the attention of commentators because of its intellectual sophistication. It must be understood, however, that for all its intellectual virtuosity, central features of the theory are unlikely to have been original to the text. The *Hsun Tzu*'s naturalistic view of T'ien is most likely derivative, reflecting what were probably the dominant trends of late Warring States metaphysical speculation. Similar theories appear in texts associated with various types of naturalistic philosophy, and we will see that at the time that the *Hsun Tzu* was composed, naturalism was, indeed, the dominant philosophical mode of the day. Theories of T'ien as Nature, in one form or another, were not uncommon. The distinctive achievement of the *Hsun Tzu* was to coopt this type of theory and apply it in a typically Ruist way, to reinforce the Ruist commitment to ritual.

The key function of this first theory was to respond to naturalistic philosophies, which legitimized Nature as a source of ethical value by identifying it with a primary ethical term: "*t'ien*." The *Hsun Tzu* accepted that identification, but denied to T'ien-as-Nature the ethical significance traditionally associated with the word "*t'ien*."

The second theory of T'ien differs from the first in a subtle but important way. It, too, views T'ien as Nature, but it does not seek to divest T'ien-as-Nature of ethical significance. Rather, portraying this natural T'ien as normative, it seeks to show ethical continuity between the natural realm and the primary artifact of human perfection: *li*. In this theory, man's ritual-making ability is pictured as a manifestation of a normative natural endowment possessed innately by man. *Li* is portrayed as an extension of natural patterns, and T'ien-as-Nature is presented as a prescriptive model which the Ruist Sage alone is able to emulate.

This second theory has not been generally recognized by commentators.

It takes a variety of forms in the text, the most prominent of which are a portrait of human psychology endowed with normatively described "T'ien-like" qualities, a theory of the continuity of *li*: "ritual," and *li*ª: "natural principle," and a doctrine that proclaims an ideal "trinity of heaven, earth, and man." all of these ideas appear in the "Treatise on T'ien," and we will encounter them in our analysis of that chapter. The notion of a continuity between ritual and natural principle is also linked implicitly to the *Hsun Tzu's* portrait of the world of things, which we will discuss in connection with the thematic unity of the text.

As the third component of the *Hsun Tzu's* discussions of T'ien, we will encounter in the text several instances where "*t'ien*" seems to be used as a normative term without any direct reference to Nature at all. In these instances, T'ien, as god, as ethical prescript, or as fate, is employed in conventional Ruist fashion to legitimize Ruist ritual interests.

The organization of this chapter will be as follows: First, we will explore the history and structure of the *Hsun Tzu*. Our main conclusion will be that the central portions of the text are unlikely to have been the work of a single author, and that the text is best viewed as a collective work, the product of a school of Ruism founded in the state of Ch'i by the philosopher Hsun K'uang during the third century B.C.

In "The Challenge of Naturalism," we will argue that the text should be viewed as, in large part, a sectarian response to the rise in popularity experienced during the late Chou by a wide variety of philosophies, all of which shared an interest in deriving ethical value from Nature. We will briefly summarize what we know about these various "naturalistic" schools, all of which threatened Ruism because they claimed that value must be sought in the world of Nature, rather than in cultivating "non-natural" artifacts of human culture, such as *li*. We will then go on to argue, through an examination of five of the *Hsun Tzu's* most distinctive philosophical theories, that the *Hsun Tzu's* organizing theme should be viewed as a multifaceted defense of ritual and ritual self-cultivation, a theme that its theories of T'ien are intended to echo.

Finally, we will analyze directly the function of T'ien in the text, focusing in particular on those sections of the "Treatise on T'ien" that illuminate theories of T'ien different from that recognized by the consensus view.

Our conclusion will be that although in coopting a naturalistic terminology for T'ien the *Hsun Tzu* differs from the *Analects* and *Mencius*, in terms of the instrumental meaning of "*t'ien*" there is substantial continuity with the earlier texts.

1. The Nature of the Text

The text of the *Hsun Tzu*[2] has traditionally been attributed to a Warring States Ruist named Hsun K'uang (var. Sun K'uang;[3] styled Ch'ing), who flourished during the third century B.C. We know very little about Hsun K'uang's life, and what documentation we do possess tends to be confusing and contradictory.

Hsun K'uang's birth date is the subject of much dispute, and scholars vary in their choice of date by as much as three decades.[4] His death date is likewise unknown.[5] He is said to have been a native of the state of Chao in north central China. Some time between about 305 and 285 B.C., he came to study and teach at the great Chi-hsia Academy in the state of Ch'i.[6] The academy had been founded at the capital city during the mid-fourth century B.C. by the ruler of Ch'i.[7] It offered famous thinkers large stipends and state honors in return for no services other than remaining in Ch'i and expounding their doctrines. By the early third century B.C., it numbered among its members virtually all the greatest thinkers of the time, and these men and their doctrines are frequent objects of polemical attack in the *Hsun Tzu*.

In 285 B.C., the excessive expansionism of King Min brought Ch'i into a disastrous war with neighboring states. The king was killed, Ch'i nearly dismembered, and the Chi-hsia Academy dissolved.[8] One source tells us that at about this time, Hsun K'uang traveled to the state of Ch'u.[9] Later, when the Academy was reassembled under King Hsiang (r. 283-265 B.C.), Hsun K'uang seems to have returned, eventually becoming the senior scholar at the Academy.[10]

During the reign of King Hsiang and his successor, T'ien Chien,[11] the southern regions of Ch'i suffered steady encroachment by Ch'u. Between 261 and 255 B.C., Ch'u seized those parts of Ch'i that constituted the old Ruist homeland of Lu (absorbed into Ch'i during the fourth century B.C.). The seizure was orchestrated by the great Ch'u warlord Huang Hsieh, known as Lord Ch'un-shen, and he capped his triumph in 255 B.C., by appointing Hsun K'uang, the most famous Ru of his day, magistrate of the Lu town of Lan-ling.[12] Hsun K'uang seems to have served as magistrate until 238 B.C., the year of Huang Hsieh's assassination.[13]

Hsun K'uang lived during an age of peripatetic wise men, wandering from court to court in search of sympathetic rulers. The *Hsun Tzu* does not narrate Hsun K'uang's travels, but it does contain set pieces which portray Hsun K'uang in audience with the rulers and leading statesmen of the state of Ch'in and of his home state of Chao.[14] These dialogues have generally been accepted as convincing evidence that Hsun K'uang did, in fact, travel to these states as a "persuader," and they have been employed in all attempts to construct a biographical outline for Hsun K'uang. It is entirely possible that they are actually fictionalized accounts—philosophical arguments rendered more impressive and attractive by being set in the common anecdotal format of the audience.[15] But if they are valid testimony of Hsun K'uang's travels, this would mean that he was in western China between 266 and 255 B.C. or between the death of King Hsiang of Ch'i and his own appointment at Lan-ling.[16]

What we can reconstruct of Hsun K'uang's biography potentially points us in two different directions as we approach a functional analysis of the *Hsun Tzu*. If we lay great stress upon Hsun K'uang's travels among feudal courts and on his appointment to an official position, we will tend to view the text of the *Hsun Tzu* as essays directed towards rulers with the aim of securing for Hsun K'uang and his disciples positions of governmental responsibility—as Hsun K'uang's portfolio, so to speak.

If, conversely we lay greatest stress upon Hsun K'uang's long tenure at Chi-hsia and upon his apparent success as an academic there, we will tend to view the text as a philosophical polemic, directed primarily against other Chi-hsia thinkers and their schools with the aim of rationalizing the characteristic thought and activities of Hsun K'uang and his Ruist disciples.

Obviously, the model of early Ruism presented in this book suggests the greater likelihood of the latter interpretation, and I will argue for it in the remainder of this section.

Let us turn first to the matter of Hsun K'uang's appointment at Lan-ling. The fact that Hsun K'uang appears to have occupied a post of administrative responsibility has traditionally been viewed as evidence of his politically activist orientation. How, we must ask, is his tenure at Lan-ling consistent with a portrait of Hsun K'uang as a politically withdrawn Ru master?

We must examine the circumstances of the appointment. It was made in 255 B.C., at a time when Hsun K'uang was probably between sixty and eighty-five years old.[17] He held the post for eighteen years, until at least age seventy-eight, and retired only because of the death of his patron. The implication is that the post was intended as a lifetime sinecure, and this may be taken as evidence that it was little more than an honorary position.[18] Hsun K'uang's appointment was probably designed to enhance the reputation of Huang Hsieh and pacify the populace of the conquered region of Lu. We have no evidence that Hsun K'uang pursued a political career prior to his tenure at Lan-ling.[19] The post might well have been unsought, and the linkage of the appointment to Huang Hsieh's conquests suggests that Hsun K'uang may have accepted employment under some duress. His position was, in any event, far removed from the seat of Ch'u power, where any influence on state policy might have been felt. In short,

Hsun K'uang's post at Lan-ling should not lead us to portray the man as an office seeker, or to view the philosophy of the *Hsun Tzu* as springing from the motivations of political ambition.

The portrait of the *Hsun Tzu* as an academic rather than a political text is also enhanced if we question the ascription of the text to a single author. It has long been recognized that certain portions of the text were clearly not written by Hsun K'uang. The text's earliest annotater, Yang Liang of the T'ang Dynasty, conceded that chapters 27 through 32 were not the work of Hsun K'uang alone.[20] Others have noted that portions of other, more seminal chapters, such as *Ju-hsiao* ("The Ruist Paradigm"), *Yi-ping* ("Debate on the Military"), and *Ch'iang-kuo* ("Strengthening the State"), speak of Hsun K'uang in the third person by honorific, and seem to have been written by disciples.[21] It is true that great consistency of style and thought is found throughout many of the chapters and this, taken alone, might indicate the likelihood of a single author. In particular, the *Hsun Tzu* consistently employs unusual vocabulary found rarely in other pre-Ch'in texts.[22] Yet these words are used as frequently in chapters that are clearly the work of disciples as in other chapters, hence their use throughout the text cannot prove that Hsun K'uang was author of any given part.

The hypothesis that the *Hsun Tzu* is more plausibly viewed as a collective work of "Hsun Tzu's school" than as the work of a single individual is not a new one.[23] The foremost textual analyst of the *Hsun Tzu*, Kanaya Osamu, has demonstrated that consistent arguments can be offered for both views (1951).[24] The preponderance of evidence, however, points toward collective authorship. Yet little is known about Hsun Tzu's circle of followers.

The *Hsun Tzu* is written in an impersonal style and rarely interjects narrative passages about Hsun K'uang and his disciples. The text itself seems to mention the names of only two disciples,[25] and not many more can be found through other sources.[26] We know, however, that teachers at Chi-hsia had large followings, with disciples numbering in the hundreds.[27] Given Hsun K'uang's elevated status there, he too probably attracted a considerable following.[28] The outsized influence which his works exerted during the late Chou and early Han periods—no other philosophical text was so promiscuously plagerized by later authors[29]—confirms the existence of a large body of disciples who passed along their Master's wisdom.

The connection between disciples and text is also suggested by the fact that virtually none of the chapters speak of persons or events which allow us to date them post-255 B.C., that is, after Hsun K'uang's final departure from Chi-hsia. There are exceptions,[30] but a case can easily be made for the argument that Hsun K'uang added nothing to the literature after his departure to Lan-ling, and that whatever portion of the *Hsun Tzu* he may have written before his appointment at Lan-ling was left to his disciples in Ch'i to develop and edit.[31] The text belonged to the group, not the Master.

I do not mean to argue that Hsun K'uang wrote none of the *Hsun Tzu*. I believe he may have written a great deal of it and inspired the rest. The intimacy of certain polemical passages, such as the tirade against Sung Chien in the *Cheng lun* ("Rectifying Doctrine") chapter, clearly echoes the frustrations of the jealous academician and can best be read as Hsun K'uang's own words (see Hsia 1979:26). My point is that the text as a whole should be viewed as the statement of a scholastic sect over the period of, say, 100 years, and analyzed in terms of the enduring interests of that sect, rather than in terms of any supposed political ambitions of its leader. It should be viewed as a textbook for Ruist disciples, written to instruct them in self-perfection and equip them with rhetorical weapons to fend off philosophical attack—similar, in the latter way, to the *Mencius*.

The communal Ruist background of the text is, perhaps, best glimpsed in two of its more obscure chapters: the *Ch'eng-hsiang* ("In Cadence") and *Fu* ("Conundrums") chapters, each named for and written in a popular literary form. *Ch'eng-hsiang*, which is an elegant summation of the major points of the philosophy of the *Hsun Tzu*, is written as a simple rhythmical chant.[32] "*Fu*" denoted a type of riddle form during the pre-Ch'in period, and the *Fu* chapter opens with a series of riddles, followed by brief verse sections described in the text as an "eccentric ode" (*kuei-shih*) and a "ditty" (*hsiao-ko*).

Ch'eng-hsiang can be dated post-238 B.C.[33] and seems very likely to have been written after Hsun K'uang's death. Its unique style can be explained by viewing it as a summary mnemonic for beginning students of the *Hsun Tzu* school of Ruism. It is complete with cue lines, and might have been a recitation, guided by a percussive rhythm marker. The riddles of the *Fu* chapter are clearly group games—some are quite trivial—and in them we may be reading a near-transcript of a Ruist school in "recess."[34] Read as records of group recitations and games, these chapters transmit a distant echo of the cultic nature of the *Hsun Tzu* school. their anonymous speakers serve to remind us that although we know little of Hsun K'uang's disciples and successors, their influence on the text of the *Hsun Tzu* may have been great indeed.

As we examine the *Hsun Tzu*, then, we will do best to read it as the statement of one among the many scholastic sects gathered at Chi-hsia during the third century B.C., each of them busily engaged in programs of self-cultivation and philosophical speculation, vigorously disputing among one another to earn preeminence among the academic schools, attract students from the community and beyond, and retain or increase the stipends granted them by the rulers of Ch'i—all this until the whirlwind conquests of Ch'in scattered them into isolation, each school religiously elaborating doctrine and perfecting practice in the hope of future exaltation, believing that, "disciples, if you study hard, T'ien will not forget you!" (*H*:26.32).

2. The Challenge of Naturalism

The text of the *Hsun Tzu* opens with a paradox: "Study must never cease: blue dye is procured from the indigo plant, but it is bluer than indigo" (*H*:1.1).[35] Paradox is indeed a key theme of the *Hsun Tzu*, for if any single lesson permeates the text, it is this parallel paradox: Sagehood and social perfection born of non-natural *li* are cultivated in man as a natural animal, but they are far greater than anything innately in man's nature. The central goal of the *Hsun Tzu* is to demonstrate the dynamics of this paradox, which stood in direct conflict with the dominant mode of contemporary philosophy: naturalism. This is not to say that the authors of the text had only one point on their minds. No other pre-Ch'in text outside of compendia such as the *Kuan Tzu* and *Lü-shih ch'un-ch'iu* shows as much diversity of interest and genius. Not every passage of the text is linked on the single thread of ritual self-cultivation. But the predominant ideas of the text—the evil of human nature, the social nature of man, the dynamics of scarce resources, the design of a fair society, the epistemological structure of the mind—all are facets of a central project to legitimize non-natural *li* in the face of the growing authority of Nature in the late Chou philosophies.

In the course of this section, I hope to show that this is so, and to demonstrate that the urgency of formulating the arguments that comprise the *Hsun Tzu* was created by the growth of a variety of naturalistic systems of thought during the last century of the Warring States period, all of which threatened the intellectual legitimacy of the Ruist devotion to non-natural *li*.

We shall see that the *Hsun Tzu* responded to the challenges of naturalism with three basic types of argument: First, what is biologically innate in man and materially natural in the world is insufficiently valuable to serve as an ethical standard. This argument appeals to the theory of T'ien as non-purposive and non-normative Nature. Second, the forms of ritual and social order are meta-dimensions of nature because, although they are "art," they are induced through the dynamic interactions of nature with the structure of the human mind. Third, the forms of ritual and social order are the teleological culmination of the natural cosmos, and their transforming function establishes them as extensions of Nature and as ethical standards— that is, ritual order is the "final cause" of the processes manifest in biological Nature, human action being the immediate agent of that culminating order. These last two arguments appeal to the notion that T'ien, as Nature, is normative and is manifest in the ritual organization of society.

In the section below, we will briefly survey the varieties of contemporary naturalistic philosophies that challenged the legitimacy of the Ruist school in the last century of the Chou period. The following section will then portray the main outline of the *Hsun Tzu* as a multifaceted defense of ritual practice in response to the naturalistic challenge.

2.1. Late Warring States Naturalism

The earliest philosophical schools of the Warring States period, Ruism and Mohism, sought to solve contemporary issues of value by imposing humanistic interpretive frameworks on the phenomenal world: the frameworks of aesthetic ritualism and rationalistic utilitarianism. As the Warring States era progressed, however, a range of philosophical schools arose that looked to Nature as the source of values and the starting point of philosophy. These naturalistic philosophies varied in their approaches to Nature, but all stood in contrast to Ruism (and Mohism) in the ethical primacy which they granted natural processes.

In this section, we will characterize briefly some of these diverse schools and their influences on the *Hsun Tzu*. Among those we will consider are early Taoism, "Yangist" naturalism, "Sung-Yin" or "Chi-hsia" naturalism, Tsou Yen's *yin-yang* naturalism, and "divinistic" or "shamanistic" naturalism. Some of these schools differed sharply in their notions of Nature, but they are linked in that they all looked to the natural world to find guidance for human wisdom and behavior. Our brief survey will illustrate the pervasiveness of late Warring States naturalism and the hostile philosophical climate that surrounded Ru in that period.

Early Taoism
The *Hsun Tzu* shows an awareness of both the *Chuang Tzu* (*H*:21.22: "Chuang Tzu was obsessed by T'ien and did not know man") and the *Lao Tzu* (*H*.17.51: "Lao Tzu understood recession, but did not understand assertion"), and mentions other thinkers often associated with early Taoism.[36] Many early Taoist writings survive today, and this is not the place to enter into a long discussion of their views of ethics and nature. These can be found elsewhere in abundance. For us, the salient point about early Taoist thought is that it generally employed a criterion of "naturalness" to determine value and regarded ethical distinctions of the sort central to Ruist ritualism as forced, unnatural, and of no cardinal value.[37]

The *Hsun Tzu* is heavily influenced by Taoist ideas, particularly in chapters such as *Pu kou* ("Be Not Errant") and *Chieh pi* ("Dispelling Blindness").[38] However, this influence should be viewed as a cooptation of those

aspects of Taoist quietism that easily enhanced Ruist self-cultivation practice. The *Hsun Tzu* consistently qualifies its Taoistic discussions with statements asserting the absolute necessity of traditional ritual and social codes,
which are what give Ruist value to the innate qualities of mind and body
prized by Taoists.[39]

In both its cooptation of Taoist language and ideas, and in its defensive
assertions of ritual values, the *Hsun Tzu* demonstrates the intellectual pressure which naturalistic Taoism exerted on late Chou Ruism.

"Yangism"

The *Lü-shih ch'un-ch'iu*, which according to tradition was compiled in
the state of Ch'in late in the third century B.C., includes a set of chapters
that Graham and others believe to contain the ideas of the lost philosopher
Yang Chu.[40] The first of these chapters, *Pen-sheng*, begins thus:

It is T'ien which first gives birth to it; it is man who nurtures it to fulfillment. He who
can nurture what T'ien has given birth to, without hindering it, is called "the son of
T'ien" (*LSCC*:1.6).

The "Yangist" chapters celebrate the sacred nature of the bodily self as a
natural product and place the highest value upon protection of that natural
object in its spontaneous development from youth to old age.

Needham remarks that Yangism demonstrated no interest in Nature
(1956:67-68). It is true that in the small corpus of chapters ascribed by
some to Yang Chu, there is no interest in Nature as an object for empirical
observation. The high valuation on the living body as a sacred product
of Nature, however, identifies the Yangist chapters with other late Chou
naturalisms in that value is derived from Nature, which serves as an
ethical foundation.

Furthermore, as Needham notes, the possibility exists that the thinkers
who produced the Yangist texts figured in the development of immortality
and body hygiene cults that became prominent during the Han—cults that
actively took Nature as an object of study in the belief that the ultimate
secrets of life lay within its herbs and minerals. While we lack the evidence
to demonstrate that this was so, the force of the speculative linkage is
significant, and the Yangist chapters must be included in any account of
late Chou naturalisms.

"Sung-Yin" or "Chi-hsia Materialism"

At roughly the same time as the *Lü-shih ch'un-ch'iu* was being assembled
in Western China, the compendium *Kuan Tzu* was being assembled in Ch'i,
probably at Chi-hsia.[41] Among the chapters of that work are a group that
several modern Chinese scholars have identified as the lost books of Sung

Chien and Yin Wen, two philosophers of the late fourth and early third centuries B.C.[42] The identification is much disputed.[43] However the philosophical importance of the ideas in these chapters and their apparent strong influence on the *Hsun Tzu* is not in doubt. Many key phrases in the *Kuan Tzu* chapters appear nearly verbatim in the *Hsun Tzu*, and philosophical models, such as the metaphor of the mind and body as a political hierarchy, appear in both texts.[44]

These chapters of the *Kuan Tzu* present a program of bodily self-cultivation based upon a portrait of the natural self as an extension of a cosmic order. They stress the notion that quietism, suppression of desire, and strict regulation of bodily activities such as eating can give people access to the natural spirit-force of the cosmos and control over the material world.[45]

Although the chapters, as they appear in the *Kuan Tzu* today, include passages clearly intended to reconcile this asocial quietism with Ruism,[46] the primary interest of their thought is unquestionably anathema to Ruism's ritual standpoint. Value is not located in the creative acts of human beings or the perfection of an ethical society, but in the suppression of narrow human impulses and the search for a transcendental cosmic force.[47]

The primary concern of these chapters with natural forces of the universe has led Fung Yu-lan—who doubts that they were authored by Sung Chien and Yin Wen—to place them in a larger group of *Kuan Tzu* chapters, which he describes as "Chi-hsia materialism" (1962:274).

Tsou Yen's Yin-Yang Naturalism

With the exception of Yang Chu, perhaps the most elusive of pre-Ch'in philosophers is Tsou Yen.[48] According to the *Shih-chi*, Tsou Yen was highly revered in Ch'i between the times of Mencius and Hsun K'uang, that is, c.300 B.C. (*SC*:74.2344).[49] All accounts of his thought state that he formulated a detailed cosmology, based on the interaction of *yin* and *yang* and the theory of the "five elements."[50]

If we are to believe early sources, Tsou Yen's ideas were enthusiastically received in northern China. There is, however, little explicit evidence of their influence in the *Hsun Tzu*. Tsou Yen's name is never mentioned, although a brief attack is made on a doctrine of five elements attributed to Tzu-ssu and Mencius (*H*:6.11-12). Nor is any marked interest found in the notion of *yin* and *yang*—it plays neither positive nor negative philosophical role in the text (Ikeda 1965:13).

Nevertheless, given the accounts of secondary sources, such as the *Shih-chi*, which ascribe enormous influence to Tsou Yen's ideas, it would seem inappropriate to dismiss any possible influence on the *Hsun Tzu*. The apparent popularity of Tsou Yen's ideas, even if they escaped the direct criticism of the Hsun Tzu school, would have enhanced the general appeal of naturalistic ideas during the late Chou. Moreover, the effect that Tsou Yen's philosophy had upon spiritualism, described below, would in itself constitute an influence on the *Hsun Tzu*, which so actively attacks spiritualism.

Finally, we should note the intriguing possibility that Tsou Yen was initially trained as a Ru, a notion strongly suggested by the *Shih-chi* and other sources.[51] It may be that the *Hsun Tzu*'s attack on Mencius and Tzu-ssu, mentioned above, was actually a direct attack upon Tsou Yen, a possibility if Tsou were known to have belonged at one time to a Ruist faction associated with the Mencian tradition.

"Divinistic" or "Shamanistic Naturalism"

One of the best known and most celebrated aspects of the *Hsun Tzu* is its uncompromising rejection of all forms of spiritualism, from belief in ghosts to divination on the basis of natural "portents."[52] This stance is generally consistent with the religious agnosticism expressed in the *Analects*, but the *Hsun Tzu* carries scepticism much further, even to the point of flatly denying the spiritual efficacy of those religious rituals in which Ruists specialized (*H*:17.38-39).

The strength of the *Hsun Tzu*'s scepticism should be understood in the context of the divinistic cosmologies and shamanistic cults of the time. It is well established that during the Han Dynasty, Ruists and diviners (*fang-shih*) were adversaries in the struggle for imperial recognition (*SC*:28.1398). The polemics of the *Hsun Tzu* suggest that mutual antipathy flourished during the Chou as well.

Divination and sorcery were, of course, ancient arts with a hallowed tradition. It would probably be correct to label this tradition religious, rather than philosophical. Spiritualist schools differed in intellectual tone from the other naturalistic schools discussed in this section, yet they still must be considered as a part of the late Chou flourishing of naturalism. As with other naturalisms, spiritualist schools held that man must look to the processes of biological Nature to find keys to ethical action. Although spiritualist practice might, like Ruism, focus upon rituals of song and dance and incantation, unlike Ruism, these rituals were rationalized by maintaining that their efficacy was due to an entailment in the action of natural (or supernatural) processes. Nature, not human ethical standards, was the ultimate legitimization for spiritualist doctrine and practice. In this, late Chou spiritualism was aligned with other, more philosophical naturalisms.

By late Chou times, adepts of spiritualism were able to elaborate sophisticated cosmological models to rationalize their practices. The *Tso-chuan* is our primary source for information in this regard. It contains several passages where spiritualists employ complex cosmological models to rationalize their soothsaying (e.g., Hsiang 9:14.53-57). Despite roots in superstition, spiritualist systems appear to have become credible competitors of more philosophically oriented cults, such as Ruism. For example, although the *Tso-chuan* generally holds to an antispiritualist line,[53] it sometimes seems to be coopting, rather than refuting, spiritualist cosmologies, which indicates the intellectual credibility of spiritualism during the late Chou.[54]

The sophistication of spiritualist ideology seems to have been greatly enhanced by the development of late Chou naturalisms. The *Shih-chi* provides the following account of the proliferation of Chou-Han diviner-sorcerers:

From the time of the reigns of Kings Wei and Hsuan of Ch'i (i.e., c. 300 B.C.), men like Tsou [Yen] wrote treatises about the endless revolutions of the "five virtues" (*wu te*: water, fire, wood, earth, and metal). . . . [Tsou Yen's disciples] Sung Wu-chi, Cheng-po Ch'iao, Ch'ung Shang, and Hsien-men Kao were all from Yen. They practiced the magical arts of immortality, the dissolution of the body, and the ways of ghosts and spirits. Tsou Yen explicated for rulers how *yin* and *yang* controlled the revolutions of the cosmos, but the diviners of the coasts of Yen and Ch'i transmitted his arts without understanding, and from this sprang the countless hoards who dealt only with the prodigious and bizarre (*SC*:28.1368-69).[55]

This account points to early linkages between Tsou Yen's style of cosmological naturalism, portent divination, and the rise of immortality cults, so prevalent during the Han.[56]

These linkages suggest that in attacking crude spiritualism the *Hsun Tzu* might have been, in part, attacking more sophisticated philosophical views that looked to analyses of natural or cosmic forces for ethical guidance. In the same way that Taoist obsession with the spontaneous naturalness or trancendental greatness of the Tao threatened to drain all possible value from Ruist *li*, so the speculation of cosmologists like Tsou Yen and the diviner-sorcerers who used his ideas to claim esoteric transcendental knowledge threatened the ethical status of the Ruist path of Sagehood.[57]

In sum, in the intellectual environment within which Hsun K'uang and his Chi-hsia disciples lived, the most vigorous philosophical trend was clearly naturalism, whether of the subtle, paradoxical style of the *Chuang Tzu*, the protoscientific style of Tsou Yen, or the spiritualistic style of the early diviner-sorcerers. Different as they were, all these ideologies shared a conviction that human values must be founded upon the pre-human entity of Nature. What "Nature" meant for each school or philosopher varied widely. But regardless of the image in which Nature was cast, the ascription of fundamental value to it threatened to trivialize the Ruist commitment to non-natural *li*. The *Hsun Tzu* should be viewed as first and foremost a response to that threat.

3. *The Thematic Unity of the* Hsun Tzu

The proliferation of naturalistic philosophies during the fourth and third centuries B.C. left Ruism in an exposed position. A growing consensus held that man's only hope of enhancing the value of his life or his society lay in learning how he could fit into a logically pre-human cosmic scheme and bring its powers to bear through his actions. The philosophical strength of this sort of position was considerable, and it may well be that ritual-centered Ruism was, at this time, on the way to becoming an outmoded way of thought. If we eliminate Hsun K'uang and his followers from the history of the third century B.C., not much that is Ruist remains (although, were one to assign the *Ta-hsueh* and *Chung-yung* to this period, the picture would be somewhat changed).[58] But what the Hsun Tzu School achieved was a remodeling of Ruism's polemical armory that allowed Ruists to defend their commitment to non-natural *li* against the onslaught of naturalistic attacks.

Ruism's survival of the naturalistic heyday is an impressive achievement. Naturalism was, in many of its forms, a methodically rational and well-grounded approach to solving both metaphysical and ethical problems. It was also extremely adaptable, as its employment by schools as divergent as Legalism, Taoism, and divinistic shamanism suggests. In retrospect, the survival of the Ruist philosophical position seems extremely unlikely, and Ruism's ability to hold its own was surely due in large part to the fact that it numbered among its defenders the authors of the *Hsun Tzu*.

In this section, we will argue that the wide-ranging discussions of the *Hsun Tzu* should be understood largely as improvisations on a basic theme: the theoretical defense of *li* as a fundamental human value.[59] The task of providing a variety of sophisticated arguments demonstrating that human ritual can compete with natural processes as a basis of philosophical understanding is a unifying thread that ties together the text's many interests.[60]

The centrality of this issue can be discerned by exploring its pervasiveness in the text. The legitimation of *li* lies at the base of virtually every major theoretical achievement of the *Hsun Tzu*. Here we will discuss the relation of this interest of five realms of theory: (1) theory of the world as an object of knowledge, (2) political theory, (3) theory of human nature, (4) theory of education, and (5) teleological metaphysics. In each of these realms, the *Hsu Tzu* elaborates sophisticated and subtle theories that can be and are used to demonstrate the fundamental value of non-natural *li*.

Our goal in surveying the linkage of these doctrines is not to demonstrate that all were formulated in direct response to naturalistic thought—some were clearly elaborated to counter other schools, such as Mohism and the logicians. What our survey will show is that the text of the *Hsun Tzu* stands as a coherent whole. Its major doctrines are all intelligibly connected to the theme of philosophically grounding Ruist devotion to ritual by rationalizing the relation of human ritual forms to the forms of Nature.

3.1. The World of Things as a Taxonomy

The *Hsun Tzu* elaborates, sometimes systematically but most often indirectly, detailed theories of the structure of the world and the process of knowning.[61] So interesting are these theories that they are commonly analyzed in isolation, without consideration of how they represent the overall concerns of the text. These theories are structured to uphold the value of positive ritual forms. They are exemplary Ruist theories.

The core of the *Hsun Tzu's* portrait of the world of things is a taxonomical view of a world divided into categories, roles, and principles, based on the fundamental pivot of "samenes" (*t'ung*[a]) and "difference" (*yi*[h]). (The stress on "*t'ung*[a]" and "*yi*[h]," which for the *Hsun Tzu* signify sameness or difference of distinguishing traits rather than of existential identity, was characteristic of late Chou logical schools, such as the Mohists and logicians.)

This taxonomical portrait possesses obvious potential for legitimizing ritual forms. By sketching a picture of the world as naturally structured by categories and relationships, the text implicitly portrays Nature as an analogue of ritual. This structural congruity between the logic of nature and ritual order is essential to the explicit linkages between Natural principles and ritual *li*, detailed in the discussion of man's cosmic role, below. It is also of critical importance to the model of T'ien as the basis of a normative human psychology, which we will discuss in connection with the "Treatise on T'ien."

"What makes man man?" asks the text. "The ability to make distinctions" (*H*:5.23-24):

In the proper course (*tao*) of human life, everything is according to distinctions. Among distinctions, none are more important than role distinctions (*fen*). Among role distinctions, nothing is more important than *li* (*H*:5.28).

This notion is reflected throughout all sections of the text in the prevalent use of a taxonomic vocabulary. We hear frequently of "types" (*lei*), of "positions" or "roles" (*fen*), of "rules" (*fa*) and "principles" (*li*[a]). And the Sage, we learn, is a man who "ties together" (*t'ung*) related things, who "grasps" (*ts'ao*), "strings together" (*kuan*), "unifies" (*yi*[b]), "orders" (*li*[a]), or "classifies" (*lei*).[62]

This position is most systematically presented in the analyses of knowing in the *Cheng-ming* ("Rectification of Names") chapter, which is commonly and correctly viewed as a refutation of the methods of the School of Logicians, but whose implications are far broader.

Cheng-ming constructs a model of the proper function of language on the basis of the claim that the role of "names" (generally, substance words) is to distinguish differences in "realities" (*shih*ᵉ).⁶³ The world is pictured as a field of objects that are naturally ordered into sets on the basis of sameness (*t'ung*ᵃ) and difference (*yi*ʰ). Man is innately equipped to distinguish these two primal qualities.⁶⁴

The things of the world interact at complex levels which parallel, in ascending order, the logic of names, compound words, discursive speech, and valid argument (in the sense of expository theory). Hence, the structure of the world is reflected in the configuration of speech and of ideas expressed as doctrines.⁶⁵ "[Valid] argument is the mind creating an image of the Truth (*tao*)" (*H*:22.40).⁶⁶

When the mind accords with the *tao*, doctrine accords with the mind, and words accord with doctrine, then names are rectified and properly combined, the essences of this are understood, differences are distinguished without error, and distinctions according to type (*lei*) are extrapolated without contradictions; as one listens to [the Sage's] speech it is consistent with the pattern of things (*ho wen*) and his arguments exhaust primitive reality (*chin ku*) (*H*:22.41-42).

Note that the ideal and empirical worlds have unexpectedly mingled here: words and speech find their ultimate reference in the *tao* rather than in the natural world. This is not merely a digression in argumentation. It signals the primary function of the *Hsun Tzu*'s theory of the world. Although the text outlines this theory in passages of the *Cheng-ming* chapter where the argumentation is constrained to a value-free dimension, it applies that model and its terminology in ethical discussion. Outside the core sections of logical argument, we see a shift in focus from theories about objects and about knowing to ethics, and the vocabulary of the former dimensions is applied without modification to the latter dimension.

When we view the text as a whole, it is apparent that the terms "type" (*lei*) and "distinction" (*pien*) are used to refer less to objective entities than to situations, behavior, and value. For example, the notion of object type is adapted directly to ethical action: "That objects are manifest as particular types is due to their origins; people encounter glory or shame according to their virtue" (*H*:1.13). Situations occur in classes: "In passing legal judgment, apply law where codified laws exist, and where they do not, judge according to type" (*H*:9.13).⁶⁷

The notion of making distinctions (*pien*), which is no more than a "true" perception of natural divisions in the constitution of the world, is inextricably linked to the idea of creating proper order: "Making fair equity (*p'ing-chün*) universal, with all ordered according to their distinctions (*chih-pien*): in this the hundred kings were alike; this is the great role (*fen*) of ritual and law (*li-fa*)" (*H*:11.63, 11.99). "Duties (*fen*) divided without disorder above; talents without exhaustion below: this is the ultimate of order according to distinctions" (*H*:8.55).

This overlap between ethics and the text's ostensibly objective portrait of the world of things points to the doctrinal logic of the *Hsun Tzu*'s model of reality. The pivotal notion is that knowing is a recognition of class distinctions.[68] This is grounded in the text's portrait of a natural world constituted of qualitative categories. But its central function is to support a description of Sage wisdom as the ability to classify situations according to their ethical implications and respond properly to them: "to respond to things as they come, and distinguish the character of situations as they arise" (*H*:3.40, 21.93).

The educational and social context that fosters this skill of knowing is an environment that manifests ethical distinctions: the environment of ritual. "The *li* are the foremost components of law and the guidelines of classification according to type" (*H*:1.28-29). "*Li* is the ultimate of order according to distinction" (*H*:15.78).[69]

In describing a world sliced into pieces and roles, and a human mind that learns truth by distinguishing classes, the *Hsun Tzu* designs rationalizing theories that make its ritual ethics appear to be an analogue of Nature. By providing *li* with this structural affinity to Nature, it becomes possible to claim that ritual is an extension of Nature's organizing principles, a claim that the *Hsun Tzu* does make, and which we will explore below.

3.2. The Natural Logic of Social Forms

We noted earlier that the text of the *Hsun Tzu* opens with a paradox, and that paradox is central to the *Hsun Tzu*'s rationalization of the natural value of non-natural *li*. Nowhere is the method of argument from paradox more skillfully employed in this regard than in the *Hsun Tzu*'s portrait of ritual hierarchy as a natural law of social integration.

Two levels of paradox are involved. First, there is the counterintuitive anomoly that social differentiation is the root of social integration. "Unequal yet even, crooked yet simple to follow, disparate yet a unity: such are human relations" (*H*:4.77).[70]

Second, and more important, is the notion that human social forms are the consequence of natural laws:

When allotments are all equal there is insufficiency; when authority is divided evenly there is disunity; when the multitudes are all equal there is no direction. There is sky (*t'ien*) and there is earth, hence there is discrepency between what is above and below. . . . It is a natural rule (*t'ien shu*) that the equally eminent cannot serve one another and the equally humble cannot direct one another. . . . The former kings, loathing such disorder, fashioned ritual and propriety[71] to create distinctions [of rank] (*H*:9.15-18).

A considerable portion of the *Hsun Tzu* is devoted to political discussion; chapters eight through sixteen—about one-quarter of the total text—form a coherent subtext on Ruist political science.[72] No theme is more dominant in this subtext than the critical role of *li* in politics: "The fate of individuals rests with T'ien; the fate of states rests with *li*" (*H*:16.4).[73]

The power of the theme rests on the natural necessity of *li*. In chapter nine, *Wang chih* ("The Rule of the King"), the text portrays a "chain of being" that describes the distinguishing innate power of man as his sense of *yi*, or propriety. Consequently, man alone is able to form social groups (*ch'ün*).[74] "How is he able to form social groups? By [creating social] divisions (*fen*). How do social divisions work? Through the sense of propriety" (*H*:9.71).[75]

In chapter ten, *Fu kuo* ("Enriching the State"), the text expounds on the social powers of man by setting forth the basic dialectic that forces societies to take the shape they do. "People desire and dislike the same things: when desires are many and goods are scarce, conflict is inevitable" (*H*:10.4-5). For society to succeed, goods must be apportioned, and this is the function of social divisions. Social divisions distribute scarce resources among people without conflict, thus controlling their naturally inexhaustable desires.[76] "Human life cannot exist without social groups, but if groups lack divisions there is conflict; conflict leads to disorder, and disorder to poverty" (*H*:10.22-23). Thus, the distinguishing characteristic of man as a natural being is his need and ability to form social groups. Social divisions are a necessary condition for the realization of this ability.

The public manifestation of social division is ritual form. It is the vocabulary of social syntax. The trappings of ritual form—music, costume, decoration—perform the function of "bringing to light the patterns of *jen*" (*H*:10.26).[77] The tool that society's rulers use to elaborate ritual forms is economic surplus. The central thesis of *Fu kuo* is that investment of social resources in ritual forms creates an efficient social order capable of producing the economic surplus necessary to further perfect the ritual display of social structure.

Opposing the Mohist notion that scarce resources must be governed by an ethic of frugality, *Fu kuo* argues that the central issue is not the allocation of scarce resources but the creation of plenty (*H*:10.47-71).[78] This can be achieved through the perfection of social organization, a perfection only attainable through ritual forms. "Thrift must be governed by *li*" (*H*:10.10). The cultivation of the insignia of status—fine houses, clothes, and foods—"is not motivated by extravagance"; it is the means to creating efficient socioeconomic order (*H*:10.26,10.30). The culmination of aesthetic elaboration in the figure of the ruler—the investment of resources in his material display—is not only the duty of the ruler himself (*H*:10.60-63), but the natural desire of a populace creating abundance out of ritual order (*H*:10.32-35).

This type of theory is echoed in other chapters. The formula that appears in the *Chün tao* ("Way of the Ruler") chapter suggests a linkage to the text's taxonomic portrait of the world: "The Sage King molds surplus to bring to light distinctions (*pien-yi*)" (*H*:12.53-54).

Non-natural ritual forms, then, are consequences of a natural process: the interaction of innate desire with an empirically given scarcity of resources. They are a meta-natural phenomenon. This theory lies at the heart of the *Hsun Tzu's* political argument, and represents a virtuoso cooptation of naturalistic values in the defense of Ruist interests.[79]

3.3. The Cardinal Valuelessness of Human Nature

The *Hsun Tzu* has traditionally been best-known for its theory that human nature is innately evil, a view systematically expounded in its essay *Hsing o* ("The Evil of Human Nature"). This celebrated doctrine bears directly upon our analysis of the role of T'ien in the text. So extensive is the secondary literature on the subject, however, that I feel it is appropriate to make only a selective analysis of the doctrine here.[80] It should be borne in mind that while the discussion here reflects a dominant line of thought in the *Hsun Tzu*, important passages contradict it. The *Wang-chih* chapter's assertion that man can innately recognize propriety (*yi*) and the section in the "Treatise on T'ien" that discusses man's T'ien-like qualities, point towards an evaluatively positive view of human nature. Nevertheless, the negative assessment discussed here is more frequently encountered in the text and has been central to traditional interpretations of the *Hsun Tzu*.

The central tenet of the *Hsun Tzu's* theory of human nature (*hsing*) is that an examination of man's spontaneous behavioral dispositions reveals in them nothing of inherent ethical value.[81] That which is of ethical value in man's behavior is created through effort and artifice (*wei*) involving suppression of spontaneous dispositions.[82] These efforts, for the *Hsun Tzu*, constitute a value created in the human sphere rather than by the action of Nature.[83]

The *Hsun Tzu* concludes that man's ethical role is to escape the limits of *hsing* through effort. This position is generally and correctly regarded as a refutation of the Mencian theory of *hsing*, which holds that man's role is to develop his innate ethical potential. In *Hsing o*, Mencius is repeatedly attacked by name.

But the *Hsun Tzu's* position should also be viewed in contrast to doctrines of *hsing* found in some naturalistic texts. Naturalisms tended to value that which is untrained and spontaneous in human behavior because it most directly expresses man's character as a product of Nature. Taoist texts, for example, glorify the image of primal man as a plain or uncarved block of wood: "Be a flowing stream to the world; constant virtue unfragmented, you return to childhood. ... Be a valley to the world: constant virtue fulfilled, you return to an uncarved block" (*TTC*:28). "Together in ignorance, virtue unfragmented; together without desire: this is utter simplicity (*su-p'u*). In utter simplicity, the people fulfill their *hsing*" (*CT*:9.10-11).[84] The *Hsun Tzu* criticizes Chuang Tzu for his ethic of docile compliance with T'ien, or Nature (*H*:21.22-24). Its great stress on effort, *wei*, seems an obvious response to the *Tao te ching*'s doctrine of non-striving (*wu-wei*).[85] And it attacks philosophers identified as Taoists for "giving free license to the *hsing*" (*H*:6.2-3).[86]

When we explore naturalistic chapters in texts such as the *Kuan Tzu* and *Lü-shih ch'un-ch'iu*, a similar ethic of spontaneity often appears, even in chapters that pay lip service to Ruist-style *li*. The "Yangist" chapters of the *Lü-shih ch'un-ch'iu* place great emphasis upon "preserving" what T'ien endows: "He who nurtures what T'ien gives birth to without injuring it is called the Son of T'ien" (*LSCC*:1.4a).[87] The "Sung-Yin" chapters of the *Kuan Tzu*— despite Ruist admixtures—convey a quietist portrait of self-cultivation far closer to naturalistic than Ruist values.

Because the *Hsun Tzu* frequently denies any *a priori* ethical value to man's innate dispositions, the entire burden of endowing man with ethical understanding falls upon *a posteriori* education. "Without a teacher and without rules, the mind of man is just his mouth and belly" (*H*:4.52).[88] The ethical imperative for man is to "change what is primitive (*pien ku*)" (*H*:4.49).[89]

Human teachers, human codes, human effort—this is where value lies for human beings. It is upon this theoretical foundation that *Hsun Tzu* builds a philosophy of education that legitimizes the governing role of Ruist ritual forms.

3.4. Educating the Sage

"The program of study begins with the chanting of texts and ends with the study of *li*; its significance is that one begins by becoming a gentleman and ends by becoming a Sage" (*H*:1.26-27). No proposition was more central to legitimizing Ruist practice. An analysis of the instrumentality of Ruist doctrines would show that the vast majority of them were designed ultimately to promote and defend this notion.

The *Hsun Tzu*'s theory of human nature tells us that all ethical qualities are acquired through training. The totalistic model of Sagehood tells us that a person can be transformed into an ethically omniscient, perfect being, who, "Sitting in his room sees all the world; living in today understands distant history" (*H*:21.41-42).[90] Thus, the text has raised the stakes of education very high; it is essential that the absolute value of *li* in education be persuasively demonstrated.

The *Hsun Tzu* goes about this in various chapters and in various ways. At the theoretical base of its discussions of education lies a model of how and why learning occurs. What goes on in learning is an interaction between the motivation of a plenitude of innate material urges and man's unique ability to make distinctions through the organ of the mind. The fundamental distinctions the mind makes are judgments on whether options for action are ultimately appropriate for the purpose of gratifying spontaneous urges. "Desires do not await possibilities of fulfillment; they are received from T'ien. [Methods of] pursuit [of gratification] (*ch'iu*) follow possibilities of fulfillment; they are received from the mind (*hsin*[a])" (*H*:22.57-58).

As we saw above, if an individual develops according to his spontaneous nature, "his mind is just his mouth and belly" (*H*:4.52). This is a natural state of "narrow" (*lou*) perception. As an individual is broadened by experience guided by teachers and rules, he learns fundamental lessons of deferred gratification and quality of gratification.[91]

These are hard won lessons, learned gradually over human history and available to individuals through teachings and social culture. The accumulated teachings of the Sages of history—the *Poetry, Documents, li*, and music—these represent the distillation of human forethought, and thus can serve as guides to the world (*H*:4.66-68). They are legitimized by their origins in extensive human experience.

Although the mind possesses the power to acquire knowledge through the interaction of mind's distinction-making capacity with spontaneous motivating urges, this process is in itself insufficient. Without guidance, the distinction-making power of the mind operates randomly when faced with the plenitude of experience.

What man employs in knowing is his nature;[92] what he can know are the principles of things (*wu chih li*). If one takes the nature by which one knows and pursues knowledge of the principles of things without any limiting boundaries,[93] then one could continue to the end of the world and never be complete. To penetrate a million principles falls far short of bringing into coherence the changes of the world: it is the same as total ignorance (*H*:21.78-80).[94]

The natural world provides the mind with little or no guidance. That must be provided by the world of human society, with its long history of effort in thought.

Study is the study of limiting [the bounds of knowing].[95] Where are the limits? In greatest amplitude. What do we mean by "greatest amplitude?" Sagehood. Sagehood

is the exhaustive comprehension of relationships. And True Kingship is the fulfillment of good regulation (*chih*ᵍ) [of these]. . . . Thus in study, take the Sage Kings as
teachers and their regulations as rules. Follow their rules to penetrate their governing
categories (*t'ung-lei*) and to emulate their persons (*H*:21.81-83).

The individual begins self-improvement by mastering the distilled excel-
lence of human achievement: cultural codifications. These, and not natural
structures, are the embodiment of human value.

The Way (*tao*) of the former Kings is the exaltation of *jen*: cleave to the center in
following it. What is the center? Rites and propriety. This way is not the way of
T'ien, and not the way of the earth; it is that which man takes as the Way, it is the
Way trod by the *chün-tzu* (*H*:8.23-24).

The Ruist syllabus is the epitome of this Way:

The Sage is the Way's piper, and he sounds the Way to the world. The teachings of
the hundred Kings are one in this; hence the *Poetry* and *Documents*, *li* and music all
return to this (*H*:8.65-66).[96]

The notion of study as the delineation of the bounds of knowledge relates
to our earlier discussion of the *Hsun Tzu*'s taxonomic portrait of the world.
As we noted there, when the *Hsun Tzu* slices the world into pieces and
principles, it does so not only for objective entities but for life conceived as
situations and roles. This analogous structure between natural and ethical
worlds allows the *Hsun Tzu* to make an implicit but clear claim to the effect
that ritual *li* embody intrinsic principles of ethical existence fundamentally
equivalent to principles of natural existence, or "*li*ᵃ."[97] Ritual *li* are, in
essence, the extension of natural principles into the human sphere.
    This extension is signaled in the text in a number of ways. First, behavior
according to norm is described as "according to principle (*li*ᵃ)."[98] Second,
the aesthetic forms of ritual *li* are designated as "pattern-principles" (*wen-
li*).[99] "The apotheosis of ritual *li* is a plentitude of principles of pattern and
a scarcity of spontaneous actions" (*H*:19.38). Finally, in a linkage of man
and nature, ritual *li* are directly described as manifestations of principles of
natural existence. "Music is the manifestation of unchangeable harmonics;
ritual *li* is the manifestation of unchangeable principle" (*H*:20.33).[100]
    This brings us to the doctrine of human social forms as meta-natural
phenomena.

3.5. Man's Cosmic Role

In its theory of human nature, the *Hsun Tzu* draws a clear demarcation
between what belongs to the natural realm and what belongs to the human
realm. The phenomena of the physical world, up to and including that in

man which "cannot be studied or reformed through effort" (*H*:23.11) belong to Nature.[101] That which is created on human initiative and which requires study to master belongs to man The dichotomy of man and nature is a fundamental characteristic of reality.

But the division is in no way adversarial. The realms of nature and man form a continuum with a teleological direction. Man is Nature's complement in the creation of a perfect universe. It is in this sense that the artifice of ritual society can be viewed as an extension of natural principle.

The distinguishing characteristic of man is his ability to make distinctions (*pien*). That ability differentiates man not only from animals, but also from Nature itself: "T'ien can give birth to things; it cannot make distinctions among things (*pien wu*). ... The universe of things and the human race awaited the coming of the Sage to be assigned divisions (*fen*)" (*H*:19.78-79).

The portrait of the human component as the teleological completion of cosmic order is eloquently framed in the political essay, *Wang chih*:

Heaven and earth[102] are the source of life. Ritual and propriety are the source of order; the *chün-tzu* is the source of ritual and propriety. To practice these, penetrate their unity, multiply them, and love them to the full is the source of becoming a *chün-tzu*, and the *chün-tzu*, orders (*li*[a]) heaven and earth. The *chün-tzu*, forms a trinity with heaven and earth: he is the consummation of the world of things—the father and mother of the people. Without the *chün-tzu*, heaven and earth would be without order, ritual and propriety without coherence (*t'ung*).[103] ... [The social roles of] ruler and minister, father and son, elder and younger brother, husband and wife—which begin and end and begin again anew—these are guided by the same principles as heaven and earth, and are as eternal as the generations of the world (*H*:9.64-67).

We find, then, a level above both natural and human dimensions, a level from which the limits of both nature and man can be observed. From the perspective of that level, nature and man are linked. This is the meta-natural level of the teleological cosmos.

The *Hsun Tzu* has no systematic metaphysical model hypostatizing this cosmic integration as a transcendental realm of reality, but the text occasionally comes close to making one. For example, certain passages that speak of the Sage's ability to focus the mind and comprehend a unity behind the world's multiplicity describe this as "penetrating the spiritual (*shen-ming*) and forming a trinity with heaven and earth" (*H*:8.111, 23.68-69; cf. 25.15-16). It may be that in these and in some other instances, the terms "*shen*" or "*shen-ming*" are meant to suggest a transcendental reality.[104]

Elsewhere, we seem to catch a glimpse of a transcendental realm called the "Great Oneness" (*t'ai-yi*) (*H*:19.25-27), a notion we will discuss in our concluding chapter.

Whether or not we posit a cosmic realm beyond nature and man, the fact remains that the human sphere, characterized by artifice and ritual, is pictured in the *Hsun Tzu* simultaneously as an extension and as a transformation of the natural world, at least when the human world is governed according to Ruist prescripts. While the human sphere is a development from Nature, it is qualitatively different. Such a model represents an argument against any direct use of Nature as a value standard, and effectively legitimizes the Ruist exaltation of ritual forms.

Our survey of the most significant doctrines of the *Hsun Tzu* indicates that the diverse intellectual issues that the text addresses should be viewed in terms of an overarching unity of theoretical and practical concern. The wide-ranging discussions of the *Hsun Tzu* should be understood largely as variations on a single basic theme: the theoretical defense of *li* as a fundamental human value. That theme is, of course, closely linked to the core issue of pre-Ch'in Ruism: the preservation and promotion of the ritual-centered lifstyle of the early Ruist community. In exploring any single theory or doctrine in the *Hsun Tzu*, such as the role that T'ien plays in the text, the import of that doctrine must be expressed largely in terms of its relation to the core interest of the text: the defense of *li*.

4. The Hsun Tzu's Theories of T'ien: the "Treatise on T'ien"

We turn now to direct analysis of the role of T'ien in the *Hsun Tzu*. Because of the length and complexity of the text, it is not practical to attempt to discuss each instance in which the word "*t'ien*" occurs, as we were able to do in the cases of the *Analects* and the *Mencius*.

Our aim, then, will be this: to illustrate by a selective choice of passages in which "*t'ien*" appears that the *Hsun Tzu* embraces at least three different theories of T'ien—the three theories described in the opening section of this chapter. They are:

1. The portrait of T'ien as nonpurposive, non-normative Nature. This theory responds to naturalistic ideas by claiming that T'ien-as-Nature cannot be a source of ethical standards. Such standards must be sought in non-natural *li*.

2. A portrait of T'ien as Nature endowed with a clear, normative dimension. This theory pictures T'ien as the natural basis of the human ability to make ethical distinctions and create ritual order. It complements passages that portray *li* not as non-natural phenomena, but as extensions of the structure of T'ien-as-Nature into the human sphere. It answers the challenge of naturalism in a manner different from the

preceding theory, in that it seeks to reconcile human ritual with the pre-human forms of biological Nature which, for naturalism, must be the ultimate source of human value.

3. Usages of *"t'ien"* in senses other than Nature, which indicate the persistence in the *Hsun Tzu* of notions of T'ien as god, as fate, or as the direct basis of ritual order—notions we have encountered earlier in the *Analects* and the *Mencius*.

These theories are, to a large degree, mutually contradictory. While it is true that so complex an area of speculation as the relationship between man and nature or cosmos is always likely to generate philosophical confusions, the degree to which we can discern inconsistencies in the *Hsun Tzu*'s portrait of T'ien more likely reflects the indirect nature of the text's agenda. The *Hsun Tzu*, as with earlier Ruist texts, is not primarily concerned with the philosophical task of formulating consistent metaphysical theory. For all its discussion of T'ien, T'ien is not the point. The primary concern is the legitimation of *li*, and the instrumental significance of all instances of *"t'ien"* in the text *is* consistent, in that all serve the basic function of aiding the text in the task of legitimizing ritual forms and practice.

We have seen in earlier chapters that the word *"t'ien"* performs roughly similar functions in the *Analects* and in the *Mencius*. To overstate the case for clarity, each text employs the word prescriptively as a source of or ethical basis for the system of aesthetic ritual conduct that lay at the heart of early Ruism, and descriptively to suggest a teleological course of history that implied that the Ruist community should, for a time, be politically obscure in order that it be prepared to assume the world's burdens when the times ripened for utopian reform.

We have already encountered in the *Hsun Tzu* an entirely different use of the word *"t'ien."* This usage denotes T'ien in a sense close to "Nature," and it signifies a non-normative process of creativity in the material world. This process—this T'ien—is precisely what human beings should *not* use as a standard for measuring ethical ideas and acts. It is nonpurposive, non-teleological, purely descriptive, and, unlike the descriptive aspect of T'ien in the *Analects* and *Mencius*, devoid of ethical significance.

This is the most celebrated meaning of T'ien in the *Hsun Tzu*. It is a clear cooptation of the naturalistic schools' identification of T'ien and natural processes with the aim of denying for those processes prescriptive meaning.[105]

But this T'ien is not the only T'ien in the text. The *Hsun Tzu* uses a nonprescriptive T'ien in a negative way to legitimize ritual forms, but what is generally overlooked is that it also uses a normative T'ien in a positive way to achieve the same end. Furthermore, the teleological interpretation of T'ien's descriptive role as an historical force *does* appear in the text, albeit very rarely. The text's use of *"t'ien"* thus includes not one but several dimensions, and among these are some that are characteristic of the earlier Ruist texts.

In the sections which follow here, our primary, though not our sole source will be the "Treatise on T'ien," which is where the *Hsun Tzu* formulates its theories of T'ien with most coherence. The "Treatise" is the single most extended discussion of T'ien in early Ruist texts, and an analysis of it in its entirety would not be out of place in a study such as this. However, the "Treatise" alone contains so much material concerning T'ien that a complete exegesis in the course of the discussion here would serve only to confuse the lines of analytical argument we are pursuing. For this reason, at this point we will deal only selectively with the "Treatise," referring the reader to an annotated translation of the entire chapter, which appears as appendix C. Peripheral issues of various meanings of the word *"t'ien"* are discussed in the notes to that translation.

(Note that in the discussion which follows, references to major subsections of text within the "Treatise" are made by means of notation which appears in the appendix. Thus, when reference is made to sections A, B, etc., the precise range of the reference can be located by consulting appendix C.)

4.1. The Portrait of T'ien as Nonpurposive Nature

Beginnings tend to capture the attention, and the consensus view of the meaning of T'ien in the *Hsun Tzu* probably owes a great deal to the fact that the most forceful presentation of that theory constitutes the initial section of the "Treatise on T'ien."

The first section of the "Treatise" describes T'ien as an uncompromisingly non-normative, descriptive entity or process. It is nonpurposive, predictable within limits, and indifferent to man.

T'ien's ways are constant: it does not prevail due to Yao; it does not perish due to Chieh. Respond to it with order and good fortune follows; respond to it with disorder and ill fortune follows (*H*:17.1).

The passage continues by raising examples that may have either political or personal significance:

Bring nurturance to completion and act only when the time is ripe, and T'ien cannot sicken. Cultivate the Way without irresolution and T'ien cannot devastate (*H*:17.2).

The section brings home a central point: events in the human sphere that have ethical significance are meaningful in an evaluative sense precisely because they are the consequence of *human* action, rather than action by T'ien-as-Nature. For example, in the case of misrule and disorder:

Though the seasons revolve as they do in ordered times, disaster and devastation arise unlike in ordered times. T'ien cannot be blamed; it is a consequence of the path [chosen by man] (*H*:17.5).

The arguments of section A should be taken as a response to contemporary schools of thought that posited that political success and failure are the consequences of either long-term influences of nonpurposive natural forces or or circumstantial consequences of supernatural purpose manifest through nature.[106]

The political argument of section A is resumed in section D (*H*:17.19-22), which claims that T'ien has no influence over whether states are well or poorly ruled. Further on, in section H (*H*:17.34-6), well-crafted arguments against omenology and shamanism make a similar point concerning the lack of influence of human religious rites on events in Nature.

Throughout all of these sections (A, D, and H), T'ien is nonpurposive, descriptive, and very close to what we mean by "Nature." These passages form the heart of the *Hsun Tzu*'s celebrated naturalization of T'ien. We note them here in order to highlight by contrast very different notions of T'ien that appear in subsequent sections of the "Treatise," notions far less celebrated, but in many ways more revealing of the text's central goals.

4.2. T'ien as Prescriptive Psychology

The second section of the "Treatise" is the longest and by far the most difficult to understand. Although it is relatively free of textual corruptions, its language is at times so vague that, in one case at least, an entire article has been written to interpret a single phrase (Kodama 1972). I believe that key portions of this section have been misunderstood. As I interpret them, these passages attempt to forge a link between two species of T'ien: a descriptive naturalistic T'ien and a prescriptive metaphysical T'ien, whose action man can and should emulate or, more precisely, fulfill. The linkage is designed to legitimize ritual study and discredit empirical investigation. My belief that the *Hsun Tzu*'s view of T'ien is more complex and typically Ruist than has been previously noted rests in large part on the interpretation of section B which follows.

Section B opens with a characterization of T'ien described by its manifest works: "That which is accomplished without action, obtained without pursuit: that belongs to the office of T'ien" (*H*:17.6). Man is urged to recognize the demarcation between the realm of human action and the realm of

T'ien's action and not to attempt to interfere in the action of T'ien. This the text calls "not contesting office with T'ien" (*H*:17.7).

All of this echoes the final sentence of section A: "He who understands the distinct roles of T'ien and man may be called the perfect man," but it does not carry forward the political frame of reference that pervades the language of section A.

After an intervening passage that gives a cosmological description of the action of T'ien (and which is very likely to be a later commentary insert, see appendix C, note 10), the text returns to pick up the thread of the "office of T'ien":

With the office of T'ien settled and the work of T'ien accomplished, the physical form is intact and the spirit is born. Love, hate, pleasure, anger, grief, and joy are assembled therein: these are called the "T'ien-like dispositions" (*H*:17.10-11).

At this point, the text embarks upon a portrait of man's psychology and ethical constitution that links man's natural being with the action of T'ien. The portrait occupies the remainder of section B. It forms the core of the text's portrait of T'ien as a *normative* natural force. The distinction between the non-normative T'ien of section A and the normative T'ien of section B is the main point I want to illustrate in this discussion of the "Treatise."

It is in the description of man as a set of T'ien-like components, beginning at *H*:17.11, that the text begins to bridge the gap between non-normative T'ien and ethically perfectable man. As we read, we see T'ien gradually extend from human faculties properly regarded as value-free to ethically significant aspects of man:

The ears, eyes, nose, mouth, and body have their [realms of sensual] encounter without duplicative ability: these are called the "T'ien-like faculties." The mind dwells in the vacant center and thereby governs the five faculties: it is called the "T'ien-like ruler" (*H*:17.11-12).

We are clearly moving here toward a normative use of "*t'ien*," and this is at odds with theories found elsewhere in the *Hsun Tzu*.[107] Note that in the description of the T'ien-like dispositions above, "desire" (*yü*), a term with generally negative evaluative overtones, does not appear. This is surprising, in light of the major role which "desire" plays elsewhere in the characterization of man's innate nature.[108] Note, too, the association of T'ien with the operation of the mind, which possesses the ability to make distinctions and refine desires. Elsewhere in the text, the capabilities of the mind are assigned to the human rather than the natural sphere. While the mind is naturally innate, its *governing function* is characteristic of human training. Without training, the mind is precisely the mouth and the belly (*H*:4.52); until it learns the art of concentration it is "without discrimination" (*H*:21.46-47).[109]

Section A of the "Treatise" prepared us for a theory stressing the sharp division of T'ien and man, but here T'ien has spread rather thoroughly through man's being. With the ascription of a governing role to the T'ien-like ruling mind, the term "T'ien-like" is clearly bordering on a normative sense.

The two phrases that follow are, I believe, the most crucial to understanding this section of the "Treatise." They also present great exegetical difficulties. My interpretation differs sharply from previous commentaries and translations. Let me give it here, preceded by the translations of Chan and Watson:[110]

To plan and use what is not of one's kind to nourish one's kind—this is called "natural nourishment." To act in accord with [the principle and nature of] one's own kind means happiness, and to act contrary to [the principle and nature of] one's own kind means calamity. This is called natural government (Chan 1963:118).

Food and provisions are not of the same species as man, and yet they serve to nourish him and are called heavenly nourishment. He who accords with what is proper to his species will be blessed; he who turns against it will suffer misfortune. These are called the heavenly dictates (Watson 1963:81).

[The mind] molds things not of its species in order to nurture its species: this is called "T'ien-like nurturance." It judges (*wei*ᵃ) things which accord with their species to be fortunate and judges things which discord with their species to be ill fortuned: this is called "T'ien-like rule" (*H*:17.12-13).

The most obvious difference here is that Chan and Watson interpret the interest of the entire passage as shifting abruptly from a psychological to a social or political focus. Aside from creating a problem of lack of continuity, their interpretations pose other problems. For example, they read the text as raising a somewhat irrelevant point: that man feeds on things not of his own species. This seems hardly worth mentioning unless the passage is meant to do little other than to make a list of things that can be assigned the name "T'ien-like" or "natural." A further problem of significance arises immediately below, where misguided people are characterized as forsaking their "T'ien-like nourishment," a charge that is difficult to understand if we abide by Chan and Watson.

Moreover, both Chan and Watson (particularly Watson) fail to deal successfully with the word "*wei*ᵃ" in the second phrase. "T'ien-like rule," if we follow the text, does not mean that things will encounter good or bad fortune according to the degree to which their actions accord with their proper roles; it means that human judgment should be passed on the value of conduct according to this rule.

To deal with the issue of continuity first, continuity can be partially restored to the passage by making the "T'ien-like ruler" the grammatical subject of these phrases.[111] If we posit the mind as subject, we are at least able to suggest a formal extension of the psychological focus. But this does not eliminate other problems. The sudden political admixture remains, as does the problem of philosophical vacuity.

The solution lies in understanding the use of the terms "mold" and "nurturance" in the first phrase of the passage.

The word for "mold" is "ts'ai[a]": "riches," or "riches of nature" (cognate "ts'ai"). Commentary tradition has correctly taken this verbal usage as a loan for "ts'ai[c]": "to cut cloth," with the sense of "adapt objects for use."[112] Watson, Chan, and most other commentators, take the notion of "ts'ai wu" to refer to agriculture. This renders the current passage of little interest. In fact, "ts'ai wu" here refers us to an entirely different notion, one of great philosophical interest.

We find a notion that appears several times in the Hsun Tzu to the effect that the man who simply gratifies his spontaneous desires in the end becomes the servant of things (yi yü wu), but the Sage makes objects serve him (yi wu). This theme appears in the Hsiu shen and Cheng ming chapters (H:2.20, 22.82-88), and in each instance is associated with the notion of "nurturance" (yang). (A similar association appears in the Kuan Tzu, confirming the importance of the theme.)[113] Although the phrase "yi wu" does not appear in the specific phrases we are discussing here, it does appear soon thereafter. Toward the end of section B, we are indeed told that the outcome of fulfilling one's T'ien-like qualities is that "the things of the world will serve you (wan-wu yi)" (H:17.15). The description of "molding things" clearly seems to refer not to agriculture but to this ideal, and it denotes the exercise of human control over the world for ethical human purposes.

In several other places, the Hsun Tzu touches on the notion of molding things for nurturance, and these instances can enlighten our reading of the "Treatise." In some of these instances, the meaning of "molding things" (ts'ai wu) might be limited to the economic notion of husbandry for subsistence (e.g. H:6.18, 8.13, 9.54), and these would tend to support traditional interpretations of the phrase as used in the "Treatise." But the term is also used in a broader sense to refer to the appropriation of surplus resources to enhance the human condition through the creation of ritual social forms: "The Sage molds (ts'ai[a]) economic surplus to make distinctions manifest" (H:12.53-54). Ritual social forms, in turn, create the order necessary to increase economic productivity and further ritualize society (H:9.71-74; 10.30-31).[114] (These issues are discussed in more detail in section 3.2 above.)

As for the notion of "nurturance," this word too refers frequently to ritual cultivation, rather than agricultural subsistence, as in the doctrine that nurturance of the mind and bodily spirit *(ch'i)* is most effectively achieved through ritual study (*H*:2.18). The *Hsun Tzu* fully articulates this facet of ritual in its systematic discussion of the doctrine that *li is* nurturance per se:

> The former kings detested the [natural] chaos [of human relations], and so fashioned ritual and propriety in order to create distinctions among people, to nurture their desires, provide them their wants ... thus *li* is nurturance (*H*:19.2-3).

Here, "nurturing desires" means something close to "cultivating tastes"; that is, refining natural urges so that they find satisfactions within the measured bounds of ritual society. It does not signify the base satisfaction of desire, but rather the molding of human dispositions in order to create a more perfect social being. Thus, fine foods nurture the palate, fine perfumes nurture the sense of smell, fine carvings and patterns nurture the eye, and so forth. (*H*:19.3-5). In short, "Ritual and propriety, pattern and principle are the means by which natural dispositions are nurtured" (*H*:19.10). Nurturance, then, does not signify mere subsistence, but a process of self-transformation through cultivation of the sensual self. It is not sustenance but growth.[115]

Returning to the phrase at issue–"the mind molds things not of its species in order to nurture its species"–we may interpret it as meaning that the mind has the capacity to direct the appropriation of the things of the world in order to cultivate the innate dispositions and faculties, thereby accomplishing the improvement of the human species. This clearly normative ability, replete with ritual significance is called "T'ien-like nurturance," which is the ability of the human mind to transform the nature of the human species into an ethical object.

The passage then proceeds to describe how the human mind goes on to create value in a concrete way; it grounds ethical judgments by measuring human actions against this evolving species description. This may sound unduly sophistic, but its simple sense can be made clear by paraphrasing the entire passage: The mind appropriates the riches of the nonhuman world in order to refine the human species; it then defines propitiousness according to the degree to which individuals act in accordance with this refined species ideal.[116]

Such a portrait of human capacities, with its clear functionality in supporting ritual self-cultivation against naturalistic challenges, makes perfect sense in a text such as the *Hsun Tzu*. What is somewhat surprising is that these capacities should be called "T'ien-like," in view of the *Hsun Tzu's* restriction of the meaning of "*t'ien*" elsewhere to non-normative Nature. It is quite clear that "*t'ien*" is used here as a normative term, and the

traditional rhetorical authority of the word is being employed to bring legitimacy to a theory of the "natural" psychological origins of ritual society.
T'ien has crossed the boundary between human nature *(hsing)* and human
effort *(wei)*. It is no longer confined to the narrow limits of instinct that
man must transcend, but now plays a role in normative social capacities
that man–in a Mencian fashion–must aspire to fulfill.

We can summarize section B to this point: the operation of T'ien as Nature
creates the forms of the world, one of which is man. Man possesses innately
a set of T'ien-like organs and capacities, which includes spontaneous dispositions, sense faculties, intellect, and the power of the intellect to delineate man's species character by using the objects of the world to train and
refine his dispositions and faculties and to form ethical value judgments on
the basis of this self-created species role.

The "Treatise" goes on to link the fulfillment of these capacities to the
teleological notion of the "completion of T'ien's work":

> To darken one's T'ien-like ruler, disorder one's T'ien-like faculties, forsake one's
> T'ien-like nurturance, discord with one's T'ien-like rule, contravene one's T'ien-like
> dispositions, and so dissipate T'ien's work: this is called "greatest evil." The Sage
> clears his T'ien-like ruler, rectifies his T'ien-like faculties, fulfills his T'ien-like
> nurturance, follows his T'ien-like rule, nurtures his T'ien-like dispositions, and so
> brings completion to T'ien's work (*H*:17.13-15).

"Completing T'ien's work" echoes the homily: "Heaven and earth give birth
to it, the Sage completes it" (*H*:10.39, 27.35),[117] summarizing the cosmic
role of ritual social action described earlier in this chapter.

The final passage of section B reformulates this lesson in language that
recalls the discussion of the office of T'ien.

> Thus if one understands what he is to do and not to do, then heaven and earth will
> fulfill their proper functions and the things of the world will serve him. Acts fully
> ruled, nurturance fully realized, in life suffering no agony: this is called "knowing
> T'ien." Thus the greatest craft lies in acts not taken, the greatest wisdom in thoughts
> not pondered (*H*:17.15-16).

The passage is suggestive not only of the "Treatise's" division of the offices
of T'ien and man, but of the *Hsun Tzu*'s theory of education. Recall that for
the *Hsun Tzu*, study produces wisdom not through the random accumulation of empirical facts, but by "limiting" the vision of the student to those
lessons that are of value to man (*H*:21.78-83). The student's goal is not to
broaden his knowledge, but to "unify" it (*H*:1.43-45): to learn "linkage"
(*H*:1.46), "classification" (*H*:2.37), and "penetration" to an elevated, totalistic viewpoint (*H*:8.111, 15.57, 23.69).

According to the "Treatise," then, this limitation of vision to man's ethical missions of self-cultivation and transformation of the world is a fulfillment of all that is T'ien-like in him: it is the realization of a teleology implicit in the Nature that gives birth to man. This is the Ruist way to know T'ien, and it stands in sharp distinction to the cosmological speculations of a Tsou Yen, to the spiritualistic manipulations of a shaman or diviner, to regimens of breath control or diet, or to the Taoist ideal of nonpurposive spontaneity.

It also stands in contrast to ideas found elsewhere in the *Hsun Tzu*, for in extending what is T'ien-like in man to include his powers of ritual self-transformation, the "Treatise" resembles the *Analects* and the *Mencius* far more than some of the *Hsun Tzu*'s other essays, such as *Jung-ju* ("Glory and Shame"), *Cheng-ming*, and *Hsing o*, where the action of a non-normative T'ien-as-Nature is specifically excluded from the normative aspects of the human psyche.

We can conclude, then, that the *Hsun Tzu* displays major inconsistencies in its theories of T'ien. We encountered similar inconsistencies in the *Analects* and the *Mencius*, and once again we should read them as confirmation that the motivation giving rise to these theories was not an abstract philosophical interest in T'ien, but a need to manipulate theories of T'ien to serve more concrete Ruist interests.

4.3. Forming a Trinity with Heaven and Earth

Earlier in this chapter we discussed the *Hsun Tzu*'s theory that ritual social forms, *li*, are, at root, merely extensions of principles of nature, *li*^{a}, which govern every aspect of the cosmos. In this theory, Nature, or T'ien-as-Nature, is tied to the normative dimensions of ritual social behavior.

In the "Treatise on T'ien," there is a second dimension to the portrait of T'ien as a *normative* natural force, apart from the psychological model laid out in section B, and it relates closely to the notion of the continuity between natural principles and ritual forms.

This dimension appears in section E of the "Treatise,"[118] a section that enlarges upon a statement that appears earlier, in section A,[119] to the effect that man has the capacity to "form a trinity with heaven and earth."

The notion of the trinity is a pervasive one in the *Hsun Tzu*. The formula is explicitly stated in eight different essays (*H*:3.13-14, 8.111, 9.65, 13.46, 17.7, 23.69, 25.13, 26.6, 26.11), and triadic comparisons between heaven, earth, and the Sage appear elsewhere (e.g., *H*:1.50-51, 6.31 19.36).[120] The formula employs "heaven and earth," the equivalent of T'ien,[121] as a prescriptive model of perfection for man to match, and thus gives T'ien a normative sense, again somewhat inconsistent with statements rejecting T'ien as a source of value. The "Treatise" makes this normative dimension explicit by portraying the disinterested action of T'ien described in section A from a different perspective, one that finds moral meaning in what had seemed to be a phenomenon outside the sphere of value:

Heaven does not suspend winter because people dislike cold; earth does not contract its breadth because people dislike [traveling] great distances; the *chün-tzu* does not curtail his actions because of the clamor of petty people. Heaven has a constant way; earth has constant progressions; the *chün-tzu* has constancy of person (*H*:17.22-24).

Heaven and earth, in the sense of Nature, are prescriptive ideals that reinforce the *chün-tzu*'s assurance of the value of constant ethical action. Just what that action consists of is spelled out by a citation from a lost poem:

The *chün-tzu* takes what is constant as his way; the petty man calculates his credits. The *Poetry* says: "[Undeviating in ritual and right], why be concerned what others may say?" (*H*:17.24).[122]

Interestingly, then, Nature is being used here as a prescriptive model ensuring the value of non-natural *li*. This is the paradox of the "trinity" throughout the text; it is just where man most radically departs from Nature that he gains the power to be Nature's equal.

Although in section E, the trinity model serves to legitimize *li* only indirectly, elsewhere in the "Treatise" it is used in a slightly different way to support a claim for the value of *li*:

In heaven, nothing shines more brightly than the sun and moon; on earth, nothing shines more brightly than water and fire; among objects, nothing shines more brightly than pearl and jade; amidst humanity, nothing shines more brightly than ritual and propriety (*H*:17.40-41).

This sort of mechanistic parallelism, which brings Nature to the support of *li*, appears in other essays of the *Hsun Tzu* with somewhat more provocative metaphysical implications. For example, the *Wang chih* chapter, which draws parallels between Sage government and the action of Nature, holds that social roles exemplify the same principles that govern the patterns of heaven and earth (*H*:9.67; translated in section 3.5 above). A passage in the *Li-lun* ("Treatise on *Li*") makes a similar claim for the cosmic basis of *li* (*H*:19.26). Such passages suggest an underlying ambivalence in the *Hsun Tzu*'s stress upon the ethical dichotomy of T'ien and man.

The content of T'ien-as-Nature—its ethical valuelessness as manifest in man's innate nature—is the negative model away from which man must aspire to climb. But the grandeur and perfection of T'ien as Nature nevertheless serves as a positive model, and represents the goal of human aspiration. T'ien, like Sagehood, embraces in a totalism all worldly phenomena. The Sage, like T'ien, "embraces the universe within him" (*H*:21.43).[123] Nature is what man must transcend to become ethical, yet the greatest of goals toward which man can strive is to become Nature's equal.

4.4. T'ien as a Historical Force

The Portrait of T'ien as a normative force of the natural world is the most important theoretical departure from the theory of a non-normative T'ien-as-Nature that commentators have long represented as the sole "theory of T'ien" in the *Hsun Tzu*. The two theories—T'ien as non-normative Nature and as a normative natural force—are fundamentally contradictory, but they are consistent in that both are designed to counter the devaluation of non-natural *li* by contemporary naturalisms. The first denies the possibility of finding value in the natural sphere, the second posits an essential continuity between normative nature and normative ritual behavior.

In the following sections, we will complete our analysis of the role of T'ien in the *Hsun Tzu* by examining other meanings of T'ien in the text, in particular, meanings that apparently have little or nothing to do with Nature. We will see that scattered throughout the text are uses of *"t'ien"* in a variety of traditional, and mutually inconsistent senses. These instances will reinforce the conclusion that forging a consistent theory of T'ien was by no means a primary concern of the *Hsun Tzu*. T'ien was a malleable notion, embracing an evolving variety of possible meanings. The *Hsun Tzu*, like other Ruist texts, used the term *t'ien* in any sense consistent with its primary motive of legitimizing *li* and perpetuating the Ruist ritual community. In this section, we will examine passages in the "Treatise" and elsewhere where T'ien appears to have a descriptive sense close to the notion of "fate."

In both the *Analects* and the *Mencius*, T'ien was pictured descriptively as a teleological force of history, directing a flow of events that rationalized the contemporary political submergence of Ruism as a preparatory phase, to be ended when the times were ready for the Ruist school to grasp the reins of government and lead man toward a ritual utopia. This philosophical message was linked in both texts to the individual political failures of Confucius and Mencius, who constituted the literary foci of those texts.

The *Hsun Tzu* is a different sort of book. Hsun K'uang is by no means a focus of the text, and even when he makes an infrequent appearance, his personal history is not relevant.[124] His persona is merely a vehicle for rhetorical expression. Nor is other history of great moment to the text, except as philosophical grist: the book is profoundly ahistorical, totally free of narrative.

This formal aspect of the *Hsun Tzu* probably accounts, in large part, for the general absence of any portrait of T'ien as a descriptive historical force. Moreover, unlike the other texts, in the *Hsun Tzu* we miss the implicit audience of disciples that lies behind even the most context-free proverbs of the *Analects* and *Mencius*. Without the context of disciples, an important dimension of the need to rationalize Ruism's political failures is missing: the need to encourage disciples by assuring them of T'ien's teleological plan.

A very few chapters, such as *Ch'eng-hsiang* and *Fu*, do seem to provide such an implicit audience—though their relation to Hsun K'uang is questionable.[125] And in the latter chapter, sure enough, we do encounter the teleological T'ien of the other texts in a poignant rhyme:

> Oh dark is the world, plunged so in blindness,
> Should T'ien's light not return my cares will be boundless.
> A new start every thousand years, so goes the ancient rule;
> Disciples, study hard! T'ien will not forget you!
> The Sage clasps his hands; the time is almost come (*H*:26.31-3).

These lyrics reflect better than any text I know the political alienation of the Warring States Ru and their consequent faith in T'ien's teleological direction. But elsewhere in the text the portrait of T'ien as a historical actor is rarely glimpsed.

In section E of the "Treatise on T'ien" we encountered an injunction reminiscent of Confucius' admonitions to disciples to exemplify forbearance in the face of society's hostility to right Ruist action: "The *chün-tzu* does not curtail his actions because of the clamor of petty people." It goes on to speak of the *chün-tzu's* adoption of what is "constant" as his guide.

A similar formula appears in the *Jung-ju* chapter, and there the issue of just reward for moral action is closer to the surface:

Jen and *yi*, virtuous conduct: these are the arts of constant security; nevertheless, they do not guarantee that one will never be in danger. Deviousness, lying, violence, and thievery are the arts of constant danger; nevertheless, they do not guarantee that one will never be comfortable. Thus it is that the *chün-tzu* takes as his way what is constant (*ch'ang*) while the petty person takes as his way what is accidental (*kuai*) (*H*:4.41-42).

Thus, the *Hsun Tzu* clearly holds, with other Ruist texts, that right conduct is, in the "usual" course of things, eventually rewarded. It recognizes, however, that circumstances frequently dictate other results.

In section F of the "Treatise on T'ien" the injunction to act according to prescript despite consequent social obscurity is related to T'ien, here clearly portrayed as a historical force:

That the king of Ch'u may have a retinue of a thousand chariots does not mean that he is wise. That a *chün-tzu* may have only beans to eat and water to drink does not mean that he is stupid. These are due to the rhythms of circumstance. To be refined in purpose, rich in virtue, and clear in thought; to live in the present but be devoted to the past—these things are within one's power. The *chün-tzu* attends to what is within his power and does not aspire to that which is within the power of T'ien alone. The petty person defaults on what is within his power and aspires to that which is within the power of T'ien alone. Thus the *chün-tzu* ... goes forward day by day, and the petty person ... goes backward day by day ... (*H*:17.24-28).

T'ien here has nothing to do with Nature. It is a controlling force that determines the "rhythms of circumstance" (*chieh*) a term whose meaning is virtually indistinguishable from "*ming*": "fate." It is, in fact, defined elsewhere in the text as "*ming*" (*H*:22.6; see *HTCC*:11.28). The passage brings out the ethical gulf between Ruist prescript and T'ien-guided history in a manner closely resembling the earlier Ruist texts (*A*:14.35; *M*:7A.3).

The significance of the passage has been generally misinterpreted.[126] Once understood, it is clear that T'ien is used descriptively, but not in the sense of non-purposive Nature. In itself, the passage does not provide enough information for us to say that the *Hsun Tzu*, like the *Analects* and *Mencius*, rationalized the descriptive role of T'ien in history through a teleological model. However, if we were to take it together with the passage from *Jung-ju* cited above, which holds that good conduct generally yields material rewards in life, then we could claim that T'ien's action in controlling events in the amoral mode of the *Hsun Tzu*'s day was viewed by the *Hsun Tzu* as unusual and the unfavorable times seen as an aberration in an ethical order. If we go further and add here the millennial passage in the *Fu* chapter, we can claim a skeletal teleology that pictures the late Chou as a "last times," much as the *Mencius* does (*M*:2B.13). Although the doctrine is rarely glimpsed in the *Hsun Tzu*—which might be function of the text's chosen style of abstract and seemingly objective argumentation—instances in other chapters confirm that a teleological role for T'ien is an occasional undertone (*H*:2.44-45, 8.50-51, 27.75, 28.33-34).

4.5. Miscellaneous T'iens

For additional meanings of T'ien, we have to look outside the "Treatise on T'ien." With our analysis of section F we have encountered the last instance of a major new usage in that chapter.[127] Interestingly, T'ien is not mentioned in the Treatise after section L (*H*:17.46), and the final portion of the Treatise is largely a discussion of the value of *li*, a shift in topic that should seem intelligible in light of the close connections we have seen between the text's theories of T'ien and its interest in *li*.

As we look through the entire text of the *Hsun Tzu*, searching for instances where "*t'ien*" is employed in ways other than those predicted by the consensus view of the text, we find most frequently examples of "*t'ien*" being used in the sense of a deity. Ikeda Suetoshi has identified these passages (1965:20), and the list he has compiled includes nine such instances in seven chapters.[128] Ikeda maintains that these passages are evidence that the primary theory of T'ien in the text is a belief in T'ien as a god, but this clearly goes too far. While passages such as, "T'ien gave birth to the teeming multiudes" (*H*:4.25), and, "In *li*, one serves T'ien above and the earth below" (*H*:19.15), clearly demonstrate that the notion of T'ien as god was intelligible to the authors and readers of the *Hsun Tzu*, its use in the text is primarily rhetorical, not theoretical.

A somewhat more intriguing usage of *t'ien*, appears in the *Ta lüeh* ("Great Summation") chapter. Were it not that *Ta lüeh* falls on the edge of the range of chapters we are treating as the "core" of the text, I would stress this usage, as it fits into my overall theory of Ruism with great elegance.

In *Ta lüeh*, the word "*t'ien*" twice occurs in the compound "*t'ien-fu*": "the storehouse of T'ien." The "storehouse" is defined thus: "The breadth of the six arts is the storehouse of T'ien" (*H*:27.79),[129] and, "Ever studying without surfeit, unceasingly loving the [example of] gentlemen: this is the storehouse of T'ien" (*H*:27.94-95). The imagination need not roam far to see the ethical perfection of any and all traditional T'iens suffusing the syllabus and membership of the Ruist study group.

Summary

The role of T'ien in the *Hsun Tzu* differs significantly from its role in the *Analects* and *Mencius* in that a portrait of T'ien as non-normative Nature is introduced. Despite the innovation that this portrait represents for Ruism, its role has been overstressed by most commentators.

The description of T'ien as Nature was not original to the *Hsun Tzu*. Similar doctrines appear in the texts of several naturalistic schools, and some of these, the *Chuang Tzu* "Inner Chapters" for instance, clearly predate the *Hsun Tzu*. Nor is this the only dimension to T'ien in the *Hsun Tzu*. T'ien is used in a normative way to legitimize Ruist devotion to ritual. In some instances, T'ien as Nature is interpreted normatively as the source of man's ability to transform himself from a being characterized by desires to one governed by style and principle. This is the meaning of section B of the "Treatise on T'ien." In other instances, nonpurposive Nature is portrayed as an exemplar of perfection that can form a model for man's effort to achieve a distinctive perfection: the ethical perfection exemplified by ritual order. This is the doctrine of man's potential to form a trinity with heaven and earth. In a few instances, T'ien appears to play a teleological historical role, and its descriptive action is used in formulas that exhort adherence to Ruist prescript.

The overriding point about the role of T'ien in the *Hsun Tzu* is that regardless of whether T'ien is pictured as nonpurposive Nature, as a normative natural force, as fate, or as a purposive deity, its instrumental function remains always the same—to legitimize ritual forms, ritual study, and ritual society. The sense of T'ien as Nature predominates in the text because such a usage provided the most effective way to respond to the challenges to ritual presented by the ethical valuation of Nature characteristic of contemporary naturalism. T'ien-as-Nature, in itself, is *not* an object of interest to the *Hsun Tzu*, as the text makes explicit. It is *li* that is of interest, and T'ien is addressed only to the degree that contemporary theories of T'ien affect *li*.

The instrumental use of T'ien in a framework legitimizing *li* is a characteristic Ruist usage, closely resembling the role played by T'ien in the *Analects* and *Mencius*. It also integrates the *Hsun Tzu's* theories of T'ien with its other major theories: its theories of the world of things and of knowing, its political theory and its theory of education. All these areas of theory join in the text to complete a central mission: the development of a coordinated theoretical rationalization of *li*. On the basis of such an array of theories, the late Chou Ruist community could persevere in their unique ritual practices without fear that they would ever be unarmed in defending their eccentric lifestyle against philosophical attack.

Sagehood and Philosophy

Conclusion

W hen this study was begun several years ago, it was with a simple goal: to find a unity underlying multiplicity in the meanings of *"t'ien"* in early Ruist texts. In the continuities of instrumental meanings we have found in the *Analects, Mencius*, and *Hsun Tzu*, we have at least partially achieved that goal.

But in the course of the study, the notion of unity has been more consistently applicable to what might be a far more philosophically interesting aspect of early Ruism than T'ien: the ideal of Sagehood. Indeed, Sagehood was the dominant issue of early Ruism, and we have discovered in the course of this study that in many ways the meaning of T'ien was always a function of the Ruist commitment to that ideal. Consequently, in this concluding chapter, we will examine once again the ideal of Sagehood in terms of its concrete implications for Ruist thought and practice, and also in terms of our own philosophical interests, as delineated in the introduction.

We close this study, then, with a short summary analysis of early Ruist Sagehood, with the particular aim of getting beyond explicit doctrine in order to glimpse the experiential basis that led Ruists to establish this ideal and to pursue it with so deep a commitment. It is the connection between this experiential basis and the synthetic form of Ruist philosophy that ultimately constitutes the philosophical nature of Ruism and makes plausible the claim that a school that was grounded in the ascription of cardinal value to accidental patterns of social custom can be considered philosophical.

To place this analysis in perspective, we will begin with a brief overview of the main outlines of this study that have led us to this point.

A Philosophical Recap

If we were to select a single philosophical theme to summarize the significance of what we have found in this study, it would be this: skills or skill systems are central to determining meaning and truth for individuals, and the philosophical energy of Ruism was devoted to tailoring every disciple's repertoire of skills to determine how he would see meanings and truth in the world. In this sense, Ruism was quintessentially a synthetic philosophy: its methodology lay not in an eloquence of syllogistic reasoning, but in an elegance of educational design.

Fung Yu-lan once observed that Chinese philosophy, "as far as regards dialectical method and elucidation, holds a humble position when compared with the philosophies of the West or of India" (1931:8). While enthusiasts of Mohism or the early school of logicians might disagree, this statement is certainly true for early Ruism, whose texts are filled with arguments from authority, specious reasoning, and logical gaps. Ruists were, in fact, doctrinally hostile toward analytic rigor in argument; they tended to view it principally as a means of obscuring rather than elucidating truth.[1]

The rigor of Ruism did not lie in its analytic proof of philosophical claims. It lay instead in the care with which it designed a system of education that made those claims seem self-evidently true to the trained disciple. This is what a "synthetic philosophy" must do: it must organize the way in which synthetic thought is generated (see the discussion in the introduction). Its articulate doctrine merely describes insights that follow. Proof cannot lie in analysis; it must lie in duplicating the governing skill matrix.

In chapter II, we examined in some detail the Ruist syllabus that generated the skill systems governing Ruist Truth. We saw that the syllabus was varied and specific. Mohists complained that the syllabus could not be mastered in a lifetime (*MT, Fei Ju*:9.21a). Yet despite its breadth, Ruist education was unified by the central theme of self-cultivation through *li*: the ritualization of the self through progressive mastery of an ancient choreography of daily life. Once the thread of self-ritualization had been grasped, individual lessons and skills could be strung upon it. As the *Hsun Tzu* puts it, Ruist education does not lie in broadening knowledge, but in unifying it (*H*:1.44-45).

The *Hsun Tzu* also tells us that education lies in learning limits (*H*:21.81), and this has a particularly apt application to Ruist ritual education. It is easy to overlook the fact that the basis of Ruist education, *li*, consisted of rules rather than skills, while the ultimate goal of Ruist education was not knowledge of rules but skill in action. This suggests a lacuna in Ruist synthetic methodology. In theory, an unbridgeable gap exists between rules and acts. Rules are inflexible and limited: to apply a rule in action requires a secondary rule of application, and it is simple to see that this leads us to an infinite regress. In short, rules and acts are different logical species, and the gap between them cannot be bridged analytically. However, we are, in fact, able to bridge this gap in ordinary life; we do it synthetically, that is, by practice—trial and error, repeated until we are satisfied that skill has captured and transcended prescript. To apply rules in life requires not logic, but art.[2] This art is the limiting boundary of rule learning; once it is mastered, the guiding role of explicit rules becomes secondary. The *Hsun Tzu's* formula makes sense: the goal is not the learning of ever more numerous and detailed rules, it is superseding rules with the organizational unity of a skill system.

This point is central to the Ruist doctrine of the unity of knowledge and action, a notion of great importance to Ruism throughout its history. This doctrine, which claims that knowledge is not complete until it has been applied in action, implicitly recognizes that cognitive knowing and skill application are categorically distinct. One cannot possess a skill until one has applied the rules which govern it—haphazardly at first, then with increasing competence. "Study ends with application (*hsing*ᶜ). When one applies [what one has learnt], one comprehends; comprehending is Sagehood" (*H*:8.102-3).

The Mohists misunderstood Ruism to be teaching an endless set of rules, when in fact it was teaching a single art. That art was a product of the educational integration of a broad variety of skill systems: archery, textual study, music, dance, and so forth. These discrete skill matrices were linked through a framework of normative doctrine and aesthetic affect, and they were intended ultimately to generate a single all-encompassing master matrix: Sagehood. For Ruists, Sagehood born of such study was ample enough to comprehend holistically the interrelated significance of all phenomena.[3] We explored this notion briefly in chapter III, where we described it in the theory of practical totalism.

This Sagehood, which for Ruists was an ultimate breadth of vision, must seem to us a product of narrowness. It was determined by a range of skill systems which, from our cultural standpoint, was clearly limited and arbitrary. Ruists were under no illusions about the source of their ideal—they understood that it was a product of a limited set of skills. The *Hsun Tzu* explicitly celebrates this process, which it regarded as far more reliable than any abstract attempt by the mind to penetrate universal truths on its own: "Ordering the mind is not as good as choosing one's skills. . . . When the proper skills are mastered, the mind will follow them" (*H*:5.2-3).[4] Ruists understood the genetic basis of their Sagehood, but, unlike us, they saw it as a foundation of ethical breadth. For the Ru, their ritual skills were the culmination of a world of history and the acme of social and ethical perfection. If, as practical totalism implies, there can be only one species of true Sagehood, what single set of skills could be more legitimate than these with which to generate it?[5]

In sum, Ruism was a rigorous, synthetic philosophy, which aimed to cultivate in disciples a comprehension of meaning and truth born of ritual skill mastery. In our quest for the Ruist meaning of T'ien, we have had to return always to this educational source of the Ruist vision.

But to know T'ien thoroughly—to see it in ritual and to watch it change in meaning in the light of political failure and philosophical threats—to know what this changeable notion was to Ruists over the early years, we would have to master Ruist skills and become Ruists. As we have argued, Ruist Truth is not demonstrated in argument, but in a narrowly delimited educated understanding.

We cannot be Chou period Ru, so we cannot, in the end, know what they knew or what T'ien meant to them. But we can, I think, learn something more about it if we find a modern analogue for Ruist Sagehood, a model that might appeal directly to contemporary personal experience, thereby giving us greater empathy with the experiences of Ruist disciples. This is what I hope to do in the next two sections. The first will compile from the early texts a descriptive portrait of Ruist Sagehood. The second will draw on some recent studies of the psychological concomitants of the exercise of skill mastery to suggest commonalities between seminal Ruist experiences and our own.

The Elements of Sagehood

As we indicated in the introduction, the presumptions of the modern scholarly point of view lead us to be sceptical about whether Ruists ever achieved in their persons anything similar to the perfection idealized as Sagehood. Nevertheless, given the commitment to that ideal evidenced by generations of Ru, it would be cynical to maintain that this notion of ritual perfection and social omniscience was an arbitrary claim made by Ruists simply to glorify their sect and its leaders. It is reasonable to believe that the notion was not arbitrary, but merely an idealization of an attainable level of human accomplishment and reward that Ruists experienced in the course of their studies and practice.

This is essentially a question of sincerity and intellectual honesty. When, for example, we encounter a passage such as Mencius' description of the flood-like energy (*M*:2A.2), unless we are willing to argue that Mencius was a charlatan, we must believe that his Ruist self-cultivation had led him through at least one profoundly moving experience of which his statements were descriptive.

The *Hsun Tzu* contains a passage which is even more convincing on this score. It seems to describe a Ruist ritual experience we might call mystical, but to allow that the same experience can be achieved in a non-Ruist way.

All *li* begins in sparse outline, becomes complete in patterned style (*wen*), and ends in taking joy in its confines. Thus, in its most complete form, spontaneous feelings (*ch'ing*) and stylization are both fulfilled. The next best is for spontaneous feelings and styles to overcome one another in turn. And lower still, one can revert to spontaneous feelings and, even so, return to the Great Oneness (*H*:19.25-26).[6]

Now, the Great Oneness (*t'ai yi*) is described earlier in the same passage as an experience available through ceremonial action (*H*:19.21). The term itself suggests an encounter with some transcendent level of unity, but we have no further information about it, and speculation on so hazy a notion would be unproductive. What is remarkable about the passage, though, is the final phrase, which allows that the experience, whatever it may have been, could be encountered through what appears to be an ecstatic rather than a stylized approach; that is, it could be achieved in a non-Ruist manner. This is a doctrinally disinterested statement, and as such it is convincing evidence that this is a *sincere* description of actual experience, and not simply self-serving rhetoric cast in a mystical mode. It is strong testimony, which lends credence to a wealth of textual descriptions of Sagehood, all of which may hence be read as exaggerations or idealizations of real experiences.

If we gather some of these together, and organize them by common elements, we can arrive at a general description of the components of the root experiences of Ruist Sagehood. The description includes four major elements: (1) focus of concentration; (2) integration of phenomena; (3) a sense of total control; and (4) feelings of freedom and joy.

Focus of Concentration

In the *Analects*, Confucius says that a *chün-tzu* never for an instant deviates from *jen*. No matter what the circumstances, his task "must be here" (*A*:4.5). This idea that one must learn to focus one's attention on the task of self-perfection pervades all three of our texts, and represents both a method for becoming a Sage and a characteristic of the Sage.

Focus has two elements: it means narrowing one's vision to include only the field of ethical action, and it also means concentrating all one's attention on that field.[7] This second element becomes increasingly important as a mark of Sagehood. When Mencius talks about the proper method for cultivating the "flood-like energy," he says it comes from the accumulated practice of right action and describes that process by saying that "the matter must always be there, and the mind must never forget it nor force it" (*M*:2A.2).[8] In this way one can nurture an "unmoved mind." If the mind strays for an instant; then its proper path becomes overgrown (*M*:7B.21).[9] One must unify one's dispositions and thus focus the natural energies of the body upon one's ethical task (*M*:2A.2).[10]

In the *Hsun Tzu*, this theme is repeatedly stressed. One must focus (*yi*[b]) the mind, because "the eyes cannot look at two things and see clearly; the ears cannot listen to two things and hear clearly" (*H*:1.20-22). In every facet of self-perfection, the key is to "unify all and never be divided" (*H*:8.110-11).

Integration

The second element of Sagehood is the ability to grasp the meaning of phenomena in terms of a unified view of the world. In the *Analects*, this concept is expressed in the formula, "I link all upon a single thread," which we have already examined in chapter III.[12]

In the *Mencius*, this idea of integration is expressed in statements such as "the world of things is complete within me" (*M*:7A.4), and "he who exhausts his mind ... knows T'ien" (*M*:7A.1). This totalistic understanding is often described as an extension of ordinary ways of thinking, and a substantial technical vocabulary reflects this idea. In addition to "exhausting" (*chin*) the mind, the *Mencius* tells us to "fill out" (*ch'ung*) our innate moral inclinations (*M*:2A.6, 7B.25, 7B.31), to "extend" (*t'ui*) them (*M*:5A.7, 5B.1), to "complete" (*ta*) them (*M*:7A.15, 7A.19, 7B.31).[13] This extension is precisely equivalent to an unswerving devotion to *jen* and to right action.[14]

In the case of the *Hsun Tzu*, we have already discussed a similar technical vocabulary (chapter VI, section 3.1), within which the notion of *lei*, inference from type, plays a leading role.[15] The Sage has developed the faculty of moral inference to perfection. "He grasps what is deep by means of what is shallow, what is new by means of what is old, the many by means of the one (*H*:8.97-98; cf. 5.31-32). "He measures all by means of himself. . . . He can look upon random things and not become confused" (*H*:5.35-37).

Sense of Total Control

Because the Sage has a unified understanding of the world, he always knows what to do. This means that the Sage always responds properly to contingencies, and also that he controls events.

We have seen how, in the *Analects*, the Sage is never anxious, perplexed, or afraid. Confucius (and Yen Yuan) always understood when it was proper to serve a lord and when not to. As the *Mencius* puts it: "Confucius was the Sage of timeliness (*shih*)" (*M*:5B.1).[16]

The Sage's totalistic understanding allows him to act with far greater subtlety than the ordinary person. Having mastered the comprehensive art of ritual action, he is no longer bound by limited moral rules. Thus, Confucius perceives in a great minister's apparent cowardice a higher principle of action, and praises him as *jen* (*A*:14.16-17). And Mencius tells us that the Sage's words and actions might not conform to ordinary standards of morality (*M*:4B.11). The Sage alone can weigh and evaluate all the consequences of his acts.[17]

The *Mencius* tells us that the Sage "rights himself and the world of things is righted" (*M*:7A.19). The *Hsun Tzu* agrees: he grasps the unity of the total-ism and "all things take their proper place" (*H*:21.53). This is because the Sage "controls things," he is not "controlled by things" (*H*:2.20).

Moreover, the Sage meets every contingent circumstance with an abso-lute perfection of movement. It is worth repeating the *Hsun Tzu*'s dance-like description:

He moves along with time; he bows or arches as the times change. [Fast or slow, curled or stretched,] a thousand moves ten thousand changes: his Way is one (*H*:8.86-87).[18]

Freedom and Joy

Confucius tells us, in the *Analects*, that at age fifteen he set his heart on study, and when he was seventy, he could follow the desires of his heart and never transgress (*A*:2.4). As a master of ritual art, he had become a source of moral law, and he could confidently enjoy perfect freedom to do as he pleased. For the *Hsun Tzu*, this is the inevitable outcome of Sagehood, for having perfected the totalistic understanding, what need would there be to force or restrain oneself in order to do what is right?

The Sage gives free rein to his desires, embraces his spontaneous dispositions, and all he controls is perfectly ruled. What need to force, to restrain—what danger could there be? Thus the *jen* person walks along the Way without purposive effort (*wu wei*); the Sage walks along the Way without striving. The thoughts of *jen* people are decorous (*kung*); the thoughts of the Sage are joyful (*H*:21.66-67).

The *Hsun Tzu* even states that the Sage need not plan his action; his unpremeditated impulses not only will be moral, they will perfectly suit each contingency (*H*:5.5, 17.16).[19]

And in his state of supreme wisdom, the Sage finds tranquility and joy. In the *Analects*, both Confucius and Yen Yuan are described as men of joy, unaffected by circumstance (*A*:6.11, 7.19). Mencius, too, believed he had mastered an unswerving tranquility: an "unmoved mind" (*M*:2A.2). The *Mencius* speaks of a feeling of freedom born of loving right action, and it describes a joy so intense that all unaware, "the feet prance and the hands dance" (*M*:4A.27).

Many other aspects of Sagehood could be cited, political prowess being one. This was an aspect of Sagehood read into history, rather than contem-porary society. In the Ruist view, the Sages of the past had invented society and been its kings—they were Sages as leaders. In addition to mastering the art of responding to contingencies, they were able to transform the world.

We have limited ourselves here to nonpolitical aspects because they are descriptive of the Sage as opposed to the Sage King, and so applicable to the real experiences of late Chou Ruists, and also because I believe that taken just this far, these descriptive qualities are comprehensible as a whole and suggest believable human attributes.

The Ruist texts, unlike some Taoist texts, do not generally claim powers for the Sage that conflict with the physical limitations of man, such as the ability to fly. The Ruist ideal is still a mortal man, albeit a perfect one. Although there are probably few people in the modern West who would admit that such totalistic perfection is possible in a human being, this description of the Sage becomes recognizable to us as a persona encountered in life if we slightly alter its context. Rather than trying to apply this idealized description to a person as he lives through the varied scenes of his life, our Ruist Sage will become a plausible and entirely familiar figure, only slightly exaggerated, if we narrow the scope of his powers by comparing him to a skilled Master in the process of performing a special and limited art.

The Phenomenon of Mastery

The structure of skill performance is sometimes difficult to isolate. Virtually every act performed during the course of a lifetime can be described as the performance of skills. Actions are not, however, usually interpreted in this way; they are generally understood in instrumental context, that is, they are entailed with the events of life, and it is the consequences of an act to which we tend to pay attention, rather than the structure of the act itself. Its meaning is a function of its context.

However, we do recognize areas in which skill performance is relatively (although not completely) disengaged from life, areas such as the arts, athletics, and games. The relative noninstrumentality of these activities allows us to see more clearly attributes that characterize skill performance.

Recent studies by psychologist Mihaly Csikszentmihalyi have examined some characteristics of skill performance in these relatively noninstrumental contexts, and the descriptions that subjects give of their experiences tally well with Ruist descriptions of Sagehood. Successful performance of skills is associated with a focus of concentration upon a limited phenomenal field, facilitated by the fact that the skilled actor is completely acquainted with the limited possibilities which that field offers for his or her skill.[20] The infinite contingencies of normal experience have been narrowed: "[E]verything needed for acting in the situation is available—all the information is there, all the tools are at hand."[21] The skilled performer (pianist, fencer, skier, dancer) adopts a single, unified point of view from which all relevant particular phenomena are comprehensible in relation to the whole.[22]

The result is a totality of control experienced in no other type of activity. The master performer has a balance of "inner" skills and "outer" challenges that engenders a feeling of complete control over situations.[23] And this sense of control is confirmed by an ability to act in extraordinarily appropriate ways. Decisions seem to the actor unpremeditated, yet are unfailingly correct.[24] Within the context of mastered skill, it is possible to become a Sage.

Complementing this exercise of skill is a profound affective element, described as a calmness, or harmony, an "aliveness": we find a deep sense of joy.[25] This feeling is sometimes described as a special type of energy or a sense of "Oneness" with something greater than the self, descriptions that remind us of passages from our Ruist texts. Compare Mencius' description of the "food-like energy" with dancers' statements that when a performance is going well and concentration is complete, there is "no area where you feel blocked or stiff. Your energy is flowing very smoothly." "I am in control. I feel I can radiate an energy into the atmosphere. . . . I become one with the atmosphere." " I want to expand, hug the world."[26]

The significance of statements such as these for understanding Ruism can only be appreciated when we recall that what Ruists were perfecting during their long years of self-cultivation were precisely skills suited for this type of noninstrumental action: skills in the human arts. In the course of their study of ritual, music, and dance, Ruists more than likely encountered the very sorts of totalistic experiences described by modern artists, athletes, and others. Such experiences of complete cognitive and motor competence could have provided the model for the totalistic Ruist portrait of Sagehood.[27]

Did they? I believe they did. My feeling is that in descriptions of the psychological concomitants of skill mastery we encounter the root of early Ruist practice and its elaborating doctrine, and the generation of two millennia of Ruist history. The hypothesis is not subject to proof or, more telling, to disproof. It is merely speculation. Nevertheless, this speculation makes sense and is enlightening, and it is legitimate to accept it for what it is—a satisfying and consistent conclusion to an exploratory philosophical quest.

At the outset of this book, we suggested that the paradigmatic role of the Ruist philosopher was as a Master of dance, and our reinterpretation of early Ruism has frequently employed dance as a guiding metaphor. The metaphor has formed a linking theme on several levels.

Ruists studied dance and were dancers. The Chou ceremonial dances they practiced integrated an artistic mastery over ritual music and song, the bearing of ritual costume, and the ritual dance steps themselves. While ritual dance may not have occupied Ruists daily to the degree that other forms of ceremony did, it stood as the ultimate expression of Ruist aesthetic mastery, combining many aesthetic skills, and exemplifying the basic task of all ritual study: the choreography of ordinary existence. Its meaning was self-fulfilled, as the *Hsun Tzu* recognized:

How do we come to know the meaning of a dance? . . . Our eyes not seeing for themselves, our ears not hearing for themselves, we look down and up, we curl and stretch, we advance and retreat, we quicken and slow—in all we are strictly ruled. We exhaust the strength of muscle and bone, constraining ourselves to the converging rhythms of gong and drum without the slightest deviation—and gradually, the meaning becomes clear (*H*:20.39-40).[28]

Then, too, dance exemplifies the perfect bonding of social ritual: the ideal that Ruists prefigured in their millennial vision. As in their utopian world where the prescripts of delineated social roles would unite all individuals in a predictable, largely repetitive, but supremely rewarding web of social action, just so dance unites its members in the aesthetic satisfactions of integrating the motions of individuals in a perfect figure of social cooperation.

Finally, as an arena of noninstrumental skill, I know of no activity that more universally elicits the exultant experiences of skill mastery we have discussed in this chapter. Since beginning this study, I have encountered numerous individuals who have told me of a devotion to dance based on precisely these sorts of rewards, and I expect that they are common property of artistic and ritual dance in all societies.[29]

When we look for a Ruist meaning of T'ien, we must anticipate that meaning to be fundamentally a function of the core rewards of Ruist practice: the joy concomitant to skill mastery. Whether T'ien was invoked as part of a doctrinal structure that legitimized and defended that ritual practice, or whether it was simply revered as a projection of Ruists' devotion to their art and its rewards, the Ruists' T'ien always prefigured the sense of the world as seen by the Master of ritual choreography, the model of the Sage.

The dance of Ruism possessed self-fulfilled meaning; the meaning of T'ien must be sought in the dance.

The Origins of the Term "*T'ien*"

Appendix A

The etymological origins of the term "*t'ien*" are obscure. The earliest unambiguous instances of usage date from the early Western Chou, that is, the eleventh century B.C. This fact is central to the most popular theory concerning the origins of the term, first proposed by Herrlee G. Creel in 1937. Creel proposed that T'ien, as a term and as a deity, was a Chou innovation. An alternative to Creel's theory that relies on an attempt to demonstrate that the term "*t'ien*" appears with frequency in pre-Chou sources was proposed by Shima Kunio in 1958. Both theories are plausible, but each also involves flaws in evidence and argumentation. A complete picture would probably include elements of both theories, as well as information considered by neither.[1]

By noting here both the contents and lacunae in the models of Creel and Shima, and supplementing these earlier theories with speculations along independent lines, we can glimpse the complex history of the term "*t'ien*" that formed the background to Ruist usage.[2]

Creel's Theory of T'ien as the Chou Ancestral Kings

Creel's theory is simply stated:

This theory holds that the character T'ien is a variant form of the character *ta* [大]. *Ta* is a pictograph of a large or great man, and it no doubt had that sense originally among the Chou people as well as the Shang. But among the Chou a particular form of *ta* became specialized to refer only to the greatest men, the Kings, and especially the dead Kings, who were even more powerful. . . . Thus, T'ien came to mean the group of ancestral Kings (1970:502).[3]

This is, I think, a well-reasoned theory; however, there are problems with it. The most evident problem is one that Creel himself notes: there is practically no textual evidence to support it. But while this is unfortunate, it is also likely to be true of any theory that tries to get at root meanings of "*t'ien*." If the lack of evidence means the theory cannot be proved, it does not mean that it is not plausible: there is no textual evidence to refute it either.[4]

A more serious problem lies in Creel's assumption that the word "*ta*" meant "a large or great man." Other problems involve the fact that a graph identical to "*t'ien*" is used in the *Shang* texts in the sense of "great," and difficulties connected with Creel's suggestion of a phonetic evolution from "*ta*" to "*t'ien*." Let us consider these problems in turn.

Creel's theory relies heavily in the gloss of "*ta*" as "large or great man." But we are able to trace "*ta*" back through the oracle texts, and nowhere do we find strong evidence of such a meaning.[5] The word seems consistently to mean "big" and the fact that the oracle graph (大) appears to be *of* a big man does not necessarily mean that "*ta*" ever *denoted* a big man, any more than the graph 陟 , meaning "ascend," ever denoted two feet, one on top of the other.[6] Creel has confused two principles of character formation, the "portrait of form" (*hsiang-hsing*) with the "indication of affairs" (*chih-shih*).

Creel wishes to show that "*t'ien*" was used as a loan for "*ta*" in the sense of "great" and in this he is certainly correct; there is much evidence to bear him out (1970:497-99).[7] However, some of the implications of this work against Creel's theory. The loan relationship appears in Shang oracle texts as well as in Chou texts, and the graph used in the Shang texts (大) does not, as Creel notes, denote T'ien in the sense of a deity. What Creel is suggesting then is that for the Chou, "*ta*" evolved into "*t'ien*" in the sense of "heaven," with a graphemic (and phonetic) development accompanying the semantic one, while for the Shang, an identical graphemic development occurred independent of semantic (or phonetic?) change. This seems improbable.

A key element of Creel's theory is that the Chou ruler was called "T'ien-tzu": "the son of T'ien," which supports the notion that "*t'ien*" basically denoted the former Kings (Creel 1970:503-04). But just here is where the relationship between "*ta*" and "*t'ien*" may be critical, because "*t'ien-tzu*" may mean "great son" as easily as "son of T'ien." Evidence that it did can be found in two related Shang bronze inscriptions, the *To-ya Sheng yi* and the *Sheng ku*. The first of these inscriptions reads:

辛 巳 王 酓 多 亞 聊 亯 京 □ … 用 乍 大 子 丁 □

On hsin-ssu, the king wined the [leader of the] gravemen (?) Sheng at the sacred shrine . . . wherefore [I, Sheng] make this ?-vessel for Ta-tzu Ting (Shirakawa 1963-64:1.13).

The second reads:

大 子 聊 乍 父 丁 彝

T'ien-tzu Sheng makes this *yi*-vessel for Father Ting (Shirakawa 1963-64:1.16).

The inscriptions present problems of interpretation, but the essential fact seems to be that "*ta-tzu*" and "*t'ien-tzu*" are equivalent, with Sheng succeeding to his father's title, while his father is still referred to by that title in the earlier inscriptions.[8] This would indicate that the original meaning of *"t'ien-tzu"* was not "son of T'ien" but "great son."

Finally, Creel's assertion that the graph 大 was originally a form of *"ta"* but "came to have its own pronunciation, 't'ien,'" is puzzling (Creel 1970:502). The two words, *d'âd/ta and *t'ien/t'ien, were not very close phonetically. How Creel proposes to get from one to the other is unclear. I think it is more likely that no evolution from *d'âd to *t'ien occurred, but that we are dealing with two distinct words that shared a graphemic form and became confused through loan associations. It seems likely that the Shang graph 大 was pronounced identically with 大 as *d'âd, but that the Chou graph 大 was pronounced differently and represented a different word. In Chou texts where the graph 大 signified "great," it was probably read *t'ien, but a Shang person, construing the form as a graphemic variant, might have continued to pronounce it *d'âd.

In evaluating Creel's theory, we must conclude that his arguments are not adequate to support the claim that *"t'ien"* was a form of *"ta"* meaning "great men," and by extension "the former Kings." However, it is equally true that the *basic* idea that *"t'ien"* denoted the former Kings remains plausible and unaffected by flaws in Creel's argumentation. Building on very little evidence, Creel's theory is reasonable and remains important.

Shima's Theory of T'ien in Shang Oracle Texts

The principal attraction of the theory of *"t'ien's"* origins proposed by Shima Kunio is that, if his theory is correct, it would allow us to track the origins of T'ien through the Shang oracle texts. Shima's theory can be divided into two parts. The first part holds that the word *"t'ien"* does indeed appear in the oracle texts, represented by the graph 口, which is also used to denote the cyclical sign *tieng/ting 丁. The second part holds that this graph, when used in the sense of T'ien, was equivalent in meaning and usage to *"ti"* 帝, a term denoting the Shang high god or gods, together with the sacrifice name *"ti"* 禘 (Shima 1958:174-86).[9] Shima argues the validity of the first part of his theory by citing the second part. We will distinguish the two parts clearly here because our conclusion will be to reject the second part. while allowing the plausibility of the first.

Shima's theory is designed to cover a range of instances of the graph 口, but not all of them. The functions of the graph as a cyclical sign are completely distinct from its hypothetical function as T'ien. The first step in evaluating the theory is to delimit the corpus of texts to which it is meant to apply.[10] Once this is done, Shima identifies two functions of the graph: to denote a type of sacrifice, and to denote a deity (1958:179-80).

Shima holds that as a sacrifice name, □ is equivalent to 帝, and as a deity, □ is equivalent to 天 (1958:179-80, 184). His arguments rest on an extremely tenuous base of ambiguous "loan" relationships and tortuous reasoning. These arguments are inadequate to overcome a central difficulty, which is that the functions of these graphs are almost completely disjoined in the oracle texts. In the case of the sacrifice names, they have no sacrificial objects in common, and the styles of divination applied to the two types are completely different.[11] The differences are equally clear in the case of the two deities. The portrait of Ti conveyed by the oracle texts is of one or many high gods that actively influence a wide variety of human affairs, but that are rarely, if ever, direct objects of sacrifice (Eno 1984:53-65). Unlike Ti, the deity denoted by □ is rarely pictured as actively influencing events, and is the recipient of a wide variety of sacrifices.[12]

Despite all this, the hypothesis that the Shang graph □ represents the same word as the Chou graph 天 remains to be explored.[13]

The most persuasive evidence that □ might, indeed, have denoted the deity T'ien is that sacrifices to □ occasionally were performed on a truly impressive scale. Three inscriptions record the sacrifice of 300 human victims to □.[14] With one possible exception, I believe these are the only cases of so many human victims being offered to a single deity.[15] Apart from this, the evidence that □ denoted T'ien is largely negative; if it is once conceded that □ here does not function as a cyclical sign denoting a particular ancestor, then what deity other than T'ien could it denote? Given the size of these sacrifices, alternatives to T'ien are not easy to justify. Further, the phonetic relationship between *tieng/ting 丁 and *t'ien/ t'ien 天 is quite close; conceivably, the graph for the former was loaned to provide a graph for the latter.[16]

We find other instances of □ in the oracle texts that might provide evidence of a correspondence between that graph and "t'ien." In one divination formula, □ appears in parallel usage with Mountain and River, and the sense of these texts appears to indicate that rain prayers were made to these deities by decapitating female human victims.[17] This may suggest that □ was a nature god, which would bring it closer to "t'ien" in the sense of "sky." Another series of divinations refers to the "ting-jen" □ 人 of certain places or temples, these people all being women (S:2866).[18] In Chou bronze inscriptions, the phrases "t'ien-chün" 天 君 and "t'ien- yin" 天 尹 seem to have the meaning of "consort" in some cases; "ting- jen" might possess a related meaning here.[19]

If Shima's theory were correct, what root meanings of "t'ien" would we be able to discern? The graph □ is itself so simple as to allow almost any interpretation, and many have been suggested.[20] There might be a hint among the inscriptions where the graph seems to function as a sacrifice name.

In these inscriptions, ▫ functions parallel or subordinate to the word "*tsung*" 宗, which in these cases apparently carries the concurrent meanings of "shrine" and "shrine sacrifice."[21] Three formulas appear: (1) 宗 其 宁 : "*tsung*-sacrifice perhaps a set of beasts";[22] (2) ▫ 其 宁 : "*ting*-sacrifice . . .";[23] (3) 宗 ▫ 其 宁 : "*tsung-ting*-sacrifice. . . ."[24] "*Tsung*" seems to denote a sacrifice here by virtue of being the place where the ritual is performed. If we take "*ting*" as parallel, it, too, would represent a ritual place, but because it is also subordinate to "*tsung*" we would expect it to represent a ritual area within the *tsung*-shrine.[25] If we allow that the graph might not be a loan graph, then we may go further and suggest a square shaped ritual place.

Turning to other members of the graphemic family to which *tieng/ting 丁 belongs, we can, in fact, find a certain amount of support for the notion that ▫ represented a raised sacrificial altar of levelled earth. The relevant family members include: *tieng/ch'eng 成: "complete," with a secondary gloss of "level";[26] *dieng/ch'eng 城: "the [square] walls around a city"; *tiěng/cheng 正: "upright"; *tiěng/cheng 整: "even, neat"; *d'ieng/ ting 定: "settled"; *tieng/ting 頂: "the top."[27]

If it were true that ▫ represented the deity T'ien, we could argue from this evidence that the word as used in the Shang texts referred ambiguously to the sky and to the square altar upon which sacrifices to T'ien as sky-god were made and whose shape might itself have been symbolic of the sky. This essential ambiguity would be hidden in the divination texts themselves, because the language of the texts generally does not distinguish between the meanings "sacrifice to" and "sacrifice at" (Keightley 1979-80:29).

If, indeed, "*t'ien*" originally carried a meaning of "altar," then that sense of the word would appear to have died out during the Chou. But one of our earliest reliable Chou texts, the *Ho tsun* inscription, might indicate that this meaning was still available soon after the Chou conquest. That inscription contains four references to T'ien, and at least two are problematical. If we allow that the word "*t'ien*" may have ambiguously denoted a deity and an altar at once, these problems might be resolved to some degree. The four passages, translated according to this hypothesis are these:

1. 隹 王 初 鄰 宅 于 成 周 復 亩 珷 王 豐 禱 自 天

It was when the King first removed his residence to Ch'eng-Chou, carrying on anew the rites of King Wu, [he performed] *fu*-sacrifices [starting] from the *t'ien* (altar of T'ien).[28]

2. [珷 王] 廷 告 于 天

[King Wu] made a courtyard announcement at the *t'ien*.

3. 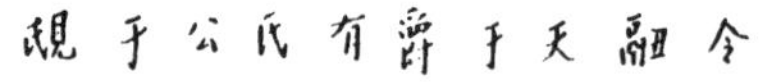

Look to [the example of] your noble clansman, who [earned the honor of] having a vessel [dedicated to him] at the *t'ien* by carrying out his duties.[29]

4. 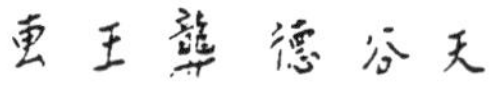

May the King's reverent virtue bathe the *t'ien*.[30]

In the first passage (1), the fact that "*t'ien*" denotes a temple location is agreed upon by most commentators.[31] Here the ellipsis of the shrine name is explained by taking the sense as implicit in the word "*t'ien*" itself. The second passage (2) exhibits the same ambiguity of "to" and "at" as we find in the oracle texts. An announcement "at the *t'ien*" would be identical to an announcement "to T'ien." In the third passage (3), the odd idea of "having rank with T'ien" is explained by sticking to the concrete imagery of the text. In the last case, the troublesome image of the King somehow being able to bathe (or cover) the sky or a sky-god with his virtue is resolved by using the concrete image of the altar.[32]

All of this provides considerable circumstantial support for the main point of Shima's thesis, that □ denoted "*t'ien*," but it falls well short of proof. Questions remain: If □ was a sky-god, why are so few indications of its power over nature found? Why is it never associated with weather phenomena? If it represented a god of such stature, why does that god appear so passive, never sending down aid or approval? Criteria for identifying which inscriptions use the graph as a cyclical sign and which as T'ien need to be developed, otherwise the argument that all instances of □ in the sense of a deity refer to *ting*-sign kings remains plausible. In other words, although Shima's theory has a great deal to offer, it remains a theory based on little evidence. One would expect that if the theory were right and these inscriptions were referring to a deity of T'ien's stature, the issue would not be in doubt.

T'ien and the Sky-Borne Dead

As a last attempt to get at the roots of T'ien, I would like to offer a hypothesis constructed largely from clues scattered through late philological sources, such as the *Shuo-wen chieh-tzu*, a work of the late Han period. Because of the late date of much of the material, this can at best be a speculative theory, but due to the great difficulty of extracting helpful information concerning T'ien from reliably early sources, I feel the attempt is justified. What we will find here are the possible traces of a tradition that pictured T'ien as the sky in the very literal sense of the direction taken by the ashes of people burnt upon a pyre. We will suggest that this might have reflected an early ritual tradition of human sacrifice, one which might have given way to more symbolic popular shamanistic rituals during the Chou.

Our starting point is the definition of "*t'ien*" found in the *Shuo-wen*. *T'ien/t'ien is defined there as *tien/tien 顛: "the top," a word to which it is phonetically related. Now, one of the reasons that the root meaning of "*t'ien*" is so difficult to trace is because the graphemic family to which the word belongs is almost devoid of other members.[33] What we are going to do here is to take the methodologically arbitrary step of associating "*t'ien*" with the graphemic family of its *Shuo-wen* definiens. We can only hope that the discoveries resulting will tend to confirm the justice of this step.

"*T'ien's*" foster family is ruled by the phonetic and semantic element *t̂ịĕn/chen 真, a word that late Chou Taoists associated with spiritual perfection and also with death.[34] The *Shuo-wen* defines the word in this way: "An immortal changing form and ascending to T'ien" (*SWCTKL*: 8A.3635-37). The "immortal" in this case is a person who is a *sịan/hsien 僊, whose cognate *ts'ịan/ch'ien 遷 is defined as "rising high" in the sense of "flying on fire" (*SWCTKL*:3A.1144a).

Let us assume that "*t'ien's*" new family is involved with the image suggested here of a person being burnt and ascending to the sky. Is there other evidence to support this? If we allow ourselves somewhat more speculative leeway than is usual, we might consider the following family members: *t̂ịĕn/ch'en 瞋: "bulging eyes"; *tien/tien 䐜: "a swelling of the belly"; *d'ien/ch'en 嗔: "filled up with breath"; *t̂ịĕn/chen 鬒: "thick (charred?) hair"; *tien/tien 顛: "toppling over" (*SWCTKL*:4A.1439b; 7B.3314b; 2A.596b; 9A.3976b; 2B.889b). These all appear applicable as descriptions of a person being burnt upon a pyre.

Consider also the family member *d̂ịĕn/shen 慎, which the *Shuo-wen* defines as "careful," going on to note that the "old script" form for the graph was 𢖻, which bronze inscriptions confirm (*CWKL*:10.344-45). This graph is also apparently a semantic element in the graph for *lịog/liao 尞, which is defined as a burnt offering to T'ien (*SWCTKL*:10A.4452b).[35]

Another graphemic family comes into the picture here, one which is phonetically close to the 真 family, members of the two families being frequently associated in loan relationships.[36] This is the family led by the word *tịən/chen 今 (also written 朁). This family includes the members *?/chen 仈: "to sprout wings and fly," and *d'ịən/t'ien 殄, which means "to exhaust" in the sense of "to die," or, as the *Lun-heng* states, it means "the equivalent of death" (*SWCTKL*:4B.1716b).[37]

All this seems to point to an association of T'ien with a ritual where people were burnt in order to send them to the sky, the home of the transformed "immortals." But was there such a ritual? We know from abundant archaeological evidence that the Shang and Chou peoples buried their dead, they did not burn them on pyres. However, indications are found that cremation was practiced by peoples to the west of the Chou polity, and this might have included the area of the ancient Chou homeland. Perhaps the echoes of such a tradition may have persisted through the Chou period.[38] It is at least true that one of the names for the death of a Chou ruler was the very term used to name the barbarian practice of cremation (*LC, Chü-li* II:1.21a).[39]

Furthermore, evidence exists that suggests shamans and witches were burnt upon pyres as a rain prayer ritual during both the Shang and the Chou.[40] Perhaps it is significant that a graph used in the oracle texts to denote this ritual was *kŏg/chiao 焚 (烄), which is defined in the *Yü-p'ien* as a burnt offering to T'ien (*Daikanwa*:7.393a). It seems more than coincidental that the grand sacrifice to T'ien during the Chou period was called *kŏg/chiao 郊, a cognate word.

Indications, then, suggest that T'ien was conceived in one tradition as the sky, in the sense of the destination of the flame-borne dead. Originally, this may have involved the act of burning people, but later the meaning must have become more a symbolic one, shamans perhaps flying toward T'ien in thought, rather than in flame. The transformation is suggested by the presence of the 真 semanteme in "old script" forms of the words "*chai*" 齋 (齋): "to purify oneself for sacrifice by fasting," and "*tao*" 禱(禱): to pray" (*SWCTKL*:1A.43-44; 1A.72-73).

Summary

Because a reliable body of evidence for tracing the earliest meanings of "*t'ien*" is lacking, efforts to isolate those meanings necessarily result in theories that are rather speculative. In this section, we have considered three such theories. H. G. Creel's theory leads us toward the image of T'ien as the rulers of the past, collectively conceived as living in heaven. Following Shima Kunio's theory, we arrived at a possible root meaning of "*t'ien*" as concurrently the sky or sky-god and the altar of that god. A third speculative theory led us to think of T'ien as the destination of the ashes of cremated sacrificial victims, a meaning of "sky" linked to the image of death by fire.

Investigations of "original meanings" generally aim at the discovery of a root referent so concrete as to explain all ambiguities of term usage as functions of later development of intellectual abstractions. It might be, however, that the deep-seated ambiguities that pervade all our research into the origins of the term "*t'ien*" indicate that varieties of referents and intellectual abstraction were characteristic of the function of the term from its beginnings. What *was* T'ien: the sky, the dead who lived there, the victims who were burnt and sent there, or an altar where they were burnt? In many ways, it makes little difference. Perhaps T'ien really "was not." Perhaps even in its most concrete sense T'ien was a vanishing point, representing the apex rather than the object of reverence. In a religious matrix, the sky, the spirits, the holy altar—any of these could have been T'ien, and all with equal rhetorical force. And at one time or another, all might have been.

A Theory of the Origins of the Term "*Ju*"

Appendix B

Oone potentially enlightening tactic for filling out our portrait of the early Ruist community would be to explore the early meanings of the term that was used to denote the group: "*ju*"儒.[1] Unfortunately, the sources of the term are obscure: its meaning and significance have been subject to long debate. It is possible to outline a theory of the origins of the term that offers strong support for the portrait of the Ruist community developed in this essay: a theory that links the term "*ju*" to traditions of dance. The theory, however, is speculative. It shares with many other explorations in Chinese philology the methodological weakness of focusing on a single thread of loan connections among words without offering a balancing scale of probability to weigh the conclusiveness of each link in the chain. Moreover, in my view at least two links of the chain I will attempt to forge below are too weak to allow the analysis to stand alone as a demonstrated hypothesis. As a result, the persuasiveness of the theory must rely in part upon the coherence of the central arguments of this book. For this reason, it is included as an appendix, rather than as a supporting argument in the main text.

The Silence of the Pre-Confucian Ru

Before turning to an etymological analysis of the term "*ju*" we must ascertain whether the term, in its Warring States usage, was applied exclusively to the followers of Confucius or had a broader range of application. The core of this question reduces to a simpler one. Was there a group of people known as "Ru" prior to the time of Confucius, or was Confucius the first Ru?

Most commentators hold that there were pre-Confucian Ru: ritual specialists at feudal courts, whose ranks were probably filled on the basis of heredity. The theory was most eloquently stated at the turn of the century by Chang Ping-lin (*CSTS, Kuo-ku lun-heng*:125-28). Chang, relying on statements from the *Chuang Tzu*, held that the original Ru had been astrologers and meteorologists, and that "*ju*" became a generic name for all types of "skilled" (*shu*術) ritualists.[2] Many scholars have followed Chang's major thesis, while differing with specifics of his argument.[3]

Chang's theory implies that at some point "Ru" denoted two types of people: the successors of the pre-Confucian Ru, court ritualists, perhaps of hereditary lineage, and Confucius' followers, who resembled the original Ru in their interest in *li*, but who were drawn from society at large, and who also subscribed to specific doctrines preached by Confucius that might not have been known to or accepted by all "original" Ru.

There is no question that theories of this nature are intuitively plausible. The main problem with them is the virtual absence of supporting evidence. To my knowledge, only one passage exists in verifiably pre-Ch'in literature that appears to use the term *"ju"* to refer to a group of men other than the followers of Confucius. That instance occurs in the *Analects* (6.13), wherein Confucius instructs his disciple Tzu-hsia to be a *"chün-tzu* Ru" rather than a "vulgar Ru." Hu Shih argued that the language of the passage proved beyond a doubt that *"ju"* was used as a generic name prior to Confucius' time (1934:5-6).

A:6.13 is good evidence to support such a claim, but it is not conclusive evidence, and it stands virtually isolated. The word *"ju"* is used only this once in the *Analects*, and it appears nowhere in pre-Confucian texts, such as oracle or bronze inscriptions, the *Poetry*, nor even in the *Documents*. In the *Mo Tzu* and the *Mencius*, the word is already employed solely as a name for Confucius' school, as it is in later works.

Perhaps the most persuasive case against the existence of pre-Confucian Ru is an argument from silence based on the evidence of the *Tso-chuan*, a Ruist text that presents a romanticized history of the centuries immediately preceding Confucius' time. Such a text might well be expected to give pre-Confucian Ru a significant role, and it seems the most likely place to turn to find an instance of the term *"ju"* applied to pre-Confucian figures. Surprisingly, the *Tso-chuan* uses the word *"ju"* just once: it appears in the compound "Ru-books' (*ju-shu* [Ai 21:30.45]), where the term is employed in direct reference to an incident involving Confucius' disciples (cf. Ai 17:30.39-40), and the word "Ru" clearly denotes them and not any pre-Confucian group.[4]

The failure of the *Tso-chuan* and other early texts to confirm the existence of pre-Confucian Ru leaves the status of *A*:6.13 very much in question. To date persuasively individual passages in the *Analects* or to evaluate their authenticity as historical accounts is notoriously difficult. But given the isolation in which *A*:6.13 stands in terms of evidence of pre-Confucian Ru, sustaining the presumption that it accurately reports words uttered during Confucius' lifetime is difficult.

In sum, groups of men professionally skilled in ceremonial practice in ways similar to Confucius and his followers unquestionably existed prior to Confucius' time: however, virtually no evidence is found to suggest that the word "*ju*" was ever used to describe them.[5] The term seems to have been an innovation originally intended to denote the new sect founded by Confucius.[6]

The Sources of the Term "Ju"

If the word "*ju*" was coined as a name for the followers of Confucius, the original meaning of the term should be of great interest in developing a portrait of that community of disciples. Currently, our understanding of the word is so shallow that the name by which the Ruist community was known adds almost nothing to our insight into the nature of the group.

Traditional Approaches

The starting point for all etymological work in ancient Chinese is the *Shuo-wen chieh-tzu*, a dictionary compiled by the late Han scholar Hsu Shen about A.D. 100. The *Shuo-wen* gives us the following definition of "*ju*": " '*Ju*' means 'flexible' (*jou* 柔); it is the name given gentlemen of skill (*shu-shih* 術士)" (*SWCTKL*:8A.3483). The word "*jou*" has additional meanings of "soft," "weak," and "to comfort." Of these, the meaning "weak" has attracted the attention of interpreters most often.[7]

Hu Shih linked the idea of "weakness" to a comprehensive theory he held that viewed pre-Confucian Ru as the descendants of Shang ritualists who, as the priest class of a conquered people, prized the value of submissiveness (1934). Hu's theory was disputed by Fung Yu-lan, who believed that the name of "Ru" was applied in the sense of "weak" to the followers of Confucius to distinguish them from the martially skilled Mohists (1935).[8] Liu Chieh, adopting portions of Fung's arguments, stressed that the name "Ru" postdated Confucius' time and was probably a satirical term, coined by Mohists who disapproved of the non-military nature of the Ruist syllabus (1943:218).[9] All these theories remain tenable, but we do not have adequate evidence to adjudicate between them.

A common flaw that pervades most of the theories we have mentioned is that they do not account for the term "*ju*" but rather for the term "*jou*," the *Shuo-wen* definiens. While it is true that *Shuo-wen* definientia are often etymologically related to the words they define, the relation is sometimes more oblique than straightforward. Any attempt to penetrate the sense of the term "*ju*" should begin by adopting a different methodology.[10]

The Dwarf Dancers

The primary reason why scholars have been driven to examine "*jou*" rather than "*ju*" lies in the fact that the word "*ju*" virtually never appears in pre-Ch'in texts in any sense other than "Confucian." The only exception is its appearance as the second element of a binome: the word "*chu-ju*" 侏儒, meaning "dwarf dancer," a species of performer, part acrobat, part shaman, of questionable reputation.[11] The semantic contribution of the element "*ju*" in this compound is not clear. "*Chu*" in itself means "dwarf," but no instances are found of "*ju*" appearing independently to confirm a gloss of "dancer." It is a characteristic of ancient Chinese that in binomes in which both elements rhyme, the second element often makes no semantic contribution. If the binome "*chu-ju*" (*t̑iu-n̑iu) were a true "rhyming binome" then we could infer no information concerning the character "*ju*."[12]

It is possible, however, that "*chu-ju*" is not a true rhyming binome and that both elements of the term make semantic contributions. Examples of apparently related binomes are found in which second syllable does make a semantic contribution. For example, the *Kuang-yun*, a word book dating from the sixth century A.D., equates the meaning of a cognate binome *chu-nou* 侏儒 with its second element.[13]

Similar instances shed further light on the meaning of "*chu-ju*" and of "*ju*." The binome *·iu-gliu/yü-lou 傴僂 : "hunchback," is both phonetically and semantically similar to *t̑iu-n̑iu/chu-ju侏儒. The element *gliu/lou 僂 has an independent meaning of "hunched" (*TC*, Chao 7:21.68), and appears with that sense in other phonetically similar binomes.[14] The phonetic and semantic similarity between *gliu 僂 and *n̑iu 儒 may indicate that the two graphs originally denoted a single word, signifying a hunched, dwarfish figure. Cognates of "*ju*" such as "*ju*" 孺: "small child" (*Shih-ming, Shih chang-yu*:3.42: "a child first starting to walk"), and "*no*" 懦: "fearful" (cowering?), could easily reflect such a meaning.[15] An elegant linkage of the ideas of dwarf and dance could be achieved by suggesting that the hunched quality of the "*ju*" may not have been a characteristic of his person, but rather of the dances performed. In particular, flowing movements for which dancers were necessarily arched or bowed might have suggested an association with the hunchback form.[16]

The implications are that the character "*ju*" may have possessed an independent meaning either identical with the overall sense of "*chu-ju*," "dwarf dancer," or with the simple meaning of "dancer." On so narrow a basis of evidence, however, such a conclusion must be judged speculative.

The Flexibility of the Ape

To make such speculation persuasive, the most promising approach would be to demonstrate that the word "*jou*," the *Shuo-wen* definiens, was likewise connected to the notion of dance, *and* that the characters for "*ju*" and "*jou*" were, in fact, simply alternate graphs for a single word, as demonstrated by significant indications of loan use (a relation that characterizes many of the definienda and definientia in the *Shuo-wen*). As it turns out, the word *"jou"* does indeed have close connections to dance; however, significant indications of loan use are lacking.

Bronze inscriptions dating from the early Chou make clear that the character *"jou"* was commonly written with a graph that evolved into the character *"nao"* 獿 (in the early Chou these were most likely homophonous).[17] *"Nao,"* the *Shuo-wen* informs us, was "an avaricious beast; some say it is a mother ape who resembles a person" (*SWCTKL*:2326b).[18]

On the basis of the bronze forms, we can infer that *"nao"* represents the original graph for the word *"jou,"* which later came to be represented by a far simpler graph. the *Shuo-wen* definition for *"jou"* is: "the straightening and bending of wood," whence the sense "flexible." The meaning of "flexible," which the *Shuo-wen* rather forcibly connects with wood on the basis of the wood semanteme in the later graph, was more directly conveyed by the crouched figure of the ape, represented in the earlier graph.

The Ape Dancers

The word *"nao"* leads us into a cluster of phonetic cognates that include the elements *ńiôg/jou 柔 and *ńiog/jao 獿.[19] Ikeda Suetoshi has conducted an extensive study of words in this phonetic/graphemic cluster, and demonstrated that many of them were connected to ritual dances performed in animal masks or costumes (1955:72-74). Important ceremonial dances of the Shang and early Chou periods, Ikeda argues, frequently involved dancers wearing headdress and costume miming ape-like figures. Terms that describe important aspects of ritual and religious significance bear the traces of these most visible aspects of archaic ceremony. Prominent among the words in this group is the term *"yu"*優: "dancer," a word that leads us back to our *"chu-ju"* dwarfs of a somewhat later period.[20]

The type of dancer denoted by the word *"yu"* was similar to that denoted by the binome *"chu-ju,"* and these dancers were also often referred to by compound words, such as *"p'ai-yu"* 俳 優 and *"yu-ch'ang"* 優 倡. The use of these terms in late Chou and Han texts indicates that these were comic dancers, associated with performances considered lewd by contemporary conservatives. Additionally, in this regard they were explicitly linked to the *chu-ju* dancers. Consider the following passage from the *Li-chi*, a Ruist text likely to date from the early Han:

Tzu-hsia said, " . . . In today's new music the ranks of dancers are all crooked, and lascivious sounds unceasingly overflow. And then the *yu* and *chu-ju* mingle male and female, like apes (*nao*) who cannot distinguish parent from child (*Yueh-chi*:11.15b).[21]

If Ruists derived their name from association with dancers of such a type, they would have been unlikely to welcome such a linkage. The term would surely have been intended satirically: a means of mocking Ruist obsessions with the artistry of orthodox music and dance. Perhaps it was in a specific effort to parry the thrust of such a jibe that Ruists elaborated the tale of the most dramatic episode in Confucius' biography: his role as a minister to Duke Ting of Lu at a meeting with Duke Ching of Ch'i at Chia-ku, in 500 B.C. In the *Shih-chi* account, Confucius confronts Duke Ching's lack of ritual propriety so effectively that Ch'i is prompted to return to Lu, with apologies, three parcels of Lu lands that Ch'i had formerly annexed. Here is how Confucius made his point:

The Ch'i Master of Ceremonies hurried in saying, "We ask permission for a performance of palace music." "Granted," responded Duke Ching. The *yu-ch'ang* and *chu-ju* began their acrobatics. Confucius hurried forward up the dais steps, calling as he began, "Commoners who daze the minds of lords must suffer execution! Let the masters of ceremonies be ordered accordingly!" The masters of ceremonies carried out the law; hands and feet were scattered in all directions. Duke Ching was moved with fear (*SC*:47.1915).

With such a climax to the political career of their founder, Ruists would have blunted at least some of the negative effects of their unfortunate title.[22]

Yet although it may seem obvious to us why Ru might feel uneasy at being named after comic or lewd dancers who recalled the forms of female apes, there is no evidence that Ruists made any direct attempt to reject the name "*ju*," or expressed dissatisfaction with it. This may merely be a lapse in the record, but it does not serve our theory. Perhaps another explanation can be found.

The Masked Dance Masters

The word "*jou*," as Jao Tsung-yi has stressed, can have a positive sense, as is exemplified in the phrase "*jou yuan neng erh*" 柔 遠 能 邇 , generally interpreted as meaning: "comfort the distant, be kind to the near" (Jao 1954:112). But the word "*jou*" in such instances may mean more than "to comfort." Both etymology and commentary tradition suggest that in these cases, "*jou*" is cognate with the word "*jao*" 擾 , "to tame," as in to tame wild animals—not surprising because both words belong to the family of words governed by "*nao*," the ape.[23]

The word "*jao*" is used in the sense of "taming animals," but it is also used in the sense of "educating the people." For example, in the *Chou-li*, the high office of T'ai-tsai includes "responsibility for establishing the state by means of the six constant codes." Of the "code of instruction," the text tells us: "It is used to bring peace to the state, to instruct its officials, and to educate (*jao*) the myriad people" (*CL*:1.10a). The term suggests a process of pacifying through enlightened training.

As we saw in chapter II, for Ruist texts such as the *Chou-li*, the process of education was built around training in music and dance: the idealized education institutions of such texts are presided over by music masters, and the curricula consist largely of graduated courses in ceremonial dance. The words "*jao*" 擾, "*jou*" 柔, and "*ju*" 儒, all might refer to such an educative function cast in the terminology of ancient mask dance. If this theory were correct, the term "*ju*" or "*ju-che*" 儒者, would have an original meaning very close to "dance master," where the master is pictured at once as the masked animal dancer and the tamer of animals. If such were the roots of the term "*ju*," it would explain the apparent satisfaction with which the Ruist school bore its name.

Colorful as this line of speculation is, further evidence will be required before the theory can be regarded as more than plausible.[24] The absence of straightforward loan relationships between words of the phonetic class of "*ju*" and those of the class to which "*jou*" and "*jao*" belong remain troubling.[25] One closing instance that bears on the theory, however, might be worth noting in brief.

In the section of the *Documents* that purports to record events at the courts of the Emperors Yao and Shun, a section probably composed by Ruist authors late in the Warring States period, two similar passages appear that seem suggestive. These passages focus on a personage named K'uei 夔, a semi-demonic culture hero whom we recognize from Shang oracle texts. In those texts, K'uei appears only as a featureless object of sacrifice—the way in which the Shang diviners thought of him is unclear—but later texts inform us that he was a one-footed monster. The ancient graph of his name (夔) seems to bear this out, as it pictures a figure with an oversized, misshapen head—unmistakably masklike—a bent body, and one great foot. As it happens, it is the graph for "*nao*," the ape and ape-masked dancer (late script evolution established a small distinction between the two characters).

K'uei, then, seems to have been a "*nao*," and so it is not surprising to find that in his Ruist incarnation in the *Documents*, he is cast as the royal music master at the court of the Emperor Shun. "K'uei!" commands the Emperor:

"I order you to codify the music and instruct the noble sons. . . . Let them speak their minds with poetry; let them chant their speech in song; let them link their chants to the tones of the scale; let their melodies bring the tones in harmony. The eight instruments in tune with one another, none usurping another's role—thus may spirits and men join in harmony." "Oh, yes," replied K'uei. "For when I strike the chime of stone it sets the hundred beasts to dancing" (*Shun tien*:1.11).[26]

Surely, if K'uei was a *nao*, though a *nao* were an ape, a Ru could be well satisfied to be called one as well.

Hsun Tzu
Treatise on T'ien[1]

Appendix C

[A][2]

(1)[3] T'ien's ways are constant: it does not prevail due to Yao; it does not perish due to Chieh. Respond to it with order and good fortune follows; respond to it with disorder and ill fortune follows. Strengthen the root[4] and regulate expenditures, and T'ien cannot impoverish. (2) Bring nurturance to completion and act only when the time is ripe, and T'ien cannot sicken.[5] Cultivate the Way without irresolution, and T'ien cannot devastate. Flood and drought cannot bring starvation; extremes of cold and heat cannot bring sickness; (3) prodigies and freaks cannot bring ill fortune. Let the roots shrivel and spend extravagantly, and T'ien cannot enrich. Skimp nurturance and act contrary[6] to the times, and T'ien cannot complete. (4) Abandon the Way and act wantonly, and T'ien cannot bring good fortune. There is starvation without flood or drought; there is sickness without extremes of cold and heat; there is ill fortune without prodigies and freaks. (5) Though the seasons revolve as they do in ordered times, disaster and devastation arise unlike in ordered times.[7] T'ien cannot be blamed: it is a consequence of the way [chosen by man]. He who understands the distinct roles of T'ien and man may be called a perfect man.

[B]

(6) That which is accomplished without action, obtained without pursuit, that belongs to the office of T'ien.[8] Though it be profound, man adds no thought to it; though it be great, man adds no ability to it; (7) though it be keen, man adds no insight to it. This is called "not contesting office with T'ien." T'ien (the heavens) has its seasons, earth has its riches, man has his rule: this is what is meant by "forming a trinity." (8) To discard the means for joining with the other two and instead to aspire to their [likeness]: this is delusion.[9]

The ranks of stars revolve in procession, the sun and moon shine in turn, the seasons succeed one another, the forces of *yin* and *yang* [alternate] in great transformation, (9) the winds and rains give broad nourishment, the things of the world each obtain a harmony [of forces] whereby they come to life; each obtains nurturance to grow to completion: the process unseen but the finished work manifest–this is called "spirit." (10) All know it by that which it brings to completion, but none know its formless being–that is called "T'ien." Only the Sage does not seek to know T'ien.[10]

With the office of T'ien settled and the work of T'ien accomplished, the physical form is intact and the spirit is born.[11] (11) Love, hate, pleasure, anger, grief, and joy are assembled therein: these are called the "T'ien-like dispositions." The ears, eyes, nose, mouth, and body have their [realms of sensual] encounter without duplicative ability: these are called the "T'ien-like faculties." (12) The heart dwells in the vacant center and thereby governs the five faculties: it is called the "T'ien-like ruler." It molds things not of its species in order to nurture its species: this is called "T'ien-like nurturance." (13) It judges things that accord with their species to be fortunate and judges things that discord with their species to be ill-fortuned: this is called "T'ien-like rule."[12]

To darken one's T'ien-like ruler, bring disorder to one's T'ien-like faculties, forsake one's T'ien-like nurturance, discord with one's T'ien-like rule, (14) contravene one's T'ien-like dispositions, and so dissipate T'ien's work: this is called "greatest evil." The Sage clears his T'ien-like ruler, rectifies his T'ien-like faculties, fulfills his T'ien-like nurturance, follows his T'ien-like rule, (15) nurtures his T'ien-like dispositions, and so brings completion to T'ien's work.[13]

Thus, if one understands what he is to do and is not to do, then heaven and earth will fulfill their proper functions and the things of the world will serve him. (16) Acts fully ruled, nurturance fully realized, in life suffering no injury:[14] this is called "knowing T'ien." Thus, the greatest craft lies in acts not taken, the greatest wisdom in thoughts not pondered.[15]

[C]

(17) What man seeks from T'ien (the sky) should merely be its manifest images, by which time may be marked. What man seeks from earth should merely be that which may be appropriated from it,[16] which may be husbanded. What man seeks from the four seasons (18) should merely be their regular sequence, to which he can act in response. What man seeks from the forces of *yin* and *yang* should merely be their harmonies, which he can employ to create order.[17] Functionaries keep track of T'ien; you must keep to the Way.[18]

[D]

(19) Are order and disorder determined by the [action of] the heavens (*t'ien*)? [I] say: the [regularities] of the sun and moon, stars, planets, and constellations were identical for both Yü and Chieh. Yü created order thereby; Chieh created disorder. Thus, order and disorder are not determined by the heavens. (20) Are they determined by [the action of] the seasons? Proliferation and growth in spring and summer, harvest and storage in autumn and winter, this, too, was identical for Yü and for Chieh. Yü created order thereby; Chieh created disorder. Thus, order and disorder are not determined by the seasons. (21) Are they determined by the land? He who acquires land is able to live; he who loses his land will die: this, too, was identical for Yü and for Chieh. Yü created order thereby, Chieh created disorder. (22) The *Poetry* puts it thus: "T'ien created the mountain tall, King T'ai brought cultivation to it; he having done so, King Wen brought peace to it."[19]

[E]

T'ien does not suspend winter because people dislike cold; (23) earth does not contract its breadth because people dislike [traveling] great distances; the *chün-tzu* does not curtail his actions because of the clamor of petty people. T'ien has a constant way; earth has constant progressions; (24) the *chün-tzu* has constancy of person.[20] The *chün-tzu* takes what is constant as his way; the petty person calculates his credits.[21] The *Poetry* says: "[Undeviating in ritual and right,] why be concerned what others may say?"[22]

[F]

That the king of Ch'u may have a retinue of a thousand chariots (25) does not mean that he is wise. That a *chün-tzu* may have only beans to eat and water to drink does not mean that he is stupid. These are due to the rhythms of circumstance.[23] To be refined in purpose, rich in virtue, and clear in thought;[24] (26) to live in the present but be devoted to the past[25] –these things are within one's own power. The *chün-tzu* attends to what is within his power and does not aspire to that which is within the power of T'ien alone. The petty person defaults on what is within his power (27) and aspires to that which is within the power of T'ien alone. Because the *chün-tzu* attends to what is within his power and does not aspire to that which is within the power of T'ien alone, he goes forward day by day. Because the petty person defaults on what is within his power (28) and aspires to that which is within the power of T'ien alone, he goes backward day by day. Thus, the [pivots of] the *chün-tzu*'s daily progress and the petty person's daily regress are [at root] one. The difference between the two lies in this.

[G]

(29) When stars fall or trees sing, the people of the state all ask in terror, "What does this mean?" [I] say it means nothing. These are the changes of the heavens and the earth, the transformations of *yin* and *yang*, (30) rare events in the world of things. It is proper to wonder at them; it is wrong to fear them. Eclipses of the sun or moon, unseasonable rain or snow, the occasional appearance of strange stars: (31) there has never been an age without them. If the ruler is enlightened and his government stable, then though these appear in series during his rule, no harm will be done. If the ruler is benighted and his government reckless, then though none of these things occur, (32) it will be of no use. The falling of the stars, the singing of the trees, these are the changes of the heavens and the earth, the transformations of *yin* and *yang*, rare events in the world of things. It is proper to wonder at them; it is wrong to fear them.

[H]

(33) Among events that may occur, those which should be feared are human portents.[26] When careless ploughing causes crops to suffer and those who weed leave weeds behind, when government is reckless and loses the support of the people—the fields unkempt, the crops meager, grain sold dear and people starving, (34) corpses lying in the road: these are what I mean by human portents. When government directives are unenlightened, the populace summoned to labor out of season, agriculture left in disorder: these are what I mean by human portents. (35) When ritual and propriety are not cultivated, public and private affairs not properly distinguished, when male and female mix wantonly and father and son doubt one another, when superior and inferior become estranged, when banditry and invasion appear in tandem: these are what I mean by human portents. (36) Such portents are born of chaos; if all three types occur at once, there can be no peace for the state. The reasons[27] are so near at hand; the catastrophe so tragic!

[I]

When labors are unseasonable, cows and horses give birth to one another's progeny and prodigies appear among the six types of livestock.

(37) It is proper to wonder at this; it is wrong to fear it. The teachings say: The prodigies of the world of things should be recorded but not explained.[28] Analyses that have no application, investigations that do not proceed from urgency: these should be discarded and not cultivated. (38) As for the proprieties governing ruler and minister, the affinities governing father and son, and the role distinctions governing husband and wife, these should be unceasingly refined.[29]

[*J*]

When performance of the great rain dance is followed by rain, what does this mean? [I] say it means nothing. It is as though the rain dance had not been performed and it had rained. (39) The rituals of "saving" the sun and moon when they are eclipsed, of performing the rain dance in times of drought, of divining with bone and milfoil before deciding a great matter, these are not performed as means of gaining an end; they are means of ornamenting (*wen*) [action]. (40) The *chün-tzu* understands them as ornamental, the populace understands them as spiritual. Understanding them as ornamental leads to good fortune; understanding them as spiritual leads to ill fortune.

[*K*]

In the heavens, nothing is more brilliant than the sun and the moon. On earth, nothing is more brilliant than water and fire. (41) Among things, nothing is more brilliant than pearls and jade. Amidst mankind, nothing is more brilliant than ritual and propriety. If the sun and moon were not high, their brilliance would not shine. If water and fire do not collect into masses, (42) their [powers to] brighten and moisten will not be spread abroad. If pearl and jade are not polished then kings and dukes will not regard them as treasures. If ritual and propriety are not applied to the state, then the fame of its accomplishments will not become known. Thus it is said: (43) The lifespan of a man resides with T'ien; the lifespan of a state lies in *li*.[30] If he who rules men exalts *li* and honors the worthy, he will rule as king; if he lays stress on laws and values the people, he will rule as hegemon; if he loves profit and proliferates deceit, he will rule in danger; if he relies on calculating schemes, (44) subversion and perilous secrecy, he will be totally destroyed.

[*L*]

Exalt T'ien and contemplate it?
Rather, husband its creatures and so regulate it!

Follow T'ien and sing hymns to it?
   Rather, regulate T'ien's mandate and use it![31]
(45) Look upon the seasons and await them?
   Rather, respond to the seasons and exploit them!
Accept things as they are and increase them?
   Rather, give rein to talents and transform them!
Contemplate things and treat them as givens?
   Rather, create order among things and
     (46) unfailingly [seize their potential]!
Long for the source from which things are born?
   Rather, promote the means whereby they are
   brought to completion!

Hence, to set aside man and contemplate T'ien is to mistake the basic nature of things.[32]

[M]

(47) That which [abided] unchanged through the reigns of the hundred kings [of antiquity] may serve as the linking thread of the Way. Respond to the transience of affairs with this thread; all principles will be linked without disorder. If you do not know how to link [things in this way], you will not know how to respond to change. The essence of this linking thread has never ceased to be.[33] (48) Disorder is born of deviating from it; order exhausts its every aspect.

Hence, [in pursuing] the goodness of the Way, follow what fully accords with it; what distorts it one must not do; to mistake it is the greatest confusion. When men wade across rivers, (49) they mark the deep pits. If the markers are not clear, others will drown. Those who rule people [must]mark the Way. If the markers are not clear, there is chaos. The *li* are the markers. To reject *li* is to darken the world, and a darkened world is in greatest chaos. (50) Thus, if the Way is made thoroughly clear, if inner and outer are distinctly marked, if there is regularity in the hidden and the manifest, then the pits which drown the people will be removed.

[N]

The world of things is but a corner of the Way; one [species of] thing is but a corner of the world of things. A foolish man is but a corner of one [species of] thing, (51) yet he believes he knows the Way. He is without wisdom.[34]

Shen Tzu could see [the advantages of] being last, but could not see [the advantages of] being first. Lao Tzu could see [the advantages of] being bent, but could not see [the advantages of] holding straight. (52) Mo Tzu saw [the advantages of] of equality, but could not see [the advantages of] inequality. Sung Tzu saw [the advantages of] few [desires], but could not see [the advantages of] many.

If all are last and none first, then there can be no gateway for the masses. If all are bent and none hold straight, (53) then the eminent and the humble cannot be distinguished. If all are equal without inequalities then commands of government cannot be carried out. If all have few [desires] and none have many, then there is no means of transforming the masses. The *Documents* puts it this way: (54) "Do not love doing any one thing; [only] follow the Way of the king. Do not hate doing any one thing; [only] follow the path of the king."[35]

Notes

Introduction

1. Frequently, statements in Confucian texts that seem highly suggestive in terms of traditional Western philosophical categories are not developed sufficiently to allow us to do more than adumbrate Confucian answers to Western questions. This is not a matter of undisciplined thinking on the part of Confucians, it reflects differences in the philosophical enterprises in Chinese and Western traditions (see the discussion in Hall and Ames 1987:1-5). In the *Mencius* passage, for example, it would not be legitimate to claim that the focus on "knowing" signals an entailment with an epistemological theory. Neither the term "to know" (*chih*) nor the structure of the Confucian quest for understanding corresponds with any precision to comparable dimensions of Western epistemological theory (Hall and Ames 1987:68).
2. In our discussions, whenever the word "T'ien" appears, without italics and generally without quotation marks, the word is being used as if it were denoting a hypothetical entity in the world, much the same as if the term that appeared were "God," "Nature," or "Heaven." In this usage, the Chinese word is simply treated as an anglicized term. On the other hand, whenever the term itself, rather than the hypothetical entity, is being discussed, it appears italicized and in quotation marks: "*t'ien*."
3. I have rendered Fung's terms somewhat differently from Bodde (Fung 1952:31). Fu Pei-jung has recently developed an expanded list based on Fung's categories as part of a sustained study of the role of T'ien in early Confucianism and Taoism (Fu 1984). Fu's analysis focuses on expanding the categories of T'ien as Ruler or God and T'ien as Nature, and his finely nuanced model represents an improvement on Fung's basic scheme.
4. Fu Pei-jung (1984) is an exception in that he does not focus on an evolutionary model.
5. These translations do not necessarily represent the interpretations I would choose for each of the passages (see chapter IV). The meaning of "*t'ien*" in several of them has been the subject of debate. I have rendered the passages here so as to illustrate the issue of ambiguity.
6. This point has been made by Paul Seligman, from whom the phrase "key term" is borrowed (1962:4).

7. John Dardess has illustrated how the vagueness of the term "Confucianism" can be subversive of clear analysis even in the context of late imperial China, the era whose history tends most to color our use of the term (1983:7-8).

8. Transcribing the Chinese term for Confucians as "Ru" rather than "Ju" departs from the norms of the modified Wade-Giles transcription system used in this book. I do this because the word and its anglicized derivatives are central to this study, and I do not wish to burden readers unaware that a Wade-Giles "j" is close to an English "r" with so recurrent a pronunciation trap. "Ruism" is an unlovable mongrel, but at least it looks as it sounds. (Problems of the origin and meaning of the term "*ju*" are discussed in appendix B.) It should also be noted that the transcriptions in this book employ umlauts only to avoid phonetic ambiguity, not, for example, in syllables such as "*hsu*" or "*yuan.*"

9. I would not like to claim that this accurately describes the ontological assumptions of all Western philosophy, but I do think it represents an enduring ground of philosophical commonsense. The most explicit statement of this point of view of which I am aware is that given by Wittgenstein in his "Tractatus" (1922:2.1-2.2, especially 2.18). The early Wittgenstein, of course, recognized that there might be more to the world than this, but barred the remainder from the arena of philosophy.

10. These ideas inform the portrait of human beings as intrinsically relational, which is the focus of chapter III.

11. This idea is fully compatible with the notion of a Confucian "ontology of events," described in Hall and Ames 1984: "Confucian philosophy entails an ontology of *events*, not one of *substances*. Understanding human events does not require recourse to 'qualities,' 'attributes,' or 'characteristics' "(15).

12. "*Tao*" may mean "a path" or "a method," or the verb "to speak," all of which senses seem to lie behind its use to mean "a teaching." An excellent discussion of the word appears in Hansen 1983a.

13. The Taoist philosopher Chuang Tzu seems to claim that a *tao* is inherently a system of practice, and as such not subject to discursive judgments of true and false. It is the growth of the verbal component into a rational system, which commits the teaching to an ontology—for Chuang Tzu a necessarily invalid commitment—that renders a *tao* inauthentic as a practical matrix and false as doctrine (*CT*:2.23-26).

14. Mohist commitments to logic are most evident in neo-Mohist analytics, which have been extensively studied by A. C. Graham and Chad Hansen. But the Mohist conviction that universally held powers of

reason can adjudicate issues of truth is equally evident in the earlier discourses. For example, in its famous chapters on "Universal Love," the *Mo Tzu* repeatedly concludes its semi-syllogistic arguments by appeal to a common power of people's minds to see their self-evident validity: "Having heard of this explanation of universality, I cannot see any reason why men would think to confute it"(*MT, Chien-ai* III:4.11-12).

15. An important impetus for this approach was Gilbert Ryle's argument that the boundary between motor and cognitive skills is not absolute (1949: Ch.2).

16. "The first evidence of capacity to organize appears in the development of habitual actions [termed] *schemata*. Their chief characteristic, whatever their nature or complexity, is that they are organized wholes, frequently repeated ... " (Beard 1969:3). Piaget's schemata represent the lower level of the spectrum of skill acquisition as it generates conceptual/ behavioral structures. In light of Ryle's demonstration that the boundary dividing motor and cognitive skills is problematic, we can suggest that at the upper end of the spectrum we would find such structures being generated from skill manipulation fully displaced into cognitive activity. Thomas Kuhn has described the networks of theory that govern each branch of the natural sciences (and Science as a whole) as "paradigms" that organize perception of the natural field and dictate the synthesis of new ideas (1962:10-11, 43-51). If we were to seriously link Piaget's schemata and Kuhn's paradigms, it might suggest that the perspectives of all intellectual activity (including analytic philosophy) and their self-evident axioms are ultimately bound to the repertoires of skill possessed by those who engage in these activities.

17. The most succinct expression of Polanyi's thought, which has greatly influenced this study, is his essay *The Tacit Dimension* (1966).

18. The power of complex skill systems to generate value perspectives and influence individual commitments is described by Alasdair MacIntyre in his theory of "practices" as ethical enterprises (1984:187-203).

19. For a discussion of this theory of embodiment and its relation to meaning, see Eno 1984: 23-27. The *Chuang Tzu* has a passage in which a master swimmer describes his skill, and the description suggests an extreme notion of skill embodiment, where an individual's nature is actually constituted, after birth, through skill mastery: "My being born on dry land and feeling at home there" the swimmer says, "is my primitive endowment (*ku*). I grew up in the water and became at home there: this is my nature (*hsing*)" (*CT*: 19.53-54). It is not surprising to find resonances of this sort between early Taoism and Ruism, as we will describe it. These two schools stand opposed to the other major schools of Mohism and Legalism in that the former were essentially

     tao-philosophies, wherein doctrine grew out of practice, whereas the
     other two were less so: for them, doctrine was the essential element.

20. An example would be *A*:17.19, in which Ruist mourning rites are rationalized in a manner that might satisfy an uncritical audience, but which
James Legge justly termed "puerile."

21. It is important to make clear that in the analyses of the term *"t'ien"*
that will occupy the second part of this book we will frequently find
ourselves involved with issues of referential rather than instrumental
meaning. This is because the Ruist texts that are our sole route of access into the school do, in fact, create an elaborate, if shaky, theoretical architecture. We will always need to set this architecture straight
in order to look beyond to the practical issues that generated it. Basically, however, the theoretical approach that governs issues of word
meaning in this study is an adaptation of "use-theories" derived from
Wittgenstein's later thought (particularly Wittgenstein 1953). This approach can be distinguished from earlier studies of early Confucian
concepts of T'ien in that previous work has implicitly adopted an
"ideational theory" in which word meanings are viewed as referential
to a "mental concept" (Alston 1964:22-25), whereas we would assume
that in each instance of usage meaning is a function of how usage
"fits" the context of the enterprise underway: that even in philosophy–
synthetic or analytic–words are employed to realize life goals and
meaning is ultimately reducible to these. (For those familiar with the
terminology developed in J. L. Austin's analyses of language, the level
of meaning of greatest interest to us is generally the "perlocution-
ary" function [1962:94-107].) These issues are discussed in detail in
Eno 1984:17-23.

22. Arthur Danto has made a number of insightful observations concerning the significance of the philosopher as model in Chinese thought
(see his "Postscript" to Munro 1985), and an excellent discussion of
the holistic role of the teacher also appears in Fingarette 1983. On
the enormous importance of the model in early Confucianism and in
Chinese thought and society in general, see Munro 1969:96-102. The
importance of mimicry in learning philosophy has not been generally
acknowledged in the West, but Merleau-Ponty observed, "I begin to
understand a philosophy by feeling my way into its existential manner;
by reproducing the tone and accent of the philosopher" (1962:179).

Chapter I

1. Compare Hsun Tzu's economic theory of the origins of *li* (*H*:19.1-3).
2. It is difficult to characterize properly the political structure of the

Shang polity. I use the term "tribe" to indicate the probable insularity and independence of the local territorial-lineage units of Shang culture, relative to the later situation under the Chou (on the ad hoc nature of Shang political structure, see Keightley 1983:548-51). The complexities of the issue of Shang political structure are well represented in Morton Fried's analysis of the applicability of the term "tribe" with regard to the Shang polity and its neighbors (1983).

3. The best overview of the process by which the oracle texts have broadened our understanding of early Chinese society in English is Tung 1964 (updated in Chinese as Tung 1974; for a recent survey, see Wu and P'an 1985). On the oracle materials themselves, Keightley's study (1978) is incomparable.

4. Some scholars have suggested that the complexity of the Shang pantheon is due in part to a process of religious cooptation, whereby early Shang rulers consolidated their influence over an expanding polity by incorporating into royal religious structures deities of border tribes newly absorbed into the Shang political network (Hsu 1984:96-7).

5. The generic term for ritual sacrifice, "*ssu*[a]," became, during the late Shang, synonymous with "*nien*" ("harvest") in denoting "year."

6. The oracle texts refer to many types of religious actors; among them: diviners, liturgists (*chu*), shamans (*wu*[a]), and scribes (*shih*[a]); on their religious origins, see Shirakawa 1974:5-17.

7. For a survey of issues concerning the rise of the Chou, see Hsu 1984:33-70.

8. The date of the conquest is according to Nivison 1983a. (Nivison himself has suggested a revised date [1982-83], but his original calculations have been defended by Shaughnessy [1985-87:56n27].) For an account of King Wu's war dance, see *KY, Chou-yü* III:3.24.

9. The most extensive English account of Western Chou political organization appears in Creel 1970:317-87. For a detailed study of Western Chou feudalism incorporating more recent archaeological finds, see Hsu 1984:139-73. As is customary in describing Chou society, I use terms drawn from European feudalism, despite the fact that Chou "feudalism" was a very different species of political structure.

10. David Nivison has compiled an impressive revised chronology of the Western Chou using both the *Bamboo Annals* and other traditional sources as well as bronze inscriptions dated according to his own complex formulas (1983). Nivison's account generally marks the crises in Western Chou politics, and if it is borne in mind that the period covered comprises two and one-half centuries, these seem few indeed.

11. Judging by accounts of the period in the *Shih-chi* and *Chu-shu chi-nien* and by the evidence of the bronze inscriptions, after King Ch'eng and the Duke of Chou put down a rebellion during the first years of King

Ch'eng's reign, Chou military activity until the early ninth century was directed against "barbarian" tribes within and outside the borders of the Chou polity, and these campaigns were generally successful, apart from setbacks under King Chao in the mid-tenth century. This would not indicate any weakness on the part of the dynasty; campaigns against barbarians could equally be a sign of vigor.

12. The portrait of the Western Chou presented here relies primarily on inscriptional material, supplemented in a few instances by sections of the *Poetry*. I do not cite material from the *Documents* chiefly because I am unsure of the historical status of that text. My scepticism extends to those twelve chapters accepted as "genuine" by Creel (1970:447-63; most scholars are less critical than Creel and accept a much broader range of chapters). The chief reasons for my scepticism, briefly stated, are as follows: (1) The tradition that *Documents* texts were faithfully transmitted over centuries because they were regarded as "sacred" is belied by the presence of acknowledged forgeries in the book and the existence of variant versions of the texts revealed through divergent citations in pre-Ch'in texts; (2) The profusion of Ruist-flavored value words in presumably authentic chapters purporting to date from the early Chou is anachronistic when compared with contemporary inscriptional material; (3) The current text of the *Documents* was only one of a number that circulated during the Han. The interested role of the Ruists who "recovered" it from the recitations of an elderly scholar (who, according to tradition, possessed a heavy dialect accent) created likely conditions for misunderstandings, tampering, or forgery; (4) With the exception of the *K'ang-kao* and possibly the *Chiu-kao* chapters, none of the other chapters accepted by Creel are cited in pre-Ch'in texts (see Matsumoto 1966:543, 641, 678-79 [chart]). For these reasons, I prefer not to rely on the *Documents* for evidence of early Chou thought and practice. I should note that my caution applies primarily to those sections of texts that purport to be "transcripts" of speeches, rather than to prefatory statements concerning historical events. It is interesting that the *Shih-fu* chapter of the *Yi Chou-shu*, which Edward Shaughnessy has persuasively argued to be a preserved pre-Ch'in version of the lost "Wu-ch'eng" chapter of the *Documents* (1980-81), is almost entirely narrative, whereas almost all chapters of the current *Documents* text are primarily of the "transcript" variety. For a fuller discussion of these issues, see Eno 1984:122-24. A discussion of Western Chou ideology and the role of T'ien in it based entirely on the *Documents* and *Poetry* appears in Fu 1984:28-75.

13. See Benjamin Schwartz's balanced assessment of the nature of the early Chou success (1985:41-45).

14. Elaborate legend clouds the historical record concerning the Duke of Chou. What seems certain is that he seized power upon the death of his brother, King Wu, about two years after the conquest, to rule as regent during the minority of the late king's son. Several of King Wu's other brothers raised a revolt, apparently in the belief that the Duke's true intent was to usurp the throne over their competing claims. The revolt was put down by the Duke's forces, protecting the legitimacy of the royal lineage. But the act constituting the Duke's greatest contribution to the sanctified aura of the Chou throne was probably the fulfillment of his vow to restore his nephew to the throne, he himself eventually retiring after order had been fully secured. An argument that the Duke's role was, in fact, far less significant than traditionally maintained appears in Barnard 1965:339-41.

15. A few inscriptions exist that are legal in nature, recording the settling of land disputes, and so forth. But even in these cases, the casting of a ritual vessel to seal the outcome and report it on the tools of ancestral sacrifice suggests a highly ritualized context of contract settlement.

16. Some sources indicate that Chou *li* was the exclusive province of the aristocratic class (*H*:10.18-19; *LC*, *Ch'ü-li* I:1.14a). Others imply that this was not the case (*H*:12.54; *KY*, *Ch'u-yü*:18:4-5).

17. See, for example, *Poetry*: 266: "How many the knights, possessing patterned virtue (*wen-te*)!"

18. See Eno 1984:204n39. For variants, see Glossary (*wen*[a]).

19. The character appears in the form of a bird (*wen*[b]) on the *Fu Ting tou* (*K'o-chai*:17.18b). The word "*wen*" was used to denote one category of dance, most likely dances in animal and bird costumes; the name for a complementary category of war dances, "*wu*," probably denoted dances with weapons (see Eno 1984:204n39). On the possible connection between ritual dances in animal costumes and the name of the Ruist school, see appendix B.

20. The earliest example of "*wen*" used in this way is the *Pao yu* inscription (Ch'en 1955-56:I.157). The piece dates from the first decades of the Chou. On the connection of the word "*huang*" with dance, see Ikeda 1955:76-77 and, especially, Kuo 1962:6-7.

21. Other well attested early meanings of the word, such as "patterned animal skin," and "tattoo," seem clearly connected with the notion of dancers costumed in animal skins or painted with their patterns. Which usage is strictly "original" is arguable.

22. As in dance, the terms "*wen*" and "*wu*" formed a complementary pair in naming kings. This usage might not have originated with the Chou; the Shang referred to a pair of kings whose sacrificial ceremonies fell on the same day of the calendrical cycle by the paired names "*wen*"

and "*wen-wu.*"

23. The graph "*li*" does not appear in early bronze inscriptions; rituals are named individually. The cognate graph "*li*ᵉ": "sweet wine," does appear in the phrase "*wang ch'ing* [=*hsiang*] *li*" "the king held a cere-monial banquet (with ritual wine?)" (*San-nien Hsing hu; Ch'ang Ts'ung ho; Shih Chü fang-yi*). Another graph, "*feng*," may have been used as a loan for "*li*" (*Ta feng kuei*; on the reliability of which, however, see Eno 1984:112n32). However, neither of these graphs was used to refer to ritual in general, only to specific instances.

In the *Poetry*, we encounter the word "*li*" in six poems, and, in con-trast to the bronze texts, the word is sometimes used to refer not to an instance of *li*, but to *li* as a body of codes, as in: "I am not plundering; my acts accord with *li*" (193/5). However, in only one instance does "*li*" seem to denote a general category of action: "A man without *li*: shall he not soon die?" (52/3). (The word does appear in the "Chou-shu" section of the *Documents*, albeit very rarely, and there it does carry the generic sense of ritual, but see note 12).

24. See the discussion in Creel 1970:93-99.

25. This had not been the case in the Shang. There are inscriptions that portray the Shang high god Ti as the potential adversary of the king and the state (see the divination examples in Ch'en 1956:570-71, where Ti is pictured as potentially destroying the capital of the Shang).

26. The virtual identity of king and T'ien seems to suggest a clear and simple structure to Chou religious practice. Nothing could be further from the truth. The mandate theory probably had little impact on the complex religious practices of the time. For a description of Chou reli-gious practice as a complex of three levels—state, clan, and popular—see Eno 1984:83-85.

27. Bronze inscriptional sources are consistent with this portrait. We occa-sionally see the king sacrifice at T'ien's altar (e.g., the *Ho tsun* inscrip-tion), but we do not see others sacrifice or pray to T'ien. Late Chou and early Han texts claim this as a rule, and deviations are condemned as unsanctioned (see Eno 1984:86-88).

28. *Ta yü ting, Ta-hsi*: 3.34a. Reign dates for Western Chou kings are according to Nivison 1983.

29. See Kuo Mo-jo's commentary in *WW* 1972:9.2-10. I am taking "*ch'ien*" as a loan for "*ch'ien*ᵃ": "to send off," rather than as a name; "*ch'ien-ling*" thus are the "marching orders" issued by the king. "*Ch'eng*" is read as "peace" a well attested use, rather than as "complete." The graph "*tu*" is read as "*yi*ᵗ," "sated," rather than "defeat."

30. Taking the first "*wang*" as "*mang*": "darkened, ignorant," to go with "*mei*" of the same sense, and changing the metaphor from blindness

to deafness. *"Ts'ai"* is read as *"tsai"* "disaster," a common loan. *"Yi"* is translated as "all," an extension of its meaning as "norm."

31. The *Pan kuei* is sometimes dated to the reign of King Ch'eng, in which case "deaf to T'ien's orders" might imply an unwillingness to acknowledge the change of dynasties. But some commentators have suggested that the vessel should be dated to the reign of King Chao (977-957) (Hsu 1984:178-79), and I suspect that calligraphic evidence might support an even later dating (see Eno 1984:127n112).

32. This contrasts with the portrait of the Shang high god Ti revealed in the oracle texts. Ti is by no means a predictable force, and little or no sense of ethical regularity to Ti's actions is found.

33. *Fu kuei, WW* 1979:4.89-90. The piece is assigned to King Li on the basis of T'ang Lan's identification of Fu with Hu, which was, according to the *Shih-chi*, the personal name of King Li. Note that Shirakawa rejects the identification (*KBTS*:18.274-75). In my translation here, I take *"p'in"* in the sense of *"she"*: "cross over a river," linked with *"chih-chiang"*: "ascending and descending," all in the sense of picturing the movement entailed in rendering service to Ti by carrying out his orders. My understanding of the inscription has benefited from suggestions by Anne Behnke and Bill Savage.

34. For the text and dating of the *Yü ting*, see Hsu 1959.

35. It is so dated by Kuo and Shirakawa (*Ta-hsi*:3.135b; Shirakawa 1963-64: 3.21). The date has been a matter of extensive dispute, with scholars placing it as early as the eleventh century B.C. and as late as the seventh (see *KBTS*: 30.689-700).

36. Reading *"min"* ("pitying") in the sense of its antonym.

37. This is an important point because it distinguishes the action of T'ien pictured in these inscriptions from the theory of T'ien's ethical perfection as presented in the *Documents*. In that text (and in certain parts of the *Poetry*), T'ien punishes kings only if they lack virtue: it is a just and responsive punishment. This formula provides for the prescriptive perfection of T'ien by assigning all evil to human beings as causes. But we do not find this idea in the bronze inscriptions. Perhaps the later kings simply did not have the intellectual power or personal inclination to shoulder the burden of keeping T'ien pure, even though the dynastic founders had given them the rhetorical basis to do so. If the early Chou chapters of the *Documents* are not viewed as genuinely early, then the doctrine of the "mandate" probably was only partially elaborated during the early Chou, holding prescriptively that the king had to work hard to be worthy of the mandate, and that the mandate could be withdrawn, but not stressing the descriptive implication that if T'ien withdrew the mandate it meant that the king had not been

worthy. If T'ien were not ethically perfect, this would not be a necessary implication, and these late kings obviously preferred not to draw
it, instead suggesting the waywardness of T'ien.

38. Note that the authenticity of this inscription (the *Shih P'ou kuei*, which
survives only in the form of a hand copy [*Ta-hsi*:3.139a]) is borne out
by a different but formally similar inscription on an attested vessel,
the *Shih Hung kuei* (Barnard 1965:365-67). (Shirakawa renders the title
as the *Shih Hsun kuei* [*KBTS*:31.710].)

39. *Ch'in Kung kuei* (*Ta-hsi*:3.247a). For the date (early seventh century
B.C.) see *WW* 1978:11.1-3, which discusses the similar text of the lately
excavated *Ch'in Kung chung*. I am reading "*mi*" as a graphic variant of
"*shang*," in accord with this latter inscription.

40. *Hsu Wang Yi-ch'u chuan* (*Ta-hsi*:3.162a). Note also the inscription of
the *Tseng Po X fu* (3.186a) that prays that T'ien will bestow its bless-
ings, a usurpation of the king's exclusive prerogative to address T'ien.

41. On the origins of the term "*t'ien*," see appendix A.

42. I take "*ch'e*" in the sense of the *Mao-chuan*, as a loan for *che*: "cart
track" (see Karlgren 1944:92; Karlgren does not accept this gloss).

43. For example, referring to the evils of King Yu's consort: "This disorder
did not fall from T'ien, it was born of a woman" (*Poetry*:264/3). In
upbraiding incompetent officials, another poem says, "The sufferings
of the people did not fall from T'ien," implying it was caused by mortal
ministers (193/7). (The language of these poems suggests that these
statements may be more ironic than substantive, perhaps better translated, "These evils did not fall from the sky.")

44. Ikeda's many examples are primarily drawn from the *Tso-chuan*; for
instance: "I have heard it said that when a country has no virtue (*wu
tao*) and the harvests are abundant, it is T'ien aiding it" (Chao 1). It is
important to distinguish T'ien as Fate, in the sense of an amoral deity,
and the idea that T'ien is moral but "works in mysterious ways," and
so may not seem moral at certain times. When Mencius says, "My not
meeting the Marquis of Lu was due to T'ien" (1B.16), he does not mean
that T'ien has done evil, but that T'ien's ethical plans required this
unfortunate interlude.

Chapter II

1. The term "*li*" may apply to ceremonial ritual, including religious ritual,
and also to most forms of social etiquette. Ruists did not generally
distinguish these two senses of the word, and it is likely that for them,
the two dimensions were not distinct. I use the term here to refer
indiscriminately to both aspects, defining *li* as "stylized behavior that

accords with explicit traditional norms." The word "*li*" can be used as a singular noun, denoting a particular rule or set of rules, or it can be used as a plural, collective noun.

2. The detail of prescript in Ruist *li* is truly remarkable. Even in the *Analects*, the detail of routine etiquette is evident in rules such as, "Once having lain down, one does not speak" (*A*:10.6), and, "One does not sleep in the position of a corpse" (*A*:10.17).

3. See, for example, *MT, Kung Meng*:12.10a. Even Ruists acknowledged that *li* were subject to change (*A*:2.23, 3.9, 9.3).

4. In discussing ritual in these terms, I do not mean to imply that no other significant aspects are found. The value of this simple schema is only that it helps us speak more clearly about how the role of ritual changed during the Chou.

5. This sort of belief might be part of a systematic cosmology that explains natural/supernatural entailments, or it might belong to unintellectualized superstition.

6. Fingarette offers a modern example of this subtle power of ritual. In democratic America, nearly everyone shakes hands upon meeting, and the form of the ritual is very narrow. But the variety and subtlety of information passed through the simple handshake—strong, fishy, hearty, cursory—is impressive indeed (1972:9-10).

7. Many instances of this ritual are described in the *Tso-chuan*. Perhaps the most intricate and moving appears at Chao 16 (*TC*:23.49-50).

8. The *Yi-li* is a collection of ceremonial codes and scripts, probably incorporating some early materials, but showing a Ruist influence that indicates a rather late date of final editing (following Liang Ch'i-ch'ao in *WSTK*:279-80).

9. These observations are consistent with the model of ritual action presented in Fingarette 1972:chapter I. Fingarette articulates this theory through a discussion of ritual acts as forms of performative utterance.

10. This interpretation relies upon *M*:3B.7 and assumes that Yang Huo is identical with the Lu usurper Yang Hu, an assumption not accepted by all interpreters. Note that although the *Analects* passage indicates preliminary assent, Confucius apparently did not serve Yang Huo.

11. This passage may have been incorporated into the text rather late (Kimura 1971:410). It appears to be an attempt to coopt the Taoist-Legalist ideal of non-striving (*wu-wei*) by giving it a ritual cast (suggested by the word "reverence" [*kung*]), and portraying it in a Ruist model.

12. On the Shang rain dance (*yü*[b]), see Ch'en 1956:599-603. Numerous references show that the dance was performed throughout the Chou.

13. Many early ritual dances were probably war dances. The *Chou-li* indicates that warriors were under the tutelage of a dance master, who

drilled them in a variety of sacrificial dances (*Ti-kuan*, Wu-shih: 3.36b-37a). The *Kuo-yü* description of King Wu's war dance, noted earlier, shows that the practice of war dance was understood during the Chou. Battles were directed by the same musical symbols that directed dance: drums initiated attacks, gongs brought them to a close (*H*:15.58-9). Terminology also suggests a link between dance and war. Leaders of troops were known as "*shih*[d]" during the early Chou (as many bronze inscriptions show). Later, the term is applied to teachers and, more particularly, to music masters. (Early evidence for this overlap appears in Western Chou sources; see, for example, the *Shih Li kuei* inscription [*KBTS*:31. 767-75].) Ikeda Suetoshi has argued that the word "*wu*": "war," was cognate with its exact homophone: "dance" (1955:74). See also Tong Kin-woon's recent demonstrations of the extensive influence of music and dance on the lexicon of the oracle texts (1983).

14. I do not mean to suggest that a complete correspondence exists between what is ethically right and what is aesthetically right, but only that the overlap is recognizable and significant enough for aesthetic criteria to serve as "rules of thumb" in guiding much ethical action. See the discussions in Hall and Ames 1987:105, 266.

15. In its earliest uses, "*yi*" seems to have denoted external standards of correct action and demeanor rather than an abstract idea of moral rightness. Chou inscriptional usage makes no graphemic distinction between "*yi*" and "*yi*[a]," and they were, at root, one (Eno 1984:201n18).

16. "If one were to exhaust *li* in serving one's lord, people [today] would take it to be toadying" (*A*:3.18).

17. This is evidenced by many passages in Mohist and Taoist texts, for example, *TTC*:38.

18. Such ethical attitudes are reflected in the challenge to Ruist ritualism that appears in the *Analects*: "A *chün-tzu* should simply be naturally honest (*chih*[b]), what has he to do with refinements of style (*wen*)?" (*A*:12.8).

19. Few topics of comparable importance in Chinese history are less accessible to us than the biography of Confucius. The real man is shrouded in a tradition of hagiography that began shortly after his death and continued unabated for centuries (see Creel 1949:182-210). For a recently published biography of Confucius that incorporates the broadest range of late material, see K'uang 1985:32-104. In this section, we are confining ourselves to the outlines of Confucius' career, upon which sources generally agree.

20. On Confucius' birth date, see Ch'ien 1956:1-2.

21. The *Mencius* reports that Confucius' early career included tenures as

a granary clerk and supervisor of crops (*M*:5B.5). The *Tso-chuan, Shih-chi*, and *K'ung Tzu chia-yü* include accounts of Confucius' life that grow increasingly detailed as their distance in time from Confucius grows.

22. "When I was young I was of humble station" (*A*:9.6). There is considerable evidence that Confucius' forbears were natives of the state of Sung and, hence, were descendants of the Shang (e.g., *TC*, Chao 7:21.67-9; *LC T'an-kung*:2.10b).

23. Shirakawa has suggested that Confucius was trained in *li* because he was the son of a sorceress (1972:16-24).

24. Certain passages suggest that Confucius held some official rank in Lu during his last years (*A*:11.8, 13.14, 14.21), but their tone and vagueness may indicate that the rank was honorary and his political influence nil.

25. Again, the living Confucius' rank seems to rise proportionate to the source's distance from his death.

26. See Dubs 1946.

27. For details of the chronology, see Ch'ien 1956:26-51.

28. According to the *Tso-chuan* (Ai 11:29.62-65, 75) and the *Shih-chi* (47.1934), the influence of Jan Ch'iu brought about Confucius' return to Lu.

29. On the date of Confucius' death, see Ch'ien 1956:58-60.

30. The traditional tale of the way Confucius became a teacher appears in the *Tso-chuan* (Chao 7:21.67-9), where the dying nobleman Meng Hsi-tzu orders that his sons be entrusted to the young Confucius' tutelage. I do not feel that the anecdote, as it stands, is historically credible.

31. On Tzu-lu's tenure with the Chi family, see *A*:16.1; *TC*, Ting 12:28.32. Although tradition has it that Tzu-lu first received political office through Confucius' recommendation, he probably was involved in politics prior to studying with Confucius (see Eno 1984:203n36). On Jan Ch'iu and the Chi family, see *A*:11.17, 16.1.

32. The sense that society was disintegrating in civil war may have been heightened in Confucius' time by the unraveling of a reasonably effective general armistace, concluded in 546 B.C., shortly after the birth of Confucius. Calculating by the *Tso-chuan* record, a sharp drop in interstate military activity in the northern areas of the Chou polity occurred during the second half of the sixth century, particularly marked in the states of Sung, Confucius' ancestral state, and Lu, his homeland. By the turn of the century, however, the era of relative peace was apparently at an end (see *TCHC*, Hsiang 27:18.42-43; Legge 1872:534-35).

33. As Mohist texts point out (see chapter V).

34. *A*:8.8 is a nine-word literary masterpiece. "Rise up" (*hsing*[b]) is a pun on the literary device used to open many odes in the *Poetry* (for a thoughtful interpretation of the term, see Chen 1974:14-24); "stand"

("*li*^c") plays on near coincidences of word imagery and sound with ritual "*li*," a device used several times in the *Analects*; the term for "complete," "*ch'eng*," was also used to denote a musical coda.

35. In the *Analects* there is sometimes a sense that style is not as important as are simple prescriptive rules and right attitudes (*A*:1.6). Elsewhere, however, it is a defining aspect of the *chün-tzu* (*A*:6.18). Perhaps we can understand this apparent conflict by reasoning that style was, in practical terms, a central Ruist concern, but that philosophically it could not be ethically legitimized independent of other ethical notions, such as *li* and *jen*. It could not be a cardinal value. But in places, the *Analects* seems to get around this by using "*wen*" in an extended sense to denote right conduct (*A*:5.15, 14.18). And in one passage, style even has a certain practical priority over *jen*: "Tseng Tzu said, 'A *chün-tzu* relies on his style to attract friends, and he relies on his friends to support his *jen*' " (*A*:12.24).

36. This approach would have distinguished the Ru from other groups traditionally committed to ritual, such as the shamans (*wu*^a) and liturgists (*chu*).

37. This distinction was never clearly worked out. Ruists consistently maintained a doctrine of natural equality that undercut the legitimacy of hereditary privilege (Munro 1969:1-16), but hereditary privilege was also a form of *li*; hence, legitimate. The only *consistent* Ruist position on hereditary privilege was that the abuse of it was contrary to *li*; hence, it could be forfeited.

38. This phrase could be a late interpolation (Tsuda 1946:141). Fingarette, who has written eloquently about this aspect of ritual behavior, refers to this as the "magic" of *li* (1972:3-5).

39. This imperative is implicit in the *Analects*' advocacy of *li* as a social program (e.g., *A*:2.3 4.13, etc.). The notion of an ideal society completely ritualized is evident throughout the "political chapters" of the *Hsun Tzu* (chaps. 8-16), for example, *H*:9.64-74, 10.29-35, 12.50-55, 16.4-5.

40. We may note that the employment of talent in preference to hereditary appointment was a growing fact of Warring States China. When the Ruists spoke of "putting the straight over the crooked" (i.e., promoting the virtuous), the "crooked" were increasingly not decadent aristocrats but political adventurers, with whom Ruists generally maintained an adversarial relationship.

41. This is, of course, not true of the ritual texts, which do describe activities. However, these texts have not captured the attention of Western writers as have the more philosophical texts, such as the *Analects*, *Mencius*, and *Hsun Tzu*.

42. A note on terminology is due here. In the course of this essay, we will

use the word "Sage" as *our* descriptive term for the Ruist ideal of human perfection. In Ruist texts, several terms can be used to denote this ideal. The term "*sheng-jen*" almost always denotes this ideal. The term *chün-tzu* (often translated as "gentleman") is sometimes virtually equivalent to "*sheng-jen*," but it can also denote a person on the path *toward* perfection, and it is occasionally used in its pre-Ruist sense of "noble son" (on this term see Hsu 1965:158-74). Other terms such as "*hsien-che*" or "*ta-jen*" can also denote the ideal of the Sage (but the former more often means something less). In general, when translating directly, we will render "*sheng-jen*" as "Sage," leave *chün-tzu* untranslated and translate other terms with words other than "Sage." However, when we interpret the sense of the texts, we will use "Sage" to denote the prescriptive ideal regardless of which term may be used in the original text.

43. The meaning of this passage should be understood in terms of the passages that precede it. *A*:3.1-2 describe usurpations of royal Chou *li* by the leading warlord families of Lu. *A*:3.3 criticizes these warlords, and also accounts for why their attempt to emulate the rituals of the Sage Kings will not result in kingly government.

44. This passage has troubled commentators. A variant reading appears twice in the *Hou Han shu* (Ch'en 1968:64), and D. C. Lau, in his translation of the *Analects*, has emended the text in accordance with it (1979: 74; see also Miyazaki 1974:92-93). I do not think that the emendation is called for, both because it does not affect what seems to be the troubling part of the passage, the second phrase, and because I think the passage makes good sense as it stands.

45. "He who rectifies his person, what difficulty can government present to him?" (*A*:13.13).

46. See also *A*:5.21, 7.11, 14.1, 14.3, 15.7.

47. The division of Confucius' disciples into two distinct generations was first proposed by Ts'ui Shu, and is explored in detail by Ch'ien Mu (1956:81-83). If the *Shih-chi* dating for the disciples is accepted, there is a rather clear division in terms of age, the senior disciples (excluding Tzu-lu, who was far senior to all) being ten to fifteen years older than the junior disciples.

48. A complete list of *Analects* entries noting disciples holding some appointive office reads like this: Tzu-lu: 11.22, 11.23, 16.1; Jan Ch'iu: 3.6, 6.4, 11.17, 11.22, 13.14, 16.1; Tzu-yu: 6.14, 17.3; Tzu-hsia: 13.17; Chung-kung: 13.2; Yuan Ssu: 6.5; Tzu-kao: 11.23 (cf. *TC*, Ai 15); Tzu-hua: 6.4.

49. See the *Tzu-chang* chapter of the *Analects*. On the preference of the junior disciples for nonpolitical studies, *A*:11.3 characterizes ten disciples by categories: virtue in action, skill in speech, skill in politics, skill

in the study of style (*wen*). Only the two disciples listed in the last category belong to the junior generation.

50. The *Tso-chuan* indicates that Jan Ch'iu continued to serve the Chi family (Ai 23:30.47). Tzu-kao and Meng Wu-po are mentioned in ritual roles (Ai 17:30.39). The senior disciple Tzu-kung, who during Confucius' lifetime seems to have been employed as a diplomatist and ritualist in Lu (Ai 7:29.23-24; Ai 12:29.78; Ai 15:30.16) might have continued to be associated with court activities after Confucius' death (*A*:19.23). (Note the tale of Tzu-kung's diplomatic skill variously reported in *SC*:67.2197-2201; *MT*:9.21b-22a; *HFT*:19.2). Tzu-kung is also said to have been the teacher of T'ien Tzu-fang, who may have carried out diplomatic missions for the ruler of Wei[a] (Ch'ien 1956:129). Among the remaining disciples, none apparently pursued political careers, although one of Tseng Shen's pupils was a judge on the estate of a warlord family in Lu (*A*:19.19).

51. While neither the *Shih-chi* nor the *Chan-kuo ts'e* can be considered fully reliable, their information is at least presented in a historical framework that allows us to make certain tests of consistency, and that provides important context for judging the historical value of a statement. Certainly in the case of the *Shih-chi* we can rely on the outline of the chronicle and on the historiographical motives of the author. Other early "free" texts may contain reliable historical material, but the motives of the authors are generally polemical, and assessing the historicity of anecdotes and other statements that appear in them is virtually impossible. The portrait of Ruism in politics that is presented here is mainly based on a survey of the *Chan-kuo ts'e*, *Mencius*, *Hsun Tzu*, and those sections of the *Shih-chi* that deal directly with Warring States history. Despite the limited base for the portrait, the evidence of the histories is so strikingly negative with regard to Ruist political involvement that it seems unlikely that our conclusions could be far off the mark—particularly if we allow that a mid-Han work such as the *Shih-chi* would seem more likely to exaggerate early Ruist political activity than to overlook it.

52. In addition to the information cited above concerning the disciples, the following represents the record of Ruism in politics during the Warring States period.
(1) The *Mencius* tells us that at one time the state of Lu contemplated giving control of administration to an erstwhile pupil of Mencius (*M*: 6B.13). There is no record that this was ever done, however. In *M*:1B.16 we learn that the pupil, Yueh-cheng Tzu did have some influence in Lu, but that this influence was not sufficient to gain Mencius an audience with the Duke (he is not mentioned in the *Shih-chi*). A more pertinent

issue is whether Yueh-cheng Tzu was a disciple. Apparently, judging by *M*:4A.23-24 and 6B.13, Yueh-cheng Tzu did not travel with Mencius. Although Yueh-cheng Tzu is named by honorific in the text, this does not conclusively indicate that he was a Ruist Master in later years (in *M*:6B.8, the general Shen Ku-li is referred to by the honorific Shen Tzu, and other possible examples of non-Ru are named in this way). Other evidence suggests that Yueh-cheng Tzu's relation to Mencius may have involved more courtesy than reverence.

There *was* a Ruist Master surnamed Yueh-cheng, but Liang Ch'i-ch'ao and Ch'en Ch'i-yu are probably correct in identifying him as Tseng Shen's pupil Yueh-cheng Tzu-ch'un (*HFTCS*:1083n10). According to the *Li-chi*, Yueh-cheng Tzu-ch'un did become the Master of a study group (*Chi-yi*:14.12b); we have no such information about Mencius' pupil. Possibly, the Yueh-cheng Tzu of the *Mencius* was a descendant of Tseng Shen's pupil. "Yueh-cheng," which originally denoted the office of Music Master, seems to have been a surname of the state of Lu (see *M*:5B.3 for another Yueh-cheng of Lu). The clan name, with its musical associations, in itself suggests a possible connection with Ruist interests. If we hypothesize that the Yueh-cheng Tzu of the Mencius studied with Mencius as a temporary pupil, with his family, by virtue of long-standing Ruist connections, arranging the employment of Mencius as his tutor, rather than as a disciple who traveled with Mencius and identified himself as a Ru, this would seem to match the portrait of the man visible in the *Mencius*: a man with Ruist antecedents and political ambitions.

(2) The *Mencius* also tells us that during the reign of Duke Mu of Lu (r.c. 415-383 B.C.) Ruists occupied positions in government (*M*:6B.6). An echo of the story appears in the *Shih-chi* (119.3101-2), but its context is anecdotal, and its historical value is questionable.

(3) A famous example of greater reliability is the case of the philosopher Hsun Tzu, who was appointed a magistrate in the town of Lan-ling in Lu by the warlord prime minister of the state of Ch'u, which had just conquered Lu (*SC*:74.2348, 78.2395). The significance of the appointment is unclear, however. By some reckonings, at the time of the appointment (255 B.C) Hsun Tzu was over eighty years old, and the post may have merely been a formal recognition of his intellectual eminence. In any event, we find no record of Hsun Tzu seeking a political position, and the circumstances of Ch'u's conquest might have made this one difficult to decline. (These issues are discussed further in chapter VI.) Another version of this incident holds that soon after being appointed to govern Lan-ling, Hsun Tzu was dismissed and went to the state of Chao, where he was made a high minister (*ch'ing*[b]),

which post he soon resigned in order to return to his post in Lan-ling (*CKT*:5.38b-40a). The tale probably arises out of the fact that Hsun Tzu's style name was Ch'ing, and he was from Chao. The historicity of this tale was questioned as early as the mid-Ch'ing by Wang Chung, and his scepticism is endorsed by Ch'ien Mu (1956:432). Knoblock, however, accepts the episode (1982-83:41).

(4) After Hsun Tzu's time, the only record of a Ruist holding a government post is a brief statement in the *Shih-chi* that a descendant of Confucius, known as Tzu-shen or Tzu-shun, held high office in the state of Wei[a] (*SC*:47.1947). However, the records of that state, as found in the *Shih-chi*, do not mention him (Ch'ien 1956:490). Possibly the post was a ritualist position (see note 105).

This handful of examples—plus the special case of Mencius, which is discussed elsewhere—represents virtually the entire roster of men who were unquestionably Ruists and who held administrative positions in government during the Warring States period, based on our best sources. In addition to these examples, however there are a number of other instances where men who *might* have been Ru appear in political positions.

(5) Among these are a group of shadowy figures, about whom we know next to nothing, who appear briefly in the *Shih-chi*. These men speak or act like Ru, but they are not identified as such, and they appear to be more like legendary characters or pure literary devices than genuine historical figures. These include Kan Lung and Tu Chih (*SC*:5.203, 68.2229), Chao Liang (68.2233-35), and Niu Hsu (43.1797), who is said to have been a court tutor in Chao. Few of these figures are definitely identifiable as Ru, but they are made to mouth ideas consistent with Ruism, and their role in the text may reflect the fact that there were frequently Ruist retainers at feudal courts who were granted audiences or were allowed to advise their rulers occasionally, on the basis of their reputations as wise men.

Apart from these examples, we encounter a few certifiably historical figures who are classified as Ruists in some sources, but who possibly or probably were not.

(6) Of these, perhaps the most elusive is Yü Ch'ing, whose lost book *Yü-shih ch'un-ch'iu* is listed among Ruist works by the *Yi-wen chih* (*HS*:30.1726). Yü Ch'ing was, for a time, Prime Minister of Chao, but was he a Ru? The evidence is very slim. His *Shih-chi* biography mentions no Ruist connections; it calls him a "wandering persuader" (*yu-shui chih shih*). The record of his tenure in Chao indicates that he engaged in amoral intrigue such as any other politician of his day. But he does stand out because he reportedly resigned his post for ethical

reasons, to protest the unjust persecution of a friend by the Chao ruler, who was bending to pressure from Ch'in. As for the classification of his book as Ruist in the *Han-shu*, its reliability is undermined by the inclusion of a number of manifestly non-Ruist books in the same category (Eno 1984:212). Probably any text titled a "ch'un-ch'iu" was so classified, regardless of content.

(7) We must mention, finally, the surprising description of Li K'o and Wu Ch'i as Ruists. Both men were renowned as militarist thinkers, and their fame rested solidly on their skills in warfare and diplomatic intrigue. However, evidence reports that both studied under Ruist Masters for a time, and some sources classify them as Ruists. Li K'o is listed as a student of Tzu-hsia (Ch'ien 1956:132), but the reliability of the record is cast in doubt by the fact that Mo Tzu's disciple Ch'in Ku-li is also so listed (*SC*: 121.3116). Li K'o and Tzu-hsia both served at the court of Marquis Wen of Wei[a], and the belief that Li was a student of Tzu-hsia may have arisen from no more than this coincidence. Wu Ch'i is said to have studied with Tseng Tzu for a time (*SC*:65.2165), and the *Pieh-lu* listed him as a transmitter of the *Tso-chuan* (Ch'ien 1956:156). But if either of these men did, in fact, study under Ruist Masters, in achieving political prominence it seems they must have abandoned every principle of Ruist doctrine, and relied on skills utterly divorced from their Ruist studies. Li K'o was known for his ability to plan strategic warfare on the basis of topographical advantage: "Wei[a] employed Li K'o, who could exhaust the advantages of topography to strengthen his lord. Henceforward, all competed in war, valuing cunning and force and despising humane righteousness ..." (*SC*:30.1442; cf. 74.2349, 129.3258). (However, see also *SC*:44.1840, where Li K'o is portrayed in a way consistent with Ruist values.) Wu Ch'i's skill lay in battle tactics: "Marquis Wen asked Li K'o, 'What sort of a man is Wu Ch'i?' 'Greedy and lustful,' replied Li K'o. 'But in disposing troops, [none] can surpass him'" (*SC*:65.2166). If these two men had Ruist backgrounds, they must be considered exceptions that prove the rule, for if they represent Ru who followed their political ambitions to achieve power and fame, then they also show that only a complete rejection of their Ruist personas could allow them to follow this course.

53. One writer who seems to have noted the early Ruist detachment from politics after Confucius is H. G. Creel (1949:176). It is interesting to speculate on how this politically withdrawn period of Ruism came to an end. My own view is that Ruism was, not surprisingly, politicized by the persecution it suffered under the Ch'in. During the revolt of Ch'en She, Ruists participated as partisans of the insurgent (*SC*: 121.3116).

Subsequently, they appear to have sided actively with Hsiang Yü, who possessed a fief in the Ruist homeland of Lu. The language of the *Shih-chi* seems to imply that the Ru were at least partially responsible for the state of Lu being the last part of the Empire to surrender to Liu Pang (*SC*:7.337-38, 121.3117). If this were true, we would expect the Ru to have been persona non grata during the early Han, and indeed, it was several decades before the Ru attained any significant influence at the Han court.

54. The scale of such patronage could be impressive. After resigning his post as a senior advisor in Ch'i, Mencius was offered an honorarium sufficient to support him and all of his disciples, simply for remaining within the borders of Ch'i to serve as a moral exemplar for the people (*M*:2B.10). He declined.

55. Even the "agriculturist" Hsu Hsing, a man of no discernable political wisdom, was granted an audience and a stipend in T'eng (*M*:3A.4). For a brief survey of the scope of this type of patronage, see Yang 1980:401-3.

56. On the Marquis' policy of honoring worthies (which was probably intended to legitimize his rule—he was a usurper), see Ch'ien 1956:129-34.

57. Mencius traveled to Ch'i during the reign of King Hsuan, a noted patron of worthies (*SC*:46.1895). The inference that T'eng was following a similar policy is suggested by the account of Hsu Hsing (*M*:3A.4). As for Sung, in about 328 B.C., the ruler of Sung took the title "King." Judging from *M*:3B.5, Mencius traveled to Sung at about this time, probably in the expectation that the ruler would try to legitimize his title by proclaiming an ethical policy of honoring worthies (see Ch'ien 1956:345; but see also Lau 1970:211 for a different view).

58. Confirmation of the nonpolitical character of Ru at court can also be found in the *Chuang Tzu*, which classifies wise men into six groups, one being wise ministers of court, and an entirely separate one being those who "speak of righteousness, devotion, and faithfulness, respect, prudence, and courtesy, and devote themselves completely to self-cultivation" (*K'o-yi*:15.1-4).

59. Warlords, too, could enhance their stature and defuse objections to their usurpations of feudal prerogative by patronizing worthies. During the third century B. C., the great warlords of Ch'i, Chao, Wei[a], and Ch'u vied to patronize wise men and knights-errant, even as they pursued ruthless policies of expansion (see Yang 1980:403). The *Shih-chi* summarizes one year's achievements by Ch'u's great warlord Prime Minister Lord Ch'un-shen by noting: "On behalf of Ch'u he attacked the North and extinguished the state of Lu, and he appointed [Hsun Tzu] magistrate of Lan-ling" (*SC*:78.2395).

60. We should be aware that in many instances, the presence of Ruist-

style rhetoric in a text might reflect not the substance of an historical speech, but the literary or ideological interests of the author of the text. In the case of the *Chan-kuo ts'e*, the authors cannot be suspected of Ruist loyalties (but see Ch'ien 1956:452). However, the nature of the text skews its historical value and may account for the occasional intrusion of Ruist rhetoric. As James Crump has demonstrated, the basic attitude of the text was less historical than literary; it was a compendium of rhetorical techniques, which could serve as a handbook for "persuaders" of rulers and warlords (1964). While its authors were not themselves Ruists, the text aptly shows that they were interested in the art of manipulating Ruist rhetoric, just as they were interested in manipulating Taoist and Legalist rhetoric. Hence, Ruist arguments are likely to appear in contexts where they clearly do not belong (e.g., the courtly Ruist debate over the adoption of barbarian dress in Chao [*CKT*:6.16b-23b]).

As for the *Shih-chi*, we should bear in mind that Ssu-ma Ch'ien was educated as a Ru, studying at least briefly under Tung Chung-shu (*SC*:130.3297). Although he might have been attracted to Taoist ideas, the overall outlook of his history is clearly Ruist, and any Thucydidean attempts to provide the gist of missing speeches might have been influenced by this. In addition, he apparently relied heavily on forms of the *Tso-chuan* and *Chan-kuo ts'e*, and thus perpetuated the skewed histories of those texts, with their transformations of Ruist ideas into historical incident. (On the bias of the *Tso-chuan*, see appendix B, note 4.)

61. Although the text probably fabricates the Ruist arguments (which are formulated in a cynical fashion), it is likely that only Ruist arguments could have been employed to persuade a king to cede his throne in this way.

62. The role of Chung-shan has become known through inscriptions on bronze vessels recently excavated in Hopei (*WW* 1979:1.1-31). The phrases quoted here are from the *Chung-shan fang-hu*. The rhetoric of the inscriptions, forged soon after the civil war in Yen, contains a great many Ruist ideas. But, in addition to damning the decadence of Yen, the text does not fail to emphasize that the value of Chung-shan's invasion lay also in the expansion of the state's narrow borders. The *Chan-kuo ts'e* tells us that at about the time these vessels were cast, Chung-shan was pursuing a policy of honoring worthies (*CKT*: 10.17b-18a), and this is borne out by the inscriptions, which duly celebrate this policy. It is not unlikely that Ruist retainers were available to compose these inscriptions (as well, perhaps, as other proclamations) legitimizing the conduct of the government. Whether the rulers of

Chung-shan actually sympathized with these Ruist sentiments is a moot point (see Li 1979:40).

63. Judging from the text of the *Mencius*, a high minister of Ch'i paid an "unofficial" private visit to Mencius and in the course of it asked him whether he thought that the conduct of Yen was deplorable and worthy of punishment. Mencius replied that it was. Ch'i subsequently attacked Yen, and the fact that the rulers of Ch'i used Mencius' words to justify their actions is suggested by the *Chan-kuo ts'e* account and also by the *Mencius'* depiction of someone asking Mencius, "Is it true that you urged that Ch'i attack Yen?" (*M*:2B.8). Mencius makes clear that he had not understood the consequences that his remark would have.

64. The most prominent of these militarists were Yueh Yi and Chü Hsin. The philosopher Tsou Yen was said to be among those who responded to Yen's call and received high honors, but he was apparently granted no role in government (*SC*:34.1558, 80.2427-28; but see Ch'ien 1956:439 on Tsou Yen).

65. Other examples of the insincere manipulation of Ruist rhetoric include the use of such rhetoric by the pragmatic persuader Su Ch'in to deceive a ruler whom he wished secretly to undermine (*SC*:69.2265).

66. The *Analects* tells us that Tzu-chang studied with Confucius with such a goal in mind (*A*:2.18). No evidence exists that he ever received political appointment, which might indicate Confucius' success in reorienting his ambition. It is also possible that *A*:2.18 refers not to seeking political posts but to seeking other types of employment, such as court ritualist.

67. Note the clear sense of being freed from an onerous burden. *A*:15.32 might be interpreted as having a similar message: "The *chün-tzu* aims at the Way, not at food for his table. In farming, there is a starvation; in study, there is a reward. The *chün-tzu* worries about the Way, not about poverty." This reading, which takes "*nei*ᵃ" (starvation) and "lu" (emolument) as figurative, was suggested to me by William Ts'ai.

68. Compare *A*:5.6.

69. This is the disciple Tsai Wo. The *Analects* does not mention Tsai Wo as holding any posts, but it nearly always portrays him in an unflattering light (*A*:3.21, 5.10, 6.26, 17.19). The *Shih-chi* tells us: "Tsai Wo was a noble of [Ch'i]. He joined T'ien Ch'ang in the latter's revolt, resulting in the execution of his entire clan. Confucius was ashamed of him" (67.2195). If this were true, it might account for the negative portrait encountered in the *Analects*. (See Ch'ien 1956:54-8, where an attempt is made to restore to Tsai Wo his good name.)

70. Mencius' willingness to meet with the Duke of Lu (*M*:1B.16) seems to have been an exception, but he might have had to overcome his scru-

ples when his erstwhile student Yueh-cheng Tzu managed to make arrangements for the Duke to visit Mencius. When, after all, the plan falls through and the Duke does not arrive, Mencius does not seem much disturbed.

71. I feel that the text of the *Mencius* makes this clear. Commentators are divided on the question of Mencius' actual responsibilities in Ch'i (Ch'ien 1956:236-37).

72. Other passages that indicate Mencius' negative attitude towards political involvement include *M*:4A.18, 7A.8, 7A.9.

73. The significance of the structure of the *Hsueh erh* chapter was first noted by Takeuchi (1939:90).

74. "Kung Meng Tzu came to see Mo Tzu wearing a ceremonial patterned hat and waist tablet, in Ru-clothes . . . . [He said,] 'The *chün-tzu* must speak and dress in ancient fashion before he can be *jen*' " (*MT, Kung Meng*: 12.9a-b). The *Chuang Tzu* refers to the prevalence of Ru-clothes in Lu and provides a description of them (*CT*:21.38-44). A passage in the *Li-chi* denies that Ru wore special clothes, an implicit indication that they did (*Ju-hsing*:19.3b-4a).

75. Note that the *Fei Ju* passage requires emendation (*MTCK*:9.33). *A*:7.18 indicates that the use of court dialect may have been confined to study sessions and ritual occasions.

76. On the question of whether Confucius was the first to be called a Ru, and on the origins of the term, see appendix B.

77. Examples include *A*:5.4, 5.9, 6.10, 7.24, 11.15, and 11.21, the last of which is particularly poignant. In it, Confucius' favorite disciple, Yen Yuan, whose early death was the bitterest moment of Confucius' life, catches up to the group after having fallen behind during a time of peril. "I took you for dead," says Confucius. "While you are alive," replies Yen Yuan, "how would I dare to die?" Of course, moral meanings might be and were read out of every *Analects* passage, but it seems to me that the story was passed on and included in the text in order to make future disciples weep.

78. Confucius' son predeceased Tzu-lu by about three years according to Ch'ien Mu's dating (1956:615). We may wonder whether Tzu-lu was here taking over the responsibilities of a deceased or a living son.

79. Passages such as this seem provocative when cast against the background of the Ruist interest in filiality. Commitment to the Ruist master and study group might not always have been consistent with commitment to parents, particularly if disciples lived and traveled with their Masters (a fact noted in the *Yen-t'ieh lun* [5.2a]). For evidence that the Ruist stress on filiality may have been a response to an initial perception of the sect as heretically *un*filial, see Eno 1984:222n93.

80. The *Tzu-chang* chapter of the *Analects* presents portraits of the disciples as Masters of their own study groups.

81. Disciples such as Wan Chang and Kung-sun Ch'ou were among those who appear to have traveled with Mencius extensively. If one accepts Kanaya Osamu's thesis that the second book of the *Mencius* is a roughly chronological account authored by Kung-sun Ch'ou (1950-51:24), then according to Ch'ien Mu's chronology (1956:314-17), Kung-sun Ch'ou would have been with Mencius through the entire course of his travels. (On Kung-sun Ch'ou, see Eno 1984:363n11.)

82. On the identification of Kao Tzu as a Ru, see chapter V, note 53.

83. We know very little about Hsun Tzu's study group. The *Hsun Tzu* is generally written in an impersonal style and might have been composed by several authors over a period of decades (see Kanaya 1951). Virtually none of Hsun Tzu's disciples appear in the text. But portions of the text offer clues about the life of the Ruist group in Hsun Tzu's time. These chapters, *Ch'eng-hsiang* and *Fu*, may be records of Ruist group chants and games, and they seem to offer a glimpse of a cohesive, dedicated, and socially alienated order (they are dicussed further in chapter VI).

84. See the *Fei shih-erh tzu* chapter and the attacks on Mencius in *Hsing o*.

85. See Hu 1919:120 for a schematic classification of these factions.

86. I translate *"hsueh"* as "study" rather than as "learn" or "learning" because I do not believe that the sense of completed action that is conveyed by "learn" is appropriate. *"Hsueh"* generally denotes the process rather than the result of learning (A:1.7 would be an exception). Although the word "study" has its own problems, chiefly its connotation of book learning, it is frequently used in broader senses close to those in the Ruist texts, as in "studying dance." (For contrary views, see Lau 1979:44 and Hall and Ames 1987:43-4; 339n12.)

87. The various accounts of Western Chou education are discussed and compared in Ch'en P'an's excellent survey (1974).

88. The only formal institution for education that we know definitely existed during the early Chou was the archery training hall (Creel 1970:407). The hall may also have been where warriors were trained to dance, as is suggested by the *K'uang yu* inscription, "King Yi had the Hsiang dance performed at the archery hall" (*Ta-hsi*:3.8b). The *Kung-yang chuan* also mentions a pavilion that was almost certainly the archery hall (*TCHC*: 11.48-9) as being used to store musical instruments (*Kung-yang chuan* Hsuan 16:16.11). On varieties of other possible early institutions, see Eno 1984:224n101.

89. A:9.2 indicates that these studies were not evaluated as highly as others. Creel has argued from this that Confucius did not teach them (1949:82).

90. The *Yi-li* includes an account of the village archery match, which in itself might indicate that Ruists studied archery as a ritual mode, if we view the text as a ritual handbook, studied in class. Note also that archery is sometimes used as a simile in ethical discussions (e.g., *M*:7A.41), whereas martial arts like swordsmanship, which Ru seem not to have studied, are not.

91. Of the three citations of "Documents" in the *Analects* (excluding the *Yao yueh* chapter, which is undoubtedly a late addition to the text), one, *A*:2.21, cites a passage that does not appear in any part of the "New Text" (genuine) *Documents*, nor is it cited in any other pre-Ch'in text. Its invocation (*shu yun*) might not refer to the *Documents* we know. In the case of *A*:8.20, the passage is probably an insertion from the fourth century B.C. (see Eno 1984:294-95). This would leave *A*:14.40 as the sole citation of the *Documents* that might date from the earliest days of Ruism.

92. A discussion of the rules of citation appears in *TC*, Hsiang 4:14.16-19.

93. It is only when one takes into account the ritual role of the *Poetry* in formal speech that *A*:13.5 makes sense: "Though one may be able to recite the three hundred odes, if upon being given governmental responsibility one cannot convey his ideas [by means of them], or if when sent as emissary to distant lands one cannot [use them] to respond on his own initiative, then though [one has studied] much, of what use is it?" Study of the *Poetry* by noble sons was probably widespread during the late Chou (see, e.g., *CKT*:3.76b).

94. Ruist textual study early grew to include the *Spring and Autumn Annals* (*M*:7B.2; *H*:1.30, 34), and the *Yi ching* (e.g., *H*:27.39). On the latter, the *Tso-chuan* shows an intense interest in the text, but it is not mentioned in the *Mencius*, and the single possible reference to it in the *Analects* (7.17) might not prove that it was studied by the earliest Ruists (see Dubs 1928). In addition, Ruist texts refer to unnamed sources (*chuan*) and show thorough knowledge of the doctrines, and perhaps the books, of contemporary thinkers (verbatim knowledge of contemporary texts is suggested in Riegel's analysis of *M*:2A.2 [1979:437-38]).

95. This is discussed in the context of a utopian vision of a fully ritualized society, where every individual's *li*-determined material environment cultivates the precise virtues proper to his designated station.

96. But note also that *li* could be the beginnings as well as the end of study (*A*:19.12).

97. The *Hsun Tzu* satirizes Ru who are unable to bring off the delicate stylization of the ideal man (*H*:6.45-48). The intricate choreography of finely executed *li* is well illustrated in *A*:10.1-4, which describes the behavior of the *chün-tzu* at court.

98. See also *A*:15.42, where we see a music master come to visit the study group.

99. It might indicate that Confucius instructed court music masters about the proper occasions for performing certain pieces.

100. Two post-Ch'in sources mention this: the Mao commentary to *Poetry*: 91/1, and Wei Chao's commentary at *KY*, *Lu-yü*:5.15b. Confirmation in pre-Ch'in texts appears at *MT*, *Kung Meng*:12.11a; *TC*, Hsiang 16:16.3. See also Ikeda 1955:75; Chen 1974:31.

101. On the translation of "*feng*[a]," see Eno 1984:226n114. The passage is probably a late addition to the text (see *WSTK*:454, 458; Kimura 1971:353). It may be viewed as a commentary on *A*:5.8. In that passage, the first three of the disciples are characterized in terms of the personal goals set out in 11.24, and Confucius notes in each case that whether they are *jen* is doubtful. If 11.24 was composed with the earlier passage in mind, the implication would be that Tseng Tien's answer encapsulates *jen*.

102. *A*:7.7 indicates that a tuition gift, however small, was expected of disciples (but note that Cheng Hsuan offered a very different interpretation [Ch'eng 1965:388]). Stress has traditionally been laid on the fact that the passage shows that Confucius was democratically willing to accept as tuition even the smallest class of ritual gift, thus not excluding poor students. But the passage also suggests that he accepted tuition from this level "on up", and there may have been a tradition of "from each according to his means." *M*:2B.10 implies that Masters supported their disciples, but the more general rule may have been one of sharing resources within the group.

103. The role of Ru as popular teachers is suggested by the *Chou-li*, which refers to them as "those who employ the Way to attract the people" (*T'ien-kuan*, T'ai-tsai:1.15b-16a), and lists them along with "elders" and "teachers" (*Ti-kuan*, Ta ssu-t'u:3.17b).

104. Occasionally, feudal lords might even bestow unsolicited gifts on prominent Ru, as a way of demonstrating their own virtue (*M*:5B.6).

105. A number of Ru are seen occupying positions as "*hsiang*," a term that could denote a high political post, but that could also mean "master of ceremony" at a ritual or diplomatic event. It is in this latter role that Ruists appear in the *Tso-chuan* (e.g., Confucius: Ting 10:28.21-24; Meng Wu-po: Ai 17:30.39).

106. Discussions appear in *A*:17.19; *M*:3A.2; *H*:19.79-91; and throughout early Ruist texts. For an important discussion of the three years mourning ritual, see Hu 1934:27-35.

107. The economic interest that Ruists had in promoting funerals is viciously satirized in the *Mo Tzu*'s caricature of early Ruists, which is

worth quoting at length:

> [The Ru] lives in poverty . . . He turns his back on what is basic by refusing to work, and contents himself with laziness and arrogance. He has no means of keeping himself from starving in times of shortage and freezing when it grows cold. . . . In the summer he begs for grain, but once the harvest is in, he goes chasing after big funerals. All his children follow him there, to eat and drink their fill. If he can manage a few of these, it will be enough to get by. . . . When a wealthy family requires a funeral he is delighted. "Here," he says gleefully, "is the spring from which food and clothing flow!" (*Fei Ju*:9.17a-b).

The *Chuang Tzu* includes a portrait that is even more unsavory, if that is possible. It pictures Ruist funeral experts piously robbing graves (*CT*:26.16-18). The degree to which these caricatures are accurate is certainly questionable, but they do alert us to the popular views of the cult, and seem to show that the picture of Ru as impoverished was widespread and surely had a basis in fact.

108. It is possible that not all Ruists were reconciled to the necessary compromises that social living entails. There are indications that some preferred to reject paths of economic opportunity and withdraw into eremetic lifestyles. One of Confucius' disciples, Yuan Hsien (Ssu), is said to have done this (*SC*:67.2208), and the elusive philosopher Lu Chung-lien, if he was, in fact, a Ru, may be another example (*SC*: 83.2460-69; *CKT, Chao ts'e*:4.52-54). In addition, certain parts of the *Analects* suggest eremetic tendencies (e.g., the *Wei Tzu* chapter), and parts of the *Hsun Tzu* seem to have been written precisely to combat an eremetic branch of Ruism (*H*:4.57-58, 5.40-41, 6.11-12).

Chapter III

1. Totalism is a nonstandard philosophical term that has been applied in various ways in connection with China. Robert Lifton has used the term in Erik Erikson's sense to refer to "a tendency towards all-or-nothing emotional alignments" (1961:129). Lifton's use of the term is narrower than ours, but is probably compatable as one aspect of Ruist totalism.
2. Compare *H*:21.41-42: "Sitting in one's room, one can see throughout the four seas; living in today, one can see the order of distant ages."
3. The phrase appears in several chapters: *KT, Hsin-shu* II:13.5a; *Pai-hsin*: 13.7b; *Nei-yeh*:16.4a. For a discussion of these chapters as representative of a "Chi-hsia school of materialism," see Fung 1962:274f. On their authorship, see the contrasting views in Hou 1957:397-99 and Fung 1962:168. The same phrase also appears in a late chapter of the *Chuang Tzu* (*CT*:23.34-35).

4. Metzger's description is appropriate for neo-Confucianism, with its great emphasis on theoretical coherence, but even in the neo-Confucian case extending the notion of totalism to cover action might be warranted. As Metzger himself notes, for neo-Confucians the importance of thinking was tied to the quest for action standards (1977:66). The explicit linkage of cognition and action as an enduring theme of Confucian (and post-Confucian) philosophy has been analyzed by Donald Munro in his model of the clustering of knowing, feeling, and promptings to act in traditional Chinese concepts of mind (1977:26-37).

5. This narrow dogmatism can be greatly modified in texts such as the *Chuang Tzu*, where identification with the Tao can be attained through mastery of almost any skill: swimming, butchering, or catching cicadas on a pole (but apparently not through ritual mastery). However, no intrinsic value is found in these activities or in becoming skilled in them. Ultimately, despite a plurality of paths to the totalism, there is no pluralism of values in the Taoist world.

The closed portrait of human perfection entailed in practical totalism may bear upon the issues raised by Rosemont concerning the "openness" of Ruist ideal society (1970-71). The fact that the guiding philosophy of the Ruist state would reject a pluralism of values might predispose it to development in a "closed" direction. This issue is related to the nature of moral choice in Ruism, which, as Fingarette has noted, becomes a unitary issue of following or not following the Ruist Tao (1972:chapter 2).

6. The use of the word "*jen*" varies in the *Analects*. It can be used in both a weak and a strong sense (paralleling the use of the word "*chün-tzu*"). Used in the weak sense, it means little more than "goodness." Examples of *jen* used in the weak sense include A:12.22, 15.33 (for *chün-tzu* in the weak sense, see A:11.1, 14.6). In discussing *jen* as the key to the Sagely totalism, we are excluding passages where it is used in this weak sense.

7. The mystery of the term may be related to the fact that, as far as we can tell, Confucius seems to have been the first historical figure to use the word as a major ethical term. It is rarely encountered in pre-Confucian sources, and when we do find it, it does not seem to carry a great deal of weight. For a detailed discussion, see Lin 1974-75. Lin arrives at a root gloss of "manly" for *jen*. (178-80). Note that the reconstructed Chou reading (*ńięn) might have been cognate with *ning* (*nieng): "glib," and the graphemics of this relationship would tend to enhance Lin's argument. (All phonetic reconstructions are based on *GSR*.) If this relation between "*jen*" and "*ning*" were pursued, it might increase our understanding of *Analects* passages such as A:5.5.

8. *A*:6.30 is a notable exception, but in that case, Confucius' response, which stresses that *jen* is *far* simpler than what his disciple suggests, might merely reverse the direction of the problem of *"jen"* rather than solve it (compare *A*:7.30).

9. A few commentators do not agree that Confucius grants the quality of *jen* in this passage (see Ting 1949:3.3). I am grateful to Yan Shoucheng for alerting me to this.

10. I have taken *"li*ᵈ*"* as a verb parallel to *"ch'u,"* based on *M*:2A.7, 4A.11 (see Wang Ying-lin's commentary to *A*:4.1 in Ch'eng 1965:197). *Jen* and wisdom are repeatedly linked in the *Analects* (*A*:4.2, 6.23, 9.29, 15.33). In most cases, they should not be taken as either independent or mutually exclusive, as, for example, Waley's interpretation of *A*:6.23 (VI.21) suggests (1938:120, 239-40).

11. The comprehensiveness of *jen* is indicated in other passages, where it is prior to filiality (*hsiao; A*:1.2), devotion (*chung; A*:5.19, 13.19), purity (*ch'ing*ᵃ; *A*:5.19), and vigilance (*ching; A*:13.19) among others (cf. *A*:17.5). There is a passage in the *Analects* where *jen* seems to be superseded by the term "Sage" (*sheng; A*:6.30). Tsuda took this to mean that in a hierarchy of virtues, "Sageliness" was superior to *jen* (1946:135). However, *A*:6.30 is a paradoxical reply to a question about *jen*, stressing the ease of achieving *jen* in contrast to the interlocutor's high-flown portrait. *"Sheng"* probably carried a special rhetorical force because it was a traditional term for mythical Sages, whose stature it would be all but impious to aspire to surpass. These Sages, as past kings, not only came complete with all virtues but with breathtaking political achievements already on record. They were both good and successful. The notion of *jen* addresses virtue, but not success (except perhaps in *A*:14.17-18). It is not that the *sheng-jen* is better than the *jen-jen*, but that the former term carried different rhetorical overtones. On problems of rationalizing the *Analects'* hierarchy of terms, see Hall and Ames 1987:185-88.

    In a related matter, we might note that what was perhaps the primary pre-Confucian virtue, *"te,"* also plays a role in the *Analects*. It is used as a noncontroversial term denoting "high virtue," as distinguished from the provocative new term *"jen,"* whose meaning was not fully delineated by traditional use. The two words have roughly similar weight in the *Analects*, and they tend to obey a "law of avoidance" (they appear together only in *A*:7.6 and 14.4). They, too, should not be compared according to their status in a hierarchy of virtue. They essentially belong to different terminological sets.

12. Literally: ". . . I would tap it at both ends and empty it." There seems to be a metaphor operating, but I cannot identify it.

13. The *Mencius* contains a very eloquent passage that describes the teaching of the ineffable totalistic skill:

> The *chün-tzu* deeply immerses [his student] in the Way: he wishes him to find it for himself. Once he has found it, he will learn to dwell in it at ease. Once he dwells in it at ease, he will learn to draw deeply from it. Once he draws deeply from it, then as he takes it to himself he will encounter its source to his every left and right. Hence the *chün-tzu* wishes him to find it for himself (*M*:4B.14).

Previous translations have taken the object of the *chün-tzu's* teaching to be himself, which runs counter to the grammar of the passage and, as Dobson noted, renders the meaning very dubious (see Dobson 1963:148n31).

14. Tseng Shen was only about twenty-six when Confucius died (Ch'ien 1956:615-16), one of the youngest disciples. He probably would not have been so deeply initiated as this passage suggests. It was probably composed by pupils of Tseng Shen (he is named by honorific), and if so, his remarks would represent his mature interpretation of the "single thread." The passage might have been inserted in Book 4 after the book had already taken shape; it is the only interruption in the stylistic homogeneity of the book (excepting the final entry, attributed to Tzu-yu and probably appended). An examination of the functions of the disciples in the *Analects* suggests that Tseng Tzu and the subtle Tzu-kung are cast in competition as authoritative interpreters of Confucius' ideas.

15. See, for example, *LYCY*:82 and, more recently, Ch'ien 1963:129. This also seems to be the final position of Fingarette, who has made a detailed analysis of the passage (1979a:397-98).

16. Loan instances are found between "*chung*" and "*chung*[b]" (*H*:25.33, 29.3-5). On the meaning of the latter word as "inner recesses of the mind" (a sense common in the *Tso-chuan*), see Ikeda 1968:27, 30n8.

17. Only one passage in the *Analects* allows us to distinguish whether "*chung*" denoted loyalty to persons or to duty; all others permit the ambiguity. The passage is *A*:5.19. It reads:

> Tzu-chang asked, "The Grand Minister Tzu-wen was thrice appointed as Grand Minister and never displayed pleasure. He was thrice discharged and never displayed displeasure. Invariably, he reported to the incoming minister the affairs of his term in office. What would you say of him?" "That he was *chung*," replied the Master.

"*Chung*" appears to signify a complete submergence of self-interest in scrupulous devotion to duty. The passage tends to confirm glosses of "*chung*" as "exhausting the mind" (*SWCTKL*:10B.4658b, Tuan Yü-ts'ai's gloss) or "exhausting integrity (*ch'ing*)" (Huang K'an citing Wang Pi [Ch'eng 1965:232]).

Fingarette, in his analysis of *A*:4.15, stresses the notion of *chung* as loyalty to persons (1979a:389, 393). In places, however, he seems to equate this with loyalty to responsibilities (390).

18. Note, however, that in texts such as the *Tso-chuan, Hsun Tzu, Ta-hsueh,* and *Chung-yung*, "*shu*" seems to mean something closer to "do not demand from others what you are not yourself competent to do." The word "*shu*" does not appear in pre-Confucian sources. It appears only twice in the *Analects* (4.15, 15.24), and much of both of these passages may be borrowed from other entries in the text (15.3, 5.12, 12.2). One cannot help but wonder whether Confucius himself ever used the word.

19. The *Shuo-wen* gives the variant form (*SWCTKL*:10B.4672b). Note that because no instances of loans are found to confirm this etymological analysis of "*shu*" (so far as I am aware), it must be considered speculative.

20. It is interesting to consider Cheng Hsuan's comment to the preface of the first ode of the *Poetry*: " '*Chung*' means to feel for another (*shu*) from the heart's core (*chung*ᵃ)." (The gloss seems odd in context, and Cheng may have borrowed it.) Note that from our perspective, *shu* is, perhaps, more likely to have entailed a process of projecting one's own needs rather than internalizing the needs of others. This is particularly so in light of a tendency in Chinese thought, both early and late, to take as an a basic axiom the assumption that human needs and emotions are innate and universal. The result has been that Chinese thinkers have not stressed the need to make allowances for important differences among individuals, and the parameters governing ethical prescripts to empathize have been narrow. I am grateful to Donald Munro for bringing this to my attention.

21. I have supplied here an additional phrase from a parallel passage (*H*:5.46-47). In this latter passage, the dance metaphor is more completely drawn, but becomes mixed with other metaphors. I have supplied the phrase for illustrative purposes; I do not mean to suggest that the text should be emended.

22. Waley objected to the interpretation of "*k'o*" as "conquer" (1938:162n1), but relevant passages in the *Tso-chuan* (Chao 10:22.26; Chao 12:22.54, to which Waley alludes) indicate that the evidence does not support his gloss of "to be able" (although that is, of course, a common meaning of "*k'o*" in early texts).

23. See, for example, Tu 1968:33-34. Benjamin Schwartz's recent discussion of the relation of *jen* and *li* also reflects a commitment to rationalize

the priority of *jen* over ritual (1985:80-82).

24. Lin Yü-sheng has made points similar to those I am making here (1974-75:193-96). Note that the *chün-tzu* will always act according to *li* after "throwing away his books." However, he will have more leeway to act than others. As the *Mencius* states: "The great man will not always be true to his word or follow through to the end: he cleaves to the right" (4B.11; see also the discussion of *ch'üan* in 4A.18). The Sage fully embodies *li* and, as such, becomes a creator of *li* in the manner of the great Sages of the past.

25. Many ideas in this analysis owe a debt to Fingarette 1972: chapter 3.

26. Fingarette's claims have been strongly rejected by H. G. Creel (1979: 410-12) and Benjamin Schwartz (1985:78-80), but neither has offered sustained arguments to disprove these claims or attempted to explain why the *Analects* is so reticent concerning the affective dimension of decision-making.

27. The doctrine associated with Plato is most explicit in *Alcibiades* I: 129-30. Although the authorship of the text may be spurious, it is consistent with other dialogues, such as the *Phaedo*.

28. For example, *A*:4.17; cf 12.4.

29. I am building on the *Shuo-wen* definition of *"ssu"* as grain and the use of the term to denote the private field in *Poetry* 277.

30. See *A*:9.22, where Yen Yuan is also described through the metaphor of ripening grain using the term *"fa*ᵃ*."* The use of *"fa*ᵃ*"* in the sense of grain ripening appears in *Poetry* 277.

31. The fact that *"hsing*ᵃ*"* here denotes inspection rather than introspection is signaled by the absence of the modifier "inner" (*nei*). However, in the *Hsun Tzu* the term *nei hsing* is used to refer to self-examination of one's public conduct (11.96). Compare *A*:1.4, which seems to bridge public and private: "I daily inspect (*hsing*ᵃ) my person on three counts: Have I been conscientious when planning on behalf of others; have I been faithful in dealings with friends; have I practiced the teachings I pass on?"

32. Several factors might have contributed to this sort of portrait of the self. The link of private and public realms is consistent with assumptions about the nature of cognitive processes pervasive in Chinese philosophy. Donald Munro has demonstrated that cognitive acts were conceived in a manner that intrinsically entailed them with action dispositions and that this manner of "clustering" mental processes that we demarcate rigidly is built into the meaning of the verb "to know" (Munro 1977:27-37). The differences between Chinese and Western views of self may also have been fostered by the radically different linguistic grammars that influenced the structure of ontological assump-

tions. Chad Hansen has argued that Classical Chinese lacks principles of noun individuation that are characteristic of Indo-European languages (1985:41-42), and this might have militated against the search for a core substance of individuation such as guided Western approaches. Hansen's claim that the Classical Chinese equational sentence expresses a part-whole relationship rather than a substance-predicate one fits well with the notion of individual persons as intrinsically social.

33. On the atomic portrait of the individual, see Lukes 1973:73-78.

34. Munro's account describes the resonance between traditional Chinese views of human nature as social and those of Marx. For Marx's critique of the exclusion of social dimensions from portraits of human nature, see Lukes 1973:75-76.

35. The *Mo Tzu* adopts a Hobbesian picture of precivilized society in the *Shang-t'ung* chapter (*MT*:3.1-2), and this could indicate a belief that social attributes are not intrinsic. However, the *Hsun Tzu*'s somewhat similar portrait (19.1-2) is reconciled with intrinsic social dispositions.

36. My suggestion that the notion of human nature as social may have been a pre-philosophical consensus is based on familiarity with Chou bronze inscriptions. The unfailing linkage of individual to ancestors and progeny in those texts seems to me to reflect a fundamental vision of the individual as bound to the context of family and clan. The persistence of the portrait of the individual as social, demonstrated in Munro's work, further suggests that the Ruist portrait was a "transmission" rather than an "innovation."

37. On the theories of the *Hsun Tzu*, see chapter VI.

38. For glosses of *jen* as "person," see *M*:7B.16; *CY*:20. For "person" as "*jen*," see *Shih-ming, Shih hsing-t'i*:2.51.

39. *Hsiao ching*:1 indicates that filiality was viewed as the basis of all relational roles.

40. The *Chuang Tzu* speaks of the futility of discovering a true inner self through an inventory of subjective faculties (2.16-18). This indicates that notions comparable to Western portraits of the self were not alien to contemporary ways of thought. That the *Chuang Tzu* was sceptical that an inner self could be found in this way does not, of course, indicate that the text subscribed to the view of man as innately social. The Taoist schools dissented from the mainstream, and this probably is as true for *hsien*-Taoists (to use Creel's term) as for the authors of the *Chuang Tzu* and the *Tao te ching*.

41. Donald Munro, suggests a contrast between neo-Confucian views of the self and an Augustinian model. Munro notes that for Augustine, the pivotal axis on which selfhood revolves is a vertical link between the individual soul and God: the self of the *Confessions* is one increas-

ingly alienated from its social surroundings in an inner search for the link to God. For Chu Hsi, the axis is horizontal: the search for the self is carried out through alert social practice—it is through links with other humans that one discerns, and then shapes one's true nature (1988:105-6). In this respect, Chu Hsi is faithful to the early Ruist approach. The influence of Augustinian self-scrutiny in later Christian views of the individual is noted in Lukes 1973:94-98.

42. Hence, Mencius' remark that those who allow their innate moral qualities to be submerged in other elements of their natural endowment seem no different from animals (*M*:6A.8 cf. 4B.19).

43. On these dimensions in Western portraits of the individual, see Lukes 1973:67-77.

44. In *M*:5B.1 we are presented with a variety of Sages, each with his own personality, from the intolerantly upright Po Yi, to the altruistic Yi Yin, to the affable Liu Hsia-hui. However, the case for individuality is somewhat vitiated by the latter portion of the passage, which exalts Confucius far beyond any of these men. The passage seems cognate with *A*:18.8.

45. One might argue that by omitting individual personality from discussions of the individual, Ruists in fact shielded idiosyncratic thought and behavior from the negative implications of their ritualist doctrines. While self-regarding dispositions were always subject to attack, idiosyncrasy underwent a benign neglect that left Ruism in a position to absorb aspects of Taoism in conceiving well-rounded models of the *chün-tzu*, particularly from the T'ang period on, models that could sanction the influence of a Li Po on a Tu Fu, or the eccentricities of a Su Tung-p'o.

According to the theory of skill systems outlined in the introduction, what we refer to by the term "personality" might correspond closely to the individual's repertoire of skills. Ruism's commitment to a monolithic set of ritual skills tends, in theory, to imply a convergence of personalities among Ruist Masters. But once again, theory and experience diverge. Our notion of skill systems is a descriptive tool and encompasses all aspects of personal skill, not merely skills acquired through formal training. Our model tends to predict that the members of the Ruist community striving for Sagehood through *li* would reflect the sort of personality convergence that characterizes any professional cohort when viewed from the outside. Viewed from within, variety of personality appears as an obvious fact.

Chapter IV

1. In preparing translations and commentary interpretations of the *Analects*, I have taken the *LYYT* text as standard, and I have relied on Ch'en

1968 for information on textual variants. Passage citations conform to
LYYT numbers. For traditional commentaries, I have relied heavily upon
Ch'eng 1965, which includes a broad range of materials with pre-Sung
interpretations well represented. I have also referred to the *Lun-yü
cheng-yi* [*LYCY*], a nineteenth-century commentary by Liu Pao-nan. I
have consulted and benefited from the following English and Japanese
translations: Legge 1894; Waley 1938; Chan 1963 (partial); Kaizuka
1973; Miyazaki 1974; Lau 1979. All translations appearing in the chapter are my own.

2. The simplest theory of the origins of the *Analects*, to which almost all
scholars subscribe in one form or another, is stated in the *Yi-wen chih*
chapter of the *Han shu*: "The *Lun-yü* [*Analects*] contains the teachings
that Confucius spoke in responding to disciples and contemporaries,
and the lessons learned from their Master that the disciples spoke to
one another. Each disciple of the time made his own record. After their
Master's death, his followers collectively edited and collated these;
hence, they are called the 'collated teachings' (*lun-yü*)" (*HS*:1717).
In fact, we possess no testimony concerning the composition of the
Analects predating the first century A.D., the *Yi-wen chih* and the
Cheng-shuo chapter of Wang Ch'ung's *Lun-heng* being our earliest
sources on this matter. Neither text is able to report specifics of compilation or transmission of the text prior to the early Han.

The *Lun-heng* tells us that during the early Han, until the reign of
Wu-ti (140-87 B.C.), no copies of the text were generally known due to
the great Ch'in book burnings. (The *Yi-wen chih* does not report this,
but its testimony may be consistent with Wang Ch'ung's report [Kimura
1971:165].) Possibly no text known as the "Lun-yü" existed during the
pre-Ch'in period, which could indicate that the final editorial stages
occurred as late as the Ch'in or early Han. (D. C. Lau believes that
an explicit citation from the "Lun-yü" in the *Fang-chi* chapter of the
Li-chi proves that the text existed in its current form prior to the
Ch'in [1979:220]. However, the date of the *Fang-chi* chapter is uncertain and is by no means necessarily pre-Han [see Itō 1969:30-35, also
Tsuda 1946:47-54]. The fact that the name "Lun-yü" is mentioned in
no other pre-Ch'in work is good evidence that the name, at least, was
a Han invention.)

Very powerful evidence supporting the notion of a late editing date
is provided by the *Hsun Tzu*. At least six passages in that text appear
to be near verbatim citations of the *Analects* (compare: *H*:1.6, *A*:15.31;
H:1.32, *A*:14.24; *H*:8.96, *A*:2.17; *H*:9.68, *A*:12.11; *H*:27.9, *A*:17.9; *H*:27.122,
A:13.25), yet none of these is attributed to Confucius or to any text
(note, however, that *H*:1.6 appears in the *TTLC* version attributed to

Confucius [7.6]). These statements are all presented as if original to Hsun Tzu. Furthermore, none of the many statements attributed to Confucius in the *Hsun Tzu* appears in the current text of the *Analects* (although there is thematic overlap, e.g., *H*:28.31, *A*:9.19). Hsun Tzu was famous for his erudition in Ruist texts (according to Liu Hsiang's *Sun Ch'ing hsin-shu hsu-lu* [*HTYT*:110-12]). He also spent many years at the Chi-hsia Academy in Ch'i, the center for scholastic learning during the third century B.C. It seems inconceivable that the text of the *Analects* we possess today could have existed in its current form at that time, given the evidence of the *Hsun Tzu*.

For information about the vicissitudes of the text during the Han, see the brief summary in Lau 1979 (220-22) or the more detailed accounts in Takeuchi 1939 (72-86) and Tsuda 1946 (83-101).

3. Arguments from his *Lun-yü yü-shuo* appear in *WSTK* (454-59).

4. The most detailed of those I know are Takeuchi 1939; Tsuda 1946; Kimura 1971. These three studies rely upon different fundamental assumptions and parameters of analysis, and they differ significantly in their conclusions. Takeuchi attempted to reconstruct the composition process by analyzing the current text in light of the types of variant texts reported by Wang Ch'ung to have been extant during the early Han. His model relies heavily upon the notion that the individual books of the *Analects* were coherent and independent units from very early on. Tsuda's analysis stresses the need to challenge assumptions that the editing process was largely completed during the early stages of the text's development. He cites the evidence of unattributed *Analects* passages in late texts to support his view that the organization of entries into books was a late development. For Tsuda, the structure of the text as we have it today offers only minimal clues to the provenance of individual entries. Kimura attempts to tread something of a middle path. Faced with Tsuda's findings, but lacking his sceptical outlook, Kimura tries to solve the problem by stressing the importance of "linked" entries: contiguous entries within a single book that share a single principle of organization. Tending to assign to passages the earliest date of origin he deems possible, Kimura arrives at a detailed schematic model of the dating and geographical or factional classification of the nuclear linked groups. My own view falls between those of Kimura and Takeuchi. I believe that Kimura is correct in considering linked groups as the nuclear literary unit of the text (although I would identify many specific groups differently from Kimura). However, I have come to feel that more than one-half the books constitute coherent arrangements of these linked groups in such a way that we should be wary of attributing groups of passages within a single book

to diverse factional origins, a view more in tune with Takeuchi. Tsuda's counsel of despair is best employed as a cautionary device rather than as a methodological priciple.

5. Even the most credulous of interpreters must follow the *Yi-wen chih* in taking the compilation of the text to have begun after Confucius' death, and most commentators would agree that an analysis of terms of appelation in the text indicates that full-scale editorial work was most likely initiated no earlier than the second generation of disciples (*A*:14.1 providing, perhaps, the most prominent challenge to this principle). Thus, even a traditional approach to the text leaves a considerable gap between Confucius and his editors, which creates problems for those who wish to discover Confucius' ideas through a detailed analysis of precise phraseology.

6. Where relevant, analyses of the dating of individual passages will appear in the course of our discussion. However, in order to alert the reader to implicit biases in my presentation, I will state briefly my current approach to dating *Analects* entries.

Following Takeuchi and most other interpreters, I see the division of the text into books as providing significant clues to discovering relative dates of composition and factional origin. I take Books 3-7 to have been joined at a relatively early date; they are on the whole stylistically and philosophically compatible, and, together, they contain no reduplicated material. They include, however, passages that I believe were inserted or appended after the books were joined (e.g., 5.13-14; 6.29-30). I am inclined to view portions of Book 8 (2, 8-17) as belonging to this group of books, perhaps as a brief, final book on the theme of ritual study. (For an analysis of the tripartite structure of Book 8 and its significance, see Eno 1984:294n53.) Because Books 5-7 contain many idiosyncratic portraits of disciples and other contemporaries of Confucius, it seems likely that this "core" text (Books 3-8) incorporates some of the oldest material in the *Analects*. None of the material from these books appears unattributed in the *Hsun Tzu*, which may also point to an early date (4.1 and 7.34 appear, attributed to Confucius, in the *Mencius* [2A.7, 2A.2]).

The *Analects* is usually considered as possessing two "halves," Books 1-10 and 11-20. If Books 3-8 form a core in the "upper half," Books 11-15 seem to form a somewhat more loosely organized core in the "lower half." They may also have been joined at an early date, although the presence of some partially reduplicated material (compare 12.2, 15.24; 14.30, 15.19) may indicate that portions were developed independently. Material from most of these books appears in the *Mencius*, and also in the *Hsun Tzu*, where it is unattributed, indicating perhaps a late date of final editing. Certain entries appear to be particularly late (e.g., 11.24).

In general, I think it is correct to say that these two core groups represent the heart of the text. The two groups show stylistic differences that might indicate divergent factional or geographical origins, but they are not philosophically inconsistent. Duplicated material (e.g., 4.15, 15.3; 6.2, 11.7, and so forth) might indicate common sources.

Among the remaining books in the "upper half," I follow Takeuchi in considering Book 1 a late summary text (1939:93-94). His speculation that it constituted a pair with Book 10 makes sense in light of Huang K'an's report of the chapter order of the "Ku-lun," one of three versions of the text that circulated during the Han (1939:88).

I feel that the disparate materials in Book 2 suggest a late date, as does the concern with filiality (2.5-8), atypical for the *Analects* (see Eno 1984:222n93). *A*:2.5 contains material attributed to Confucius by the *Analects* but to Tseng Shen by the *Mencius* (3A.2), and this strongly suggests that this portion of the text was at least reshaped after Mencius' time, perhaps to support Ruism's growing interest in filiality.

Takeuchi offers many arguments for considering Book 9 to be late (1939: 95-98). It contains an unusual amount of material found in variant form in other books (compare 9.5, 7.23; 9.10, 10.18; 9.11, 6.27, and 12.15; 9.12, 7.35; 9.14, 5.7; 9.18, 15.13; 9.25, 1.8; 9.29, 14.28). I think we should conclude that this book was incorporated into the text very late, but might have existed as an independent "*lun-yü*," drawing on original sources used for other parts of the text from an early date (although, assigning an early date to some of its entries, such as 9.9, would be difficult).

Ts'ui Shu argued that Books 16-20 were all of a relatively late date. I agree with regard to Books 16, 18, and 20 (but see Kaizuka 1951 for a different view of Book 16). These books probably were added after the text was essentially complete, and they sometimes seem philosophically inconsistent with the rest of the book, particularly Books 16 and 18.

An unusual proportion of entries in Book 17 appear in the *Mencius* and *Hsun Tzu* (e.g., *M*:7B.37 links *A*:17.11 and 17.16; compare also *M*:3B.7 and *A*: 17.1). It seems most likely that the book postdates the *Mencius*, but that much of the material in it is older.

Ts'ui Shu regarded Book 19 as late because it records only the statements of disciples after Confucius' death. This reflects an optimistic view of the early date of the bulk of the text, but from our standpoint, there seems to be no reason to assign a particularly late date to the chapter. The final six entries, all quoting Tzu-kung, differ in style and content from the rest, and might be of independent origin, but, altogether, the book could be viewed as one of the earliest in the entire text.

For a somewhat different summary approach, see Lau 1979:222-33.

7. Significant references to T'ien appear scattered among twelve of the twenty books of the *Analects*. Contrast the distribution of references to another important notion, filiality, which are almost all centered in the first four books, most in a single cluster of entries in Book 2.

8. The *Mo Tzu* often seems to ignore the problem in its discussions of T'ien. See, for example, the *T'ien-chih* chapters (especially 7.2), where it is not only claimed prescriptively that righteousness should be followed because T'ien wishes it, but also that empirical observation shows that T'ien always rewards the righteous.

9. Taoist texts sometimes (but by no means always) seem to suggest that T'ien is ethically neutral (e.g., *CT*:2.29, 2.40; *TTC*:73).

10. In the following analysis, we will adopt what might be called a "principle of overinterpretation." This is based on the notion that the *Analects* should be viewed as a carefully composed canonical text. From an early date, both editors and disciple-readers probably viewed the text as brimming with symbolic meaning, and such meaning may often have determined whether or not a given entry was included in the text. When we explore for "original" meanings in the *Analects as an edited text*, we are justified in carrying our interpretations several steps further than we would if we were dealing with a less "sacred" text, or if we were looking at the text simply as a record of Confucius' words.

11. Which, if any, conventional image we are expected to attach to T'ien is left vague. If we are correct in reading a sense of purposive action into T'ien's "engendering" virtue, an anthropomorphic god would fit. But the passage could be read to mean that virtue itself protects Confucius, in which case he might possess it through the action of T'ien as Nature without any implications of divine purpose.

12. For analyses of the root meaning of "*te*," see Munro 1969:99-108, 185-97; Jao 1975; Nivison 1978-79; Hall and Ames 1987:216-22.

13. In the case of *A*: 7.23, a greater than usual possibility might exist that the *Shih-chi* account reflects an early tradition. The *Analects* entry is so terse as to suggest that traditional contextual material must have been transmitted orally with the text. In other cases in which the *Shih-chi* adds contextual material, this may not have been the case, and Ssu-ma Ch'ien's account is more likely to reflect late embellishments of traditional material.

14. The fact that *A*:7.23 and 9.5 are two versions of one tale is noted by Dubs (1958:248n2) and Miyazaki (1974:248-49). Cheng Hsu-p'ing, relying on the evidence of the *Shih-chi*, claims that these record distinct events several years apart (1963:88).

15. Commentators frequently interpret "*wen*" as denoting "culture," as in the later compound "*wen-hua*." In the *Analects*, it is actually used to

suggest conventional patterns of style and behavior, a sense very close to *li*. It should be compared to the use of the compound "*wen-li*" in the *Hsun Tzu*. On the etymology of "*wen*," see the discussion in chapter I.

16. In this translation, I have taken "*ku*[a]" as a loan for "*ku*," a frequent loan relation (*Daikanwa*:3.65d). (The *Lun-heng*'s version of the passage uses "*ku*" [Chen 1968:147].) I have interpreted "*ku*" as "what is original or basic" in light of Graham's analysis of the term (1967:216).

    There has been much debate over the meaning of the word "*chiang*." I have translated it "great" in light of *H*:32.30.

17. Miyazaki 1974:249 takes "*chün-tzu*" in this passage to denote "nobleman," in contrast to "humble"(compare *A*: 11.1). Overtones of such a meaning might be found in the passage. Perhaps "sage" was applied to commoners in an ironic sense.

18. Concerning the imagery denoted by "*t'ien*" in this passage: I feel that the thrust of Tzu-kung's remark—particularly if one interprets "*ku*" as I have—suggests that "T'ien allows him" means, "he is endowed with the ability by nature." If this were true, T'ien would not necessarily be pictured as a purposive deity, but as a natural process.

19. *A*:9.7 reads: "Lao says: 'The Master said, I have not been employed, hence I am skilled in arts.'" Numerous problems exist with this brief entry. Considering its content, it is clearly a comment on *A*:9.6 (many interpreters regard *A*:9.6-7 as a single passage). For a detailed argument for regarding the passage as a late commentary intrusion (including an admission of bias), see Eno 1984:291n45.

20. The last phrases of *A*:9.6 have sometimes been taken to mean that a *chün-tzu* should *avoid* acquiring many talents (see the pre-T'ang commentaries cited in Ch'eng [1965:504]). A more accurate interpretation would be to say that "the quality of being a *chün-tzu* does not lie in possessing many abilitles." The negative particle "*pu*": "does not," should be read as approximating "*fei*": "is not" (parallel examples may appear at *A*:2.12, 6.25).

21. Some question might arise whether to regard Tzu-kung's statement in *A*:9.6 as true or as a disciple's mistaken reply. Confucius does not address it in his own remarks, and seems to shift the subject from "Sagehood" to the "*chün-tzu*." The *Analects* tells us that Confucius refused to accord himself the labels of "Sage" or "*jen*" (*A*:7.34), but it is quite clear that the *Analects* itself presents him as both (see, e.g., *A*:19.23-25). Because Confucius does not actually criticize his disciple's reply (as he does at, e.g., *A*:3.21), I think we are safe in concluding that Tzu-kung's statement represents the position of the *Analects* on Confucius' virtue, and that Confucius' change of subject should be interpreted as mild modesty.

22. Both T'ien and "man's nature" probably should be considered as metaphysical notions here. The *Shih-chi* version of the passage (47.1941) refers not to man's "nature" (*hsing*) but to his "natural decree" (*hsing-ming*), a phrase generally associated with the *Chung-yung*. If my interpretation of the passage seems somewhat Mencian, it is because I take it to be a post-Mencian retrospective of Confucius' original teaching. The passage is a clear intrusion in *Analects* Book 5 (see Kimura 1971: 296), and the interest in *hsing* would be typically post-Mencian. The root meaning of "paradigm of style" is discussed below.

23. Sung commentators took this approach. See, for example, Chu Hsi's commentary (Ch'eng 1965:279-80).

24. I am referring here to the lengthy passages of the *Yao tien* that detail the charges to the Hsi and Ho clans. Liu Pao-nan points out the relevance of these passages (*LYCY*:166). The notion that the symbolic interpretation of natural forces was the primal basis of social order is a prominent theme in the "wings" of the *Yi ching* (e.g., *Hsi-tz'u chuan*:II.2).

    I feel that *A*:8.19 is very strong evidence that the image of T'ien as Nature or as natural object is present in the *Analects*. Interpreters who wish to prove that it is not (e.g., Fung 1931; Hou 1957; Ikeda 1965) conveniently ignore this passage in their analyses. Whether this proves that Confucius himself thought of T'ien as Nature is a different matter. See the discussion on the dating of *A*:8.19 in Eno 1984:294n53.

    Concerning the role of Yao as first Sage King, this is based on the view of history expressed in the philosophical texts, such as the three we are analyzing here. Later Ruist texts do, of course, use the "pre-Yao" mythology, as do texts such as the *Tso-chuan*.

25. The translation of "calendar" for "*li-shu*" "successive numbers" follows Liu Pao-nan. I do not know why English translations have so carefully avoided this simple gloss. The "wages of T'ien" (*t'ien-lu*) denotes the royal throne, the Sage King pictured as T'ien's stipended agent.

26. For instances of such usage, see, for example, *CT*:1.30; *H*:5.43, 19.4. The *Poetry* (177/4) includes a description of barbarian army banners as "woven patterns of bird insignia" (*chih-wen niao chang*). The basic meaning of "*wen-chang*" is avoided by Lau, who translates it "accomplishments," and by Legge ("display of principle" or "regulations"). Waley and Chan split "*wen-chang*" into two, "culture and its insignia" or its "manifestation," which comes closer, but which forces them to translate *A*:5.13 as if it were referring to Confucius' *views* about *wen-chang*; it is not referring to his views but to his example.

27. The ritual implications of *A*:8.19 may be reinforced by those of a nearby passage, *A*:8.21. In the latter, which appears to be an attempt to

coopt the patron saint of Mohism, the Emperor Yü is portrayed in typical Mohist fashion but with an added Ruist component: "He dressed in shabby clothes, but wore ritual robes and caps of consummate beauty." Both *A*:8.19 and 8.21 may share the function of ascribing Ruist ritual values to legendary Sages.

28. Following most commentators, I have chosen to disregard the variant which reads *"fu"* for *"t'ien"* reportedly occurring in the Han period Lu-version of the text.

There has been considerable debate over whether this passage pictures T'ien as Nature or as an anthropomorphic god ruling Nature. Fung Yu-lan at one time claimed that the proposition "T'ien does not speak" implied that T'ien could speak but chose not to. He used this to prove that *A*:17.17 pictures T'ien anthropomorphically (1931:83n). Fung's argument is unsound, however, as reference to *H*:3.28-29 quickly shows ("T'ien does not speak, yet people infer its great depth; the four seasons do not speak, yet the people plan by them. . . . "). Fung himself has moderated his stance (1962:102), but his original view has been influential (Hou 1957:154; Ikeda 1965:4). I feel that as it stands, there is no evidence that T'ien is portrayed anthropomorphically in *A*: 17.17, and because T'ien is clearly linked to the natural order, the hypothesis that T'ien is pictured as a natural force is to be preferred. Whether this means that Confucius himself pictured T'ien in this way is another matter. On the possible late date of *A*:17.17, see Tsuda 1946:284.

29. For example, see Mencius' defensive reaction to the accusation that he enjoys sophistic debate (*M*:3B.9), and the *Hsun Tzu's* repeated attacks on the sophistic distortion of language. In the *Analects*, "glibness" (*ning*) seems to be the opposite of *jen* (*A*:5.5, cf. 1.2, 12.3).

30. For example, "When a *chün-tzu* perfects his virtue, he is silent but understood" (*H*:3.29). See also *M*:7A.13, 7A.21.

31. Ts'ui Shu thought that this passage, along with *A*:6.29-30, was a late appended entry. *A*:6.29-30 are, indeed, prime candidates for a late date; Ts'ui might be correct about all three.

32. This passage seems related to *A*:17.4.

33. Tales of Confucius' exemplary behavior in Wei may have been fabricated in response to rumors that he did, in fact, compromise his ideals there. *M*:5A.8 reports such a rumor.

34. *A*:3.13 might echo certain themes of surrounding entries in addition to those we have noted. *A*:3.12 speaks of the importance of psychological piety during sacrifice. *A*:3.14 celebrates the beauty of Chou ritual style. Standing between these, the political message of *A*:3.13 might suggest that political purity is a manifestation of ritual devotion.

35. The introduction of a teleological metaphysics suggests that early Ruism was "future oriented." I believe that this is essentially correct. Although Ruists celebrated the past eras of the Sage Kings as a golden age, this does not mean they were pessimistic about the future, only that they placed a low valuation on the present. We should not misinterpret the Ruist belief that the past should be a model for the future as pessimism about the future. Both the *Mencius* and *Hsun Tzu* suggest that the ethical course of history is cyclical (*M*:2B.13; *H*:26.32), and the *Analects* might even suggest a progressive course (*A*:3.14, 9.23).

36. As Chu Hsi noted, the wooden bell metaphor might also point to the peripatetic nature of Confucius' late career, since criers who rang the bell walked as they called out their message.

37. The doctrine of deferred teleological consequences is linked to the Ruist notion of "timeliness" (*shih*), on which, see the discussion in chapter V.

38. This and related problems, such as the question of the value of human effort, are entailed in the deterministic implications of the teleological model. The *Analects* neither addresses nor solves these problems. It does seem to suggest, however, that the Sage has solved them, as we will see.

39. As, for example, *A*:1.1, which portrays the *chün-tzu* as a man whose devotion to ritual self-cultivation and Ruist group study is unsoured by his political obscurity. See also *A*:14.38, where Confucius is called, "he who does what he knows to be in vain."

40. *A*:2.4 is employed by Hall and Ames (1987) as the framework for their study of Confucianism. While I find the many interpretive discussions therein stimulating and in general compatible with the arguments here, my reading of *A*:2.4 differs from theirs in several respects, particularly with regard to the latter half of the passage.

41. The following points suggest a relatively late date for *A*:2.4: it is highly schematic in style; it is immodest, atypical for a self-characterization by Confucius; the notion of "knowing T'ien's decree" is associated with late sections of the text (*A*:16.8, 20.3) and with Mencian doctrine; Book 2 is probably a late compilation (see note 6 above); the particle "*yüᵃ*" that appears in this passage in most editions of the text (Ch'en 1968: 21) is atypical of the grammar of the text as a whole. Finally, as I hope to show, *A*:2.4 is crafted with a high degree of conscious symbolism, which suggests a systematic doctrinal motive underlying its composition, rather than the personal motive of reflective self-characterization. Note, however, that these arguments, while numerous, fall short of being conclusive.

42. This linkage is noted by many traditional commentaries (Ch'eng

1965:64; see also the discussion in Hall and Ames 1987:85-86). The phonetic association between the two words should not be overstressed. Karlgren's reconstructions are *gliəp (*li^c*) and *liər (*li*).

43. Pre-T'ang commentary interpreted the decree in political terms, much as I do here. T'ang and Sung interpreters, beginning with Han Yü and Li Ao, took a more metaphysical tack, along the lines of *M*:7A.1 and *CY*:1 (see Ch'eng 1965:65-66). Among modern writers, interpretations vary from Fung Yu-lan's claim that Confucius was describing a new perspective on natural truth (1962:115) to Dubs' remark that Confucius' discovery was that T'ien had ordained him to teach the people (1958:247). Kaizuka (1973:34), T'ang (1974:515), and Miyazaki (1974:173) interpret the phrase much as I do.

44. Among the translations, only Waley's explicitly links the two phrases as I have. I am unable to make much sense out of translations such as, "At sixty I was at ease with whatever I heard" (Chan 1963:22), or "At sixty my ear was attuned" (Lau 1979:63), although the interpretation given Lau's reading by Hall and Ames is an insightful essay on the Ruist idea of the Sage (1987:253-304). Note that in the Tun-huang text, this phrase appears as *"liu-shih ju shun"*: "At sixty I was compliant" (Ch'en 1968:22).

45. This is close to Kaizuka's interpretation (1973:34).

46. The word *"chü"*: "proper bounds," has been glossed by most commentators as *"fa"*: "prescriptive rule" (Ch'eng 1965:68-69). Fung takes it to denote *li* (1962:116). Its root meaning is the carpenter's square. No other instances of its use are found in the *Analects*.

47. The relation between *"chih"* and *"ta"* discussed here has not, to my knowledge, been previously noted.

48. The notion that T'ien planned Confucius' failure for a purpose might be echoed in *A*:9.12, which reads:

> The Master fell ill. Tzu-lu had the followers act as though they were feudal retainers. When his illness eased, the Master said, "How long Yu has practiced deception! Pretending to have retainers when I have none, whom do I deceive? Do I deceive T'ien? Moreover, would I not rather die in the hands of you disciples than in the hands of retainers? And even if I do not receive an elaborate funeral, am I being left by the roadside to die?"

The passage clearly celebrates the value of belonging to the Ruist community in contrast to belonging to the community of amoral political actors (how much better disciples than retainers!). Tzu-lu had not yet grasped, as had Confucius, that T'ien had destined Confucius to teach rather than to govern. How could Confucius deceive the director of his destiny with a charade—and having embraced that destiny as superior to the one he had once wished for, why would he want to?

While I think that this interpretation makes sense in terms of the *Analects'* overall treatment of T'ien, I much prefer the nonphilosophical interpretation presented in section 3 of this chapter and would be content to omit this passage from inclusion in the editors' theory.

49. As in *A*:9.6, I read "*ku*ᵃ" as "*ku*." This avoids the tortured sentence division advocated by many commentators (see Ch'eng 1965:888), one that underlies Waley's translation.

50. On the matter of the decree, some interpreters would take issue with my linkage of *ming* in *A*:14.36 and T'ien in *A*:3.13 and 14.35. These writers draw a sharp line between the *ming* that T'ien decrees, as in *A*:2.4, which is prescriptive in their view, and the *ming* that is fatalistically predetermined (see the remarks of Ch'en Chi-t'ing, cited by Yen Jo-ch'ü in Ch'eng 1965:65). T'ang Chün-yi bases his theory of the decree in the *Analects* on his belief that both sorts of *ming* are, for Confucius, identical in meaning "righteousness" (*yi*) (1974:515). While I do not agree with T'ang, I do believe that the *Analects* sometimes uses "*ming*" in the sense of "*t'ien-ming*," and that passages such as *A*:2.4 and 14.36 are talking about the same thing. In my view, all senses of "*ming*" in the *Analects* are essentially descriptive, not prescriptive (thus the gloss of "righteousness" is, I think, flawed). However, not all of these uses are "deterministic." In some cases, T'ien's decree has meaning beyond the simple fact of its existence: it is a puzzle for the Sage to find normative value in its descriptive action. The purely deterministic sense of *ming* is used only in connection with the meaning of "lifespan" (*A*:6.3, 6.10, and so forth). (On the matter of *A*:11.18: "Ssu's wealth increases despite his not receiving *ming*; his speculations are frequently on the mark," which is frequently taken to mean that Tzu-kung somehow refused to accept T'ien's decree and aimed at wealth, my inclination is to follow Chiao Hsun's interpretation that "*ming*" here denotes an order to assume office [Ch'eng 1965:698]. I do not feel that the strong condemnation of Tzu-kung implied in the traditional interpretation makes sense in terms of his role in the *Analects*.)

For a fuller discussion of the meanings of "*ming*" and its role in early Ruism, see chapter V.

51. *A*:14.37 deals with eremeticism and begins: "The worthiest shun the world." *A*:14.38 includes the famous characterization of Confucius as "he who does what he knows to be in vain." *A*:14.39 records a passerby's advice to Confucius: "If no one knows you, then give up." I would translate Confucius' response as: "Were this right, it would all be so easy!"

52. Here *ming* should be understood in the narrow sense of one's allotted years. The parallel usage of *ming* and T'ien serves to emphasize the

descriptive action of T'ien. But note that in assigning to T'ien the descriptive determination of social status, Tzu-hsia does not imply that T'ien is not normative. As other passages indicate, the ritual diligence of the *chün-tzu*–while not determined by T'ien–does accord with T'ien as a prescriptive notion.

53. T'ang Chün-yi relies on the passage to formulate his model of the decree of T'ien in the *Analects* (1974:515). Fung Yu-lan even finds a mystical element in it (1962:102), presumably with *M*:7A.1 in mind.

54. The passage is one of a series, each reciting a list of three things. No additional contextual material appears. Since *whatever* the decree of T'ien might be we would expect the *chün-tzu* to respect it and the small man not to know it, the passage really provides little that would support one interpretation of the decree against another.

55. *A*:11.10 records how Confucius' wailing at the funeral of Yen Yuan overstepped the proper bounds.

56. The functional equivalence of T'ien and *tao* is sometimes encountered in Taoist texts. There the *tao*, as with T'ien for the Ruists, can function both as a prescriptive model for people and as a descriptive cosmic force. In Ruist texts, however, "*tao*" is used only prescriptively.

57. This count includes all instances except those where "*t'ien*" appears as an element of the binomes "*t'ien-tzu*" or "*t'ien-hsia*."

58. A theory exists that Confucius did not speak of T'ien because, although he held a traditional view that T'ien was prescriptively ethical, he felt that in light of the chaos of the times no one would believe him if he said so (Hou 1957:152; Dubs 1958:246-47; Yang 1973:115-17). The theory cannot be decisively disproved, but it conflicts, with what we do know about Confucius, and it ascribes to Confucius either a mysticism or a stubborn dogmatism for which there is no evidence.

59. Note that in *A*:7.21, "*shen*," might not mean "spirits" but "spirit-power."

60. *A*:3.12 is generally interpreted as expressing simultaneously religious piety and agnosticism. It reads: " 'Sacrifice as though present': sacrifice to the spirits as though they were present. The Master said, 'If I do not take part in a sacrificial rite, it is as though I had not sacrificed.' " The text seems to be corrupt (the second phrase may be an interpolation), but the sense is clear. What is important about sacrifice is not feeding the spirits (whose real existence seems to be questioned by the phrase "as though"), but personally expressing reverence.

Concerning the "agnostic" passages we have been discussing, Ikeda, who wishes to prove that Confucius held a traditional pietistic religious viewpoint, argues that none of them actually disputes the existence of gods and spirits, while some, on the contrary, stress the need to respect them (1965:4-5). He cites Hou (1957:155), who notes the evident contradictons in an agnostic philosophy that celebrates religious ritual. Hou cites the argument of the *Kung Meng* chapter of the *Mo Tzu*: "To hold that there are no spirits and study sacrificial ritual is like . . . setting out fish nets when there are no fish" (12.11b-12a). What Ikeda ignores is that in the context of a religious society, passages like *A*:6.22, which fall short of endorsing spiritualism, have the effect of expressing agnosticism. (Compare the example of Socrates, whose unwillingness to assert a belief in divinities as opposed to divine agencies was seen as a clear token of atheism by his contemporaries— correctly, perhaps.) The cited *Mo Tzu* passage (and other passages in the *Mo Tzu*) make clear that early Ruism was perceived as an atheism, and that despite the fact that its interest in religious ritual was contradictory, it apparently embraced that contradiction.

61. On the other hand, a variant rendering of the same tale at *A*:7.35 does seem to say something about religious metaphysics when it expresses scepticism about the value of verbal prayer. On *A*:9.12, see note 48.

62. Dubs interprets this instrumental effect perfectly (1958:252). A similar instrumental interpretation should be applied to *A*:14.36 (which we discussed earlier), and has been by Creel (1949:121).

63. Dubs takes this passage to show that "Confucius felt himself personally dependent upon Heaven" (1958:247). I cannot see how he arrives at this conclusion.

64. These two passages have closely parallel structures, a fact noted by Tsuda (1946:125). In both, Confucius makes a statement, Tzu-kung questions it, and Confucius responds with a rhetorical question concerning T'ien. While I suspect that neither entry records an actual conversation (they seem too carefully crafted for that), if we suppose that they do, they can be interpreted as examples of didactic playfulness. In both instances, Confucius' opening statement is surprising and starts Tzu-kung thinking, and the concluding questions about T'ien serve to keep the issues of the passages unresolved and keep the disciple pondering over the value of worldly success or doctrinal argument. It seems significant that Tzu-kung repeatedly plays this role in the *Analects*, in passages that are philosophically provocative (e.g., 5.4, 11.16, 14.17, 15.3).

65. The dating of *A*:2.4 is discussed above. On *A*:8.19, see Eno 1984:294n53. I follow Ts'ui Shu in taking Book 16 to be a very late text. Note that for my theory concerning Confucius' doctrinal silence to be valid, it is not necessary that any *Analects* passage referring to T'ien be proven to be an accurate record of Confucius' speech.

Chapter V

1. In preparing translations and commentary for the *Mencius*, I have taken the *MTYT* text as standard. For traditional commentary, I have used the *Meng Tzu cheng-yi* [*MTCY*], a mid-Ch'ing work by the brothers Chiao Hsun and Chiao Hu that includes the notes of Chao Ch'i (d. 201 A.D.), the Han editor of the text. I have consulted and benefited from the following English translations: Legge 1894, Dobson 1963, Chan 1963 (partial), Lau 1970. All translations are my own.

2. The history of the text is obscure; we know very little about it prior to Chao Ch'i's second century A.D. editorial work. According to Chao's introduction, the text was highly revered during the early Han, and the government even appointed an exegete specializing in the *Mencius*, as it did for the recognized classics (*MTCY*:10). However, the post lapsed at some unknown time, and we have no other record of the course of the text during the Han apart from the fact that it was noted in Liu Hsin's *Ch'i lueh* and the *Yi-wen chih* as having eleven books. When Chao Ch'i annotated the text, he chose not to include the final four books, which he regarded as inferior and spurious, and they were eventually lost. See Kanaya 1950-51:20-21 and Lau 1970:220-22.

3. Certain passages, such as *M*:4B.33 might have been appended to the original text. A number of entries in Book 4B have an unusual narrative style that could indicate a late date (e.g., 4B.29, 31).

4. Kanaya, for example, feels that Book 4 represents Mencius' earliest thought, and Book 7 his latest (1950-51:24, 42).

5. In *M*:1A.1, King Hui of Liang addresses Mencius by a term generally reserved for elders (*sou*). The king was himself well on in years, having reigned approximately fifty years at the time (according to Ch'ien Mu's chronology).

6. The *Shih-chi* claim that Mencius was trained in the Tseng Tzu/Tzu-ssu faction of Ruism seems borne out by the many references to these men in the text of the *Mencius* (and also by remarks in the *Hsun Tzu* [6.14]). However, the *Mencius* also frequently cites the words of an early Ru named Kung-ming Yi, who may have belonged to the Tzu-chang faction of Ruism (*LCCC*:180).

7. Mencius' personal obscurity is remarkable and reinforces our impression of the general obscurity of Ru during the Warring States period. Even Mencius' "style name" (*tzu*) is unknown (but see *HS*:30.1728n3). On early legends about Mencius, see Lau 1970:214-19.

8. The chronology of Mencius' travels is a matter of dispute (varieties of models are conveniently listed in *Daikanwa*:3.838c). We can deduce certain facts from the text of the *Mencius*, but others remain problem-

atic. As certain points of interpretation hang upon such issues, developing a reliable chronology is of some importance. The chronology that lies behind the account here accepts Ch'ien Mu's theory that Mencius made two visits to the state of Ch'i, which allows us to account for the otherwise inexplicable fact that after the disastrous breach of etiquette recorded in *M*:2B.2, Mencius was still able to receive high honors in Ch'i. Our model of Mencius' itinerary runs: Ch'i (prior to 319 B.C.), Sung (after 328), Tsou, T'eng, Ch'i (after 319, including 314-312), Lu (retirement). The visit to Liang occurred somewhere between the two trips to Ch'i. These issues are treated in greater detail in Eno 1984:360-62.

9. According to Ts'ui Shu, Mencius continued to pursue his travels after leaving Ch'i. However, the model we are using here concludes Mencius' career with his resignation in Ch'i. The notion that Mencius' resignation in Ch'i was for the announced purpose of retirement is implied in the use of the word *"kuei"* in *M*:2B.10. Note that the incident in Lu recorded in *M*:1B.16 could have occurred in Mencius' retirement, particularly because Mencius' homeland of Tsou was essentially a part of the somewhat larger state of Lu (although *M*:1B.12 indicates they were still politically distinct).

10. The point most often cited to prove this is the use of posthumous titles to refer to rulers in the text. Some of these rulers, at least, probably died after Mencius, who would therefore not have known them by the names used in the text. Ch'ien Mu has argued (1956:374) that because the ruler of Sung—the last of these men to die—alone is not referred to by posthumous title, the text was probably edited before his death (286 B.C.), but after the death of the next latest lived ruler (Liang Hsiang Wang, d. 296 B.C). This narrows the dates of the text nicely, but the theory suffers because it is not apparent from the text that there was any occasion to name the ruler of Sung at all: he is never referred to in a narrative passage.

11. Kanaya offers a theory of Book 2 as Kung-sun Ch'ou's record of his adoption of Mencius as a teacher (1950-51:24). Jeffrey Riegel (1979: 450n4) has offered an interesting theory that Kung-sun Ch'ou was not a disciple at all. Reigel's theory, however, seems to conflict with the apparent fact that Kung-sun Ch'ou traveled with Mencius. For a more detailed discussion, see Eno 1984:363n11.

12. Kanaya (1950-51:25) notes this division and mentions that the first to describe it was Itō Jinsai (1626-1705).

13. For example, the *Tso-chuan*, a Ruist history, puts the following speech into the mouth of the ruler of Chu: "If something benefits the people, it benefits me. T'ien gave birth to the people and established rulers for their benefit" (Wen 13:9.14).

14. This figure was probably not Mencius' invention. It is a part of a theory of historical cycles found in the *Shih-chi* (27.1344).
15. Doctrines such as "timeliness" were not restricted to Ruism. They appear in Taoist and Legalist texts as well. The term *"shih"* does not appear in the *Analects* in the sense of "timeliness" except at *A*:10.21, which might be a late appended entry (see Ts'ui Shu's comments in *WSTK*:458). The sense of the doctrine is, however, a pervasive theme of the text.
16. It can be argued that all of Mencius' discussions of true Kingship implicitly involve a theory of T'ien, because the theory of the "Mandate of Heaven" underlies them. In fact, the mandate theory plays an explicit role only in *M*:5A.5-6 (it is also referred to in a cited passage in *M*:4A.8), and Mencius is never shown mentioning the theory to a political actor. In view of this, I have chosen not to read the theory into passages where it is not explicitly mentioned.
17. Compare *M*:2B.8. I have rendered *"ti^b"*: "match," as "enemy" without meaning to reject the gloss of "peer." The idea is that such a ruler would have no rival in virtue or in politics.
18. The two rulers who are noted as honoring smaller states are T'ang, who honored the Ko people (*M*:3B.5), and King Wen, who honored the K'un-yi people (see the discussion in *MTCY*:65-66). The rulers who submitted to powerful states are King T'ai, the progenitor of the Chou line, who submitted to the Hsun-yü, and Kou-chien, the ruler of Yueh, who submitted to the state of Wu.
19. "Without expanding its borders or increasing its population, if [Ch'i] were to practice humane government no one could stop its ruler from becoming a [true] King" (*M*:2A.1).
20. "The *Documents* says: 'T'ien set down the people and created for them rulers and teachers. . . .' King Wu brought peace to the people of the world in a single burst of wrath. If you would also bring peace to the world, the people would fear only that you did not love [wrathful] valor" (*M*:1B.3).
21. There is, however a passage that directly contradicts this. In *M*:4A.8 Mencius claims that by following the proper policies, the leader of even a small state can come to rule the Empire within seven years. *M*:1B.14 and 4A.8 cannot really be reconciled. Their essential difference might be that in *M*:1B.14, Mencius is actually addressing the ruler of a small state, and so risks any predictions he makes being put to a test. *M*:4A.8 merely quotes Mencius' teachings out of context, and he might have been speaking (or the author/editor writing) in a more theoretical vein.
22. It is interesting that Mencius does not discuss these Sage Kings in his persuasions of rulers. The models he offers them, T'ang of the Shang,

Wen and Wu of the Chou, were Sage Kings by conquest rather than
by pure virtue.

23. It is difficult to believe that the bow that Mencius here makes to
spiritualist religious notions was intended to be deeply philosophical. It is, to my knowledge, the only pre-Ch'in spiritualistic passage
in a Ruist philosophical text (by contrast, the historical text *Tso-
chuan* includes several of them). As noted, the passage goes on to
discuss the will of T'ien as being expressed through the action of
people, and the action of the spirits is not emphasized. See the following note.

24. In this passage, the word "*hsiang*" should probably be interpreted as including a religious sense of "master of ritual ceremony" (a common use
of the term). In saying the action of T'ien allowed Shun to act as *hsiang*
for Yao for a prolonged period, Mencius seems to be saying that no
natural disasters occurred throughout this period, proving that the
spirits (i.e., T'ien) were satisfied with state sacrifices of which Shun, as
Prime Minister, might have been in charge. By this interpretation, the
spirits, and T'ien, are reduced to the status of descriptive "action and
event" in the natural sphere, and are at least partially rationalized.

25. Mencius cites these words from the *T'ai shih* chapter of the *Documents*,
now lost. Similar language appears in the extant *Kao Yao mo* chapter.

26. This rule appears to foreclose the possibility of righteous conquests
such as those that founded the Shang and Chou Dynasties. In order to
make his main point—the legitimacy of hereditary rule—Mencius seems
willing to ignore numerous contradictions in his arguments.

27. My interpretation of this passage is closer to Dobson (1963:63) than to
Legge or Lau. I take "*chih*" in the sense of "bestow" (*SWCTKL*:5B:2317b),
rather than in the sense of "bring about," and so take the "*ming*" of
this passage to refer specifically to the royal mandate, rather than to
the more general notion of fate.

28. Both *M*:5A.5 and 5A.6 have the effect of delegitimizing arbitrary cession of thrones and of supporting the institutional status quo. The
motivation to argue against the cession of the throne might have been
tied to Mencius' actions in Ch'i where his condemnation of the Yen
ruler's abdication was used to help justify an invasion of Yen by Ch'i
(see chapter II). These passages might have been intended to answer
critics of Mencius' actions in Ch'i.

On a broader scale, these passages illustrate Mencius' institutional
conservatism, a facet of his thinking that seems at times to conflict
with his populist doctrines and that has led some communist writers
to brand him as violently reactionary (see the discussion in Hou 1957:
382-87). Mencius seems at times to oppose the replacement of incum-

bent officeholders with talented newcomers (M:1B.7, but see Munro 1969:205n) and includes hereditary appointments for all offices as part of his ideal government (M:1B.5). These statements indicate a devotion to traditional Chou political values. On the other hand, Mencius was not averse to serving usurpers: he does not mention to the rulers of Liang and Ch'i that their thrones were not legitimately obtained by their lineages, nor does he seem concerned, when in Sung, that the ruler has recently usurped the title of King; on the contrary, that seems to have induced him to go to Sung.

Mencius' institutional conservatism seems to follow the path of least resistance, and suggests that he was willing to overlook deficiencies in the pragmatic institutions of the Warring States period in order to work within them. Mencius faced two practical problems of considerable difficulty: finding a man to convert into a new King—one who really stood a chance of fulfilling millennial prophecy—and supporting a large entourage of disciples (on the size of his following, see M:3B.4). The men best able to solve both these problems for Mencius were those best placed within the existing political system, and Mencius did not quarrel with their legitimacy.

Perhaps we could generalize on Mencius' behalf and say that for him the possession of political power represented an ethical opportunity to establish a higher legitimacy by creating an ethical world. This attitude would account for the language we find in M:5B.3, where Mencius refers to the throne of a feudal state as the "office of T'ien," a phrase properly applied only to the Chou throne.

29. The exception is Yueh-cheng Tzu, about whom we know somewhat more (see chapter II, note 52).

30. The totalism is also implicit in discussions of Sage models, such as Yao and Shun, who are represented as essentially perfect men.

31. These are the four sprouts: *jen, yi, li,* and *chih*[a], sometimes translated as "humanity," "righteousness," "ritual," and "wisdom." While the last of these is an adequate translation, problems arise with the other three. For the sake of consistency, I will refer to all four sprouts by transcription only.

32. Passages of the *Mencius* occur almost verbatim in the *Chung-yung* (e.g., compare M:4A.13 and CY:20). The authors of the *Chung-yung* and *Ta-hsueh* have traditionally been taken as Tzu-ssu and Tseng Tzu, the founders of Mencius' faction of Ruism. See Tu 1976:21-22.

33. The most straightforward presentation of the two-schools model I know of appears in Takeuchi 1936, chapter 3. (Takeuchi does not assign Hsun Tzu to either school because of certain statements made in the *Fei shih-erh tzu* chapter of the *Hsun Tzu.*) See also Levenson and

Schurmann 1969:43. The model I refer to in the text is implicit in many discussions of Ruist philosophical diversity; usually, however, the opposition of the schools is discussed in terms of contrasting "idealist" and "materialist" tendencies.

34. See, for example *H*:3.27-28, which is very close in language and spirit to *CY*:23. Similar ideas appear in different terminology in the first two chapters of the *Hsun Tzu*, which lay their greatest stress on the value of ritual study. Other chapters, such as *Chieh-pi* and *Ch'eng-hsiang* share the meditative interests of the *Chung-yung* and *Ta-hsueh*.

35. This is particularly true of Tseng Shen, as he appears In the *T'an kung* chapter of the *Li-chi*, and more particularly, in the so-called Tseng Tzu chapters of the *Ta Tai li-chi* (chaps. 49-58).

36. Although I believe that any model that divides Ruism into schools that are pro-*li* and neutral toward *li* is inaccurate, early Ruism certainly was highly factionalized. Disciples of Mencius and Hsun Tzu may be said to have belonged to different traditions of Ruism, but not in the sense of the two-schools model described here.

37. Although the *Mencius* does not name Taoism or any philosopher unquestionably Taoist, I regard it as possible that his attacks on Yang Chu were directed against the Taoist school. See note 41 below.

38. See, for example, the attacks on Ruist ritual ideas in the *Fei Ju, Fei yueh, Chieh tsang*, and *Kung Meng* chapters of the *Mo Tzu*. The figure in the *Mo Tzu* most ridiculed for slavish adherence to *li* is Kung Meng Tzu, who is probably a caricature of Mencius. (The possibility that this is so makes it questionable whether we should take Kung Meng as a double surname, and this is why I have avoided doing so.) The fact that the *Kung Meng* chapter of the *Mo Tzu* includes references to Mencius' contemporary Kao Tzu increases the possibility of the identity of Kung Meng Tzu and Mencius (Meng Tzu). Note, however, that traditional identifications of Kung Meng Tzu have differed [*MTCK*:12.12]).

39. The *Mencius'* polemical attitude is best exemplified by *M*:3B.9, wherein Mencius responds to the "charge" that he enjoys argument. Mencius' reply is itself a demonstration of rhetorical skill, as he defensively rationalizes his propensity to debate by describing his missionary impulses to rescue people from false doctrines. The *Mencius* is entirely lacking in the graceful humility that the *Analects* portrays in the figure of Confucius (e.g., *A*:5.9, 7.34, 17.3). In passages such as *M*:2B.2, there is almost a sense of desperation in the rationalization of Mencius' most arrogant behavior.

40. Some of the main themes of this analysis are recapitulated in Graham 1978:15-18.

41. Elsewhere, I have discussed at length the difficulties I have with Graham's

theory (1984:370-72). To note the main problems briefly: (1) If Mencius'
antipathy toward Yang Chu were based on the latter's doctrine of *hsing*,
why was Yang Chu's name never connected with *hsing* in the *Mencius*
(nor in any text before the *Huai-nan Tzu*)? (2) Graham reconstructs
Yang Chu's philosophy largely from chapters in the *Lü-shih ch'un-ch'iu*
that consist of material found also in the *Chuang Tzu*. Why associate
the ideas with Yang Chu rather than Chuang Tzu (per his later ghost-
writers)? (3) Graham's theory fails to provide insights into the issue
of why Yang Chu's philosophy vanished. Such answers are provided by
the controversial theory that Yang Chu was a variant name for Chuang
Chou (see Ts'ai Yuan-p'ei's presentation in Yen 1971:12.139-40). This
latter theory itself involves several difficulties, but none, to my mind,
is fatal, and the logic behind it is strong.

42. "*Yi*" was a traditional ethical term adopted by Ruists for special stress.
It appears in pre-Ruist materials such as attested bronze inscriptions.
As noted in chapter III, "*jen*" seems to have been transformed into an
important ethical term by Confucius himself.

43. The *Mo Tzu* stresses the cognate meanings of "*yi*": "right" and "*yi*ᵃ":
"standard." See the *Fa-yi* chapter and also *Shang-t'ung* I:3.1-2.

44. On *jen*, see, for example, *MT, Chien-ai* II:4.3a. On *yi*, see, e.g., *Fei kung*
III:5.7b-8a.

45. In this respect, the *Huai-nan Tzu* report is confirmed by the many
references to the Hsia founder Yü in the *Mo Tzu*. Yü is generally
regarded as the Mohists' ideal model.

46. For information on Mohists as craftsmen, see Graham 1978:6-7, 11. On
their connection with the martial arts, see Fung 1948:37,50.

47. For an extended example of an explicit attack on Chou *li* as relative,
see *MT, Chieh tsang*:6.14b-15a.

48. See also *MT, Fa yi*, which many interpreters consider to be a late chapter.

49. I do not mean to contend that the equivalence of the two terms is
complete in the text. In some passages "*yi*" clearly refers to political
acts undertaken in compliance with the doctrine of timeliness (e.g.,
M: 5A.8: "Confucius advanced according to *li* and retired according to
yi"). My point is that *li* and *yi* overlap in such a way as to allow Mencius
to portray the arena of *li* as the root of the less doctrinally problematic notion *yi*, when the latter term is under close analysis.

50. On the aesthetic dimensions of this overlap in Ruism, see the discussion in chapter II.

51. Riegel (1979:444) translates: "It is what is produced by joining with
propriety," following Chao Ch'i's gloss of *chi* as *tsa* (var. *tsa*ᵃ). But Chao's
gloss does not suggest a linkage of two elements as Riegel's rendering
suggests, but the intertwining of many threads into a cloth (in the root

sense of *"tsa"*). It should be understood as an attempt to use graphemic resonance to give a descriptive interpretation of the way in which cultivating one's inclinations toward *yi* progressively nurtures a reciprocal growth of the *ch'i.* The metaphor is completed by the term *"hsi,"* in the sense of "a suit of clothing" (I am indebted to Neil Bolick for this suggestion).

52. Flood-like energy (*hao-jan chih ch'i*) is sometimes taken to refer to practices of breath control. *"Ch'i"* could literally denote the breath (on its root meaning of "vapor" see Riegel 1979:453n24), and judging from some sections of the *Chuang Tzu* and *Kuan Tzu,* meditational practices involving breath control existed in early China. However, *"ch'i"* had other meanings as well. In *M:*2A.2, the discussion of the flood-like energy is presented as Mencius' version of doctrines that other thinkers phrased as techniques to cultivate valor. *"Ch'i"* did carry a meaning of righteous wrath or bravery. For example, the *Han Fei Tzu* records this tale: "The King of Yueh was considering a campaign against Wu, and wished his countrymen to regard death as a matter of no importance. Setting out one day, he spied a furious frog and bowed to him from his carriage. 'What is there to honor in him?' the King's followers asked. 'He has *ch'i!*' answered the King" (*Nei ch'u-shuo* I:9.8b). A more theoretical discussion of *ch'i* in the context of bravery can be found in *LSCC, Chüeh sheng*:8.7b.

   Mencius tells us that the path to the *hao-jan chih ch'i* is *yi,* righteousness, a term linked to active *li* practice rather than to passive breath control. Mencius may have been describing feelings of righteous self-confidence acquired through a stylization of personal behavior which made "right" action feel spontaneous.

53. The last two of these entries are not part of the "debate with Kao Tzu," although they enlarge on Mencius' arguments there. In the interests of brevity we will not deal with them here.

54. The *Mencius* does not explicitly state Kao Tzu's philosophical affiliation. Mencius' implicit praise for Kao Tzu's level of self-cultivation itself argues for a Ruist identification (*M:*2A.2), and there are other indications that this is correct. Kao Tzu's concern with *jen* and *yi* narrow the possible alternatives to Ruism and Mohism, and his statement at *M:*6A.4: "I love my brother, I do not love the brother of some man from Ch'in" is clearly a slap at the Mohist doctrine of universal love. In the *Kung Meng* chapter of the *Mo Tzu,* we find Kao Tzu appearing as an anti-Mohist (12.16b-17a). Graham has demonstrated that Kao Tzu's ideas appear in a completely Ruist context in the *Chieh* chapter of the *Kuan Tzu* (1967:228-31).

55. This may be the implication of Mencius' remark that Kao Tzu achieved an unmoved mind before he himself did (*M:*2A.2).

56. Jeffrey Riegel's recent study of *M*:2A.2 (1979) has suggested some important new ideas elaborating Kao Tzu's theory that "*yi* is external." Riegel
argues that the essential meaning of Kao Tzu's theory is not expressed
directly in the *M*:6A debates, but is contained in a teaching that Mencius
attributes to Kao Tzu and cites in *M*:2A.2: "If you do not get it from the
word do not seek it in the mind; if you do not get it from the mind do not
seek it in the *ch'i*" (trans. Riegel). Riegel paraphrases Kao Tzu's theory
thus: "[Never] seek, nor indeed hope to find in the mind what is not got
from doctrines and teachings and never . . . seek, nor hope to find in the
natural dispositions . . . what is not got from the mind" (439-40). Riegel's
insight into the importance of 2A.2 in this context is excellent, but I do
not agree with his interpretation of Kao Tzu's doctrine, which I believe
was an aspect of his attack on Mohism. If we follow Riegel in linking this
formula to Kao Tzu's position on *yi*, its balanced structure suggests
that it is a version of the entire bipartite doctrine, namely that *yi* is
external but that *jen* is internal. If we interpret the passage in this way,
its sense may be paraphrased thus: "Whenever one faces an issue of
propriety (*yi*), if a given course of action does not accord with teachings [sanctioned by Kao Tzu], do not seek to rationalize it by finding
grounds for it in inclinations of the mind—they are not relevant to propriety. Whenever one faces a situation that relates to *jen*, then if a
course of action does not tally with the inclinations of the mind (e.g.,
Mohism's universal love [cf. 6A.4]), then do not seek to overrule the
inclinations of the mind with voluntaristic energy (as Mohists do)." In
this way, Kao Tzu allows for ritual prescript to overrule spontaneous
inclinations in matters pertaining to *yi*, and implicitly characterizes
Mohist altruistic utilitarianism as "un*jen*": a well-thought Ruist position.
For a more detailed discussion, see Eno 1984:374-76.

57. We might note that there is little reason to insist that there ever
occurred an actual debate between Mencius and Kao Tzu such as the
one described in *M*:6A.1-4. Kao Tzu, Mencius' senior, may have been
long dead at the time the debate was composed. The speeches put
into Kao Tzu's mouth are probably Mencian constructions, which would
explain why Mencius is always able to have the last word.

58. On the explication and functionality of the arguments in these passages, see Lau 1970:234-63, especially, 234-43.

59. The central issue of these three passages is whether people have innate
species-specific ethical dispositions. Kao Tzu's analogies are consistent
with a position that people possess *no* norms apart from those common
to all animal species (although his analogies are intended only to assert the indeterminacy of most ethical dispositions). In *M*:6A.3, Mencius pins Kao Tzu by invoking the commonsense notion that animal

species have distinguishing properties. In *M*:6A.6, he indicates that the properties that distinguish mankind are specifically ethical.

60. The legendary model of Yi Yin, who according to *M*:5A.7 turned the founder of the Shang Dynasty into a true King, might exemplify the scenario Mencius pictured for his own career.

61. Donald Munro has noted, "One reason why Mencius held that man's nature was good was his logical confusion of the ideal man with the actual man" (1969:72). In terms of Mencius' political aspirations, the confusion was not truly logical, it was practical. Without it, Mencius would have had no political career at all.

62. On the notions of moral motivation that supported Mencius' extravagant hopes, see Nivison 1979.

63. The first book of the *Mencius* makes no mention of *hsing* either, but it includes only "persuasions" of rulers, and we might not expect Mencius to raise with them what was then a technical philosophical issue. Note that in Book 3, the sole reference to *hsing* occurs in the opening phrases of the book, in a narrative introduction. The reference describes the content of a persuasion; however, the persuasion we see does not refer to the doctrine of *hsing*, but to the related nontechnical formula that "any man can become Yao or Shun." The use of the word "*hsing*" in *M*:3A.1 might reflect the fact that the editors of the text understood that the two doctrines were equivalent and not that Mencius explained the theory of *hsing* to the Duke of T'eng. My suspicion is that at the time Mencius was in T'eng speaking to the future Duke, he probably had not yet reformulated the early theories of "any man can be Yao or Shun" and the four sprouts into the doctrine of the good *hsing*.

64. The proximity of the proofs of the internality of *yi*, which equate *yi* with the feeling of respect (*ching*), probably accounts for the fact that the *M*:2A.6 description of the sprout of *li* as "a sense of deference" (*tz'u-jang*) is reformulated in 6A.6 as "a sense of respect" (*kung-ching*), making it equivalent to *yi* in the previous passages. For the purposes of persuading rulers that their minds contained moral impulses, the proof of the internality of *jen* was probably sufficient. The proof is not repeated at 6A.6, and this is perhaps because it is irrelevant to the debate with Kao Tzu, where the issue is the status of *yi*.

65. Graham wishes to extend this sort of usage throughout early Chinese texts, but I doubt that this is warranted. Certainly the *Hsun Tzu* frequently uses "*hsing*" in a sense restricted quite narrowly to "what is possessed at birth." For the argument that "*hsing*" always meant simply "what is inborn" in pre-Ch'in texts and that the character used during the period was graphemically identical with "*sheng*ᵃ" to be

born," see Fu 1940, especially I:33b-39a. On Mencius' concept of *hsing* as pointing to man's potential for growth, see Lau 1953:561.

66. Graham has made a detailed analysis of this passage (1967:251-54). I am indebted to it, but my interpretation is somewhat different.

67. The interpretation of "*ku*" as "primitive" follows Graham. Previous translations of this passage have differed from mine in taking "*chih-che*" to refer to a type of person, a wise or clever man. However, the word is used interchangeably with "*chih*," just as "*ku-che*" and "*ku*" are used, and I think that by understanding "*chih-che*" in the sense of the abstract noun "*chih*": "intelligence," the many difficulties of the passage become soluble.

68. I am taking the second instance of "*ku*" here to denote "innately," consistent with the usage in *M*:4B.26. The interpretation eliminates the awkward syntax suggested by the usual gloss of "therefore."

69. Mencius' opinion of himself was not low. When asked if he was a Sage, he professed shock at the thought of such presumption, but only to the extent of noting that even Confucius did not *claim* to be a Sage (*M*:2A.2). The point is that Mencius surely did regard himself as virtuous enough to test the assertion in question.

70. The teaching that Ch'ung Yü quotes back to Mencius appears as Confucius' comment on his own political failures in *A*:14.35. When Mencius replies, "that was one time, this is another," both he and Ch'ung Yü probably understood this to mean, "Confucius' failure was a function of the social realities of his time; according to the realities of our time, my mission should not have failed, hence Confucius' words do not apply here."

71. My phrase "personal decree" is not a translation. I use it to distinguish this doctrine of *ming* from the doctrine of the Mandate of Heaven, which applies only to kings.

72. The graphemic form used is "*ling*."

73. Excavated vessels that used the word in this sense include the *Shih Yü chung*, the *Fu Shu ting*, and some of the *Hsing chung* inscriptions (*WW* 1975:8.58; 1976:1.94; 1978:3.7).

74. The *Mo Tzu* raises this issue in several places, for example, *Fei ming* I:9.1b.

75. The ruler-subject metaphor cannot he stretched too far in this passage; the notion of "knowing T'ien" seems to fall outside of it.

The fluctuations of the imagery used to speak of T'ien in *M*:7A.1 leads Fung Yu-lan to speak as if Mencius were talking about two T'iens here, an ethical one and a fatalist one (Fung 1962:225-26; compare Li 1961: 45-46). Ikeda (1965:7-8) seems to think that T'ien in this passage represents something close to Natural Law. A widespread school of interpretation takes passages such as 7A.1 to indicate that Mencius believed in an ontological idealism, where "the objective world loses the basis of its existence" (Hou 1957:396). I feel very strongly that descriptions of Mencian philosophy as an "idealism," while convenient for categorizing, represent a distortion of the type of philosophy Mencius was doing and are a misapplication of the comparative method. It is akin to reading Mencius between the lines of Wang Yang-ming's works.

The references to lifespan in *M*:7A.1 are a play on the second meaning of "*ming*," but should not be misunderstood as the operant meaning of the term in the passage.

76. The final phrase is a reference to the doctrine of timeliness and is a warning against incautious political activism.

77. The function of the word "*ming*" here essentially is no different from the way the word "*shih*" is used in the doctrine of timeliness. Compare the following two passages: "The *chün-tzu* simply acts according to rule to await his *ming*" (*M*:7B.33); "The *chün-tzu* studies broadly, plans deeply, cultivates himself and acts uprightly to await his *shih*" (*H*:28.40-41).

78. The idea expressed here is also evident in Mencius' interpretation of the *Poetry* couplet: "Ever matching T'ien's decree, seek for fortune through yourself" (*M*:4A.2). The resemblance of these Mencian ideas to Stoic philosophy in the West is striking.

79. On this point, see Kanaya 1956:48. Several ideas in this section have been influenced by Kanaya's analysis.

80. The phrase "moral tropism" has been used by Arthur Danto to describe the action of perfect wisdom in the Ruist Sage.

Chapter VI

1. I have not seen Itano's article. It is familiar to me only through the description of its major theme in Matsuda 1975:65.

2. In preparing translations and commentary for the *Hsun Tzu*, I have taken the *HTYT* text as a standard. For traditional commentary, I have relied on the *Hsun Tzu chi-chieh* (*HTCC*), a Ch'ing period commentary by Wang Hsien-ch'ien, and the *Hsun Tzu chien-shih* (*HTCS*) a Republican period commentary by Liang Ch'i-hsiung. I have consulted and benefited from the following partial English translations: Dubs 1928a; deBary 1960; Chan 1963; Watson 1963.

3. In the text of the *Hsun Tzu*, the name appears both as Sun Ch'ing Tzu and Hsun Ch'ing Tzu. The earliest edition of the text, compiled by Liu Hsiang late in the first century B.C., was entitled *Sun Ch'ing hsin shu*, or "The New Book of Sun Ch'ing." During the late Chou, the variant characters prob ably were near homophones (*GSR* readings are *sịwĕn/hsun and *swən/sun).

4. The variety of birth dates assigned to Hsun K'uang range from Ch'ien Mu's 340 B.C. (1956:333-35) to John Knoblock's suggested range of 315-305 B.C. (1982-83:34). Intermediate theories include c.335 B.C. (*HTCS*: 420) and 316 B.C. (Hsia 1979:25-26). The central issues dividing the "early daters" from the "late daters" are inconsistancies among the accounts found in the *Shih-chi* and in Liu Hsiang's preface to the *Hsun Tzu* on the one hand, and in the late Han work *Feng-su t'ung-yi* on the other. The former two works state that Hsun K'uang first came to Ch'i at age fifty, but the third tells us that he was fifteen. Both Liu Hsiang's preface and the *Feng-su t'ung-yi* suggest that Hsun K'uang arrived in Ch'i during the reigns of King Wei (r. 357-320 B.C.) and King Hsuan (r. 319-301 B.C.), but Liu's preface inverts the names of the kings, raising the question of whether the text actually refers to Kings Hsuan and Min (r. 300-284 B.C.) (Ch'ien 1956:334).

Scholars inclined to assign an early birth date to Hsun K'uang cite an account in the *Han Fei Tzu* that places Hsun K'uang in Yen in 316 B.C. (*HFT*:16.3b). Their opponents can point to an account in the *Yen-t'ieh lun* that indicates that Hsun K'uang was active as late as c.220 B.C. (*YTL*:4.7b).

5. Most sources agree that Hsun K'uang survived Huang Hsieh, who died in 238 B.C.

6. I am following the emended Liu Hsiang account and interpreting it to mean that Hsun K'uang arrived in Ch'i late in the reign of King Hsuan or during the reign of King Min.

7. The identity of the founding ruler is uncertain. It was either King Wei or King Hsuan (see Ch'ien 1956:232).

8. On the vicissitudes of the Chi-hsia Academy, see Ch'ien 1956:231-33.

9. *YTL*:2.14a.

10. *SC*:74.2348; *Sun Ch'ing hsin-shu hsu-lu* (*HTCC*:20.46); *FSTY*:7.2.

11. T'ien Chien was the last ruler of the Chou state of Ch'i; he was given no posthumous title.

12. Considerable confusion abounds with regard to dating Ch'u's encroachment upon Ch'i and the seizure of Lu. Ch'u first seized portions of the greater Ch'i realm in 284 B.C., when Ch'u aligned with a number of northern states against Ch'i, and procured the area known as Huai-pei, which probably designated a strip of land between the Huai and Sui Rivers (*SC*:40.1729-30). In 261 B.C. Ch'u again attacked Ch'i, seizing more of Ch'i's southern territory, this time portions of the old state of Lu between the Sui River and the Rivers Ssu and Tan, a piece of land known as Hsu-chou (*SC*:33.1547). Finally, in 255 B.C., Ch'u, under the leadership of Huang Hsieh, seized those portions of Lu north of the Ssu, which included the town of Lan-ling (*SC*:78.2395). (Geographical

interpretations are based on *CKLSTTC*:1.43-44.)

Clarity concerning the sequence of events is crucial in evaluating the theories of Ch'ien Mu concerning Hsun K'uang's tenure at Lan-ling (1956:431-34). Ch'ien maintains if that Hsun K'uang did indeed serve at Lan-ling, then it must have been during his first (and, for Ch'ien, only) stay in Ch'u, beginning c. 284 B.C. This theory, which entails extensive revision of Hsun K'uang's biography, requires the assumption that Ch'u received possession of Lan-ling in 284 B.C., which conflicts with all *Shih-chi* accounts.

13. *SC*:74.2348. An elaborate tale appears in several sources, describing how, soon after assuming the post of magistrate, Hsun K'uang was dismissed by Huang Hsieh, traveled to Chao, where he was appointed a High Minister, and was, at last, induced by a repentant Huang Hsieh to return to Lan-ling (*CKT*, Ch'u Ts'e:5.38b-40a; *Sun Ch'ing hsin shu hsu-lu* [*HTCC*: 20.47]; *HSWC*:4.13b-15a). The authenticity of this tale was questioned as early as the eighteenth century by Wang Chung (*HTCC*, *K'ao-cheng*: 34-35). As Wang pointed out, it is implausible on the surface, and furthermore, the *Chan-kuo ts'e* and *Han-shih wai-chuan* versions incorporate in the tale sections of the text of the *Hsun Tzu* and material found independently in other contexts in the *Han Fei Tzu* (cf. *HFT*:4.12b-13a). These sources give no indication that the material was in any way connected with a correspondence between Hsun K'uang and Huang Hsieh, as the anecdotal versions claim. (See, however, Knoblock's chronology, wherein the facticity of the tale is accepted [1982-83:30-34, 41].)

14. See the *Ju-hsiao, Ch'iang kuo,* and *Yi ping* chapters. Note that the *Han Fei Tzu* tells us that Hsun K'uang was in Yen about 316 B.C. (*HFT*:16.3b).

15. The highly idealized "transcript" of Hsun K'uang's debate with Lord Lin-wu in the *Yi ping* chapter, wherein even Lord Lin-wu cannot help but marvel at the brilliance of Hsun K'uang's arguments, should alert us to the anecdotal nature of these "historical" audiences. This does not mean that the accounts are not based on real incidents, but it does require that we treat the material with caution.

16. The *Yi ping* chapter tells us that Hsun K'uang was in Chao during the reign of King Hsiao-ch'eng (r. 265-245 B.C.). In *Ch'iang kuo*, we see him in conversation with Fan Sui, who was Prime Minister of Ch'in from 266 to 257 B.C. In *Ju-hsiao*, Hsun K'uang addresses King Chao of Ch'in (r. 306-251 B.C.). Note that the conversation between Hsun K'uang and a Prime Minister of Ch'i in *Ch'iang kuo* would indicate, if historical, that Hsun K'uang was in Ch'i between 261 and 255 B.C., after Ch'u had captured Hsu-chou but before the seizure of the northern portions of Lu.

17. Ch'ien Mu's chronology diverges from this (1956:431-34), but see note 12 above on the problems of his model.

18. I know of no certain evidence that it was not customary in Ch'u or elsewhere that non-hereditary magisterial posts be lifetime appointments. However, when we encounter a case where the incumbent was in office at an age of between seventy-eight and one hundred and three, we may at least suspect that the post could not have been administratively burdensome and was likely to have either been initially or become substantially honorary.

19. Passages in the *Hsun Tzu* that portray Hsun K'uang in audience with political leaders of Chao and Ch'in (if accepted as factual) do not indicate ambition for political responsibilities. Audiences were sought for many reasons other than solicitation of a political post, for example, securing court lodgings and stipends for oneself and one's followers. The text also portrays Hsun K'uang in audience with political figures in the state of Ch'i, and his persuasions there are clearly part of his duties as a sinecured retainer. If factual, they would signal no ambition for political duties.

20. See his commentary at *HTCC*:19.1.

21. For example, see Liang Ch'i-ch'ao's remarks in *WSTK*:621.

22. For example, the *Hsun Tzu*'s use of the word "*ch'ü*" to mean "completely," the word "*lung*" to mean "exalt" or "the exalted," and the word "*ch'i*" to mean "maximize."

23. See Yang 1938.

24. Note that Knoblock has recently devised a chronology of the text based on a theory of single authorship (1982-83:35-46). Although I do not agree with Knoblock's basic assumptions, he has isolated many datable elements that indicate *termini a quo* for various chapters of the text.

25. *H*:15.72 portrays Li Ssu, known from other sources to have studied with Hsun K'uang (e.g., *SC*:87:2539), in conversation with Hsun K'uang. This suggests that Ch'en Hsiao, mentioned in a nearby parallel passage (*H*:15.66), was also a student of Hsun K'uang's.

26. See Kanaya 1951:28.

27. Witness the remark addressed to T'ien P'ien, a Chi-hsia master, in the *Ch'i ts'e*: "Now you, sir, are given no official duties, but receive a stipend of a thousand measures and maintain a following of a hundred disciples" (*CKT*:4.16b-17a). The fact that such a phrase made sense, even if the source is more fiction than fact, indicates the scale of Chi-hsia followings.

28. The *Shih-chi*, Liu Hsiang's preface to the *Hsun Tzu*, and the *Feng-su t'ung-yi*, all state that Hsun K'uang became the senior master at Chi-hsia. We are also told by the first two of these sources that he

"was thrice charged with the wine sacrifices," a phrase Ssu-ma Chen interpreted to mean that during three different terms of tenure, Hsun K'uang was the senior participant in banquet or other ritual ceremonials (*SC*:74.2349n5).

29. Extensive sections of the *Hsun Tzu* text appear in the *Li-chi, Ta Tai Li-chi, Han-shih wai-chuan*, and *Shih-chi*. For an interesting, if somewhat overstated, survey of the influence of *Hsun Tzu* Ruism on Han Ruist traditions, see the remarks of the Ch'ing commentator Hu Yuan-yi cited in *HTCC*, K'ao-cheng: 68-70.

30. The most notable exception is the *Ch'eng-hsiang* chapter, which seens to mention the death of Lord Ch'un-shen in 238 B.C. (*H*:25.9). The commentator Lu Wen-chao maintained that this reference to Huang Hsieh was a corruption of the text (*HTCC*:18.5). Ch'ien Mu agrees, and cites supporting arguments by Liu Shih-p'ei (1956:433). I do not find their arguments convincing. In any event, we argue elsewhere that the *Ch'eng-hsiang* chapter was not written by Hsun K'uang, regardless of this status of the reference to Huang Hsieh.

   We might note that the chapters *Ju-hsiao*, which refers to King Chao of Ch'in (d. 251 B.C.) by his posthumous name, and *Yi ping*, which refers to King Hsiao-ch'eng of Chao (d. 245 B.C.) by his posthumous name, were probably put in their present form after Hsun K'uang's final departure from Chi-hsia. As noted above, these chapters refer to Hsun K'uang by honorific and were obviously composed or at least edited by disciples. No other chapters among the first twenty-six must necessarily be dated later than 261 B.C.

31. An early separation of Hsun K'uang from the development of the *Hsun Tzu* text might account, in part, for the fact that despite the enormous influence that the *Hsun Tzu* exerted during the early Han (see note 29 above), Hsun K'uang himself is rarely mentioned and passages from the *Hsun Tzu* cited in other texts are virtually never linked to his name.

   Another factor that bears on this point is the problematical form of the *Hsun Tzu* prior to the Han. When Liu Hsiang edited the text toward the end of the Western Han, he wrote: "The texts of Hsun Ch'ing's book [collected in the Imperial Library] which I have edited numbered three hundred and twenty-two chapters. I compared these and excised duplications amounting to two hundred and ninety chapters, settling upon a text of thirty-two chapters" (*HTCC*:20.46). Liu Hsiang called his edited text "The New Book of Sun Ch'ing" (*Sun Ch'ing hsin-shu*) which indicates that prior to his edition, no completely organized text attributed to Hsun K'uang (Sun Ch'ing) existed. Judging from his introductory remarks, the essays that comprise the *Hsun Tzu* text as we have it today probably were originally circulated independently or in small groups. The organization of the extant text, which groups chapters with similar themes, may reflect early, more circumscribed books of "Hsun Tzu's" writings. Kanaya Osamu has gone so far as to suggest that these subsections of the text reflect the division of Hsun K'uang's school of Ruism into factions with specialized interests (1951:21-28), a theory that implies that a substantial portion, if not most of the text, springs from the hands of first or second generation disciples, rather than from Hsun K'uang's own.

32. "*Ch'eng-hsiang*" means a cadence created by the beat of a pestle. It resembles the modern "*hsiang-sheng*" chant, which is performed by two people who alternate lines.

33. The text appears to mention with grief the downfall of Huang Hsieh, which occurred in 238 B.C. See note 30.

34. For a different view of *Ch'eng-hsiang*, see Tu Kuo-hsiang's essay on the chapter in Tu 1962.

    The composition of the *Fu* chapter is particularly unusual. The group nature of the dialogue in the opening riddle section cannot be doubted. Each riddle is followed by a confession of puzzlement, such as, "your servant is foolish and does not know the answer, may I ask the King?" And then the "King" or some other persona replies. The impression that this is a record of group play seems inescapable. Furthermore, the *Yi-wen chih* records a book of poems in the *fu* style by Hsun Tzu, in ten chapters. This suggests that the records of Ruist group play were at one time far more extensive (but for a different explanation of the *Yi-wen chih* entry, see Hu Yuan-yi's remarks in *HTCC*, K'ao-cheng:65).

35. This is not a true paradox: there is neither a logical nor a chemical contradiction here. But it is treated as a paradox in the text. The importance of paradox to the *Hsun Tzu* is noted in Akatsuka 1958:13.

36. These include Shen Tao and T'ien P'ien (*H*:6.8).

37. See Munro 1969:132-33.

38. Note Wang Nien-sun's commentary to *Pu kou* (*HTCC*: 2.15); on *Chieh pi*, see Kanaya 1951:27.

39. For example, in *Pu kou*, the Taoistic description of the *chün-tzu*: "Without stepping down from his dwelling the essence of all within the seas is accumulated within him" (cf. *TTC*:47), is preceded by the following description of the path to this perfection: "The *chün-tzu* examines the ways of the later kings (see below), and [extrapolates so that] he can describe what was prior to the hundred kings as though in casual conversation; he extrapolates from the guiding rules of ritual and propriety, distinguishes right from wrong . . ." (*H*:3.36-37). *Chieh pi* concludes a discussion of perfecting the mind, which is filled with vague and seemingly mystical language, with a description of the path to

wisdom as the bounding of wisdom through study–study which "takes the Sage Kings as teacher and their regulations as rule, conforming to their rules and seeking their guiding categories in order to emulate their persons" (*H*: 21.83). (Note that in the Taoistic *Chieh pi*, Chuang Tzu is attacked; cf. *H*:21.22).

The passage from *Pu kou* alerts us to an important textual side issue, namely, that in resolving arguments with an appeal to authority, the *Hsun Tzu* frequently endorses reliance on what it calls the "later kings" (*hou-wang*). Who these later kings were is disputed. For a review of the literature on the issue, and a defense of the position that the term refers to the Chou founders, see Eno 1984:458-59.

40. For a discussion of Graham's theories of Yang Chu, see Eno 1984:370-72. As suggested in chapter V, note 41, I would prefer to view the "Yangist" texts as a sub-corpus of Taoist texts, without any claim of linkage to Yang Chu.

41. See the discussion in Rickett 1965:12-13.

42. This theory is discussed in detail in Kuo 1945:210-32; see also Hou 1957:351-59.

43. Rickett 1965:157-58; Fung 1962:168.

44. See the comparisons adduced in Hou 1957:531-49.

45. Some passages from *Nei-yeh* ("Inner Tasks") illustrate: "The essence of things is transformed [following Ting et al., see Kuo et al. 1956:781] and becomes life; born below, it is the five grains; above, it is the ranks of stars; flowing between heaven and earth it is called 'ghosts and spirits'; hidden in the breast it is called 'the Sage' [*KT*:16.1a].... The Way has no fixed place; it settles peacefully in a good mind. If the mind is tranquil and the breath regular, the Way settles therein.... The essence of the Way, how can it have thought [see Kuo et al. 1956:784] or sound? Cultivate the mind, quiet the thoughts, and the Way may be reached [*KT*:16.2a].... The mean between gorging and starving one-self is called perfect harmony. The vital essence dwells within and knowledge is therein born [*KT*:16.4b]...." (These translations make use of Rickett 1965:158-68.)

46. See Rickett 1965:153. These passages are poorly reconciled with the general thrust of argument in these chapters. As with certain sections in the *Chieh Lao* ("Explication of the *Lao Tzu*") chapter in the *Han Fei Tzu* (6.1b-2a), these passages may be viewed as syncretic insertions, either added by the composer of the text to link together older materials, or directly inserted after the compilation of the text.

47. The notion of suppressing desire does not inherently conflict with interest in *li*. The *Mencius* suggests suppression of desire as a self-cultivation device (*M*:7B.35). The *Hsun Tzu* takes a strong position

that *li* nurtures or edifies (*yang*) desire (*H*:19.1-3), but that desires are innately unexpungeable (e.g., *H*:22.55-63). A number of its arguments concerning desire are directed against Sung Chien (*H*:18.114-22), who, according to some, was an author of the *Kuan Tzu* texts at issue.

48. An extensive discussion of Tsou Yen and his philosophy appears in Needham 1956:232-44. (Note that major omissions occur in the translation of *SC*:76.2370 that appears on page 237; the meaning of this important passage is significantly altered.) See also Fung 1931: 200-209; Henderson 1984:31-35.

49. The accuracy of the *Shih-chi* accounts has been widely questioned. See Ch'ien 1956:439.

50. *SC*:28:1368-69; 74.2344; Tso Ssu, *Wei tu fu* (cited in Fung 1931:202); Liu Hsiang, *Pieh-lu* (cited *SC*:74.2348n3). The phrase for "five elements" in Tsou Yen's philosophy seems to have been "*wu te*," rather than the "*wu hsing*" that played so great a role in Han cosmology. For an argument asserting that the portrait of Tsou as an innovator is a Han projection, see Henderson 1984:32-5

51. As Fung Yu-lan notes (1962:439), the *Shih-chi* groups the biographies of Mencius, Tsou Yen, and Hsun Tzu together, and this in itself may suggest that Tsou Yen was originally a Ruist who developed his cosmological interests until they overshadowed his early training. The *Shih-chi* states that, "If [Tsou's doctrines] are reduced to their fundamentals, they inevitably return to *jen*, *yi*, restraint, frugality, and the operation of the relations between ruler and minister, superior and inferior, and the six familial relationships; it is merely that his beginnings developed without restraint" (*SC*: 74.2344). The *Yen-t'ieh lun* also speaks of Tsou as a Ru (2.14b).

52. See, for example, *H*: 17.29-40, 21.74-78. See also the discussion in Dubs 1927:64-73.

53. The *Tso-chuan*'s stated views on spiritualism often resemble those of the *Hsun Tzu*. Certain passages focus on the rationalistic debunking of shamanism and superstitious omenology, for example, *TCHC*, Hsi 16:6.2; Hsi 21:6.18-19; Chao 1:20.34-35; Chao 3:20.56; Chao 5:21.41. In all of these instances, the logic of omenology and shamanism is described as benighted and rationalist arguments for the primacy of human action are offered. These passages can all be characterized as denigrating action guided by a concern with the supernatural. However, the *Tso-chuan*, unlike the *Hsun Tzu*, does not generally deny the existence of spiritual beings and supernatural forces. Some passages contradict the main anti-spiritualist leanings, for example, Chao 7:21.57-58; Chao 10: 22.20. Others, while not prescribing an interest in spirits, implicitly acknowledge their existence (Hsi 5:5.31-32), or, in one instance, actually

recount their appearance while scorning those who would cater to them (Chuang 32:3.93-94).

54. Although most of the *Tso-chuan* deals with pre-Confucian history, some of its heroic figures are depicted in the narrative in the image of later Ru. The greatest of these is Tzu-ch'an, Prime Minister of Cheng. Tzu-ch'an frequently is shown adopting an antisuperstitious stance, but in doing so, he displays a comprehensive grasp of cosmology, demonology, and the interpretation of dreams (Chao 1:20.28-33; Chao 7:21.61-62), and acknowledges that men, upon dying, may become spirits (Chao 7:21.64-65). The *Tso-chuan*, therefore, apparently reconciled an interest in cosmology with Ruist humanism by prioritizing the two—human effort is the only practical path, but in cultivating comprehensive wisdom, the Sage will also learn about the world of spirits. Indeed, Ruist-style Sages, such as Tzu-ch'an, will obtain a deeper grasp of spirit lore than the spiritualist and so be able to refute superstitious prescriptions issued by spiritualist pretenders to wisdom.

55. On Tsou Yen in Yen, see also *SC*:34.1558, 74.2345, 80.2427-28. Elsewhere, the *Shih-chi* traces the origins of diviner-sorcerers to Ch'ang Hung, a native of Chou who flourished c.500 B.C. (*SC*:28.1364).

56. On the origins of these cults, see Needham 1974:94-95. On the traditional linkage of them to Tsou Yen, see also Welch 1966:96-97.

57. The cosmologies of diviners and shamans may have portrayed Nature as a purposive, even an ethical force, far different from its role in, say, Taoism. Yet the ideologies of omenologists and Taoists share the crucial feature of locating value in a nonhuman sphere and searching for human guidance in the manifestations of the natural world.

58. The dating of these two essays, which appeared as chapters of the *Li-chi*, a Han text that brought together both Han and pre-Han materials, is disputed. Various portions of both essays bear close resemblance to the *Mencius* or to the *Hsun Tzu* (compare, e.g., *M*:4A.13 and *CY*:20; *H*:3.26-33 and *TH*: 1,7), and the texts also show evidence of Taoist influence (they are sometimes classified as Taoist). I believe that the texts are either very late Chou or early Han and postdate both the *Mencius* and the *Hsun Tzu*. My principal reasons for dating the texts in this way are: (1) the fact that the essays are not internally identified with any one Ruist Master and incorporate the teachings of more than one pre-Ch'in Ruist faction; (2) the style of argument is highly systematic and shows a great interest in metaphysical speculation (particularly the *Chung-yung*), a hallmark of Han Ruist texts. These arguments are far from conclusive; however, I have chosen to be guided by them and to exclude the essays from my discussions of pre-Ch'in Ruism for the sake of simplicity and

because they represent my own views. For more on the dating of these essays, see Tu 1976:13-15.

59. This is, of course, the same theme I suggest as the primary subject of the *Mencius* in chapter V. The texts differ radically in their strategies and the resulting tenor of discussions on *li*, but their agendas were, I believe, largely identical.

60. In these discussions, we will consider only the first twenty-seven chapters of the *Hsun Tzu*. The remaining five chapters are generally thought to have been appended to the text at a later time (*WSTK*: 621-22). Yang Liang placed them at the end of the text because he considered them largely derivative (*HTCC*:20.1). Their philosophical agenda is rather different from the other chapters.

61. I am not using the terms "ontology" and "epistemology" here, in order to avoid inappropriate implied comparisons with Western philosophical traditions.

62. A number of these terms are frequently used throughout the text: words such as "*lei*" (approximately sixty-five occurances), "*li*ª" (more than 100 occurances), and "*t'ung*" (approximately thirty occurances). The character "*pien*": [to make] distinctions, itself appears about seventy-five times, not including uses of the cognate "*pien*ª" as a loan. Others of these terms are used less frequently, but with great emphasis, as in the case of "*ts'ao*," which plays an important role in the early chapters of the text.

63. "The True Kings regulated names such that when names were determined realities were distinguished" (*H*:22.6-7).

64. "Things which are of identical type and essense are perceived by the T'ien-like faculties [i.e., sense organs] identically.... The mind, in addition, [has the power to] understand through verification (*cheng chih*) .... Thus through reliance [on the senses] one is able to [distinguish] sameness and difference" (*H*:22.16-21).

65. Interpretation of the *Hsun Tzu*'s theory of language has focused on the phrases, "Names have no intrinsic appropriateness" (*H*:22.25), and, "Names have no intrinsic reality" (*H*:22.26), to argue that the *Hsun Tzu* takes a conventionalist approach to language (see Hansen 1983:81). However, when viewed as a whole, the *Hsun Tzu*'s theory of language is realist. Although individual words are initially chosen arbitrarily, their consistent use and syntactic relations in language create a perfect correspondence between the elements and structure of language and the objects of the world and their relations. It is this characteristic of language that allows the text explicitly to limit its conventionalism: "Names can be intrinsically good: those that are straightforward and simple, without contradiction (*fu*ª) are called good names" (*H*:22.27). Implicitly, names *may* "contradict" reality.

66. Throughout the chapter, the word *"pien"*: "to make distinctions," is used as a loan for *"pien*ᵃ*"*: "argument." The loan relationship appears frequently in the text and might be an intentional indication of the *Hsun Tzu's* belief that valid argument is a verbal representation of natural distinctions.

   In rendering the word *"tao"* as "Truth" in this instance, I do not adopt Chad Hansen's theory that "Chinese philosophy had no concept of truth" (1985a:492). I believe that it had the concept, but that it was not articulated as a philosophical object. In Hansen's terms, ideas parallel to what we refer to as "truth" played "a role in theories," but, they did not become the focus of theories. This is a position of "soft linguistic determinism," and I believe Hansen ultimately returns to this less categorical claim when he restates his conclusions as "Chinese philosophers did not focus on a distinct notion of semantic truth" (515-16). Hansen argues brilliantly, but I think that his habitual linkage of the term "truth" to correspondence theories of language might have led him to give inadequate stress to the fact that, deplorable as analytic thinkers might find it, assertions of truth sometimes really do entail no theory of language. Nevertheless, much of Hansen's model is persuasive, and I will not be surprised if further argument finds me converted.

67. See also *H*:1.28, 2.37, 9.47-48.

68. On the pervasive importance of the notion of class distinctions in the text, see Katakura 1978. Katakura illustrates both descriptive and prescriptive dimensions of the notion.

69. See also *H*:5.28 and *H*:11.63, translated above. On the notion that *li* trains the senses and the mind, see the discussion on "Educating the Sage."

70. Compare *TTC*:22. The phrase "crooked yet easy to follow" (*wang erh shun*) carries a sense of "odd yet naturally pleasing." We find no conflict here with the Ruist adherence to a doctrine of descriptive equality, stressed in Munro 1969. The *Hsun Tzu* simply maintains that rank differentiations are descriptively necessary to the socialization of human beings. Rank differentiatons are dictated by organizational needs rather than disparities in innate character.

71. We will tend, in this chapter, to translate *"li-yi"* as "ritual and propriety." The compound is fundamentally a linkage of explicit conventional rules and a more abstract ethical notion, close to "right." The linkage is often understood as a way of enlarging the prescriptive range of ritual, allowing individuals to act according to what seems ethically right even if it is not in absolute accord with convention. This is correct, but as we saw in chapter V, the linkage has a complementary function of circumscribing the realm of ethical rightness to keep it closely aligned with ritual prescript.

The *Hsun Tzu* makes no effort to establish *"yi"* as a value standard independent of convention. On the contrary, in its most generalized usage as the distinguishing characteristic of man (*H*:9.70-71) *"yi"* is described as an ability to establish and act according to role differentiations. The translation of "propriety" seems most apt.

72. See Kanaya's divisions (1951:20).

73. This appears also at *H*:17.43.

74. To make this even approximate empirical reality, we must assume that by *"ch'ün"* the text means not mere society, but hierarchical society. This meaning is suggested by the text's etymological observation that "A 'ruler' is one who is good at good at 'grouping' " (*H*:9.75), which is a play on the cognate relationship of the words *"chün"* and *"ch'ün."*

75. Cf. *H*:5.26-28.

76. The doctrine is most elegantly delineated in the *Li lun* ("Treatise on *Li*"): "What is the origin of *li*? People are born with desires. If those desires are not satisfied, individuals cannot but seek to satisfy them. If people seek satisfaction without rule or limit, boundary or degree, they cannot but conflict. From conflict comes chaos; from chaos comes poverty. The former kings detested chaos among people, and so fashioned ritual and propriety to create distinctions [among them], to nurture their desires, to provide for their wants, to ensure that desires would not exhaust [available] resources" (*H*:19.1-3). On the importance of this doctrine, see Munro 1969:90. This theory and its corollary that *"li* is nurturance" are discussed in detail in section 4.2.

77. Cf. *H*:17.48-49, where the role of *li* in society is likened to the role of signal buoys in a river.

78. This argument constitutes a brilliant response to one of the most powerful doctrinal weapons used by Mohists in their attack on Ruist *li*.

79. Many portions of the political chapters do, of course, dwell upon matters of politics without direct reference to ritual. Even the most purely political chapters, however, continually lead their arguments back to issues of ritual social order. Note, for example, *H*:11.63 (in the *Wang pa*, or "Kings and Hegemons" chapter) and *H*:15.78 (in *Yi ping*: "Discussions on the Military").

The ritual concerns of the political chapters belie the characterization of the *Hsun Tzu* as a "legalist" text, a position not uncommon among scholars in the PRC. It is true that the *Hsun Tzu* shows some adaptation of Legalist theories, but the influence of Legalism on the text is far less than the influences of Taoism and "Sung-Yin naturalism." It is also true that the *Hsun Tzu* shows a persistent interest in "laws" or "rules" (*fa*), the keynote of Legalism. But for the *Hsun Tzu*—and this is a crucial point—*fa* are always compatible with, and frequently an aspect of, *li*. "The *li* are the foremost components of law" (*H*:1.28); see also *H*:2.48, 4.49-52, 8.59-60, 10.92, 11.63, 12.57, 15.99-100, 23.25.

80. See, for example, Dubs 1927: chapter 6; Lau 1953; Graham 1967.

81. This is usually described as the *Hsun Tzu*'s doctrine that man is, by nature, "evil." Kanaya Osamu has noted that the term "evil" in this context appears only in the *Hsing o* chapter, which in style and content differs sharply from the rest of the text (1951:30-31). He argues that Hsun K'uang did not write it, and the word "evil" (*o*) would then appear in this sense in no portion of the text that Hsun K'uang may have written. I do not feel, however, that *Hsing o* conflicts philosophically with the rest of the text—whose relation to Hsun K'uang is, at any rate, frequently unclear. While I agree that the *Hsun Tzu*'s theory of human nature is best described as holding that human nature includes nothing intrinsically ethical, rather than as holding that it is evil, I do not hesitate to include *Hsing o* as part of the main corpus of the text.

82. This does not mean that the desires are eliminated, only that they are controlled. See the criticism of asceticism at *H*:6.3-4, and the discussion of desires in section 4.2.

83. It is, of course, possible to view all actions of man—who is born of Nature—as being realizations of Nature. This would, however, be a purely descriptive approach and would not distinguish values among man's actions. The *Hsun Tzu* clearly wishes to acknowledge value in some human activity. Its method of allowing this is to draw a sharp line between the components of man's character for which Nature and man are responsible respectively. The line is drawn on the basis of how skills are acquired: "That in man which cannot be acquired by study or reformed through effort is called 'nature' (*hsing*). That which is mastered by study or achieved by effort is called 'art' (*wei*)" (*H*:23.12-13). This is a key circumscription of the notion of "innate" and militates against Lau's reconciliation of the *Mencius* and the *Hsun Tzu* through the notion of developmental character (1953).

84. The passage continues with an attack on *li* (*CT*:9.11-13). See Graham 1967:222-23. The *Hsun Tzu* expresses the limited value of the *hsing* by describing it as the "unadorned abilities" (*ts'ai-p'u*), a clear response to Taoist doctrine (*H*:19.76).

85. Lao Tzu is criticized by the *Hsun Tzu* as understanding "contraction" (passivity) and not "extension" (purposive activity), with the result that "the exalted and the humble are not distinguished" (*H*:17.51-53).

86. One philosopher so attacked is identified by Needham as a founding thinker of the longevity cults that flourished later, during the Han (1974:94).

87. Cf. *LSCC*:4.5b-6a, which, however, includes Ruist elements.

88. Compare *H*:8.108: "Without teacher and rules, man exalts his nature; with them, he exalts acquired [skills]."
89. As *Hsing o* makes clear, this is, for the *Hsun Tzu*, not a "natural" but a human process (see note 83).
90. See the discussion of practical totalism in chapter III.
91. Given the scarcity of resources, man's hungers must generally be satisfied at low levels to ensure continuity of satiation. The mechanics of this natural law teaches man prudence: deferred gratification. Similarly, man learns that by investing his resources properly, rather than consuming them immediately, he can improve his material rewards. He learns, for example, that by using grain to feed livestock rather than himself, he can, in the end, improve the quality of his diet. These ideas are set forth at *H*:4.42-71.
92. This seems to be inconsistent with other passages (e.g., *H*:22.19); we would expect man to employ the mind (*hsin*ᵃ) here. This formula might point to the motivating role of desire, as in *H*:19.1-2.
93. The word "*yi*ᵉ" is used in the sense of "restraint" and has been glossed as "*ting*": "settle," by Yü Yueh. Yang Liang noted the variant reading "*ning*ᵃ": "congeal," perhaps: "slow down" (*HTCC*: 15.25).
94. Compare *H*:8.25-27, emending *cheng* to *chih*ᵈ, following the *Ch'ün shu chih yao* version (*HTCC*:4.10).
95. Compare *H*:1.44-45: "Study is the study of unifying."
96. Apart from the formal syllabus per se, the cultural forms of ritual serve as an ongoing structure refining society at large. The *Li-lun* underscores this point in the theory of *li* as nurturance (*H*:19.3-13), which maintains that ritual forms train the senses and sensitize them to the aesthetically good. This creates in society a level of cultivation at which values other than simple material gratification have become institutionalized.
97. It is this overlap in empirical and ethical principle that prevents *li*ᵃ from developing a scientific dimension in the *Hsun Tzu* and in later Ruist thought. As Kanaya points out, to the degree that it is interested in natural phenomena, the *Hsun Tzu* only looks to Nature to find ethical lessons for man. Empirical observation is ended as soon as a moral meaning is construed (1970:5-6).
98. See *H*:2.14, 2.47, 3.17-18, 3.28, 7.21, 11.114. Note the apparent loan of *li*ᵃ for *li* at 22.45.
99. The meaning of the term "*wen-li*" seems frequently indistinguishable from ritual itself (cf. *H*:9.95, 10.108, 19.10, 19.103). In particular, note: "The ways of the filial son are the pattern-principles of ritual and propriety" (*H*:23.20); "Its (*li*'s) pattern-principles form [a manifest] insignia (*chang*)" (*H*:26.1).

100. See also *H*:19.20-21: "In the monthly sacrifice [to one's ancestors] one tastes the great [plain] broth, and eats one's fill of the various delicacies: this is honoring one's roots [by proffering food] while [putting the food] to personal use. Honoring the root is embellishment (*wen*); putting this to personal use is principle (*li*[a]). When the two combine into a single pattern (*wen*) to return to the Great Oneness, it is called the great exaltation [of ritual]" (taking *ch'i*[b] as *chi*[a], following Yang Liang rather than Yü Yueh [*HTCC*:13.7-8]). This curious passage seems to say that the ceremonial sacrifice, having no supernatural effect, is simply an embellishment of human life (cf. *H*:17.39-40), while the entailment of ceremony into practical life (through eating ritual foods), in accord with natural principles (the satisfaction of hunger), integrates embellishment and practicality into a pattern of entailed ritual activity, which is linked to a transcendental holism (on the Great Oneness, see the conclusion). Pattern-principles, then, are precisely the ethical transformation of natural processes (such as eating) as they enter the ritual human sphere.

101. See note 83. The rendering of *shih*[b] as "reform through effort" is a modification of Kubo's interpretation [*HTCC*:17.3].

102. On "heaven and earth" (*t'ien-ti*) see appendix C, note 1.

103. "*T'ung*" here indicates an integrating intelligibility that gives significance to the realm of ritual.

104. Cf. *H*:9.81-82, 15.57. "*Shen*" is also used as descriptive of the human virtues embodied in Sagehood (*H*:3.27, 3.45, 8.64, 9.62, 21.44). On the role of the term in the *Hsun Tzu*, see also Ikeda 1965:19-20.

105. It is obviously beyond the scope of this chapter to illustrate the ways in which the naturalisms we have identified use the idea of T'ien (or *t'ien-ti*) as Nature in a normative sense. We can merely indicate a few of these uses. T'ien/Nature as a value source and role model: *TTC*:9, 73, 77; *KT*, *Hsin-shu* I:219.11-13; *Hsin-shu* II:222.10-11; *Pai-hsin*:224.11-12. T'ien/Nature and man as one in Tao: *TTC*:39; *CT*: 4.18. T'ien/Nature transcends and trivializes human values: *TTC*:5; *CT*:2.29, 5.53; *KT*, *Pai-hsin*:225.14-15. A purposive T'ien/Nature as a responsive field of human portents: Tsou Yen's philosophy, as reflected in *LSCC*, *Ying-t'ung* (also called *Ming lei*):13.4 (see Fung 1931:201-202).

106. The former notion would fairly characterize important aspects of Tsou Yen's cosmological naturalism (cf. Fung 1931:201-202). The latter view was characteristic of late Chou omenology, which was a component of divinistic or shamanistic naturalism.

107. See the analysis of section B in Matsuda 1975:70-71.

108. "Desire" is included in a list of innate affective responses appearing at *H*:22.19 (but it is missing at 22.3). The classic formula of the "seven

emotions" (*ch'i-ch'ing*) which appears in the *Li-yun* chapter of the *Li-chi* does include "desire" (*LC*:7.6b). On the philosophically constructive role of desire in the *Hsun Tzu*, see Kanaya 1951a.

109. But the issue is somewhat confused at *H*:22.3-4, wherein the mind seems to have an innate ability to make choices on behalf of the emotions (excluding desire), which leads directly to creative artifice.

110. Dubs (1928a: 176) renders the passage thus: "To use what is not of one's kind to nourish one's kind [note: e.g., animal flesh to nourish mankind]—this is what is meant by the natural nourishing. To act according with one's station is what is called happiness; to act contrary to one's station is called calamity—this is what is meant by the natural government."

111. This is the suggestion of Kodama 1972:52, following Tsukada Ōmine. Neither phrase has a stated subject, and, while this might imply a verb-subject, it is equally likely in such cases that the subject of the antecedent sentence is implied. Note that all of the preceding sentences in the passage have stated subjects that differ from the preceding phrase. They cannot, then, be used to refute the notion that the elision of the subject indicates, in this instance, the extension of one subject over several phrases.

112. The interpretation dates from Yang Liang (*HTCC*:11.25). Kodama's unique analysis of this passage rests on a departure from this tradition. He takes "*ts'ai*[a]" as a loan for "*ts'ai*[b]": "abilities." He argues that man's innate abilities are what he uses to nurture, or transform, his mind and faculties. He paraphrases thus: "Man's motor abilities are not of the same class as his T'ien-like faculties, but they nurture the T'ien-like faculties; his cognitive abilities are not of the same class as the T'ien-like ruler, but they nurture the T'ien-like ruler. Thus motor and cognitive abilities are called the T'ien-like nurturance" (1972:57). While I agree with Kodama's scepticism of traditional interpretations, I find his own solutions confusing, both grammatically and philosophically (see Eno 1984:472n112).

113. "The Sage molds (*ts'ai*[c]) things, he is not directed by things" (*KT*, *Hsin shu* II:13.5a). Here the notion of molding things clearly goes beyond agricultural subsistence.

114. Cf. *H*:10.1: "The various things of the world inhabit the same spatial realm but possess different bodies; they have no innate appropriateness but have uses for man."

115. Note that Watson misses this sense of "*yang*," and his translation of the *Li lun* chapter is consequently flawed. The notion of refining the senses is discussed also at *H*:11.46-49.

116. Recall that man's distinguishing characteristic is the ability to make distinctions (*pien*), both cognitive—through recognition of sameness

and difference—and social, by establishing proprieties of social roles (*H*:5.24-28, 9.69-74).

117. Compare *LSCC*:1.4a, which uses a similar formula, limiting the reference to the body and its innate nature.

118. We are moving here directly from section B to section E. The functions of the intervening sections may be summarized as follows: Section C divides T'ien into the realms of sky, earth, seasons, and *yin-yang*, and cautions that inquiry into these should not go beyond those manifest regularities that, as with natural objects, can be manipulated by man for his own purposes: to keep time, to plan agriculture, and so forth. The ideal man does not concern himself with these properties of Nature; his mind is focused on the human social sphere: "Functionaries will keep track of T'ien; you must keep to the Way" (*H*:17.18). Section D expands upon the proposition set forth early in the "Treatise" that political order depends upon the function of human government, and is not determined by nonpurposive T'ien. Its dominant images are agricultural and calendrical, and the section should be viewed as a recapitulation of the earlier characterization of bad rule: "Though the seasons revolve as they do in ordered time, disaster and devastation arise unlike in ordered times" (*H*:17.5).

119. The statement appears at *H*:17.7.

120. A similar notion appears in the "Sung-Yin" chapters of the *Kuan Tzu*, for example, *KT*:13.5a, 16.2a.

121. The equivalence is demonstrated at *H*:25.13, 26.6. See appendix C, note 1.

122. The insertion follows citations in the *Wen hsuan* and the *Cheng-ming* chapter of the *Hsun Tzu* (see Yü Yueh's commentary in *HTCC*:11:28, followed by all subsequent annotators).

123. See also *H*:6.31.

124. The text's only assessment of Hsun K'uang's life appears at the end of the final *Yao wen* chapter (demonstrably a post-Ch'in addition), at *H*:32.27-37. He is there judged a political failure who was defeated because he "did not encounter his [proper] time," precisely in the mold of Confucius and Mencius.

125. See the discussion on the nature of the text.

126. Commentators have followed Yü Yueh's incorrect gloss of "*chieh*" as "what is suitable" (*HTCC*:11.28). Yang and Liu T'ai-kung correctly gloss it as "fate." Watson follows Yang but fails to make the point of the passage clear.

127. The remainder of the "Treatise" concentrates on two main themes: the nonpurposive character of Nature and the ethical irrelevance of natural phenomena, and the ethical centrality of *li*. Sections G, H, and I (*H*:17.29-38) attribute mechanistic natural causes to phenomena widely

interpreted by shamanistic and divinistic schools as ethical omens, and maintain that the true locus of ethical omens is the sphere of social phenomena. The text prescribes the unceasing cultivation of ritual social order. Section J (*H*:17.38-40) is remarkable in its explicit detachment of spiritualism from the ritual realm. Ritual ceremonies that take the form of spiritualist worship–in this case the great sacrifice for rain–are redefined as "embellishments" (*wen*) of social life. Sections K and M (*H*:17.40-44, 46-50) are straightforward exaltations of *li* as the perfection of human action and as the guiding light of social order. The intervening Section L (*H*:17.44-46) attacks Taoist quietisitic attitudes toward T'ien-as-Nature in favor of an activist policy of exploiting Nature for human use. Finally, section N (*H*:17.50-54) attacks various philosophies as one-sided. It closely resembles portions of the *Chieh pi* chapter (*H*: 21.21-24), and seems to have little to do with the rest of the "Treatise."

128. Ikeda notes the following passages: *H*:3.16, 4.21, 4.25, 5.18, 16.7, 18.69, 19.15, 19.114, 28.33. In almost every instance, with the possible exception of 3.16, I think T'ien is invoked as either a rhetorical flourish or, in the cases of 19.15, and 19.114, in the context of traditional religious explanations for sacrificial ritual. The one anomoly is 28.33, and there we have stepped outside the core chapters of the text.

129. On the reading of "six arts" for *liu erh*, see *HTCC*:19.24.

Conclusion

1. Relevant passages include *A*:1.3, 5.5, 11.23; *M*:3B.9, 7B.26; *H*:2.29-31.

2. Michael Oakeshott has argued to a similar conclusion from a different starting point. His basic claim is that propositions about skilled conduct (rules) can have no meaning for individuals unless the individual already has had some degree of practice in the skilled conduct in question at some level, no matter how rudimentary. Rules, then, are merely guidelines for refining skills already acquired through prior practices, observation, and trial and error (1962:90).

3. Hall and Ames have suggested several notions that bear directly on these points and relate them to a model of Ruist metaphysics derived from the *Analects* but consistent with all early Ruist texts. They picture the metaphysics implied in the *Analects* as involving a notion of the universe as a web analogous to a hologram, in which every part "reflects or contains its whole in some adumbrated sense" (1987:237-38). Within this cosmos, T'ien "is the source of meaningfulness," which "encompasses the traditional past as the cumulated products of human activity" (248). The Sage grasps this universe through "an aesthetic understanding, an *ars contextualis*, in which the correlativity of 'part'

and 'whole' . . . permits the mutual interdependence of all things to be assessed in terms of particular contexts defined by social roles and functions" (248). Focusing on the Ruist interest in music and dance, Hall and Ames characterize this Sage as a "virtuoso," his action in the context of the holistic universe being analogous to the performance of a musical artist improvising within the parameters of a configured musical form (275-83; the music analogy is one that has been employed frequently by Fingarette). These ideas are clearly compatible with the main themes of this study, although we would anchor any such metaphysical portrait upon the ground of a history of sectarian experience with *li* as the source and context of meaning. The metaphysics of the *Analects* is crude at best; it is its ritual foundation that is fully articulated, T'ien serving as a rhetorical vehicle for celebrating the world perceived through a ritual *habitus*.

The relation of these ideas to the synthetic nature of Ruism can be clarified if we view them through an extension of Hall and Ames' notion of a Ruist "ontology of events" (1984:15). We saw in chapter VI how the *Hsun Tzu*, when embarked on a project of developing a fully articulated portrait of the world of things, made an unexpected leap from what appeared at first to be a taxonomy of entities distinguished by characteristics of sameness and difference to a picture of the world as an array of situations each perceived by the Sage in relation to the *tao*. An ontology of atomic entities possessing substance and attributes has little appeal to the enterprise of Ruist philosophy, and while the analytic thrust of later Mohism might have prodded Ruists such as Hsun Tzu to attempt analytic inventories of the furniture of the world, the notion of things as components of norm-laden contexts seems to have been a stronger thrust. In the *Ta-hsueh*, a work that we have placed just beyond our main corpus of pre-Ch'in Ruist texts, we are told; "Things have roots and branches; affairs end and begin again (*shih yu chung-shih*). To know the sequential succession of things is to be near the Tao" (*TH*:1). The key term here is "*chung-shih*," and our rendering of it departs from the usual gloss of "beginning and end." That is a possible meaning, but the term may also be used to denote unceasing continuity, as it frequently does in the *Yi-ching* commentaries (e.g., "Kuei-mei" [54], T'uan commentary: "The marriage of maidens is the perpetuating (*chung-shih*) of human beings." Cf. also "Ku" [18], T'uan: "To end and then again begin is the motion of T'ien") and Han texts, such as the *Ch'un-ch'iu fan-lu* (e.g., *Yin-yang chung-shih*, 12.1a). An instance of the same term in the *Chung-yung* suggests this latter meaning. The text reads, "It is ethical completion (*ch'eng*[a]) that leads things to end and then begin again (*wu chih chung-shih yeh*); without it there would be no things. Thus, the *chün-tzu* takes extending ethical completion as of greatest value. . . . Thus, he applies [his virtue] with timely appropriateness" (*CY*:25; reading *ch'eng-chih* as denoting an objectless transitive form of the stative verb *ch'eng*ᵃ). In the *Ta-hsueh* and *Chung-yung* passages, the universe is portrayed as a field in a perpetual state of change, where objects have no fixed individuating boundaries and events have no natural boundaries in time; it is a universe of situations unceasingly emerging into new configurations. The Sage is pictured as guiding the dynamic flux of events in this universe. Such a world is simply not subject to analytic study except as a rough heuristic device; it will not hold still. It is a universe of emergent situations rather than objects. Foundational knowledge of it cannot be gained though verbal analysis; to know such a universe is to master it through skills.

4. In the text, these phrases are part of an argument against phrenology. Their original context in a passage of little philosophical interest has led commentators to overlook their importance.

5. On the relation between practical totalism and the closed model of wisdom, see chapter III.

6. This difficult passage appears with variants in the *Shih-chi* (23.1170) and *Ta Tai li-chi* (*Li san pen*:2.11a). I have read "*t'o*" as "sparse," following Ssu-ma Chen. The reading of "*hsiao*ᵃ" as "confines" is drawn from the *Shuo-wen* gloss:"a wooden jail" (*SWCTKL*:6A.2611a).

7. *A*:2.16 can be interpreted in this sense as, "Attacking [matters] from different starting points is harmful" (see Tai Chen's commentary in Ch'eng 1965:92). *A*:10.6 may also reflect this sort of attitude when it enjoins us not to speak while eating or when lying down to sleep.

8. I have interpreted the phrase "*pi yu shih yen*" in light of the *Hsun Tzu's* description of complete integrity as "*wu t'a shih yen*": "There is no other matter there" (*H*:3.27).

9. The same idea is expressed, in the closing lines of *M*:6A.8: " 'Grasp it and it is saved, loose it and it is lost; if it comes and goes erratically, none will know where it resides': is this not a description of the mind?"

10. The idea of focus is expressed in *M*:2A.2 by the term "*yi*ᶜ." The passage in question is Mencius' response to a request that he explain two statements: "Wherever one's dispositions go, one's energy will follow," and "Keep hold of your dispositions; do not dissipate your energy." Mencius explains the two in turn: "When the dispositions are focused they move the energy" (hence dispositions lead energy); "When energy is focused it moves the dispositions" (thus one must maintain the control of energy by the dispositions, or the focus of the energy will move the mind ungoverned). Note that Riegel follows Chao Ch'i in taking "*yi*ᶜ" as a loan word meaning "blocked" (1979:442).

11. See also *H*:21.48-49: "When the mind is branched it has no comprehension; when it wavers it is not concentrated; when it is divided it is perplexed. . . . Hence the wise choose the One and focus upon it."

12. Note also *A*:5.9, 7.8.

13. For an analysis of this process of extending moral motivation, see Nivison 1979.

14. Descriptively, an extension of one's moral impulses, for Mencius, entails the same actions as following *jen* and *yi* (*M*:2A.6, 7A.15, 7B.31).

15. On the role of "type" (*lei*) in the *Mencius*, see Nivison 1979:424-25.

16. Note *A*:10.20-21, where Tzu-lu bows to a flock of birds because it exemplifies the principle of "timeliness."

17. The idea that the Sage, as a source of moral law, is able to "weigh" (*ch'üan*) all relevant contingencies before acting (much as the utilitarian's ideal ethical calculator might) may be prefigured in the *Analects* (9.30), and is a minor but significant idea in the *Mencius* (4B.18, 7A.26). The ability to weigh contingencies frees the Sage from reliance on rules, which can only approximate correct principles. The locus classicus for the doctrine of "weighing" is *Kung-yang chuan*, Huan 11:5.6.

18. See chapter III, note 21.

    The role of "responding to changes" (*ying pien*) is an important one in the *Hsun Tzu*. It is one-half of a dynamic dialectic that pictures the action of the Sage in society. The other part is the Sage's power to "transform" (*hua*) others. The dialectic of "respond-transform" (*pien-hua*) is a detailed model of the linkage of inner self-cultivation and outer worldly power of the Sage. The following passage pictures this linkage (I have reversed the order of the two sequential series to bring out the meaning as I interpret it):

    > If one practices right action with a mind of integrity, order will appear; order will bring comprehension; comprehending, one can respond. If one preserves *jen* with a mind of integrity it will become manifest; manifest, it will gain spirit-power (*shen*); with spirit-power one can transform. When response and transformation arise in turn, this is called the virtue of T'ien (*H*:3.27-28).

    Compare *M*:7A.13; *CY*:25.

19. Interestingly, portraits of exemplary figures in the Taoist text *Chuang Tzu* depict approaches and experiences very similar to those we are describing for Ruism here. The best-known example would be the tale of Cook Ting, the butcher whose dance-like carving technique is the central theme of the *Yang sheng chu* chapter (*CT*:3.2-12). The portrait of Ting's extraordinary skill, which he characterizes as "*tao*," is prefaced by an attack on the limits of fact knowledge very similar to that encountered in the *Hsun Tzu* (*H*:21.78-80, discussed in chapter VI,

"Educating the Sage"). Other instances where the *Chuang Tzu* links skill mastery to the *tao* appear in the *Ta-sheng* chapter, and include the tales of the swimmer (19.49-54) and the cicada-catching hunchback (19.17-21). A. C. Graham has noted this linkage in his discussion of the role of "responsive awareness" in the *Chuang Tzu*, a phrase that seems to echo the Ruist idea of response to change (1983:11). The variety of skill systems that the *Chuang Tzu* describes in this way suggests that the goal of grasping "the Tao" might have been attainable through a plurality of mastered skill systems, a notion that fits in well with Chad Hansen's idea that the *Chuang Tzu* essentially endorses a plurality of "*taos*" (1983a:46-51). This resonance between the *Chuang Tzu* and Ruist texts suggests that the two schools, customarily pictured as antagonists, might have been allied in endorsing synthetic rather than analytic methodology (this despite the fact that the *Chuang Tzu* is often relentlessly analytic). If this were so, the fundamental nature of their dispute would arise from the Ruist claim that history, ordained by T'ien, has evolved a single skill system exclusively legitimate for attaining the totalistic goal of Sagehood: *li*. As the *Hsun Tzu* states: "The world possesses only one *tao*; the Sage does not have two minds" (*H*:21.1). Admittedly, neither the historical authoritarianism of Ruism nor the radical relativism of the *Chuang Tzu* provides a fully satisfactory strategy for synthetic philosophy.

20. Csikszentmihalyi 1975:38-41.
21. Csikszentmihalyi 1975:67, 192.
22. Csikszentmihalyi and Bennett 1971:56.
23. Csikszentmihalyi 1975:44-45, 191.
24. Csikszentmihalyi 1975:87.
25. Csikszentmihalyi 1975:37, 44, 81, 86.
26. Csikszentmihalyi 1975:39, 44.
27. Note also that intellectual skills are not excluded (Csikszentmihalyi 1975:35). Mastering texts and doctrine could also have generated similar, if less ecstatic experiences. The *Ch'eng-hsiang* and *Fu* chapters of the *Hsun Tzu*, as interpreted in chapter VI, section 1, might be evidence of deep aesthetic pleasure associated with mastering elaborating doctrine.
28. In her survey of dance viewed through an anthropological perspective, Anya Royce analyzes dance meaning in terms of the various aspects through which dance communicates to an audience (1977:192-211). But it may be well to consider dimensions of meaning from the performer's perspective as well, and this seems to be what the *Hsun Tzu* has done in this passage. Susanne Langer makes a sharp distinction between the sense of the word "meaning" in the context of verbal speech and in the context of musical arts, preferring the term "import" in the latter case (1953:31-32).

29. I have not attempted to introduce into this study the broad literature on dance in its various aesthetic and ritual modes. For one cross-cultural study of the structures and rewards of dance, see Hanna 1979, particularly descriptions of its noninstrumental satisfactions (132).

Appendix A

1. Creel and Shima are by no means the only scholars to develop theories concerning the origins of the term "*t'ien.*" In my view, however, their theories represent the two most plausible current options. For a brief survey of general theories concerning the origins of the term, see Miura 1975:39.
2. A full analysis of the background of the term "*t'ien*" would require an investigation of the origins of the term most commonly employed to denote "high god" in Shang oracle texts: "*ti*" 帝. This involves greater detail than would be appropriate here. For such an analysis, see Eno 1984:47-66.
3. Tu Erh-wei has offered a polemical refutation of this theory (Tu 1959:1-6) but in my view fails to offer convincing arguments. His own theory that the original meaning of "*t'ien*" is "bright" is based on evidence at least as superficial as Creel's (30-32).
4. Ping-ti Ho, a critic of Creel, has pointed out Creel's reliance on an argument from silence (1975:329-30). Ho is correct in noting the weakness inherent in such an approach, but his own claims that T'ien was a Shang concept are based on arguments considerably weaker (see Keightley 1977:403-404). The plausibility of Creel's theory has been considerably increased by the recent discovery of the *Ho tsun* inscription, which demonstrates unquestionably for the first time that "*t'ien*" was used in the sense of a deity during the first years of the Chou (*WW* 1976:1.60-66; Fong 1980:198, 203-4). However, recently excavated oracle texts that appear to be products of the preconquest Chou polity seem to indicate close religious links between the Shang and Chou peoples, which would argue against the likelihood of distinct "tribal gods" (*WW* 1979:10.38-43).
5. See *S*:28b-29d. There are examples where "*ta*" apparently functions as a name, and these could conceivably be glossed instead "a big man" (e.g. *Chui-ho*:211; *S*:29a). The fact that "*ta*" does not seem to mean "big man" in the oracle texts is not, of course, conclusive proof that it never had that meaning. Such a meaning would probably be hard to isolate in most texts.
6. Creel argues that the meaning "great man" is evident in the words "*wang*" (king) and "*wei*" (rank), the graphs of which he believes to be derived from "*ta*" (大; 大; 大). If 大 and 大 were both derived from 大

by the addition of a horizontal line below, they would presumably be
identical, but they are not. In fact, Creel's interpretation of *"wang"* is
defective here (the explanation of the graph is still a matter of doubt);
the form is not graphemically related to *"ta."* *"Wei"* and *"ta"* do appear
to be related graphemically, but they are not related phonetically, and
I do not think you can argue very far on a purely graphemic relation.

7. See also Shima 1958:213-15.

8. The difficulty with the texts is that we must assume either that the
father was referred to by a cyclical sign name while alive, or called by
his title while dead. The latter is perhaps more likely. These two inscriptions might be related to a large group of other inscriptions bearing
on the ruling house of a state called Lu[a], which rebelled against the
Chou during the early years of that dynasty (see the *Ta-pao kuei*
inscription). If so, we should note that the *Lu Po Chung kuei* inscription refers to the caster's father as "King Li," indicating that this state
might have retained pretentions to independent sovereignty, and this
could bear upon the use of the honorific *"ta tzu"* during Shang times.

9. On *"ti"* as a Shang term denoting a collection of deities, see Eno
1984:58-9. On the nature of the *ti*-sacrifice, see *ibid.*, 60-65.

10. This is by no means easy to do. Certain criteria are obvious: divinations about sacrifices to be performed on a *ting*-day are probably to
ting-name ancestors; inscriptions where □ is used as a loan for 氐 can
be ruled out (but might provide semantic clues). Even so, I am able to
determine with confidence whether inscriptions apply *either* way in
less than one-third of the cases. And of these, few seem *necessarily* to
represent a nonancestral deity. See Shima 1958:178-80 on this problem.

11. The objects of the □ sacrifice include the kings from Wu-ting through
Wen-wu-ting, and the female ancestor Mu-kuei (*S*:286a, 534c-d, 535c-d,
536a-537c, 553b). The objects of the *ti*-sacrifice include the nature deities River, Mountain, and Wind, as well as the ancestral or cultural
gods Ch'i (?), Wang-hai, Shang-chia, and Hsia-yi (*S*:158d-159c). There
are, in addition, several figures whose status is unclear to me (see
Eno 1984:111n29).

12. For example, □ does not bestow or interfere with crops, bestow aid, or
influence the king's person, all functions associated with the term *"ti"*
in the oracle texts. Listing sacrifices offered to □ is difficult because of
the problems discussed in note 10, but a broad range of possibilities
appear (*S*:286-88), and if Shima is correct in taking □ as a nonancestral deity at all, assigning many of these sacrifices to it would surely
be necessary.

13. Despite the fact that we cannot confirm Shima's claim that □ denoted
a *ti*-sacrifice identical with that represented by the graph 禘 in the
Shang texts, it possibly could have denoted a related but distict type

of *ti*-sacrifice, denoted in Chou bronze inscriptions by the graph 禘 . On the distinction between these two species of *ti*-sacrifice (the former offered to high gods, the latter to the worshipper's father), see Eno 1984:60-64, 75-76.

14. *Pu-tz'u*:245; *Hsu-pien*:2.16.3; *Yi-ts'un*:570; (*S*:287b).

15. *Hsu-ts'un*:1.295 (*S*:17a) reads □ □ 卜 貞 囚 羌 三 百 于 且 □. Three hundred *ch'iang* are offered but we do not know to how many ancestors.

16. Shima believes that the 大 element was added to □ to distinguish the latter in the sense of "*t'ien*" from the sense of the cyclical sign *ting*, and also to symbolize the meaning "the top" (Shima 1958:215). It would also be reasonable to think of the 大 element as a semantic gloss of the "*chuan-chu*" type (using that term according to the theory developed in Lung 1972:107-43).

17. These inscriptions appear at *S*:356b, and they are not easy to understand. *Yi-ts'un*:153 reads: 貞 于 □ 希 年 婐 : "Divined: to □ [who] is harming the crops sacrifice a woman." But the grammar is awkward. Translating □ as "altar" here is more convenient (see arguments for this translation later in the text). The general meaning of these inscriptions is made clear by *Chui-ho*:347: 貞 希 雨 匄 于 河 : "Divined: the rain is harmed, pray to [at ?] the River."

18. Especially *Ch'ing-hua*:3; *Yi-ts'un*:675; *Ming*:387.

19. See Ch'en 1955-56:2.117. Note also the recently excavated *Kung-ch'en kuei* (*WW* 1976:5.28-29) and *Fu yü* (*KK* 1977:1.71-72), especially the latter.

20. See *CS*:14.4239-51; Shima 1958:175-77.

21. The meaning of "*tsung*" is not in doubt, but another sacrifice term appears parallel to "*tsung*" in texts of this format; it is 示 , for which the proper transcription is disputed (*CS*:2.269-75, suppl. 4431-32). Because it functions precisely as does "*tsung*," we will treat it as if it were an alternate shrine location, without effect on the general argument.

22. This form is relatively rare; I count six examples (*S*:536d, 537b-c). Several examples of the graph 示 in parallel position can be found at *S*:536c, 537b.

23. These examples are numerous (*S*:534-37).

24. See *S*:536d, 537b-c.

25. The same relation holds between □ and 示 . Note that 示 can substitute for "*tsung*" but never for □ .

26. The gloss is "*p'ing*" 平 used generally in the sense of "peace," especially in the *Tso-chuan*.

27. Several other members of this family carry a sense of "flat" or "even." *T'ieng/t'ing* 汀 is defined in the *Shuo-wen* as "even" (*SWCTKL*: 11A. 5060a); ?/ting 钉 is defined as "even argument" (3A.980a).

28. Reading 宀 as "*ping*" 稟 "to receive/to give," here in the sense of accepting the ritual formulas of King Wu. For other translations, see Fong 1980:198; Carson 1978-79:41.

29. Here reading *"yu chueh"* literally, with an extended sense of "render service [to the state]." See similar expressions in the *Lu Po Chung kuei* and *Mao Kung ting* inscriptions.

30. I am inclined to think that this actually might be a concrete description of the king pouring a libation over the altar. The word *"te"* is here written 㥁 . The inclusion of a "heart" element would be unusual at this date—the earliest such instance I know of (the element does not appear in oracle bones)—and I suggest that the element on the bottom right might be *"chiung"* ◌ (囧), indicating a possible connection with blood consecration (drawing on the meaning of the character *"meng"* 皿 [盟]). Note that the *Shuo-wen* lists 㐭 as an "old script" form of *"chih"* 良 , a cognate of *"te"*(*SWCTKL*: 12B.5714a).

31. See commentaries of T'ang Lan and Ma Ch'eng-yuan in *WW* 1976:1.60, 65.

32. T'ang and Ma read *"ku"* 谷 as *"yü"* 裕, which should be glossed "cover" (Karlgren 1948:284). If the imagery suggested in note 30 is allowed, the transcription *"yü"* 浴: "bathe" would be more appropriate.

33. See *GSR:*#361. Many struggles with the cognate *t'ən/t'un 吞: to swallow," have failed to force it to yield significance.

34. The word plays a major role in the *Chuang Tzu*, where it is sometimes conceived as a reality we return to after death (e.g., *Ta tsung shih*:6.64). It is a very common word in Taoist texts, but remarkably, it is entirely absent from early Ruist texts. Where Taoist texts tend to use the word in the sense of "real" or "true," and make a return to the "real" a goal of self-cultivation, Ruists tend to use the word *dı̆ĕng/ch'eng 誠 : "sincere." It is interesting that in a text such as the *Chuang Tzu*, which employs both words, a general "law of avoidance" appears between the two. Chapters employing one of them tend not to use the other. This correlation holds rather well throughout early texts and suggests that the two words might have been at root one. This is of particular interest to us because *"ch'eng"* belongs to the graphemic family of *ting* 丁, with which we associated T'ien in the last section. Note that the form of *"chen"* which appears in the *Chen Po yen* has an added *"ting"* element (*CWKL*:8.159).

35. The element 吞 would be a semanteme here if it were, in fact, pronounced as was *"shen,"* which would rule out a phonetic function. The *Shuo-wen* takes it as a semanteme.

36. See the comments of Chu Fang-p'u in *CWKL*:8.161-62. Chu lays out the loan relationship in detail. Note that Tuan Yü-ts'ai suggests a loan relationship between *t'ien* 殄: "to die," and *t'ien* 醄: "to get drunk" (*SWCTKL*:4B.1784b), which might suggest a handy way of reaching T'ien short of self-immolation.

37. Interestingly, the word *d'ieng/t'ing 廷 might belong to this family, its graph in Chou inscriptions being 㣙. The *t'ing* may have been a

temple court built around an altar. The *Ho tsun* phrase 廷 告 于 天 might be evidence of this.

38. References to this appear in four early texts: *MT, Chieh-tsang*:6.15a; *H, Ta-lueh*:27.63; *LSCC, Yi-shang*:14.11b; *Lieh Tzu,T'ang-wen*:1.100. Some archaeological evidence for this custom may have been found (Chang 1986:385).

39. The term is *"teng-ko"* 登 遐/假, mentioned in the *Mo Tzu* and *Lieh Tzu* texts cited in note 38.

40. Many graphs in the oracle texts seem to suggest such a rite by their graphemic form alone (*S*:176-77). The two most generally interpreted in this way are 莫 [莫] (*S*:38c) and 焚 [焚] (*S*:374a-b). Both graphs contain the "fire" element 火 [火]. Texts such as *Yi-pien*:3449 make the sense clear: 貞 今 丙 戌 焚 𡥀 㞢 其 雨: "Divined: on this *ping-shu* day *chiao*-sacrifice a *tsai*-woman, there will follow rain." Serruys translates both 莫 and 焚 as "burn at the stake" (Serruys 1974:47: see also Shima 1958: 207-8). For evidence that this custom was at least well known during the Chou, see *TC*, Hsi 21:6.18-19.

Appendix B

1. In this appendix, the Chinese term denoting the Ruist school, *"ju,"* will be transcribed in its usual Wade-Giles form. Our anglicized terms Ruism, Ruist, and Ru will be rendered consistent with the main text.

2. On the possible relationship between the words *"shu"* and *"ju,"* see Jao 1954:116; Chow 1979:18-19.

3. Among those adopting or modifying Chang's portrait of pre-Confucian Ru have been Hu Shih (1934:1-5), Jao Tsung-yi (1954:112-15), Hou Wai-lu (1957:36-39), Joseph Needham (1956:2.3), and Frederick Mote (1971:30-33).

4. The narratives of the *Tso-chuan* seem to me the primary basis for the impression that Ru existed prior to Confucius' time. The *Tso-chuan* is, for the most part, a history of pre-Confucian China, yet many of the speeches, judgments, and prophecies uttered by the characters in its narrative are permeated with Ruist (Confucian) political and ethical ideas. This tends to give the impression that Confucius was simply embellishing a traditional school of thought when he passed on his teachings and leads to the assumption that the Ru school antedates Confucius. However, it is far more likely that the Ruist content of the *Tso-chuan* narrative reflects the interests of the authors rather than the ideas of the historical actors of the narrative. The overall outlook of the text is clearly Ruist, as we can see from its great concern with *li*, its ethical vocabulary, and the fact that commentary attributed to Confucius is occasionally interjected. The text was certainly authored by

Ruists, most likely beginning sometime early in the fourth century B.C. (on the date, see Karlgren 1926; Hsu 1965:184-85; Matsumoto 1966:326-32; Wheatley 1971:154). These Ruists apparently elaborated basic historical annals—the *Spring and Autumn Annals* of Lu among them—and created a *prescriptive* text of great philosophical and literary value, which projected their own ideas into the speech of historical figures. Confusing the later Ruist outlook with the early historical setting is erroneous (Tsuda 1935:307-84; Creel 1970:475-77).

5. We might add that there seem to be no instances of possible loan substitutions for the word "*ju*" that could alter this picture.

6. There are, indeed, texts that suggest that there was an established group of Ru, prior to Confucius' time, but these texts cannot be dated with certainty prior to the Han period. Chief among them is the *Chou li*, a text of uncertain origins that came to light late in the first century B.C. and was edited by the court bibliographer Liu Hsin (see Jao 1954:114-15). The *Chou li*, which represents itself as an administrative plan of government devised by the Duke of Chou in the eleventh century B.C., refers to Ru as teachers who guide the people through propagation of the proper *tao*, usually interpreted as referring to the "six arts" of ritual, music, archery, charioteering, writing, and figures (Jao 1954:114). While the date of the *Chou-li* remains uncertain, only the most optimistic interpreters would suggest that it could predate the mid-Warring States period (*WSTK*:316-27; Creel 1970:478-80), a time when the function of *Confucian* Ru as tutors would already be well-established. The detail and systematic nature of the text makes it far more likely that it was the product of the early Han, the period in which Confucians would find it most necessary to develop detailed administrative blueprints suitable for the style of centralized government first imposed during the Ch'in. (Judging by a rough count of the first of the book's six sections, which lists more than 3,500 members in that portion of the royal bureacracy, the text was prepared with a rather sizable administrative unit in mind.) Although the authors of the text might have been well versed in available knowledge about early Chou society, the text is best viewed as a late idealization, reflecting contemporary Ruist values rather than pre-Confucian fact.

7. The interpretation of "*ju*" as meaning "weak" is supported by the meanings of cognate words: "*ju*"孺: "small child"; "*ju*"媷: "weak; a lesser wife;" "*no*"儒: "timid." Jao Tsung-yi, in an argument heavily reliant on the notion that the term "*jou*" must be consistent with exalted Ruist values, departed from the mainstream in glossing "*jou*" by the verbal sense of "to comfort" (1954:111-14).

8. The most sustained refutation of Hu's central thesis was developed by Ch'ien Mu (1954).

9. Liu's central theory involves a particularly fanciful interpretation of
   A:6.13 (see Shirakawa 1972:70).
10. One alternate method that has been attempted with limited success is
    simple graphemic character analysis. Chang Ping-lin, who believed
    that the early Ru were meteorologists (on the basis, most directly, of
    CT: 21.40), made much of the "rain" (雨) element of the graph. He
    believed that the Ru wore kingfisher-feather caps and were thus thought
    to be endowed with that bird's supposed power to forecast rain (a
    phonetic linkage can be made between "kingfisher" [*yü* 鷸] and "skill"
    [*shu* 術] [*SWCTKL*:2B.742a], and Chang also relied on this). A differ-
    ent interpretation of the rain element of the graph has been proposed
    by Shirakawa. He explains "*hsu*" 需 as a picture of a shaved shaman
    performing a rain dance, and he connects his interpretation with his
    theory that Confucius was the son of a sorceress (1972:71-74).
11. The word "*chu-ju*" could denote either dwarf dancers (e.g., *LC*:11.18b;
    SC:47.1915) or simply dwarfs (e.g., *LC*:4.17b; *KY*:10.24a-25a). (These lat-
    ter examples undercut a theory proposed by Ch'en Ch'i-yu that held
    that "*chu-ju*" did not denote a dwarf but a "master of alien music" of
    any stature [*HFTCS*:155n7].) "*Chu-ju*" was often used as a pejorative
    term (*TC*, Hsiang 4:14.28). Marcel Granet had an interesting but highly
    speculative theory about these dancers. He held that they were ritual
    representatives of their lord, and, upon their lord's death, were interred
    with him (1926:179-80, 213-25).
12. I am grateful to A. C. Graham for alerting me to this. "*Ju*" could, of
    course, have been borrowed in the sense of the entire binome and
    applied as a satirical name for Ruists even though it originally made
    no semantic contribution, but a proof of so unlikely a possibility would
    be too burdensome to consider.
13. *Kuang yun*:1.34: "'Nou' 獳 : A 'chu-nou' 朱獳; the name of a beast.
    Like a fox but with wings like fish fins. When it appears, there is fear in
    the state."
14. E.g., *kịu-glịu/chü-lou 痀 瘻[CT*:19.17]. Note, too, that both the binome
    *t'ịu-glịu/ch'u-lü 軀 膢 and its second element seem to have shared
    a gloss as the name of a sacrifice [*Daikanwa*:9.365b], suggesting both
    that the phonetic elements 區 婁 could be widely used to create bi-
    nomes and also that the element 婁 might have retained a semantic
    role throughout.
15. The association of hunchbacks and Ru has an interesting echo in the
    legend that the Duke of Chou, "patron saint" of Ruists, was deformed,
    with a twisted foot or back (*SWCTKL*:8A.3608b; see also *H*:5.5).
16. Evidence for this linkage can be found in the *Poetry* (220/3-4), where
    drunken guests are described as "*lü wu*" 屢 舞, glossed by the "Mao
    Commentary" as "repeatedly dancing," but cogently rendered "crook-

edly dancing," drawing on the attested loans of "*lou*" 婁 or "*lou*" 僂, which, as we saw above, appear to have been cognate with "*ju*" (for evidence of such loans, see *KYYS*:66.11a). A less pejorative use of the phrase "*lü wu*" appears in a work by the poet Tso Ssu of the third century A.D.: "With flowing sleeves, all arched they dance (*lü wu*), winglike as if flying" (*WH, Shu-tu fu*:61).

17. Among the vessels that employ such a loan are: *Ta k'o ting* (*Ta-hsi*: 3.121), *Wei ting* [II] (*WW* 1976:5.28); *Chin Kung chung* (*Ta-hsi*:3.250). Many other vessels attest to the interchabgeability of "*jou*" and "*nao*" as phonetic elements.
18. Some commentators regard the character for "mother" as an error (see *SWCTKL*:2326b, 2327b, for the comments of Tuan Yü-ts'ai and Ch'en Li).
19. The *Chi-yun* offers the following alternative graphs for "*nao*": 獿, 獶, 猱, and 蝚. (The phonetic group *ńî̯og/jao should be distinguished from the group *·î̯ôg/yu 憂, see Ikeda 1955:72-73. Karlgren likewise distinguishes the two groups in *GSR*.)
20. Ikeda's argument is that "*yu*," in the sense of "dancer," employs a simplified form of an original graph 優, which places it properly in the *ńî̯og/jao 擾 phonetic group.
21. The graph "*nao*" 獶 is a loan for "*nao*" 獿. The graph for "*ju*" in this instance is 儔; the *Shih-chi* version of the passage gives the usual graph (*Yueh-shu*:1222).
22. The facticity of the *Shih-chi* account is not, of course, at issue here. Other versions appear in the *Kung-yang* and *Ku-liang* commentaries.
23. Compare "*jou*" 柔 in *Poetry*:253/1 and "*jou*" 揉 in 259/8. For "*jou*" as "to become tame," see *KYC*, Chao 25 (24.5a). The word "*jao*" sometimes takes the form 獿, which makes its root meaning clear (*SWCTKL*:4390b).
24. Much of this analysis was stimulated by Ikeda's article (1955). Ikeda, as with many other superior Japanese sinologists, approaches ancient Chinese texts in a spirit resonant of classical anthropology. Like many French sinologists, these interpreters seek out the irrational elements that lay at the basis of coherent functional systems—the bricolage of ancient thought, to use Levi-Strauss's term. This is not the approach that American sinologists tend to take, and I confess to feeling rather uncomfortable with a theory that draws so heavily on such material. Our Ruist subjects appear to be less squeamish about their connections with murky traditions of religious belief.
25. It is not that such loan links are entirely absent, but those which I have found so far are extremely obscure and generally tenuous. They add no strength to the theory as now formulated.
26. A more elaborate version appears in the *Kao-yao mo* (2.12). In the commentary to the *Kuo-yü* by the third century A.D. scholar Wei Chao,

it is recorded that the "*k'uei*" is a beast with an ape's body and a human head (*KY*, Lu-yü II:5.8b-9a).

Appendix C

1. At the outset, we should note an important distinction in usage bearing heavily on our translation. The usage in question centers on the linkage of the words "*t'ien*" and "*ti*ᵃ": "earth," in the *Hsun Tzu*.

    "*T'ien*" is sometimes used alone to denote the processes of the material world holistically conceived, much as we use "Nature." For example, in the phrase, "T'ien can give birth to things; it cannot make distinctions among things" (*H*:19.78), "*T'ien*" would be well translated as "Nature," rhetorically personifying the magnificent but nonpurposive order of the physical world. Similarly, when the text characterizes man's innate qualities as "the repository of T'ien (*t'ien chih chiu*)" (*H*:22.63; 23.11), it clearly means to denote by T'ien a notion of non-normative creativity. In the "Treatise," this is a common usage, and "Nature" is frequently an apt translation. In our rendering of the text, however, we will leave the word untranslated when used in this sense.

    Nature is also denoted in the text by the composite word "*t'ien-ti*": "heaven and earth." For example, the phrase: "Heaven and earth give birth to the *chün-tzu*, and the *chün-tzu* orders heaven and earth" (*H*:9.65) employs this term. I interpret this term to be functionally equivalent to T'ien in the sense of Nature. It is frequently used to express points of great philosophical significance, as in the passage just cited (cf. also *H*:3.31, 10.39, 19.26). It is sometimes used more vaguely to denote the "universe" as a whole (*H*:12.28, 21.42). The term is somewhat difficult to translate because, as Nature, "*t'ien-ti*" represents a unified notion, but it is rhetorically divided into two elements, which are separately counted. Thus, a phrase critical to the *Hsun Tzu*'s metaphysics, "man forms a trinity with *t'ien* and *ti*ᵃ," uses a triadic image but can be analyzed as meaning simply, "man becomes the complement of Nature (or T'ien)." With this fact duly noted, we will render the term as "heaven and earth," relying on the reader to recall the essential unity of the elements of the term.

    Finally, "*t'ien*" is also used to denote the sky, generally in tandem with "*ti*ᵃ," denoting the earth. When used in this way, "*t'ien*" and "*ti*ᵃ" cannot be linked to mean Nature or the universe; they are parts of Nature, and are usually cited for illustrative purposes, as in: "The sky is the acme of height, the earth the acme of depth ... the Sage the acme of the *tao*" (*H*:19.36). "*T'ien*" is generally used in this way without particular philosophical significance, and we will reflect this by

294 The Confucian Creation of Heaven

translating it whenever possible simply as "sky." In some cases, however, English usage dictates a translation of "the heavens."

2. As with most of the chapters in the *Hsun Tzu*, the "Treatise on T'ien" appears to be an agglutination of a series of semi-independent short essays, some closely related to one another, others less so. Some sections also might be early commentary inserts (see notes 10 and 29, below). For the purposes of convenient reference, and also to demarcate what I see as possible divisions among component essays, I have labeled these component sections by letter: A, B, C, and so forth.

    I do not mean to imply that the sections of the "Treatise" all had different authors, although some might have.

3. Bracketed numbers refer to line designations in the *HTYT* text.

4. "Root" is a conventional term referring to agriculture.

5. Compare *H*:2.44, 8.89. Note that much of section A may be read with equal cogency as prescripts directed toward a political ruler or toward ordinary individuals in pursuit of Sagehood. Its main thrust, however, seems to be political, in light of its description of the consequences of action that does not accord with the Way, a description that speaks of social chaos.

6. Taking *han* as *ni*, following Yü Yueh (*HTCC*:11.22).

7. Following Watson; contra Dubs, Chan, de Bary.

8. These phrases may be compared to similar language in *M*:5A.6, and *TTC*:47.

9. The "office of T'ien" traditionally has been interpreted as the process of natural creation and action (see Yang Liang's commentary in *HTCC*: 11.23). The phrases beginning with, "Though it be profound . . ." have been seen as proscribing human inquiry into and exploitation of natural processes. While commentators have taken these phrases as interdicting futile attempts to "interfere" with Nature, they may be read in another way. The implied injunction not to contest with T'ien is surely prescriptive, but if taken to suggest a "hands-off" policy vis-à-vis Nature, it is in direct conflict with the "Treatise's" later injunctions to "husband things" (*H*:17.44) and "order things" (*H*:17.45) in Nature for the benefit of man. Furthermore, if the traditional interpretation is adopted, the phrases which follow, beginning with, "The heavens have their seasons . . ." are non sequiturs.

    The connection between this passage and the ones preceeding will appear more logical if we reinterpret the "office of T'ien"—that which is accomplished without action, obtained without pursuit—as a general reference to the givens of the natural world, with particular reference to man's innate abilities: those talents, that through effort, man can transform into ethical tools. The powers of thought, the natural abilities of the body, the powers of perception are all "T'ien-like" aspects of man (see chapter VI, "T'ien as Prescriptive Psychology") that are available to him without his action or pursuit. They are not inherently ethical qualities, but they are the basic potentials by means of which man becomes ethical. The proscription that the text urges is against trying to interfere with, and so pervert, these natural potentials, either by the imposition of artificial cognitive frameworks, such as spiritualism or sophistic logic, or by unnatural body regimens, such as might have characterized some early naturalist schools. (For evidence of such cults in the early Han, see Needham 1956:143-52. My suggestion that the *Hsun Tzu* might have been responding to the existence of such cults in the late Chou is speculative.) In this, the text approaches a Mencian valuation of human nature, but remains consistent with its stated position that the nature is not intrinsically ethical.

This interpretation more aptly fits the overall theme of section B, which describes self-cultivation in a way that bridges the ethical gap between nonpurposive Nature and self-ritualization. The "office of T'ien" introduces a normative dimension of man's relationship to Nature and suggests that to tamper with man's natural powers by trying to distort their limits would be to destroy man's potential for achieving a clearly ethical goal: forming a "trinity" with heaven and earth.

10. This entire paragraph makes best sense if viewed as an early commentary insertion. It seems to reformulate the prescript not to contest office with T'ien to mean that one should not seek for a metaphysical truth behind Nature, although one does exist.

It is a very appealing passage but for all its rhetorical attractiveness, the passage does not make a great deal of sense in the context of the rest of section B. For example, the word "spirit" (*shen*) at H:17.9 denotes a transcendental force close in meaning to "*t'ien*." But a few phrases later (H:17.10) it denotes activities of human consciousness. Then again the implied injunction that one should not seek to know T'ien is contradicted later in section B, where the Sage's perfection is described as "knowing T'ien" (see Matsuda 1975:69). Finally, we can note that, if deleted, the surrounding passages connect with far greater elegance than they do otherwise. (It is true that the passage would become better integrated into the text if the word "*kung*[a]" were supplied after "that is called T'ien." This solution was first suggested by Yang Liang and has been endorsed by many other commentators [*HTCC*:11.24]. The problem is that while this does help the passage fit better in the flow of the text, the resulting text does not make much sense and the final line of the paragraph becomes a non sequitur.)

These are not fatal problems; the passage is appealing and does link loosely with the surrounding text. Perhaps we are simply encountering a lapse in rhetorical consistency. I prefer to read the passage as an insertion, in part because it otherwise weights the sense of section B against my interpretation of the "office of T'ien" (see note 9 above). However, sufficient evidence does not exist to justify separating it from the rest of the text. Nevertheless, in light of its inconsistencies, no analysis of the overall import of section B should rely heavily on this passage (a problem with Matsuda 1975, which hinges its interpretation of section B on this passage).

11. This passage closes the discussion of the office of T'ien–which is to provide what is spontaneously available to man–and initiates a portrait of human psychology as an assemblage of "T'ien-like" elements. It mentions, as a mediate term, the "work of T'ien." If the preceding lines (*H*:17.8-10) are not taken as an interpolation, the work of T'ien would seem to mean the creation of the physical world. If we interpret it only in terms of its subsequent occurances at *H*:17.14-15 it might refer either to this general creation or to the more particular notion of human beings as the culminating objects of creation.

12. Taking *wei*ᵃ [lit.: "call"] in the sense of "judge." See the discussion in chapter VI. section 4.2.

13. Taking "*ch'i*ᵃ" as superfluous, following Ikai Keisho (*HTCC*: 11.25).

14. The meaning of "*ch'i sheng pu shang*" is not completely clear. The phrase might be a response to Yangist prescripts to "preserve the body" or "nature." Note that there was a Ruist tradition that to live prudently, avoid danger, and so preserve one's body intact was an act of filiality. It should also be borne in mind that "*sheng*ᵃ" was frequently used as a loan for "*hsing*": innate talents (see Fu 1940). Reading this instance as a loan usage would be perfectly consistent with the sense of section B, where the innate is given normative content.

15. Compare *TTC*:45.

16. "Appropriate" is a play on the sense of "*yi*ᵈ" (that which is appropriate). The things of the earth have meaning only in their relation to man's purposes (cf. *H*:10.1). The use of "*yi*ᵈ" in the sense of natural riches adaptable for the use of man is also found in the *Yi ching* (T'ai hexagram, *Ta hsiang* commentary).

17. The meaning here is vague. The phrases might well have been included merely to complete elements of a systematic cosmological description.

18. This section seems to be an attack on cosmological naturalism, such as the philosophy of Tsou Yen. The clear distinction of the "Ways" of T'ien and of man appears outside the "Treatise," most notably at *H*:8.24.

19. The quote is from the "Chou sung" section of the *Poetry*, the poem "T'ien tso." These lines are cited here to reinforce the notion that people create the world through effort; the work of T'ien merely creates the conditions that allow effort to succeed.

Section D expands upon the proposition set forth early in the "Treatise" that political order depends upon the function of human government and is not determined by nonpurposive T'ien. Its dominant images are agricultural and calendrical, and the section should be viewed as a recapitulation of the earlier characterization of bad rule: "Though the seasons revolve as they do in ordered times, disaster and devastation arise unlike in ordered times" (*H*:17.5).

20. "*Ch'ang t'i*" refers to ethical dispositions, not demeanor, as Dubs and Watson have it, although were "demeanor" understood as denoting the normative aspects of ritual form, the word would be appropriate.

21. Cf. *H*:4.42.

22. These lines are from a poem now lost. The same poem is cited elsewhere in the text, at *H*:22.48. The phrase supplied here, "*li yi chih pu ch'ien*," occurs at that location, as well as in a *Wen hsuan* version. Yü Yueh put forward arguments for inserting the "missing" phrase here (see *CTPY*:155), and his emendation is now universally accepted.

23. Rejecting Yü's gloss of "*chieh*" as "what is suitable" (*HTCC*:11.28). See the discussion in chapter VI, section 4.4.

24. Similar phrasing appears at *H*:2.8, 4.25, 18.105.

25. Cf. *H*:12.37-38.

26. The language here is difficult, although the main sense is clear. The *Han-shih wai-chuan* has a variant text, which reads: "Among disasters in the world of things, those most to be feared are human portents" (2.4b). The word "*yao*" carries the sense both of a prodigy (freakish event) and a portent of things to come.

27. "*Shuo*" is probably cognate with "*t'o*[a]" (to remove), hence: "the means of extrication are nearby."

28. Here I follow a suggestion made by Ikai (*HTCC*:11.32), who refers to a tradition in Han historical exegesis, associated with the *Kung-yang* and *Ku-liang* commentaries to the *Ch'un-ch'iu*. The tradition holds that the Sage historian records but does not explain prodigies. Ikai suggests that the conjunction "*erh*" should follow "*shu*[a]" which is taken as a verb.

29. This passage may very well be a commentary insert. It seems to recapitulate the language of the preceding sections in a rather confused way, and to introduce some rather irrelevant notions from other Ruist sources (e.g., the oblique reference to the *Poetry* passage discussed in *A*:1.15). Making the passage read with consistency of meaning is difficult.

30. Cf. *H*:16.4.

31. The two sentences seem to have a political referent, perhaps ruling houses that usurped Chou ritual songs for their own clan ceremonies. The "hymns" (*sung*), which are found in the *Poetry*, were originally songs performed at times of royal sacrifices, and they do, indeed, contain many references to T'ien, all straightforwardly encomiastic.

32. This is the last mention of T'ien in the "Treatise." Given this sudden shift of focus away from T'ien, the remainder of the chapter most likely was appended after the "Treatise" had been substantially completed.
33. The discussion of the "linking thread" (*kuan*) here seems to refer back to passages of the *Analects*. See the discussion in chapter III.
34. This entire passage seems to be closely related to the *Chieh-pi* chapter.
35. The passage appears in the extant *Hung fan* chapter of the *Documents*.

Glossary

chang 章

ch'ang 常

Ch'ang Hung 萇弘

ch'ang t'i 常體

Ch'ang Ts'ung ho 長伯盃

Chao 趙

Chao Ch'i 趙岐

Chao Liang 趙良

che 轍

ch'e 徹

chen 真

Ch'en Chi-t'ing 陳幾亭

Ch'en Hsiao 陳囂

Chen Po yen 真伯顓

Ch'en She 陳涉

Cheng 鄭

cheng 正

ch'eng 成

ch'eng[a] 誠

cheng chih 徵知

ch'eng chih 誠之

Ch'eng hsiang 成相

Cheng Hsuan 鄭玄

Cheng-po Ch'iao 正伯僑

299

Chi 季

chi 集

chi^a 嚌

Ch'i 齊

ch'i 氣

ch'i^a 其

ch'i^b 齋

ch'i^c 綦

ch'i ch'ing 七 情

Chi-hsia 稷 下

Ch'i lueh 七 略

ch'i sheng pu shang 其 生 不 傷

Chi Yu 季 由

Chi yun 集 韻

chiang 將

Chieh 桀

chieh 節

ch'ien 趨

ch'ien^a 遣

ch'ien ling 趨 令

chih 知

chih^a 智

chih^b 質

chih^c 直

chih^d 止

chih^e 志

chih^f 致

chih^g 制

chih-che 知 者

chih-chiang 陟 降

chih pien 治 辯

chih-shih 指 事

chih-wen niao chang 織 文 鳥 章

chin 畫

Ch'in 秦

chin ku 畫 故

Ch'in Ku-li 禽 滑 釐

Ch'in Kung chung 秦 公 鐘

Ch'in Kung kuei 秦 公 段

ching 徼

Ch'ing 卿

ch'ing 情

ch'ing[a] 清

ch'ing[b] 卿

ch'iu 求

Chou 周

Chou[a] 紂

Chu 邾

chu 祝

Ch'u 楚

ch'u 處

chü 矩

ch'ü 曲

Chu Hsi 朱 熹

Chü Hsin 劇 辛

Chu-shu chi-nien 竹 書 紀 年

ch'üan 權

chuan-chu 轉 注

Chuang Chou 莊周

chün 君

ch'ün 羣

ch'un-ch'iu 春秋

Ch'un-shen 春申

chün-tzu 君子

chung 忠

chung[a] 中

chung[b] 衷

ch'ung 充

Chung-kung 仲弓

Chung-shan 中山

Chung-shan fang-hu 中山方壺

Ch'ung Shang 充尚

chung-shih 終始

chung-shu 忠恕

erh 而

fa 法

fa[a] 發

fang-shih 方士

fei 非

fen 分

feng 豐

feng[a] 風

Fu 馥

fu 夫

fu[a] 拂

Fu kuei 馥毁

Fu Shu ting 馥叔鼎

Fu Ting tou 父 丁 豆

Fu yü 逋 盂

han 罕

Han Yü 韓 愈

hao-jan chih ch'i 浩 然 之 氣

Ho tsun 疴 尊

ho wen 合 文

hou wang 後 王

hsi 襲

Hsia 夏

hsiang 相

hsiang-hsing 象 形

hsiang-sheng 相 聲

Hsiang Yü 項 羽

hsiao 孝

hsiao[a] 校

Hsiao-ch'eng 孝 成

hsiao-ko 小 歌

hsien-che 賢 者

Hsien-men Kao 羨 門 高

hsin 信

hsin[a] 心

hsing 性

hsing[a] 省

hsing[b] 興

hsing[c] 行

Hsing chung 瘷 鐘

hsing-ming 性 命

Hsu 郤

Hsu-chou 徐州

Hsu Hsing 許行

Hsu Shen 許慎

Hsu Wang Yi-ch'u chuan 郐王義楚鎬

hsueh 學

Hsun Ch'ing Tzu 荀卿子

Hsun K'uang 荀況

Hsun Tzu 荀子

Hsun Yü 獂蠒

Hu 胡

Hu Yuan-yi 胡元儀

hua 化

Huai-pei 淮北

Huan T'ui 桓魋

huang 皇

Huang Hsieh 黃歇

Huang K'an 皇侃

Itō Jinsai 伊藤仁齋

Jan Ch'iu 冉求

jen 仁

jen[a] 人

jen-jen 仁人

jen-yi 仁義

Ju 儒

ju 儒

ju[a] 如

ju[b] 女

ju-che 儒者

ju-shu 儒書

Kan Lung 甘龍

Kao Tzu 告子

Ko 葛

k'o 克

Kou-chien 句踐

ku 故

ku[a] 固

ku-che 故者

Ku-lun 古論

kuai 怪

kuan 貫

K'uang yu 匡卣

kuei 歸

kuei-shih 倪詩

K'un-yi 昆夷

kung 恭

kung[a] 功

Kung-ch'en kuei 公臣餒

Kung Meng Tzu 公孟子

Kung-ming yi 公明儀

Kung-sun Ch'ou 公孫丑

K'ung Tzu chia-yü 孔子家語

Lan-ling 蘭陵

lei 類

li 禮

li[a] 理

li[b] 利

li[c] 立

li[d] 里

li^e 體

Li Ao 李翱

li-fa 禮法

Li K'o 李克

li-shu 曆數

Li Ssu 李斯

li-yi 禮義

li-yi chih pu ch'ien 禮義之不愆

Liang 梁

Liang Ch'i-ch'ao 梁啓超

Lin-wu 臨武

ling 令

liu erh 六貳

Liu Hsia-hui 柳下惠

Liu Hsiang 劉向

Liu Hsin 劉歆

Liu Pang 劉邦

liu-shih ju shun 六十如順

Liu Shih-p'ei 劉師培

Liu T'ai-kung 劉台拱

lou 陋

Lu 魯

Lu^a 象

lu 祿

Lu Chung-lien 魯仲連

Lu Po Chung kuei 象伯戚殷

Lu Wen-chao 盧文弨

Lun-yü 論語

Lun-yü yü-shuo 論語餘說

lung 隆

mang 芒

Mao Kung ting 毛公鼎

mei 惷

Meng Hsi Tzu 孟僖子

Meng Tzu 孟子

Meng Wu-po 孟武伯

mi 冪

min 敃

ming 命

nei 內

nei[a] 餒

nei tzu hsing 內自省

ni 逆

nien 年

ning 佞

ning[a] 凝

Niu Hsu 牛畜

o 惡

Pan kuei 班段

Pao yu 保卣

pi yu shih yen 必有事焉

Pieh lu 別錄

pien 辡

pien[a] 辯

pien-hua 變化

pien ku 變故

pien wu 辯物

pien yi 辯異

p'in 瀕

p'ing-chün 平均

Po Yi 伯夷

pu 不

San-nien Hsing hu 三年興壺

Shang 商

shang 賣

she 涉

shen 神

Shen Ku-li 慎滑釐

shen-ming 神明

Shen Tao 慎到

sheng 聖

*sheng*ᵃ 生

sheng-jen 聖人

shih 時

*shih*ᵃ 史

*shih*ᵇ 事

*shih*ᶜ 詩

*shih*ᵈ 師

*shih*ᵉ 賈

Shih Chü fang-yi 師遽方彝

Shih Hsun kuei 師詢段

Shih Hung kuei 師訇段

Shih Li kuei 師釐段

Shih P'ou kuei 師訇段

Shih Yü chung 師兌鐘

shih yu chung-shih 事有終始

shu 恕

shu[a] 書

shu yun 書云

Shun 舜

shuo 說

sou 叟

ssu 私

ssu[a] 祀

Ssu-ma Chen 司馬貞

Ssu-ma Ch'ien 司馬遷

ssu tuan 四端

Su Ch'in 蘇秦

su-p'u 素樸

Sui 睢

Sun Ch'ing hsin-shu hsu-lu 孫卿新書序錄

Sun Ch'ing Tzu 孫卿子

Sun K'uang 孫況

Sung 宋

sung 頌

Sung Chien 宋鈃

Sung Wu-chi 宋毋忌

ta 達

Ta feng kuei 大豐設

ta-jen 大人

Ta K'o ting 大克鼎

Ta-pao kuei 大保設

Ta Yü ting 大盂鼎

Tai Chen 戴震

T'ai-tsai 太宰

t'ai-yi 太一

Tan 丹

T'ang 湯

tao 道

te 德

te chih 得 之

T'eng 滕

Ti 帝

ti 帝

*ti*ª 地

*ti*ᵇ 敵

t'i 體

T'ien 天

t'ien 天

T'ien Ch'ang 田 常

T'ien Chien 田 建

t'ien chih chiu 天 之 就

t'ien-fu 天 府

t'ien-hsia 天 下

t'ien-lu 天 祿

T'ien-lun 天 論

t'ien-ming 天 命

T'ien P'ien 田 駢

t'ien-shu 天 數

t'ien-ti 天 地

t'ien-tzu 天 子

T'ien Tzu-fang 田 子 方

ting 定

t'o 梲

*t'o*ª 脫

To-ya Sheng yi 多亞耴彝

tsa 雜

tsa[a] 襍

tsai 災

ts'ai 材

ts'ai[a] 財

ts'ai[b] 才

ts'ai[c] 裁

ts'ai-p'u 材樸

Tsai Wo 宰我

ts'ai wu 財物

Ts'ai Yuan-p'ei 蔡元培

ts'ao 操

Tseng Po X fu 曾伯黍簠

Tseng Shen 曾參

Tseng Tien 曾點

Tseng Tzu 曾子

Tso Ssu 左思

Tsou 鄒

Tsou Yen 騶衍
　　(var. 鄒衍)

Ts'ui Shu 崔述

Tsukada Ōmine 冢田大峯

tsung 縱

tu 斁

Tu Chih 杜摯

Tuan Yü-ts'ai 段玉裁

t'ui 推

t'ung 統

*t'ung*ᵃ 同

*t'ung*ᵇ 通

Tung Chung-shu 董 仲 舒

t'ung lei 統 類

tzu 字

Tzu-ch'an 子 產

Tzu-chang 子 張

Tzu-hsia 子 夏

Tzu-hua 子 華

Tzu-kao 子 高

Tzu-kung 子 貢

Tzu-lu 子 路

Tzu-shen 子 慎

Tzu-shun 子 順

Tzu-ssu 子 思

Tzu-yu 子 游

Wan Chang 萬 章

wan-wu yi 萬 物 役

wang 亡

wang ch'ing (= hsiang) li 王 卿 (饗) 醴

Wang Chung 汪 中

Wang Ch'ung 王 充

wang erh shun 枉 而 順

Wang Hsien-ch'ien 王 先 謙

Wang Nien-sun 王 念 孫

Wang Pi 王 弼

Wang-sun Chia 王 孫 賈

Wang Ying-lin 王 應 麟

Wei 衛

Wei[a] 魏

wei 偽

wei[a] 謂

Wei Chao 韋昭

Wei ting 衛鼎

wen 文

wen[a] 彣 交 斐 玟 文 玟 玟

wen[b] 蓕

wen-chang 文章

wen-hua 文化

wen-li 文理

wen-te 文德

Wu 吳

wu 武

wu[a] 巫

wu[b] 舞

Wu Ch'i 吳起

wu chih chung-shih yeh 物之終始也

wu chih li 物之理

wu hsing 五行

wu t'a shih yen 無它事焉

wu tao 無道

wu te 五德

wu-wei 無為

yang 養

Yang Chu 楊朱

Yang Hu 陽虎

Yang Huo 陽貨

Yang Liang 楊倞

Yao 堯

yao 祅

Yen 燕

Yen Jo-ch'ü 閻 若 璩

Yen Yuan 顏 淵

yi 義

yi[a] 儀

yi[b] 一

yi[c] 壹

yi[d] 宜

yi[e] 疑

yi[f] 戲

yi[g] 舞

yi[h] 異

Yi-li 儀 禮

yi tsai nei 義 在 内

Yi-wen chih 藝 文 志

yi wu 役 物

Yi Yin 伊 尹

yi yü wu 役 於 物

Yin Wen 尹 文

ying pien 應 變

Yü 禹

yü 欲

yü[a] 于

yü[b] 雩

Yü Ch'ing 虞 卿

Yü-shih ch'un-ch'iu 虞 氏 春 秋

yu-shui chih shih 游 說 之 士

Yü ting 禹 鼎

Yuan Hsien 原 憲

Yuan Ssu 原 思

Yueh 越

yueh 樂

Yueh-cheng Tzu 樂 正 子

Yueh-cheng Tzu-ch'un 樂 正 子 春

Yueh Yi 樂 毅

yung 勇

Abbreviations

A	*Analects.*
Ch'ing-hua	Lo Chen-yü. *Yin-hsu shu-ch'i ch'ing-hua.*
Chui-ho	Kuo Jo-yü, et al. *Yin-hsu wen-tzu chui-ho.*
CKLSTTC	*Chung-kuo li-shih ti-t'u chi.*
CKT	*Chan-kuo ts'e.*
CL	*Chou-li.*
CS	Li Hsiao-ting. *Chia-ku wen-tzu chi-shih.*
CSTS	Chang Ping-lin. *Chang-shih ts'ung-shu.*
CT	*Chuang Tzu.*
CTPY	Yü Yueh. *Chu-tzu p'ing-yi.*
CWKL	Chou Fa-kao. *Chin-wen ku-lin.*
CY	*Chung-yung.*
Daikanwa	Morohashi Tetsuji. *Daikanwa jiten.*
EY	*Erh-ya.*
GSR	Bernhard Karlgren. *Grammatica Serica Recensa.*
H	*Hsun Tzu.*
HFT	*Han Fei Tzu.*
HFTCS	Ch'en Ch'i-yu. *Han Fei Tzu chi-shih.*
HNT	*Huai-nan Tzu.*
HPCTCC	*Hsin-pien chu-tzu chi-ch'eng.*
HS	*Han-shu.*
Hsu-pien	Lo Chen-yü. *Yin-hsu shu-ch'i hsu-pien.*
Hsu-ts'un	Hu Hou-hsuan. *Chia-ku hsu-ts'un.*
HSWC	*Han-shih wai-chuan.*
HTCC	Wang Hsien-ch'ien. *Hsun Tzu chi-chieh.*

317

HTCS	Liang Ch'i-hsiung. *Hsun Tzu chien-shih.*
HTYT	*Hsun Tzu yin-te.*
KBTS	Shirakawa Shizuka. *Kinbun tsūshaku.*
KK	*K'ao-ku.*
K'o-chai	Wu Ta-ch'eng. *K'o-chai chi ku-lu.*
KT	*Kuan Tzu.*
KY	*Kuo-yü.*
KYC	*Kung-yang chuan.*
KYYS	Ch'en Li. *Kung-yang yi-shu.*
LC	*Li-chi.*
LCCC	Sun Hsi-tan. *Li-chi chi-chieh.*
LSCC	*Lü-shih ch'un-ch'iu.*
LYCY	Liu Pao-nan. *Lun-yü cheng-yi*
LYYT	*Lun-yü yin-te.*
M	*Mencius.*
Ming	Ming Yi-Shih (James M. Menzies). *Yin-hsu pu-tz'u hou-pien.*
MT	*Mo Tzu.*
MTCK	Sun Yi-jang. *Mo Tzu chien-ku.*
MTCY	Chiao Hsun and Chiao Hu. *Meng Tzu cheng-yi.*
MTYT	*Meng Tzu yin-te.*
NE	Aristotle. *Nicomachean Ethics.*
Pu-tz'u	Jung Keng and Chü Jun-min. *Yin-hsu pu-tz'u.*
S	Shima Kunio. *Inkyo bokuji sōrui.*
SC	Ssu-ma Ch'ien. *Shih-chi.*
SHC	*Shan-hai ching.*
SPPY	*Ssu-pu pei-yao.*
SPTK	*Ssu-pu ts'ung-k'an.*
SWCTKL	Ting Fu-pao. *Shuo-wen chieh-tzu ku-lin.*
Ta-hsi	Kuo Mo-jo. *Liang-Chou chin-wen ta-hsi t'u-lu.*

TC	*Tso-chuan.*
TCHC	Takezoe Kōkō. *Tso-chuan hui-chien.*
TH	*Ta-hsueh.*
TTC	*Tao te ching.*
TTLC	*Ta-Tai li-chi.*
Wai-pien	Tung Tso-pin. *Yin-hsu wen-tzu wai-pien.*
WH	Hsiao T'ung. *Wen hsuan.*
WSTK	Chang Hsin-ch'eng. *Wei-shu t'ung-k'ao.*
WW	*Wen-wu.*
Yi-pien	Tung Tso-pin. *Hsiao-t'un ti-erh-pen: Yin-hsu wen-tzu: yi-pien.*
Yi-ts'un	Shang Ch'eng-tso. *Yin-ch'i yi-ts'un.*
YTL	*Yen-t'ieh lun.*

Bibliography

Akatsuka Kiyoshi 赤塚忠, 1958. "*Junshi* kenkyū no ni-san no mondai" 荀子研究の二三の問題 [A few issues concerning research on the *Hsun Tzu*]. *Shibun* 斯文 21:10-27.

Alston, William P. 1964. *Philosophy of Language*. Englewood Cliffs, N. J.: Prentice-Hall.

Analects (*Lun-yü* 論語). *LYYT*, ed.

Aristotle. *Nicomachean Ethics*, Martin Ostwald, trans. Indianapolis: Bobbs-Merrill, 1962.

Austin, J. L. 1962. *How To Do Things With Words*. Cambridge, Mass.: Harvard University Press.

Barnard, Noel 1965. "Chou China: A Review of the Third Volume of Cheng Te-k'un's *Archaeology of China*." *Monumenta Serica* 24.307-442.

Beard, Ruth M. 1969. *An Outline of Piaget's Developmental Psychology for Students and Teachers*. New York: Basic Books.

Carson, Michael. 1978-79. "Some Grammatical and Graphical Problems in the *Ho Tsun* Inscription." *Early China* 4.41-44.

Chan, Wing-tsit. 1963. *A Source Book in Chinese Philosophy*. Princeton, N. J.: Princeton University Press.

Chan-kuo ts'e 戰國策 [Intrigues of the Warring States]. *SPTK* ed.

Chang Hsin-ch'eng 張心澂. *Wei-shu t'ung-k'ao* 偽書通考 [Comprehensive studies on spurious texts]. Taipei reprint of 1954 ed.; Shanghai: Commercial Press.

Chang, Kwang-chih. 1986. *The Archaeology of Ancient China*, 4th ed. New Haven, Conn.: Yale University Press.

Chang Ping-lin 章炳麟. *Chang-shih ts'ung-shu* 章氏叢書 [Collectania of Mr. Chang]. Shanghai: Ku-shu liu-t'ung ch'u, 1924.

321

Chen Shih-Hsiang. 1974. "The *Shih-ching*: Its Generic Significance." In Cyril Birch, ed., *Studies in Chinese Literary Genres*. Berkeley: University of California Press.

Ch'en Ch'i-yu 陳 奇 猷. *Han Fei Tzu chi-shih* 韓 非 子 集 釋 [Collected annotations of the *Han Fei Tzu*]. Taipei: Ho-lo t'u-shu ch'u-pan-she.

Ch'en Li 陳 立 . *Kung-yang yi-shu* 公 羊 義 疏 [Interpretive notes on the Kung-yang commentary]. Huang-Ch'ing ching-chieh hsu-pien edition.

Ch'en Meng-chia 陳 夢 家. 1955-56. "Hsi-Chou t'ung-ch'i tuan-tai" 西 周 銅 器 斷 代 [Dates of Western Chou bronzes]. *K'ao-ku hsueh-pao*, 9-14.

———— 1956. *Yin-hsu pu-tz'u tsung-shu* 殷 虛 卜 辭 綜 述. Peking: K'o-hsueh ch'u-pan-she.

Ch'en P'an 陳 槃. 1974. "Ch'un-ch'iu shih-tai ti chiao-yü" 春 秋 時 代 的 教 育 [Education in the Spring-Autumn Period]. *Bulletin of the Institute of History and Philology*. Nankang: Academia Sinica, 1974.4:731-810.

Ch'en Shun-cheng 陳 舜 政. 1968. *Lun-yü yi-wen chi-shih* 論 語 異 文 集 釋 [Annotated variorum of the *Analects*]. Taipei: Chia-hsin shui-ni kung-ssu.

Cheng Hsu-p'ing 鄭 緒 平. 1963. *K'ung Tzu shih-chia shang-ch'ueh* 孔 子 世 家 商 榷 [Discussion of the (*Shih-chi*) biography of Confucius]. Taipei: Privately printed.

Ch'eng Shu-te 程 樹 德. 1965. *Lun-yü chi-shih* 論 語 集 釋 [Collected commentaries on the *Analects*]. Taipei: Yi-wen yin-shu-kuan.

Chiao Hsun 焦 循 and Chiao Hu 焦 琥. *Meng Tzu cheng-yi* 孟 子 正 義 [Corrected interpretations of the *Mencius*]. HPCTCC edition.

Ch'ien Mu 錢 穆. 1954. "Po Hu Shih chih 'Shuo ju' " 駁 胡 適 之 說 儒 [Debating Hu Shih's "Explanation of 'ju' "]. *Journal of Oriental Studies*, 1.1.

————. 1956. *Hsien-Ch'in chu-tzu hsi-nien* 先 秦 諸 子 繫 年 [Dating of the pre-Ch'in philosophers]. Hong Kong: Hong Kong University, reprint.

————. 1963. *Lun-yü hsin-chieh* 論 語 新 解 [New interpretations of the *Analects*]. Taipei: San-min shu-chü.

Chou Fa-kao 周 法 高 . *Chin-wen ku-lin* 金 文 詁 林 [Collected interpretations of bronze inscriptions]. Hong Kong: Chinese University, 1974-75.

Chou-li 周 禮 [Rites of Chou]. *SPTK* ed.

Chow Tse-tsung. 1979. "Ancient Chinese Views on Literature, the *Tao*, and Their Relationship." *Chinese Literature: Essays, Articles, and Reviews* 1:1-29.

Chuang Tzu 莊 子. *Chuang Tzu yin-te* 莊 子 引 得 edition; Harvard-Yenching Institute Sinological Index Series, Suppl. 20. Peking: 1947.

Ch'un-ch'iu fan-lu 春 秋 繁 露 [Luxuriant dew from the Spring and Autumn Annals], by Tung Chung-shu 董 仲 舒. *Ch'un-ch'iu fan-lu yi-cheng* 義 證 edition, Su Yü 蘇 興 ed. Taipei: Ho-lo t'u-shu ch'u-pan-she.

Chung-kuo li-shih ti-t'u chi 中 國 歷 史 地 圖 集 [Collected historical maps of China]. Peking: Chung-hua ti-t'u hsueh-she, 1975.

Chung-yung 中 庸 [Doctrine of the mean]. *Hsueh-Yung chang-chü yin-te* 學 庸 章 句 引 得 ed. Taipei: K'ung-Meng hsueh-hui, 1970.

Creel, Herrlee Glessner. 1937. *The Birth of China*. New York: F. Ungar.

———. 1949. *Confucius, the Man and the Myth*. New York: J. Day.

———. 1970. *The Origins of Statecraft in China*. Vol. I. Chicago: University of Chicago Press.

———. 1979. "Discussion of Professor Fingarette on Confucius," *Journal of the American Academy of Religions* 47.3 (suppl.):407-15.

Crump, James I. 1964. *Intrigues of the Warring States*. Ann Arbor: University of Michigan Press.

Csikszentmihalyi, Mihaly. 1975. *Beyond Boredom and Anxiety*. San Francisco: Jossey-Bass.

———, and Stith Bennett. 1971. "An Exploratory Model of Play." *American Anthropologist* 73.1:45-58.

Dardess, John. 1983. *Confucianism and Autocracy*. Berkeley and Los Angeles: University of California Press.

deBary, Wm. Theodore. 1960. *Sources of Chinese Tradition*. New York: Columbia University Press.

Dobson, W. A. C. H. 1963. *Mencius*. Toronto: University of Toronto Press.

Documents. (*Shang shu* 尚 書). *SPTK* edition.

Dubs, Homer H. 1927. *Hsuntze, Moulder of Ancient Confucianism*. London: Arthur Probsthain.

———. 1928. "Did Confucius Study the Book of Changes?" *T'oung Pao* 25:82-90.

———. 1928a. *The Works of Hsuntze*. London: Arthur Probsthain.

———. 1946. "The Political Career of Confucius." *Journal of the American Oriental Society* 66:273-82.

———. 1958. "The Archaic Royal Jou Religion." *T'oung Pao* 46.3-5:217-59.

Eno, Robert. 1984. "Masters of the Dance: The Role of T'ien (Heaven) in the Teachings of the Early Juist Community." Ann Arbor: University of Michigan Ph. D. dissertation.

Erh-ya 爾雅. *SPPY* edition.

Feng-su t'ung-yi 風俗通義 [The meaning of traditions comprehended]. *SPTK* edition.

Fingarette, Herbert. 1972. *Confucius—the Secular as Sacred*. New York: Harper and Row.

———. 1979. "The Problem of the Self in the *Analects*." *Philosophy East and West* 29.2:129-40.

———. 1979a. "Following the 'One Thread' of the *Analects*." *Journal of the American Academy of Religions* 47.3 (suppl.):407-15.

———. 1981. "How the *Analects* Portrays the Ideal of Efficacious Authority." *Journal of Chinese Philosophy* 8:29-50.

———. 1983. "The Music of Humanity in the *Conversations* of Confucius." *Journal of Chinese Philosophy* 10:331-56.

Fong, Wen. 1980. *The Great Bronze Age of China*. New York: Metropolitan Museum of Art.

Fried, Morton H. 1983. "Tribe to State or State to Tribe in Ancient China." In David N. Keightley, ed., *The Origins of Chinese Civilization*. Berkeley: University of California Press.

Fu, Pei-jung. 1984. "The Concept of 'T'ien' in Ancient China: With Special Emphasis on Confucianism." New Haven, Conn.: Yale University Ph. D. dissertation.

Fu Ssu-nien 傅斯年. 1940. *Hsing ming ku-hsun pien-cheng* 性命古訓辨證 [Determining the original meanings of *hsing* and *ming*]. Shanghai: Commercial Press.

Fung Yu-lan 馮友蘭. 1931. *Chung-kuo che-hsueh shih* 中國哲學史 [A history of Chinese philosophy]. Taipei reprint.

_____. 1935. "Yuan Ju-Mo" 原儒墨 [Origins of the terms *ju* and *mo*]. In *Chung-kuo che-hsueh shih pu* 中國哲學史補 [Supplement to "A history of Chinese philosophy"]. Taipei reprint.

_____. 1948. *A Short History of Chinese Philosophy*. Derk Bodde, ed. New York: Macmillan.

_____. 1952. *A History of Chinese Philosophy*. Derk Bodde, trans. Princeton, N.J.: Princeton University Press.

_____. 1962. *Chung-kuo che-hsueh shih hsin-pien* [A new history of Chinese philosophy]. Peking: Jen-min.

Geertz, Clifford. 1973. *The Interpretation of Cultures*. New York: Basic Books.

Graham, A. C. 1967. "The Background of the Mencian Theory of Human Nature." *Ch'ing-hua hsueh-pao* N.S. VI, 1-2:215-71.

_____. 1978. *Later Mohist Logic, Ethics and Science*. Hong Kong: Chinese University.

_____. 1983. "Taoist Spontaneity and the Dichotomy of 'Is' and 'Ought.' " In Victor H. Mair, ed., *Experimental Essays on Chuang-tzu*. Honolulu: University of Hawaii Press.

Granet, Marcel. 1926. *Danses et légendes de la Chine ancienne*. Paris: Libraire Felix Alcan.

Hall, David, and Roger T. Ames. 1984. "Getting It Right: On Saving Confucius from the Confucians." *Philosophy East and West* 34.1:3-23.

_____. 1987. *Thinking Through Confucius*. Albany: State University of New York Press.

Han Fei Tzu 韓非子. *SPTK* edition.

Hanna, Judith Lynn. 1979. *To Dance is Human*. Austin: University of Texas Press.

Hansen, Chad. 1983. *Language and Logic in Ancient China*. Ann Arbor: University of Michigan.

_____. 1983a. "A Tao of Taos in Chuang-tzu." In Victor H. Mair, ed. *Experimental Essays on Chuang-tzu*. Honolulu: University of Hawaii Press.

————. 1985. "Individualism in Chinese Thought." In Donald Munro, ed., *Individualism and Holism: Studies in Confucian and Taoist Values*. Ann Arbor: University of Michigan Center for Chinese Studies.

————. 1985a. "Chinese Language, Chinese Philosophy, and 'Truth.'" *Journal of Asian Studies* 44.3: 491-520.

Han-shih wai-chuan 韓詩外傳 [Outer commentary on the Han *Poetry*]. *SPTK* edition.

Han-shu 漢書 [Documents of the Han]. Peking: Chung-hua shu-chü.

Henderson, John B. 1984. *The Development and Decline of Chinese Cosmology*. New York: Columbia University.

Ho, Ping-ti. 1975. *The Cradle of the East*. Chicago: University of Chicago.

Hou Wai-lu 侯外廬 et al. 1957. *Chung-kuo ssu-hsiang t'ung-shih* 中國思想通史 [Comprehensive history of Chinese thought]. Vol. I. Peking: Jen-min ch'u-pan-she.

Hsia Chen-t'ao 夏甄陶. 1979. *Lun Hsun Tzu te che-hsueh ssu-hsiang* 論荀子的哲學思想 [On the philosophical thought of the *Hsun Tzu*]. Shanghai: Jen-min ch'u-pan-she.

Hsiao T'ung 蕭統, *Wen-hsuan* 文選 [Anthology of literature]. Taipei: Wen-hua kuo-shu edition.

Hsin-pien chu-tzu chi-ch'eng 新編諸子集成 [New collection of the philosophers]. Taipei: Shih-chieh shu-chü.

Hsu Cho-yun. 1965. *Ancient China in Transition*. Stanford, Calif.: Stanford University Press.

————. 許倬雲. 1984. *Hsi-Chou Shih* 西周史 [History of the Western Chou]. Taipei : Lien-ching ch'u-pan shih-yeh kung-ssu.

Hsu Chung-shu 徐中舒. 1959. "Yü ting te nien-tai chi ch'i hsiang-kuan wen-t'i" 禹鼎的年代及其相關問題 [On the date of the *Yü* tripod and related issues]. *K'ao-ku hsueh-pao* 1959.3:53-66.

Hsu, Francis L. K. 1971. "Psychological Homeostasis and Jen: Conceptual Tools for Advancing Psychological Anthropology." *American Anthropologist* 73:22-44.

Hsun Tzu 荀子. *HTYT* edition.

Hsun Tzu yin-te 荀子引得 [Concordance of the *Hsun Tzu*]. Harvard-Yenching Institute Sinological Index Series, Supp. 22. Peking: 1950.

Hu Hou-hsuan 胡厚宣. *Chia-ku hsu-ts'un* 甲骨續存 [Further preserved oracle texts]. Shanghai, 1955.

Hu Shih 胡適. 1919. *Chung-kuo ku-tai che-hsueh shih* 中國古代哲學史 [Ancient Chinese philosophy]. Taipei: Commercial Press reprint, 1961.

_____. 1934. "Shuo *ju*" 說儒 [An explanation of "*ju*"]. In *Hu Shih wen-ts'un* 胡適文存. Taipei: Yuan-tung t'u-shu kung-ssu, 1953. IV: 1-103.

Huai-nan Tzu 淮南子. *SPTK* edition.

Ikeda Suetoshi 池田末利. 1955. "Hai-yū kigen kō" 俳優起源考 [On the origins of acrobatic dancers]. *Shinagaku kenyū* 支那學研究 13:72-83.

_____. 1965. "Chūgoku koyū no shūkyō to in'yō shisō 中國固有の宗教と陰陽思想 [The original religion of China and yin-yang thought]. *Shūkyō kenkyū* 宗教研究 182 (38/3):1-28.

_____. 1968. "Tendō to tenmei (I)" 天道と天命 [The way of T'ien and the mandate of T'ien]. *Hiroshima Daigaku Bungakubu kiyō* 広島大学文学部紀要 28.1:24-39.

Itano Chōhachi 板野長八. 1968. "*Junshi* no ten-jin no bun to sono ato" 荀子の天人の分とその後 [The division between T'ien and man in the *Hsun Tzu* and its consequences]. *Hiroshima Daigaku Bungakubu kiyō* 28.1.

Itō Tomoatsu 伊東倫厚. 1969. "*Raiki: Bōki, Hyōki, Shie* hen ni tsuite" 禮記・坊記・表記・緇衣篇について [On the *Book of Rites* chapters: "Records on interdiction," "Outer records," "Black garments"]. *Tōkyō Shinagakuhō* 東京支那學報 15:17-38.

Jao Tsung-yi 饒宗頤. 1954. "Shih *ju*," 釋儒 [Explaining "*ju*"]. *Journal of Oriental Studies* 1.1.

_____. 1975. "The Character *te* in Bronze Inscriptions" (Noel Barnard, trans.) In Noel Barnard, ed., *Ancient Chinese Bronzes and Southeast Asian Metal and Other Archeological Artifacts*. Melbourne: National Gallery of Victoria.

Jung Keng 容庚 and Ch'ü Jun-min 瞿潤緡. *Yin-ch'i pu-tz'u* 殷契卜辭 [Oracle texts from Yin]. Peking: 1933; Taipei reprint, 1970.

Kaizuka Shigeki 貝塚茂樹. 1951. "Rongo no seiritsu" 論語の成立 [The compilation of the *Analects*]. *Tōhōgaku* 1:95-105.

————. 1973. *Rongo* 論語 [*Analects*]. Tokyo: Chūō Kōron-sha.

Kanaya Osamu 金谷治. 1950-51. "Mōshi no kenkyū" 孟子の研究 [Studies on the *Mencius*]. *Tōhoku Daigaku Bungakubu kenkyū nenpō* 東北大学文学部研究年報 1:18-46.

————. 1951. "*Junshi* no bunkengakuteki kenkyū" 荀子の文献学的研究 [A textual study of the *Hsun Tzu*]. *Gakushiin kiyō* 学士院紀要 9.1:9-33.

————. 1951a. "Yokubō no arikata–*Junshi* no shosetsu o megutte" 欲望の在り方荀子の諸説をめぐって [On the ideal manner of desiring– the *Hsun Tzu*'s views]. *Bunka* 文化 15.2:92-103.

————. 1956. "Kō-Mō no mei ni tsuite" 孔孟の命について [Confucius and Mencius on "*ming*"]. *Nippon Chūgokugakkaihō* 8:43-54.

————. 1970. "*Junshi* no ten-jin no bun ni tsuite" 荀子の天人の分について [On the division of T'ien and man in the *Hsun Tzu*]. *Shūkan Tōyōgaku* 集刊東洋学 24.

K'ao-ku 考古 [Archaeology]. Peking.

Karlgren, Bernhard. *Grammatica Serica Recensa. Bulletin of the Museum of Far Eastern Antiquities* 29 (1957).

————. 1926. *On the Authenticity and Nature of the Tso Chuan*. Taipei: Ch'eng-wen reprint, 1968.

————. 1944. "Glosses on the Siao ya Odes." *Bulletin of the Museum of Far Eastern Antiquities* 16.

————. 1948. "Glosses on the Book of Documents (I)." *Bulletin of the Museum of Far Eastern Antiquities* 20.

Katakura Nozomu 片倉望. 1978. "Junshi shisō no bunretsu to tōitsu" 荀子思想の分裂と統一 [Division and unity in Hsun Tzu's thought]. *Shūkan tōyōgaku* 40:14-27.

Keightley, David N. 1977. "Ping-ti Ho and the Origins of Chinese Civilization." *Harvard Journal of Asian Studies* 37.2:381-411.

_____. 1978. *Sources of Shang History.* Berkeley: University of California
Press.

_____. 1979-80. "The Shang State as Seen in the Oracle Bone Inscrip-
tions." *Early China* 5:25-34.

_____. 1983. "The Late Shang State: When, Where, and What?" In
Keightley, ed., *The Origins of Chinese Civilization.* Berkeley: University
of California Press.

Kimura Eiichi 木村英一. 1971. *Kōshi to Rongo* 孔子と論語 [Confu-
cius and the *Analects*]. Tokyo: Sōbunsha.

Knoblock, John H. 1982-83. "The Chronology of Xunzi's Works." *Early China*
8:29-52.

Kodama Rokurō 兒玉六郎. 1972. "*Junshi* ni okeru ten'yō no gainen" 荀
子における天養の概念 [The concept of the nurturance of T'ien in
the *Hsun Tzu*]. *Nippon Chūgokugakkaihō* 日本中国学会報 24:51-62.

Kuan Tzu 管子 . *SPTK* edition.

Kuang-yun 廣韻 . *SPTK* edition.

K'uang Ya-ming 匡亞明 1985. *K'ung Tzu p'ing-chuan* 孔子評傳 [A
biography of Confucius]. Chinan: Ch'i-Lu shu-she.

Kuhn, Thomas. 1962. *The Structure of Scientific Revolutions.* Chicago: University of Chicago Press.

Kung-yang chuan 公羊傳 [The "Kung-yang" commentary (to the *Spring
and Autumn Annals*)]. *SPPY* edition.

Kuo Jo-yü 郭若愚, Tseng Yi-kung 曾毅公 Li Hsueh-ch'in 李學勤.
Yin-hsu wen-tzu chui-ho 殷虛文字綴合 [Compilation of writings
from the Wastes of Yin]. Peking: 1955.

Kuo Mo-jo 郭沫若. *Liang-Chou chin-wen ta-hsi t'u-lu* 兩周金文大
系圖錄 . [Illustrated compendium of bronze texts of the two Chou
periods]. Taiwan reprint of *Liang-Chou chin-wen-tz'u ta-hsi t'u-lu k'ao-shih*
兩周金文大系圖錄考釋 . Peking: K'o-hsueh ch'u-pan-she, 1957).

————. 1945. *Ch'ing-t'ung shih-tai* 青銅時代 [The Bronze Age]. Chungking: Wen-chih ch'u-pan-she.

————. 1962. "Ch'ang-an hsien Chang-chia-p'o t'ung-ch'i ch'ün ming-wen hui-shih 長安縣張家坡銅器群銘文彙釋 [Interpretations of inscriptions on a collection of bronze vessels from Chang-chia-p'o in Chang-an County]. *K'ao-ku hsueh-pao* 1962.1:1-14.

Kuo Mo-jo, Wen I-to 聞一多, Hsu Wei-yü 許維遹. 1956. *Kuan Tzu chi-chiao* 管子集校 [Collected textual notes to the *Kuan Tzu*]. Peking: K'o-hsueh ch'u-pan-she.

Kuo-yü 國語 [Discourses of the States]. *SPTK* edition.

Langer, Susanne. 1953. *Feeling and Form*. New York: Scribner's Sons.

Lau, D. C. 1953. "Theories of Human Nature in Mencius and Shyntzyy." *Bulletin of the School of Oriental and African Studies* 15:541-65.

————. 1970. *Mencius*. Harmondsworth: Penguin.

————. 1979. *The Analects*. Harmondsworth: Penguin.

Legge, James. 1872. *The Chinese Classics, Vol. 5: The Ch'un Ts'ew with The Tso Chuen*. Hong Kong. Taiwan reprint, 1972.

————. 1894. *The Four Books*. Hong Kong. Taiwan reprint.

Levenson, Joseph, and Franz Schurmann. 1969. *China: An Interpretive History*. Berkeley: University of California Press.

Li-chi 禮記 [Book of rites]. *SPTK* edition.

Li Hsiao-ting 李孝定. *Chia-ku wen-tzu chi-shih* 甲骨文字集釋 [Collected explanations of oracle text characters]. Nankang: Academia Sinica, 1965.

Li Hsueh-ch'in 李學勤. 1979. "P'ing-shan mu tsang-ch'ün yü Chung-shan-kuo te wen-hua" 平山墓葬群與中山國的文化 [A group of funeral articles from the P'ing-shan gravesite and the culture of the state of Chung-shan]. *WW* 1979. 1:37-41.

Li Tu 李杜. 1961. "Hsien-Ch'in shih-ch'i chih t'ien-ti kuan" 先秦時期之天帝觀 [Views of T'ien and Ti in the pre-Ch'in period]. *Hsin-Ya shu-yuan hsueh-shu nien-k'an* 3.

Liang Ch'i-hsiung 梁啟雄, *Hsun Tzu chien-shih* 荀子柬釋 [Analytical explanations of the *Hsun Tzu*]. Taipei: Ho-lo t'u-shu ch'u-pan-she reprint, 1974.

Lieh Tzu 列 子 . *SPTK* edition.

Lifton, Robert Jay. 1961. *Thought Reform and the Psychology of Totalism.* New York: Norton.

Lin Yü-sheng. 1974-75. "The Evolution of the Pre-Confucian Meaning of *Jen* and the Confucian Concept of Moral Autonomy." *Monumenta Serica* 31: 172-204.

Liu Chieh劉 節. 1943. "Pien Ju-Mo"辨 儒 墨 [Distinguishing Juism and Mohism]. In *Ku-tai k'ao-ts'un* 古 史 考 存 Peking: Jen-min, ch'u-pan-she, 1956.

Liu Pao-nan劉 寶 楠 *Lun-yü cheng-yi* 論 語 正義 [Corrected interpretations of the *Analects*]. *HPCTCC* edition.

Lo Chen-yü 羅 振 王. *Yin-hsu shu-ch'i ch'ing-hua* 殷 虛 書契菁 華 [The flower of inscriptions from the Wastes of Yin]. 1914.

_____. *Yin-hsu shu-ch'i hsu-pien* 殷 虛 書 契 續 編 [Inscriptions from the Wastes of Yin: Supplementary Volume]. 1933; Taipei: reprint, n.d.

Lü-shih ch'un-ch'iu 呂 氏 春 秋 [The Spring and Autumn Annals of Mr. Lü]. *SPTK* edition.

Lukes, Steven. 1973. *Individualism.* Oxford: Basil Blackwell.

Lun-heng 論 衡 . Wang Ch'ung 王 充 . *HPCTCC* edition.

Lun-yü yin-te 論 語 引 得 [Concordance to the *Analects*]. Harvard-Yenching Institute Sinological Index Series, Supp. 16. Peking: 1940.

Lung Yü-ch'un龍 宇純. 1972. *Chung-kuo wen-tzu-hsueh* 中 國 文 字 學 [Chinese etymology]. Taipei: Hsueh-sheng shu-chü.

MacIntyre, Alasdair. 1984. *After Virtue,* 2d ed. Notre Dame, Ind.: University of Notre Dame Press.

Matsuda Hiroshi松 田 弘. 1975."*Junshi* ni okeru Jukateki rinen to ten no shisōteki ichi" 荀 子 に お け る 儒 家 的 理 念 と 天 の 思 想 的 位 置 [Ruist ideology and the conceptual role of T'ien in the *Hsun Tzu*]. *Tsukuba Daigaku tetsugaku shisōshi ronshū* 築 波 大 学 哲 学 思 想 系 論 集 1:63-91.

Matsumoto Masaaki 松 本 雅 明. 1966. *Shunjū sengoku ni okeru Shōsho no tenkai*春 秋 戰 國 に お け る 尚 書 の 展 開 [The development of the *Documents* during the Spring-Autumn and Warring States periods]. Tokyo: Kazama shobō.

Mencius (Meng Tzu 孟 子). *MTYT* edition.

Meng Tzu yin-te 孟 子 引 得 [Concordance to the *Mencius*]. Harvard-Yenching Sinological Index Series, Supp. 17. Peking: 1941.

Merleau-Ponty, Maurice. 1962. *Phenomenology of Perception,* Colin Smith, trans. London: Routledge and Kegan Paul.

Metzger, Thomas. 1977. *Escape From Predicament.* New York: Columbia University.

Ming Yi-shih 明 義 士 (James M. Menzies). *Yin-hsu pu-tz'u hou-pien* 殷 虛 卜 辭 後 編 [Oracle texts from the Wastes of Yin: Latter Volume]. Hsu Wei-hsiung 許 維 雄, ed. Taipei: 1972.

Miura Yoshiaki 三 甫 吉 明 . 1975. "Keisho yori mita ten no shisō" 経 書 より見た天の思想 [Views of T'ien seen through the classics]. *Tōyōgaku* 東 洋 学 34:38-65.

Miyazaki Ichisada 宮 崎 市 定. 1974. *Rongo no shin kenkyū* 論 語 の 新 研 究 [New studies on the *Analects*]. Tokyo: Iwanami.

Mo Tzu 墨 子. *SPTK* edition.

Morohasi, Tetsuji 諸 橋 轍 次 . *Daikanwa jiten* 大 漢 和 辭 典 [Great Chinese-Japanese Dictionary]. Tokyo: Daishukan shoten, 1955-60.

Mote, Frederick. 1971. *Intellectual Foundations of China.* New York: Alfred Knopf.

Munro, Donald. 1969. *The Concept of Man in Early China.* Stanford, Calif.: Stanford University Press.

_____. 1977. *The Concept of Man in Contemporary China.* Ann Arbor: University of Michigan Press.

_____. 1985. (ed.). *Individualism and Holism: Studies in Confucian and Taoist Values.* Ann Arbor: University of Michigan Center for Chinese Studies.

_____. 1988. *Images of Human Nature: A Sung Portrait.* Princeton, N.J.: Princeton University Press.

Needham, Joseph. 1956. *Science and Civilization in China,* Vol. 2. Cambridge: Cambridge University Press.

_____. 1974. *Science and Civilization in China,* Vol. 5, pt. 2. Cambridge: Cambridge University Press.

Nivison, David S. 1978-79. "Royal 'Virtue' in Shang Oracle Inscriptions." *Early China* 4: 52-55.

_____. 1979. "Mencius and Motivation." *Journal of the American Academy of Religions* 47.3 (suppl.):417-32.

_____. 1982-83. "1040 As the Date of the Chou Conquest." *Early China,* 8:76-78.

_____. 1983. "Western Zhou History." In George Kuwayama, ed., *The Great Bronze Age of China: A Symposium.* Los Angeles: Los Angeles County Museum of Art.

_____. 1983a. "The Dates of Western Chou." *Harvard Journal of Asiatic Studies* 43.2: 481-580.

Oakeshott, Michael. 1962. *Rationalism in Politics.* London: Methuen.

Passmore, John. 1967. "Philosophy." In Paul Edwards, ed., *The Encyclopedia of Philosophy,* Vol. 6. New York: Macmillan and Free Press.

Poetry. (Shih-ching 詩 經). *Mao-shih yin-te* edition. Harvard-Yenching Sinological Index Series, Supp. 9. Peking: 1934.

Polanyi, Michael. 1966. *The Tacit Dimension.* Garden City, N. Y.: Anchor.

Rappaport, Roy. 1971. "Ritual, Society, and Cybernetics." *American Anthropologist* 73.1:59-75.

Rickett, W. Allyn. 1965. *Kuan Tzu: A Repository of Early Chinese Thought.* Hong Kong: Hong Kong University Press.

_____. 1985. *Guanzi.* Princeton, N. J.: Princeton University Press.

Riegel, Jeffrey. 1979. "Reflections on an Unmoved Mind: An Analysis of *Mencius* 2A2." *Journal of the American Academy of Religions* 47.3 (suppl.): 433-57.

Rosemont, Henry. 1970-71. "State and Society in the Hsun Tzu: A Philosophical Commentary." *Monumenta Serica* 29:38-78

Royce, Anya Peterson. 1977. *The Anthropology of Dance.* Bloomington: Indiana University Press.

Ryle, Gilbert. 1949. *The Concept of Mind.* New York: Barnes and Noble.

Schwartz, Benjamin. 1964. "Some Polarities in Confucian Thought." In Arthur Wright, ed., *Confucianism and Chinese Civilization.* New York: Atheneum.

_____. 1985. *The World of Thought in Ancient China.* Cambridge, Mass.: Harvard Belknap Press.

Seligman, Paul. 1962. *The Apeiron of Anaximander.* London: Athlone Press.

Serruys, Paul L. M. 1974. "Studies in the Language of the Oracle Inscriptions." *T'oung Pao* 40.1-3:12-120.

Shang Ch'eng-tso 商 承 祚 . *Yin-ch'i yi-ts'un* 殷 契 佚 存 [Inscriptions from the Wastes of Yin preserved from loss]. Nanking: 1933; Tokyo reprint, 1966.

Shan-hai ching 山 海 經 [Classic of mountains and seas]. *SPTK* edition.

Shaughnessy, Edward. 1980-81. " 'New' Evidence on the Zhou Conquest." *Early China* 7:57-79.

_____. 1985-87. "The 'Current' Bamboo Annals and the Date of the Zhou Conquest of the Shang." *Early China* 11-12:33-60.

Shih-ming 釋 名 [Explanation of names]. *Ts'ung-shu chi-ch'eng* 叢 書 集 成 edition.

Shima Kunio 島 邦 男, *Inkyo bokuji sōrui* 殷 墟 卜 辭 綜 類 [Index of words in the oracle texts from the Wastes of Yin]. Tokyo: Daian, 1967.

_____. 1958. *Yin-hsu pu-tz'u yen-chiu* 殷 墟 卜 辭 研 究 [Studies on oracle texts from the Wastes of Yin] (translation of *Inkyo bokuji kenkyū,* Hirosaki). Taipei: Ting-wen shu-chü, 1975.

Shirakawa Shizuka 白 川 靜. *Kinbun tsūshaku* 金 文 通 釋 [Complete annotations of bronze inscriptions]. Kobe: Hakutsuru bijutsukan, 1962-84.

_____ 1963-64. *Kinbun shū* 金 文 集 [Collected bronze inscriptions]. Kyoto: Nigen.

_____ 1972. *Kōshi den* 孔 子 傳 [Life of Confucius]. Tokyo: Chū yō Kōron-sha.

_____ 1974. *Kōkotsubun-kinbungaku ronshū* 甲 骨 文 金 文 學 論 集 [Collected essays on oracle and bronze inscriptions]. Kyoto: Tomodachi.

Ssu-ma Ch'ien 司馬遷. *Shih-chi* 史記 [Historical records]. Peking: Chung-hua shu-chü edition.

Ssu-pu pei-yao 四部備要 [Complete essentials of the four categories]. Shanghai: Chung-hua shu-chü.

Ssu-pu ts'ung-k'an 四部叢刊 [Collected editions of the four categories]. Shanghai: Commercial Press.

Sun Hsi-tan 孫希旦. *Li-chi chi-chieh* 禮記集解 [Collected commentaries on the *Book of rites*]. Taipei: Wen-shih-che ch'u-pan-she, 1972 reprint.

Sun Yi-jang 孫詒讓. *Mo Tzu chien-ku* 墨子閒詁 [Annotation of the *Mo Tzu*]. Taipei: Ho-lo t'u-shu ch'u-pan-she.

Ta-hsueh 大學 [Great learning]. *Hsueh-yung chang-chü yin-te* 學庸章句引得 ed. Taipei: K'ung-Meng hsueh-hui, 1970.

Ta-Tai li-chi 大戴禮記 [Book of rites of the Greater Tai]. *SPTK* edition.

Takeuchi Yoshio 武內義雄. 1936. *Chūgoku shisōshi* 中國思想史 [History of Chinese thought]. Tokyo: Iwanami, reprint 1957.

———. 1939. Rongo no kenkyū 論語之研究 [Studies on the *Analects*]. Tokyo: Iwanami.

Takezoe, Kōkō 竹添光鴻, *Tso-chuan hui-chien* 左傳會箋 [Assembled commentaries on the *Tso-chuan*] (reprint of *Sashi kaisen* 左氏會箋, *Kanbun taikei* edition). Taipei: Kuang-wen shu-chü. 1977.

T'ang Chün-yi 唐君毅. 1974. *Chung-kuo che-hsueh yuan-lun: tao-lun p'ien* 中國哲學原論導論篇 [Essays tracing origins in Chinese philosophical thought: Introductory volume], 2d ed. Taiwan: Hsueh-sheng shu-chü.

Tao te ching 道德經 [Classic of the Way and virtue].

Ting Fu-pao 丁福保, *Shuo-wen chieh-tzu ku-lin* 說文解字詁林 [Complete commentaries on the *Shuo-wen chieh-tzu* dictionary]. Shanghai: Yi-hsueh shu-chü, 1931-32.

Ting Yen 丁晏. 1949. *Yi-chih-chai wen-chi* 頤志齋文集 [Collection from the Yi-chih studio]. Shanghai: privately published.

Tong Kin-woon. 1983. "Shang Musical Instruments." Middletown, Conn.: Wesleyan University Ph. D. dissertation.

Tso-chuan 左 傳 *TCHC* edition.

Tsuda Sōkichi 津 田 左 右 吉. 1935. *Saden no shisōshiteki kenkyū* 左 傳 の 思 想 史 的 研 究 [Studies on the ideology of the *Tso-chuan*]. Tokyo: Iwanami, reprint, 1958.

―――. 1946. *Rongo to Kōshi no shisō* 論 語 と 孔 子 の 思 想 [The *Analects* and the philosophy of Confucius]. Tokyo: Iwanami.

Tu Erh-wei 杜 而 未. 1959. *Chung-kuo ku-tai tsung-chiao yen-chiu: T'ien-tao shang-ti chih-pu* 中 國 古 代 宗 教 研 究 天 道 上 帝 之 部 [Studies on the religion of ancient China: On the Way of T'ien and Shang-ti]. Taipei: Hua-ming.

Tu Kuo-hsiang 杜 國 庠. 1962. *Tu Kuo-hsiang wen-chi* 杜 國 庠 文 集 [Collected works of Tu Kuo-hsiang]. Peking: Jen-min ch'u-pan-she.

Tu, Wei-ming. 1968. "The Creative Tension Between *Jen* and *Li*." *Philosophy East and West* 18:29-40.

―――. 1976. *Centrality and Commonality: An Essay on Chung-yung*. Honolulu: University of Hawaii Press.

Tung Tso-pin 董 作 賓. *Hsiao-t'un ti-erh-pen: Yin-hsu wen-tzu: yi-pien* 小 屯 第 二 本 殷 虛 文 字 乙 編 [Hsiao-t'un site—Volume Two: Texts from the Wastes of Yin: Second collection]. Nankang: 1948, 1949; Taipei: 1953.

―――. *Yin-hsu wen-tzu wai-pien* 殷 虛 文 字 外 編 [Oracle texts of the Wastes of Yin: Outer collection]. Taipei: 1956.

―――. 1964. *Fifty Years of Studies in Oracle Inscriptions*. Tokyo.

―――. 1974. *Chia-ku-hsueh liu-shih nien* 甲 骨 學 六 十 年 [Sixty years of oracle bone studies]. Taipei: Yi-wen yin-shu-kuan.

Waley, Arthur. 1938. *The Analects of Confucius*. New York: Vintage.

Wang Ching-chih 王 靜 芝 1968. *Shih-ching t'ung-shih* 詩 經 通 釋 [Comprehensive explanations of the *Poetry*]. Taipei: Fu-jen ta-hsueh wen-hsueh yuan.

Wang Hsien-ch'ien 王 先 謙. *Hsun Tzu chi-chieh* 荀 子 集 解 [Collected commentaries on the *Hsun Tzu*]. *Kanbun taikei* edition, including commentaries of Kubo Ai 久 保 愛 and Ikai Keisho 稻 飼 敬 所. Taipei: reprint, 1978.

Watson, Burton. 1963. *Hsun Tzu: Basic Writings.* New York: Columbia University.

Welch, Holmes. 1966. *The Parting of the Way: Lao Tzu and the Taoist Movement.* Boston: Beacon Press.

Wen-wu 文 物 [Cultural relics]. Peking.

Wheatley, Paul. 1971. *The Pivot of the Four Quarters.* Chicago: Aldine.

Wittgenstein, Ludwig. 1922. *Tractatus Logico-Philosophicus.* D. F. Pears and B. F. McGuinness, trans. London: Routledge and Kegan Paul reprint, 1961.

————. 1953. *Philosophical Investigations.* G.E.M. Anscombe and Rush Rhees, trans. London: Oxford University Press.

Wu Hao-k'un 吳 浩 坤 and P'an Yu 潘 悠. 1985. *Chung-kuo chia-ku-hsueh shih* 中 國 甲 骨 學 史 [A history of Chinese oracle text studies]. Shanghai: Jen-min ch'u-pan-she.

Wu Ta-ch'eng 吳 大 澂 . *K'o-chai chi ku-lu* 愙 齋 集 古 錄 [Collected old notes from the K'o Studio].

Yang Chün-ju 楊 筠 如. 1938. "Kuan-yü *Hsun Tzu* pen-shu te k'ao-cheng" 關 於 荀 子 本 書 的 考 證 [Philological issues concerning the text of the *Hsun Tzu*]. In *Ku shih pien* 古 史 辨 6:130-46.

Yang Jung-kuo 楊 榮 國. 1973. *Chung-kuo ku-tai ssu-hsiang shih* 中 國 古 代 思 想 史 [History of ancient Chinese thought]. Peking: Hsin-hua.

Yang K'uan 楊 寬 . *Chan-kuo shih* 戰 國 史 [History of the Warring States Period]. Shanghai: Jen-min ch'u-pan-she.

Yen Ling-feng 嚴 靈 峯. 1971. *Wu-ch'iu-pei chai Lieh Tzu chi-ch'eng* 無 求 備 齋 列 子 集 成 [Collected commentaries on the *Lieh Tzu* from the Wu-ch'iu-pei Studio]. Taipei: Yi-wen yin-shu-kuan.

Yen-t'ieh lun 鹽 鐵 論 [Salt and iron debates]. *SPTK* edition.

Yü Yueh 俞 樾. *Chu-tzu p'ing-yi* 諸 子 平 議 [Discussions on the philosophers]. *HPCTCC* edition.

Index

Ames, Roger, 247-48, 280-81
Analects: as canonical, 80, 82, 243; interpretation of, 80-81, 95-96; literary aspects of, 54; passages of appearing in *Hsun Tzu*, 239-40, 242; passages of appearing in *Mencius*, 241-42; textual nature of, 80-81, 239-42; timeliness in, 44, 50-51, 283; virtue terminology in, 233. *See also, Li*, in *Analects*; Sagehood, in *Analects*; T'ien, in *Analects*
Analects passage index: (1.1), 52; (2.4), 5, 89-91, 97-98; (2.9), 71; (2.10), 71; (2.16), 282; (3.3), 44; (3.12), 250; (3.13), 45, 87, 97; (3.18), 216; (3.19), 40; (3.24), 88; (4.1), 66; (4.13), 40, 44; (4.14), 52; (4.15), 67; (5.13), 85; (6.7), 71; (6.9), 51; (6.13), 191; (6.17), 66; (6.22), 96, 251; (6.28), 45, 87, 97; (7.7), 230; (7.11), 50; (7.12), 50; (7.15), 46; (7.16), 50; (7.21), 250; (7.23), 83, 97; (7.35), 251; (8.8), 39, 217-18; (8.12), 50; (8.13), 44; (8.19), 5, 85, 97-98; (9.5), 40, 83, 97; (9.6), 84; (9.7), 244; (9.8), 67; (9.12), 248-49; (10.2), 34; (10.6), 215; (10.17), 215; (11.9), 93, 97; (11.18), 249; (11.21), 227; (11.24), 60; (12.1), 40, 68; (12.2), 68; (12.5), 5, 93; (12.8), 216; (12.24), 218; (13.5), 229; (13.13), 219; (14.4), 66; (14.19), 46; (14.28), 66; (14.35), 91, 97; (14.36), 92, 251; (14.41), 40; (15.3), 67; (15.5), 35; (15.24), 68; (15.31), 55; (15.32), 226; (16.8), 93, 97-98; (16.13), 56, 90; (17.1), 35; (17.17), 5, 86, 97, 246; (19.25), 5; (20.1), 86
Aristotle, 72
Augustine, 237
Austin, J. L., 208

Bodde, Derk, 205

Chan, Wing-tsit, 159-60, 245, 294
Ch'ang Hung, 271
Chang Ping-lin (1868-1936), 190-91, 289, 291
Chan-kuo ts'e, 46, 49, 220, 225-26, 265-66
Chao Ch'i (d. A.D. 201), 252, 258, 282
Chao Liang, 222
Ch'en Chi-t'ing (Lung-cheng, b. 1585), 249
Ch'en Ch'i-yu, 221, 291
Ch'en Hsiao, 266
Ch'en P'an, 228
Ch'en She, 223
Cheng Hsuan (A.D. 127-200), 230, 235
Cheng Hsu-p'ing, 243
Ch'i (energy), 259-60
Ch'i lueh, 252
Chi Yu. *See* Tzu-lu
Chiao Hsun (1763-1820), 249, 252
Ch'ien Mu, 99, 219, 222, 228, 253, 264-66, 290
Chi-hsia Academy, 48, 134-37, 140, 231, 240, 264, 266-67
Chi-hsia materialism. *See,* Sung-Yin (Chi-hsia) materialism
Ch'in Ku-li, 223
Chou Dynasty (1045-221 B.C.). *See* Eastern Chou Dynasty; Western Chou Dynasty
Chou-li: education syllabi in, 59, 195-96, 215; textual nature of, 290
Chu Fang-p'u, 288
Chu Hsi (1130-1200), 4, 238, 245, 247
Chü Hsin, 226
Chuang Tzu, 38, 139, 150, 206, 258, 269
Chuang Tzu, 139, 143, 168, 190, 207, 224, 227, 231, 237, 276, 283-84, 288

33286577R00205

Made in the USA
Lexington, KY
22 June 2014